NATIONAL
GEOGRAPHIC

TRAVELER

egypt

TRAVELER

egypt

by Andrew Humphreys

National Geographic
Washington, D.C.

CONTENTS

**TRAVELING WITH
EYES OPEN 6**

CHARTING YOUR TRIP 8

History & Culture 13
Egypt Today 14
The Land 22
History of Egypt 26
Pharaonic Culture 42
Timeline of the Pharaohs 52
The Arts 54
Food & Drink 62

Cairo 65
Feature: Collecting Ancient Egypt 77
Downtown Cairo Walk 82
Feature: The Coffeehouse 97
Zamalek Walk: Fine Living &
Fine Art 122

Around Cairo 139
Feature: The Pyramid Builders 148
Feature: Birdlife of Egypt 154

The Delta & Suez 159
Feature: Suez Canal 168

Alexandria 173
Feature: Rediscovering Ancient
Alexandria 178
A Walk Through the Capital
of Memory 184

Western Desert 193

Middle Egypt 209
Feature: The Holy Family
in Egypt 218

Luxor 227
Feature: Making Mummies 238
Cycling the West Bank 252
Feature: Guardians & Thieves 264
Feature: Building a Royal Tomb 274
Feature: Bringing Egyptology Up
To Date 278

South of Luxor 285
Feature: Nubian Culture 292
Feature: Cruising the Nile 302
Feature: Saving the Monuments 312

Red Sea & Sinai 319
Feature: Reef Life 328
Feature: The Bedouin 340

TRAVELWISE 345
Hotels & Restaurants by Region 356
Shopping 376
Activities & Entertainment 379
Language Guide 384
Menu Reader 385
Glossary 386
Who's Who 387
Cairo Metro Map 388

INDEX 389   CREDITS 398

**Pages 2–3: Giza's great pyramids of Khufu and Khafre
Left: An herb and tea vendor in Luxor relaxes with a *sheesha*.**

TRAVELING WITH EYES OPEN

Alert travelers go with a purpose and leave with a benefit. If you travel responsibly, you can help support wildlife conservation, historic preservation, and cultural enrichment in the places you visit. You can enrich your own travel experience as well.

To be a geo-savvy traveler:

- Recognize that your presence has an impact on the places you visit.

- Spend your time and money in ways that sustain local character. (Besides, it's more interesting that way.)

- Value the destination's natural and cultural heritage.

- Respect the local customs and traditions.

- Express appreciation to local people about things you find interesting and unique to the place: its nature and scenery, music and food, historic villages and buildings.

- Vote with your wallet: Support the people who support the place, patronizing businesses that make an effort to celebrate and protect what's special there. Seek out shops, local restaurants, inns, and tour operators who love their home—who love taking care of it and showing it off. Avoid businesses that detract from the character of the place.

- Enrich yourself, taking home memories and stories to tell, knowing that you have contributed to the preservation and enhancement of the destination.

That is the type of travel now called geotourism, which is defined as "tourism that sustains or enhances the geographical character of a place—its environment, culture, aesthetics, heritage, and the well-being of its residents." To learn more about geotourism, visit National Geographic's Center for Sustainable Destinations at www.nationalgeographic.com/travel/sustainable.

egypt

ABOUT THE AUTHORS

Brought up in northern England, **Andrew Humphreys** first traveled to
Egypt in 1988 on a brief vacation, but he liked it so much he decided not to
go home. Since then his life has been divided between the color and chaos
of Cairo and the rather more leaden skies and ordered deadlines of the
London publishing world. On assignment for a variety of periodicals, including
National Geographic Traveler and *The Wall Street Journal,* over the years he has
explored every part of Egypt, cruising Lake Nasser, watching the sun rise
from Mount Sinai, and sleeping beneath the stars in the Grand Sand Sea. His
greatest fascination, however, remains with Cairo, its people, and their culture.
In 1997 he co-founded an English-language newspaper, *The Cairo Times,* all
the better to immerse himself in the goings-on of Umm al-Dunya, "the
Mother of the World." He is also the author or co-author of several guides
to Cairo and Egypt, as well as to Syria and the Middle East.

Contributions to this guide were also made by **Dr. Joann Fletcher** (Pharaonic
Culture), **Siona Jenkins** (The White Desert, Dakhla and Kharga Oases,
St. Catherine's, and Mount Sinai), and **Richard Hoath** (Bird Life of Egypt).

A native of Boston, **Chip Rossetti,** who updated and wrote new features
for the 2009 edition, worked for a number of years as a book editor in New
York while learning Arabic in the evenings. He first visited Egypt in 2003 and
moved there in 2005 to work as the senior editor for the American University
in Cairo Press, where he got to work with Arabic novelists, Egyptologists, and
historians and scholars of the Middle East. He holds a B.A. in Classics from
Harvard and is currently a graduate student in Middle East studies at the
University of Pennsylvania.

Charting Your Trip

Egypt is probably the world's oldest travel destination. With an unrivaled collection of ancient monuments and sites, a vibrant modern culture, and natural beauty, Egypt is really more like several vacation sites in one: Depending on your inclinations, it can be a place to immerse yourself in the pharaonic past, a haunting landscape of desert and coral reefs, a lively introduction to the Arab world, or any combination of the above.

Although a few tourists arrive by bus or cruise ship, the vast majority of visitors to Egypt fly into Cairo's bustling international airport. You will most likely want to use Cairo as your base of operations: Visit its sites before moving on to the rest of the country. Egypt's national airline, EgyptAir, covers most major domestic destinations. Trains are also a good, but limited, option, and a sleeper car is a great way to get down to Luxor or Aswan from Cairo (or vice versa). The crowded long-distance buses are for the more adventurous traveler, although they're a great way to meet Egyptians. For long trips, hiring a car and driver is useful, and travel agencies in Cairo (or perhaps your hotel) can set you up with reliable transport.

If You Have a Week

Many international flights arrive in Cairo in the afternoon, so it's often best to write off the first evening to jet lag and start your visit in earnest the next morning. If you're visiting Egypt for the first time and have only a week, you can visit Cairo, Giza, Luxor, and Aswan if you plan it right. Here's one way to do it:

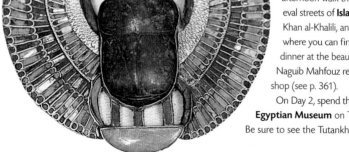

On the morning of **Day 1**, take a taxi (or hire a car and driver) to the **Giza Pyramids** and **Sphinx**—a must for any visitor. If you start off early enough, you can continue a few miles south to **Saqqara,** site of the Step Pyramid of Djoser and a raft of other Old Kingdom excavations. After lunch, switch gears and take a late afternoon walk through the medieval streets of **Islamic Cairo** and the Khan al-Khalili, an enormous bazaar where you can finish the day with dinner at the beautifully appointed Naguib Mahfouz restaurant/coffee shop (see p. 361).

On Day 2, spend the morning at the **Egyptian Museum** on Tahrir Square. Be sure to see the Tutankhamun collection

A scarab jewel from the treasures of Tutankhamun

upstairs, and the Mummy Room (the separate fee is well worth it). The museum gets crowded by mid-morning, so it's best to go early to beat the tour groups. After lunch, head down to **Coptic Cairo** by taxi or by subway to the Mar Girgis station. In addition to historic Coptic churches and the renovated Ben Ezra Synagogue, you can visit the jewel-like Coptic Museum. End the day with dessert and coffee at Groppi's café (see p. 82), a famous meeting spot in pre-1960s Cairo, and watch the passing scene in Talaat Harb Square.

A great way to pass Day 3 is by visiting the **Citadel,** which includes the palace and mosque of Muhammad Ali, some other historic mosques, and several great lookout points over the city. Immediately below the Citadel is the Sultan Hasan mosque (although you will likely need to take a taxi to get down there). That evening, take the overnight sleeper train to Luxor.

Early on Day 4, you'll arrive in **Luxor.** After checking in to your hotel, head over to Luxor Temple, conveniently sited in the middle of town, across the street from the Nile-side Corniche. After lunch, take a taxi to **Karnak,** and spend the rest of the afternoon there.

The next morning, hire a car and driver for the day to visit the **West Bank** for Day 5. You may want to start with Hatshepsut's Temple, followed by the Ramesseum, and perhaps Medinat Habu. After lunch, visit the **Valley of the Kings.** You will need to purchase a separate ticket to the valley, which lets you into any three tombs open to the public that day. Afterward, hop the three-hour train to Aswan.

NOT TO BE MISSED:

Egyptian Museum   68–76

Khan el-Khalili   87–91

The Giza Pyramids and Sphinx   128–135

Bibliotheca Alexandrina   188

The Temple of the Oracle in Siwa Oasis   200–201

Luxor's colossal Karnak complex   242–249

Valley of the Kings   271–284

Island of Philae   304–307

Abu Simbel   314–318

Diving in the Red Sea   328–331

St. Catherine's Monastery and Mount Sinai   336–339

Best Times to Visit

Though Egypt is a year-round travel spot, its high tourist season runs from November through January. During those months, Cairo can be chilly in the evenings, and Alexandria is often rainy and damp, but Upper Egypt—Luxor and Aswan—are quite pleasant. Spring and fall are the best times of year to go, although in the spring you're likely to experience the *khamsin*, hot, sand-laden winds coming from the Sudan. Summers in Egypt are extremely hot, so try to avoid visiting in June, July, or August, if possible.

On the morning of Day 6, take a felucca (small sailboat) or the local ferry to **Elephantine Island.** Visit the site of the ancient trading city on the island's southern tip, and then take a leisurely stroll north through the Nubian villages. After lunch, hire a felucca for a sail around **Aswan,** perhaps stopping at Kitchener's Island to visit the Botanical Gardens. Watch the sun go down over drinks on the Old Cataract's (see p. 371) terrace. The Nubian Museum is beautifully curated and is open until 9 p.m. most nights, making it a great post-dinner visit.

To close out your weeklong adventure, take the morning flight back to

Egyptian Money

Egypt's currency is the Egyptian pound (LE, for *livre égyptienne*, or Egyptian pound), called a guinea in Arabic. A pound is divided into 100 piastres *(irsh)*. Bills come in 25 and 50 piastre notes, and 1, 5, 10, 20, 50, 100, and 200 pound notes. Different colors and sizes make them easy to identify. There are also 5, 10, 25, and 50 piastre and 1 LE coins, although some of these you may never see at all. Egypt is a cash economy: Remember to hoard your small-denomination bills—you'll need them for taxis and tipping.

Cairo on Day 7. Return to Islamic Cairo for some last-minute souvenir shopping—perhaps with a visit to Al-Azhar mosque and then a walk south to the Street of the Tentmakers—before heading to the airport.

If You Have More Time

With more time on your hands, you can do a more expansive, thorough version of the hasty itinerary described above. For example, four-, five-, and seven-day tourist ferries regularly ply the Nile between Luxor and Aswan and stop at a number of great pharaonic sites you would otherwise miss. If you have more time in **Aswan,** reserve one day for a visit south to the awe-inspiring Abu Simbel. Buses and vans leave Aswan in a daily convoy around 4 a.m. and return in the mid-afternoon. Once back in Cairo, you can continue your trip in a number of directions. One possibility is to head to **Alexandria,** two to three hours away by train. Alexandria is worth a two-day stay: Although it lacks the pharaonic sites of Giza or Luxor, it's a charming step back into a cosmopolitan past, and harborside sites like the Citadel and the extraordinary new library are worth a visit. From Alexandria, if you're so inclined, head to the haunting **Siwa oasis** for a few days deep in the western desert (a nine-hour bus ride, though it's possible to break up the trip at Marsa Matruh).

Divers, snorkelers, and other beachgoers should consider flying directly to **Sharm el-Sheikh** or **Hurghada.** Sharm and other Sinai resorts are convenient launching points for visits to St. Catherine's Monastery, about three hours into the Sinai interior by bus.

Photography Tips

Many ancient sites in Egypt charge a camera fee of $2 to $3 on top of the admission fee. If you do not wish to pay, you may be forced to surrender your camera at the ticket office during your visit. If you do bring your camera into a site, please respect the rules and refrain from using your flash; the bright flash can damage the already faded colors on ancient walls.

Much more common is a steep price for bringing video cameras into ancient sites, often as much as $20 or $30 per site. Use caution when photographing objects other than tourist sites. For security reasons, it is illegal to photograph airports, bridges, military installations, railroad stations, or major public works like the High Dam.

Remember to use courtesy and common sense when taking photos of Egyptians. Be sure to ask permission before taking someone's photo—especially women. In many cases, however, Egyptians will be delighted to have their photos taken, and may ask you to remember to send them a copy.

Egypt's second city, adored for its Mediterranean ambiance, Alexandria recently received a five-year makeover.

Other Possibilities

Those with a hankering for Egypt's desert beauty can make a multi-day circuit of the five **western oases,** starting from either Cairo or Luxor. While it is feasible to travel by bus from oasis to oasis, hiring a four-by-four for off-road trekking is essential, so it may be more economical to hire a van and driver in Cairo for the entire trip. True adventurers may want to consider a deep-desert safari to the famous **Gilf al-Kebir** and the **Great Sand Sea**—an expedition of ten days to two weeks. Reservations should be made with desert trekking companies several months in advance.

Another less traveled route is down the scenic **Red Sea coast,** either by hiring transport in Cairo (or renting it yourself, if you feel confident of your driving) or by flying to Hurghada and hiring transport there. Aside from the diving centers and reefs around Hurghada, dive camps dot the coast from Quseir down to the deep south; the **Eastern Desert**'s little-visited ancient sites and natural vistas are also spectacular.

Harassment & How to Avoid It

Sexual harassment—from catcalls to groping—can be a real annoyance for women travelers. This is partly due to widespread perceptions about Western women among Egyptian men. Wearing loose clothing that covers shoulders and legs can help, and a loud protest will draw attention to and (hopefully) shame a groper. Single women may also want to consider wearing a fake wedding ring to deter would-be suitors. Harassment incidents are mostly confined to downtown Cairo and public beaches (though not at Red Sea resorts), but being a bit more circumspect than you might be at home can reduce your chances of getting hassled.

History & Culture

Egypt Today   14–21

Experience: Talk Like an Egyptian   16

The Land   22–25

Experience: See the Landscape by Boat   24

History of Egypt   26–41

Pharaonic Culture   42–51

Experience: Volunteer on
   an Archaeological Dig   44

Timeline of the Pharaohs   52–53

The Arts   54–61

Experience: Learn to Belly Dance   58

Food & Drink   62–64

Experience: Foods to Try   62

An "Upper Egyptian" from
the south of the country. Left:
Nefertari, "the most beautiful"

Egypt Today

Egypt is the world's original tourist destination. In one of the earliest examples of travel writing, the Greek geographer Herodotus (484–424 B.C.) pronounced: "Nowhere are there so many marvelous things, nor in the whole world beside are there to be seen so many things of unspeakable greatness." It's a statement that still holds true today.

Modern-day architects may build towers more than a hundred stories high; man may have walked on the moon and landed probes on Mars; we may have instantaneous communication between any two parts of the globe. But ancient Egyptian achievements such as the Pyramids and the Great Hypostyle Hall at Karnak leave us speechless with awe in a way that skyscrapers, rockets, and computers somehow never can. What is even more startling is that when that ancient publicist Herodotus stood before the Pyramids, they were almost as remote from his time as he himself is from ours. Small wonder that many people believe they must have been built by aliens: Egypt simply confounds.

Yet before the 19th century, Egypt was scarcely visited by Western travelers. The first recorded American to reach Cairo was John Ledyard, who died there in 1788 before he could set off on his planned exploration of interior Africa. It took a failed military expedition, led ten years later by the French general Napoleon, to awaken wider interest. Once the door was opened, Egyptomania swept Europe and America. As the first steps were being taken in France to decoding hieroglyphs, the government of the newly independent United States of America was busy incorporating the symbolism of Egypt into its civic identity, most prominently in the unfinished pyramid on the Great Seal (now to be seen on the back of every dollar bill). Cairo, Illinois? Memphis, Tennessee? They were founded in 1818 and 1819, respectively, in the first flush of excitement at the rediscovery of the antique land. American consulates were set up in Cairo and the port city of Alexandria in 1832, and at least 65 Americans are known to have visited in the decade following. Elizabeth Kirkland, wife of a former president of Harvard College, carved her name at the top of the Great Pyramid in 1830, while the Reverend Stephen Olin of Connecticut sailed up the Nile and produced two volumes on his travels in 1843. More famously, Mark Twain came and poked fun at everything except the donkeys, which he termed "indescribably gorgeous." And like a virus transmitted by the sketches, journals, and artifacts that these first intrepid voyagers carried back home, the symbols, forms, and mysteries of Egypt spread. Scarabs and sphinxes enlivened buildings in Paris, London, and New York. Pharaonic motifs decorated porcelain and furniture. Verdi wrote his

> And like a virus transmitted by the sketches, journals, and artifacts that [the] first intrepid voyagers carried back home, the symbols, forms, and mysteries of Egypt spread.

Despite millennia of history, Egypt is a young country, with 60 percent of the population below the age of 25.

bombastic ancient Egyptian opera *Aida.* The curse of the pharaohs began to claim its first victims in short stories by Edgar Allan Poe and Arthur Conan Doyle.

Judging by the conquest of the best-seller lists by Christian Jacq's historical novels set in Egypt, and Wilbur Smith's take on ancient Egyptian adventure, Hollywood's belief that there is cinematic life yet in the mummy, and the fact that Las Vegas deemed Luxor worthy of rebuilding in the Nevada desert—albeit as a casino and hotel complex—the West's appetite for Egypt has yet to wane.

EXPERIENCE:
Talk Like an Egyptian

A little bit of Egyptian Arabic will go a long way as you meet locals during your travels. Here are some words to help you get started. For a more complete glossary, see p. 386.

aywa	yes
la	no
min fadlak (*min fadlik* to a woman)	please
shukran	thank you
afwan	you're welcome
salaam aleikum (formal)	hello
ahlan wa sahlan	hello
ahlan beek	hello (said in response)
(*ahlan beekee* to a woman)	
bititkallim ingleezi?	Do you speak English?
maalesh	No problem, don't worry about it

Real Life Egypt

Egyptians tend to leave the pharaohs, their monuments, and their mysteries to the tourists. They have little choice—they are too busy with real life.

Egypt is a country that Western strategists describe as "developing," which means it's considered to be lagging behind a little in the progress stakes. If it is, that's hardly surprising. From the moment Cleopatra succumbed to the bite of the asp and Egypt fell to Rome, the country suffered continuous foreign dominion and was sucked dry of revenue and resources. That situation only ended with revolution in 1952. Subsequently, under the leadership of the charismatic President Gamal Abdel Nasser, Egypt became the diplomatic hub of the Arab world, a role it maintains today.

At peace with its neighbors, Egypt is the voice of moderation in a troubled region, and has good relations with most other world nations, particularly the United States from whom it receives some $2.3 billion annually, explicitly as a reward for being the first Arab state to make peace with Israel. However, in charge of their own destiny for little more than half a century, the Egyptians are faced with some major domestic problems. Less than 10 percent of this desert country is cultivable and into that is crammed 90 percent of a population that increases by about a million every nine months (in 2008 the figure was 81.7 million).

About a quarter of all Egyptians live in Cairo. According to the United Nations, it is the world's most densely populated urban area, with a population thought to be somewhere between 13 million and 17 million. In some central districts there are reckoned to be up to 700,000 people per square mile. The city's infrastructure gave up the ghost long ago. Housing shortages mean married children share their parents' home, probably with the grandparents living there, too. Schools operate in up to three shifts. Major roads are jammed from morning until midnight.

What keeps the city from imploding is the resilience of the Cairenes, masters in the art of making do and getting by. Just look at some of the cars on the streets: Three models welded into one, with the gaps between them covered with tinplate, run as much on sheer willpower as on fuel. It is not unusual for a wage earner to be juggling two or even three jobs, working as a poorly paid, underemployed civil servant during the day, or running a small family business, while moonlighting as a taxi driver. Strike up a conversation with your cab driver and odds are he trained as an engineer, pharmacist, or doctor.

Aiding every Cairene in his or her daily struggle is the whole of the rest of the city. There is a palpable air of "we're all in this together." Strangers fall into conversation at the first chance, and jokes and wisecracks are traded with anyone in hearing. Privacy is unheard of, but then so is loneliness.

Egyptians tend to leave the pharaohs, their monuments, and their mysteries to the tourists. They have little choice—they are too busy with real life.

The most popular TV programs tend to be homegrown soaps, peering into the loves, lives, and tribulations of working-class families. Box-office favorites at

The Pyramid of Khufu (or Cheops), the first and largest of the three Giza pyramids, covers 13 acres (5.3 ha) and is the largest pyramid ever made.

Almost a quarter of Egypt's population lives in the capital, Cairo, one of the world's most densely populated cities.

the movies are locally produced comedies in which the little guy manages, through wit and a sharp tongue, to bring some pompous and pampered types crashing down to earth. Singing and dancing play a big part, and it takes only the slightest of cues for someone to sling a scarf around her hips and break into a belly dance.

Families & Faith

Families are still the keystone of Egyptian society. Getting married and raising children are probably the main priorities of almost every boy or girl over the age of 16. However, progress toward this end is invariably slowed by the convention that requires the potential groom to provide an apartment and furnish-

ings (even if it's only a furnished room in his parents' home). On a typical salary of about $60 a month, accumulating the cash to secure a bride can take the average worker ten years or more. With sex before marriage taboo, little wonder that young Egyptian males are riveted by the casual heavy petting and bed hopping seen in the Hollywood movies that make it to the local theaters—even if the censor's scissors have snipped out all exposed flesh.

Pregnancy usually follows fast after marriage, almost invariably within the first year. Problems can arise if it doesn't. Witness the case in Alexandria in 1999, when a court of law ordered a nuclear scientist to put aside her research for a year and have a baby after her husband filed suit claiming he had a legal right to reproduce. Boys are favored, reflecting the preeminent status of men in Egyptian society. Egypt does have its high-profile feminists, such as internationally published writer Nawal al-Sadawi; but her most famous work, *The Hidden Face of Eve,* detailing the situation of Arab women, is banned in Egypt. Meanwhile women collude in their second-rank status. In a national survey of adolescents carried out in 1999, some 60 percent of girls believed that a wife must accept her husband's opinion, even if she disagrees with it, and 89 percent held that a wife should never act without his permission. While the proportion of women who enter the workforce has risen steadily in recent years, only a fifth of Cairene women work outside the home, a figure that falls dramatically once outside the capital.

Inarguably, this patriarchal attitude stems from Islam, which clearly favors the male. Religion permeates Egyptian life, although not in an uncompromisingly authoritarian manner as in Iran or Saudi Arabia—no music? no dancing? black clothes? Egyptians would never stand for that—but at a low-key, almost unconscious level. Ask after someone's health and they will reply *Alhamdilallah,* "Fine. Praise to God." Say to a tour guide, "See you tomorrow," and the answer will be *Insha'allah,* "God willing." Few pray the specified five times a day, but almost all men heed the amplified call of the *muezzin* each Friday at noon, when the crowds spill out of the mosques to block streets and sidewalks.

Likewise, the whole of the country's Muslim population is united in its celebra-

> **Singing and dancing play a big part [of Egyptian life], and it takes only the slightest of cues for someone to sling a scarf around her hips and break into a belly dance.**

tion of Ramadan, the holy month of the Islamic calendar, when all who are capable of it have to refrain from eating, drinking, and smoking, from sunup to sundown. After the endurance test of the day come the celebrations of the evening, beginning with *iftar,* the breaking of the fast. Typically a communal event, each night this takes on the appearance of a nationwide street party. Those with money to spare court blessings by sponsoring "mercy tables," where food is served free of charge to all. This being Egypt, as many turn up for the company as for the chicken and rice.

Other Islamic festivals and holidays are dotted throughout the year. A major occasion is Eid al-Kebir, the "big feast." As welcome to sheep as Thanksgiving must be to turkeys, this is a time when those who are squeamish or vegetarian should stay indoors, as backstreets become makeshift slaughterhouses.

Alongside Muslims, some five million Coptic Christians call Egypt home. Reputedly first brought by St. Mark the Evangelist (martyred in Alexandria in A.D. 63), the

Islam permeates day-to-day life for the more than 90 percent of Egyptians who are Muslim.

teachings of Christ gained a foothold in Egypt during Roman rule. The Copts of today wear their heritage proudly with crosses tattooed on their wrists. Occasional stories in the media screaming persecution of Christians by Egypt's Muslims are off the mark. But when the Egyptian government says there is no problem at all, that's more than a little disingenuous, too. The truth is somewhere in between, but it would be fair to say that interfaith relations are relatively harmonious.

Being Egyptian

Whether a person is Muslim or Copt, being Egyptian comes first. And this is perhaps a defining characteristic: the Egyptians' love

of their home country. Harsh economic realities drive many abroad, particularly to the Arab Gulf countries, where work is plentiful and well paid. It is estimated that at any one time this overseas workforce numbers about 3.5 million. In some Delta villages practically every family has at least one son working in Kuwait or Bahrain or Saudi Arabia, and the money that these workers send home constitutes one of Egypt's top three sources of income.

Living and working overseas certainly suits some Egyptians, like scientist Ahmed Zewail, who won the 1999 Nobel Chemistry Prize for his groundbreaking work at the California Institute of Technology in Pasadena, or Sir Magdy Yacoub, London-based pioneer of open-heart surgery. But most people working abroad can't wait to get home.

As you clear immigration at Cairo International Airport, look around at the other arrivals. Among the overseas visitors, edgy with anticipation of the promised sights, there will always be a handful of young Egyptian men looking like out-of-uniform Santas as they steer their luggage carts piled high with boxes and bags. They are bringing home the spoils of years spent working abroad. Their excitement is broadcast on their faces. Incoming visitors might have yellow sands, camels, palms, and pyramids to look forward to, but these homecomers have Egypt. ∎

Egyptian, Arab, or Both?

On one level, it is obvious that Egyptians are Arabs—after all, Egypt is the world's largest Arabic-speaking country, and the Arab League headquarters overlooks Tahrir Square. Depending on the context, however, Egyptians have some conflicting definitions of who exactly is an Arab: Does it mean anyone who speaks Arabic or is it someone who belongs to a tribe from the Arabian peninsula?

Traditionally, Egyptians have used the word Arab to refer to the Bedouin of the Sinai or to Gulf Arabs, while they considered themselves Egyptians first and foremost, heirs to a great pharaonic civilization. It is only in the past half century, with the emergence of Arab nationalism, that Egypt has come to embrace, sometimes with ambivalence, the idea of a common Arab identity.

The Land

Seen from a satellite, Egypt is a blank yellow expanse bisected by a single, dark blue vein that toward the top spreads in a fan to meet the sea. In this one view is the truth of the often repeated statement, "The Nile is Egypt." The country may be huge in area, but its millennia of civilization are all crammed into that one life-giving thread, the Nile Valley.

Rising in twin sources in East Africa, which converge in Sudan, the Nile flows for 4,132 miles (6,650 km) before emptying into the Mediterranean. North of Khartoum, the Sudanese capital, it describes a broad S-curve; once in Egypt it flows almost straight, from the south (Upper Egypt) down to the sea in the north (Lower Egypt). From Aswan northward to Cairo the river lies in a trench-like valley filled by a rich belt of agricultural land that gradually increases to a width of about 12 miles (19 km). This is the gift of the Nile. Each year, as a result of the heavy seasonal rainfall on the Ethiopian Plateau, the river rises, beginning in May and reaching its maximum level in August. Before the completion of the first dam at Aswan in 1902, by September every year Egypt's entire Nile Valley used to be covered by water. Its retreat a few weeks later left a thick, silty residue of the richest soil in which farmers could scatter their seeds. "These people," wrote the Greek geographer Herodotus in the fifth century B.C., "get their harvests with less labor than anyone else in the world." Far from taking their good fortune for granted, on occasion the priests of ancient Egypt would throw virgins off the cliffs at Aswan to ensure a bountiful flood. These days, the young women of Upper Egypt can sleep secure, as water management is no longer left to the gods. The completion of the High Dam in the 1970s, with its massive reservoir Lake Nasser, for the first time in history allowed the annual flood to be controlled by man. Unfortunately, there are also several negative side effects, chief of which is a decrease in fertility, and hence agricultural productivity, caused by the loss of alluvial silt.

> **The country may be huge in area, but its millennia of civilization are all crammed into that one life-giving thread, the Nile Valley.**

Nowhere are these problems more keenly felt than in the Delta, the rich, flat, bright-green fan that spreads north of Cairo. It was formed by the Nile splitting into as many as seven branches, although its waters are now concentrated in two, the Damietta Branch to the east, and the Rosetta Branch to the west. Burdened with the task of feeding the whole of the country, the land is among the world's most intensively cultivated. Farmers here grow three crops a year, with the premier produce being cotton, maize, rice, and wheat. The climate is also conducive to a vast range of fruit and vegetables, from green beans to grapes to palms laden with dates. Taking a train ride through the Delta can seem like passing through some vast and bounteous Garden of Eden. However, it is countries overseas that are the beneficiaries of the harvest because the best of the produce is exported for vitally needed hard currency. extent The lack of the annual replenishing of fresh black soil means overuse of fertilizers and

A hot-air balloon drifts over the Theban Hills, which are lit by the early morning sun.

EXPERIENCE: See the Landscape by Boat

Experiencing Egypt without a Nile cruise is like going to Las Vegas and not gambling. The traditional cruise has always been from Cairo down to Luxor (see pp. 302–303), but since the early 1990s fears for tourists' safety have meant that boats are no longer allowed to sail through Middle Egypt. Instead, cruisers sail for three or four nights between Luxor and Aswan, typically stopping off en route at Esna, Edfu, and Kom Ombo.

Every big hotel or tour operator has a boat on the Nile. In particular, Abercrom-bie & Kent's 40-passenger *Sun Boat III* and 84-passenger *Sun Boat IV* are notably luxurious and serve excellent food.

Even better than a Nile cruise is to sail the length of Lake Nasser from the High Dam at Aswan down to the magnificent temple of Abu Simbel. Among the best boats you can take are the supremely luxurious M.S. *Eugénie* and M.S. *Qasr Ibrim* (see p. 349), both designed to look like late 19th-century floating palaces; cocktails in the desert and a private sound-and-light show are highlights.

high levels of salinity. Also, inch by inch, the northern Delta, which lies only just above sea level, is being eaten away by the Mediterranean. In an effort to reverse this trend, patches of cultivable land are now being reclaimed from coastal salt marshes.

Taking to the air again, it is startling to see the division between the cultivated land and desert all along the Nile Valley. There is no gradual fade or bleed; it is a harsh precise line, green on one side, yellow on the other. The crops stop dead, there is a small bump of earth, and then the sand takes over. Egypt is in fact one great desert plateau divided unequally by the Nile into the vast Western Desert and the Eastern Desert.

The Western Desert comprises two-thirds of the land surface of Egypt, an area of about 262,800 square miles (680,600 sq km). If you ignore the political boundaries on the map, it stretches right across the top of North Africa under its better known name of the Sahara. Suffering extremes of temperature, barren and forbidding, the desert is not completely devoid of life. A series of wind-sculpted depressions allows water to come to the surface, creating a string of cultivable oases. Inhabited for thousands of years, these islands of greenery prospered in ancient times as important staging posts on trade routes between Egypt and neighboring Libya.

More recently, the Egyptian government has been attempting to develop the oases as part of the New Valley project, intended as an alternative settlement area to the Nile Valley. Since the 1950s landless farmers and city families have been encouraged to move out to the desert, and in the 1990s grand plans were announced to attract industry by linking the oases to Lake Nasser by means of a canal. Work on this pharaonic-scale scheme, known as the Toshka Canal, has yet to begin—and indeed may never happen because of cost concerns. Meanwhile the population of the Western Desert remains minimal.

Much smaller than its western counterpart, the Eastern Desert stretches between the Nile Valley and the Red Sea coast. It is devoid of sand and dunes, and instead is characterized by stony, mountainous terrain, extensively dissected by wadis (dry riverbeds). The desert is almost completely unpopulated, save for a series of small ports strung along the Red Sea coast, such as Quseir and Berenice, which served ancient trade routes between the Nile Valley and Yemen, the Horn of Africa, and beyond. Through here the pharaohs imported exotic spices, live elephants, and slaves. In return, they could offer the mineral wealth of the Eastern Desert mountains—in particular, gold. Later, the Romans quarried the same areas for porphyry, a dense roseate stone that they hacked into blocks, dragged overland to the Nile, and shipped to Rome, where it was highly prized by masons and sculptors as a raw material most suitable for imperial busts. Today the Eastern Desert remains a wilderness, and what most visitors and Egyptians alike see of it is the view from the window of an air-conditioned bus as it follows age-old caravan routes between the Nile and the coast.

The Sinai Peninsula separates Africa from Asia. It is essentially a continuation of the Eastern Desert that was ripped away about 40 million years ago, when the African and Arabian continental plates began to move apart. This tectonic shift created the shallow Gulf of Suez and the much deeper Gulf of Aqaba. The latter is part of the Great Rift Valley, which, filled with a series of rivers, gulfs, and lakes, extends from the Dead Sea for some 4,000 miles (6,400 km) all the way down the east coast of Africa to Mozambique in the south. Southern Sinai is covered by a gaunt mountain mass that includes Egypt's highest peak, Mount St. Catherine (Gebel Katerina), 8,668 feet (2,642 m) high. In the steep valleys between peaks there is enough hardy vegetation to sustain a variety of wildlife, including the rare Sinai leopard. North of this is a plateau sloping down to the Mediterranean, traditionally sparsely populated, save for roaming Bedouin tribes. However, the government has built a new pipeline, the Al-Salam Canal, to bring fresh water from the Suez Canal region. Since the 1980s, tourism has also created new population centers all along the south and eastern coasts of the peninsula. ∎

For thousands of years, Egyptians have raised their crops and livestock along the Nile River, which traditionally brought fertile silt into their desert environment.

History of Egypt

Cast your mind back to the opening scenes of the 1996 Oscar-sweeping film, *The English Patient*. Kristen Scott Thomas is copying into her notebook swimmers painted on a cave wall deep in the desert. It is a fictional episode but based on truth. In the 1930s such crudely daubed figures were indeed found at Gebel Uweinat in the Western Desert, miles from the nearest water.

Historians take this as evidence that Egypt must have been inhabited as far back as the Paleolithic period, before 25,000 B.C., when the whole of North Africa was a vast habitable grassy savanna with abundant wildlife and lakes. A dramatic change in climate turned the grasslands to desert, forcing early humans to migrate toward sources of water, either oases or the valley of the Nile. Settlements dating from the Neolithic period, about 5000 B.C., have been found in the western oases of Siwa and Kharga, and in the Fayoum. The people lived by agriculture and fishing and were sufficiently advanced to produce pottery and woven materials. Little is known about them except that by the fourth millennium B.C., they had formed two geographically defined groups: Upper Egypt along the Nile Valley, and Lower Egypt, based in the fertile Nile Delta.

Herodotus: Egypt's First Travel Guide

In his *Histories*, the 5th-century B.C. Greek writer Herodotus tells the roundabout story of the Persian Wars of his day, with long digressions on the history of the known world and descriptions of other societies. Perhaps the most famous section of the *Histories* is Book 2, which is all about Egypt, its people, its past, and its customs. Herodotus drew on his own research travels in the Delta, Siwa, Memphis, and even Aswan. Though much of his information is inaccurate, his accounts of Egypt's traditions, religious beliefs, and major sites make his an early forerunner of books like this one.

The Pyramid Builders

Lost among the overload of exhibits at Cairo's Egyptian Museum is a shield-shaped piece of slate carved with battle scenes. One side shows a king wearing the white crown of Upper Egypt about to deal a fatal blow to a kneeling figure. On the reverse is the same king wearing the red crown of Lower Egypt. Known as the Palette of Narmer and dating from about 3100 B.C., it is the museum's earliest artifact and one of its most significant. With its single king wearing two crowns, it depicts the first unification of Egypt under one ruler. This is ground zero—the event usually taken as marking the beginning of Egyptian civilization. From here begins a line of royalty that stretches for more than 3,000 years, encompassing 170 or more kings and pharaohs. The term "pharaonic Egypt" is used for this entire period, even though the king took the title "pharaoh" (see p. 42) only in the New Kingdom, starting about 1550 B.C.

The basic skeleton of ancient Egyptian history comes from a list compiled in the third century B.C. by a high priest of Heliopolis named Manetho. He divides Egypt's rulers into

An 1893 photograph of the Great Hypostyle Hall at Karnak, which was constructed in the New Kingdom and rediscovered in the mid-19th century

30 dynasties, or ruling houses. Modern Egyptologists then group these into three major periods (Old Kingdom, Middle Kingdom, and New Kingdom), each separated by periods of decline known as Intermediate Periods. Historians naturally could not rely on one uncorroborated source, and Manetho is backed up by several other ancient chronologies, including extensive "royal lists" such as that inscribed on the walls of the Temple of Seti I at Abydos (see p. 222), and a fragmentary papyrus known as the Royal Canon of Turin, after the museum in which it is to be found (the Egyptian Museum in Turin, Italy). Of course, many discrepancies exist between the various sources, with the result that the whole time frame of pharaonic Egypt is still open to passionate debate.

Nowhere is this more the case than in the Early Dynastic period, the run-up to the Old Kingdom. Next to nothing is known of Narmer, the unifier of ancient Egypt, or of those who followed, including a king called Menes, who may actually be Narmer under a different name. Menes is important because it is to him that historians have traditionally ascribed the founding of Memphis, capital of Egypt for most of the pharaonic period. Appropriately, the new city was sited at the point where Upper and Lower Egypt met, making it well suited for controlling both the Nile Valley and the Delta.

Herodotus described Memphis as a "prosperous city and cosmopolitan center," and we have to take his word for it, because next to nothing of the city has survived. We can

The shadow of more than four and a half millennia of history is cast over modern Egypt.

only get an idea of its glories through its vast necropolis, which developed in tandem with the living city during the period of the Old Kingdom (2686–2181 B.C.), a period otherwise known as the "pyramid age." These fantastic funerary monuments appeared in the 3rd dynasty, heralded by the Step Pyramid at Saqqara, built during the reign of Djoser (R.2667–2648 B.C.). During the next three dynasties some 21 other major pyramids were built, but the truly gigantic pyramids were all completed by father, son, and grandson in fewer than 80 years. Sneferu (R.2613–2589 B.C.) achieved true pyramid perfection first, at Dahshur, replacing steps with an even (on the second attempt) slope. He was outdone by his son Khufu, or Cheops (R.2589–2566 B.C.), who built his Great Pyramid at Giza even bigger. For reasons unknown, Khafre, or Chephren (R.2558–2532 B.C.) chose not to challenge his father Khufu, and built his neighboring pyramid marginally smaller.

The rise of Thebes marks the beginning of the Middle Kingdom, . . . an intermission between the glories of the Old and New Kingdoms.

This spectacular program of pyramid building speaks volumes about the power of the Old Kingdom rulers, who were able to marshal the vast workforce needed. Pyramid specialist Mark Lehner estimates that a constantly rotating workforce of 20,000 men must have labored for 20 years on Khufu's pyramid. This workforce had to be organized, fed, housed, and paid, which must have required an extraordinarily well-developed system of administration.

Khafre's was the last of the giant pyramids. Though many followed during the 5th and 6th dynasties, all were on a much smaller scale—a symptom of the erosion of the king's power. Unified rule gave way to rival principalities and, inevitably, civil war. When the dust settled, following more than a century of chaos, control of the country had shifted from the north to Upper Egypt, and to a family of princes based at Thebes, site of modern-day Luxor.

Thebes & Karnak

The rise of Thebes marks the beginning of the Middle Kingdom, which stands as something of an intermission between the glories of the Old and New Kingdoms. Continued disruption and strife held progress in check, and few of its 11 dynasties of kings are well known outside the world of Egyptology. Mentuhotep II (R.2055–2004 B.C.) is credited with reunifying Egypt, and Senusret III (R.1874–1855 B.C.) has a high profile through his granite portraits at the Cairo and Luxor museums. However, these are very minor figures compared with the great pharaoh-gods to come.

The Middle Kingdom ended with Egypt partially occupied by invaders from the north, a Palestinian people called the Hyksos. Their introduction of the horse and chariot into warfare and their skill in archery enabled them to conquer the whole of the Delta region. It was only when

the Theban Egyptians adopted this new military technology that they finally defeated the Hyksos and established Ahmose I (*R.*1550–1525 B.C.) as the first king of the 18th dynasty, and founder of the New Kingdom (1550–1069 B.C.).

So begins the golden age of the pharaohs. Over the next 500 years, Egypt would rise to unequaled greatness, and its rulers would create a legacy of awe-inspiring temples, tombs, and treasures that continue to captivate our imaginations today. Their names echo still: Tuthmose, Ramses, Akhenaten, and, most famously, Tutankhamun.

The first two New Kingdom rulers were concerned with consolidating Egypt's borders, but by the time of Tuthmose I (*R.*1504–1492 B.C.) domestic affairs were stable enough for the pharaoh to embark on a series of brilliant military campaigns. He marked his achievements by raising a stela at Abydos that reads: "I made the boundaries of Egypt as far as that which the sun encircles...I made Egypt the superior of every land."

Tuthmose III (*R.*1479–1425 B.C.) surpassed his grandfather Tuthmose I in military prowess. He made no less than 17 successful campaigns into western Asia. He was nicknamed "the Napoleon of ancient Egypt" by American archaeologist James Henry Breasted (1865–1935).

All this empire building laid the foundations for the most prosperous and stable period of ancient Egyptian history. Wealth accumulated from foreign expeditions was used to embellish Egypt's temples and palaces, not least that of Karnak, the vast complex at Thebes dedicated to Amun-Re, chief of the gods. During the almost 40-year-long reign of Amenhotep III (*R.*1390–1352 B.C.) in particular, hardly any military activity was called for and instead manpower was lavished on great building works such as Luxor Temple. There also was a flowering in all aspects of the arts during this time. Some of the country's most magnificent statuary dates from the reign of this pharaoh, including several pieces now housed in the Luxor Museum (see pp. 240–241), as well as a colossal statue of the pharaoh and his queen that stands in the main atrium at Cairo's Egyptian Museum (see p. 68).

> **Egypt would rise to unequaled greatness, and its rulers would create a legacy . . . that continues to captivate our imaginations today.**

A revolutionary period in ancient Egyptian history (see pp. 214–217) was ushered in by Amenhotep IV (*R.*1352–1336 B.C.), better known as Akhenaten. He removed the capital to Amarna in Middle Egypt—though the change was short-lived—and was married to the famous Nefertiti. His promotion of the cult of the sun disk, Aten, over

Tutankhamun's gold coffin exemplifies the pinnacle of ancient Egyptian prosperity and artistic magnificence in the New Kingdom.

Egypt's traditional gods has been called a revolution in monotheism. Akhenaten's heresy, however, caused him to be vilified by his successors when orthodoxy was restored on his death. Subsequently his name was left off the royal lists, such as the one at Abydos. Akhenaten's immediate successors suffered similarly and were also written out of history by revisionist scribes. It is ironic then that one of them, a very minor pharaoh called Tutankhamun, who took the throne at the age of nine and was dead at 18, should wind up as the best known of all of ancient Egypt's rulers, thanks to the world-famous 1922 discovery of his intact and treasure-filled tomb by Howard Carter (see pp. 276–277).

Tutankhamun's early death briefly left the succession in question. Aye, a royal official, seized the opportunity and hastily married the young widowed queen, despite the fact that she was actually his granddaughter. On the death of Aye, the throne passed not to a blood heir but to an army commander, Horemheb. On his death, the throne passed to another general, Ramses I, founder of a dynasty of warrior pharaohs. Mightiest of these was Ramses II (R. 1279–1213 B.C.), or simply Ramses the Great. Immortalized by the 19th-century English poet Percy Bysshe Shelley as the "king of kings," Ramses II is the epitome of the all-powerful pharaoh-god. His massive temple at Abu Simbel, the Hypostyle Hall at Karnak, and the great mortuary temple called the Ramesseum at Thebes practically define ancient Egypt in the popular imagination. No other pharaoh built so prolifically (and on such a scale) or raised so many colossi (or usurped those of others). For that matter, no other pharaoh fathered so many children (more than a hundred). Ramses II also gathered together the largest force of Egyptian troops ever seen, some 20,000 men, and led them against the Hittites at the Battle of Kadesh (1275 B.C.), fought in what is now Syria.

Cleopatra has long captured the imagination of writers and artists. In 1883 British painter Alma-Tadema depicted the queen on her barge on the Nile after the battle of Actium.

Ramses II may have lived to be as old as 92 years of age. Although his tomb was discovered empty, the actual body of this extraordinary ruler was found as part of the cache of royal mummies at Gurna in 1881 (see "Guardians & Thieves," pp. 264–265). In 1976 he was flown to Paris for a Ramses II exhibition where, despite being dead for 3,200 years, he was met at the airport with a full presidential guard of honor. He now lies in the Royal Mummy Room at the Egyptian Museum in Cairo.

By the time Ramses III came to power, some 30 years after his illustrious namesake, Egypt was already in decline. Disunity had once more set in, and the country was under siege from outsiders. Before long, the kings of Libya had captured the Delta, Nubians from the south had taken Thebes, and other civilizations, such as those of the Assyrians and Persians, were invading the Nile Valley. Egypt was bankrupt and powerless, and it ultimately fell to a fabled outsider to rescue the country and resurrect its former pharaonic glories.

Alexandria & the Ptolemies

When Alexander the Great entered Egypt in 332 B.C., he was hailed as a savior. The Persians, who occupied the country, had already fallen before him the year previously at Issus in what is now southeastern Turkey. He marched straight to Memphis, where he was welcomed as a pharaoh, before crossing the desert to consult the famed oracle of Amun at the oasis of Siwa.

On the Mediterranean coast Alexander founded the city of Alexandria. And then he was gone, campaigning across Asia and into India. When he died in 323 B.C. in Babylon, his enormous empire was divided among his generals. Alexander's boyhood friend Ptolemy claimed Egypt.

The newly crowned Ptolemy I (305–285 B.C.) had to defend his interest against rival claimants but did so successfully, and founded a dynasty of 15 Hellenistic rulers lasting 275 years. Although Egypt now inevitably became part of the Mediterranean world, with Alexandria supplanting Memphis and Thebes in national importance, the Ptolemies strove to maintain continuity with the age of the pharaohs. They kept the existing political and religious structures, adopted pharaonic dress and artistic styles, repaired and restored temples, and built some anew. Almost all of the most complete temples in Egypt today—Dendara, Edfu, Kom Ombo, and Philae—are Ptolemaic, not ancient Egyptian. This means that well over a thousand years separate Luxor Temple and that at Esna, 50 miles (80 km) to the south. However, the Ptolemies used the earlier temples as their blueprints, and in doing so preserved for us building forms and styles that otherwise might have been lost.

As the Ptolemaic dynasty progressed, it took on all the qualities of a murderous soap opera, full of domestic intrigue and backstabbing (literally). The result was serious internal weaknesses in the country. Rome, the rising power of the region, was quick to exploit the situation and began to involve itself in the affairs of the exceedingly wealthy Egypt. In the end, it was the actions of Cleopatra VII, *the* Cleopatra of play and movie, that provided a pretext for the Romans to invade Egypt.

> **Ptolemy I had to defend his interest against rival claimants but did so successfully, and founded a dynasty of 15 Hellenistic rulers.**

Daughter of Ptolemy XII, Cleopatra became queen on his death in 51 B.C., sharing a co-regency with her brother, Ptolemy XIII (R.51–47 B.C.), before he ousted her from power. The two siblings were set to battle it out for the throne when they were interrupted by the arrival of a Roman fleet led by Julius Caesar. He was in pursuit of Pompey, his rival for control of Rome, recently defeated and now seeking asylum in Egypt. Ptolemy had Pompey executed and presented his head to Caesar.

Far wilier than her brother, Cleopatra had herself smuggled into the palace of Alexandria in the dead of night and delivered to Caesar hidden in a rolled carpet. The next morning, Ptolemy was astonished and furious to find his sister with Caesar. Cleopatra was restored to power and kept secure there by her new lover, to whom she bore a son, Caesarion, or "little Caesar."

Contrary to the popular image of Cleopatra as a voluptuous, ravishing vamp— as she was portrayed on the big screen by Vivien Leigh (1945) and Elizabeth Taylor (1963)—Cleopatra's charms were apparently not based on her looks. "Her actual beauty... was not in itself remarkable," wrote Greek biographer Plutarch (A.D. 46–119). Her seductiveness, he reports, was in her "bold wit" and "the charm of her society."

Following the assassination of Julius Caesar in Rome, Cleopatra sailed to Tarsus in Asia Minor at the behest of the new rising star of the Roman Empire, Mark Antony. The two entered into a mutually beneficial political alliance: Antony sought money, Cleopatra wanted power and territories. They became lovers, produced two children, and later married. But Antony already had a wife, whose brother was Octavian, legal heir to Caesar. Thus Rome was turned against Antony and his queen in Alexandria, and in 32 B.C. the senate declared war. At the naval Battle of Actium the following year, Octavian defeated Antony, whom he pursued to Egypt. Antony committed suicide. Cleopatra tried her charms on Octavian to little avail. She herself then committed suicide, possibly by means of an asp (a venomous snake), preferring death to the humiliations she foresaw.

The victorious Octavian then ordered the death of Cleopatra's eldest son and heir, Caesarion, appointing himself pharaoh and bringing to an end Ptolemaic rule in Egypt.

The Nile

Until the roads and railways of the 19th century, the Nile was Egypt's only highway. The pharaohs ruled a kingdom stretched out along the river, which itself provided the means for regular tours by the king. The Nile also moved regiments, grain, and the stone used for pyramids and temples. Sailing the river demanded great skill, especially at low water, when laden vessels could run aground on sandbanks. Ships used prevailing northerly winds for travel up the river, but few boats sailed upstream during the summer inundation, when floodwaters made voyages laborious. The ancient Egyptians' world was one of flowing waters and fecund soil, of order balanced against unpredictable, menacing chaos.

Al-Qahira, the City Victorious

The Romans cared little for Egypt. For six centuries they used it as a granary, taking what they required and leaving nothing in return. Almost no monuments stand to their rule in Egypt.

The most significant legacy of the Romans' time is the emergence of the Christian faith in Egypt. Tradition has it that the teachings of Christ were spread in Alexandria by no less a personage than the gospel writer St. Mark from about A.D. 45—making the church in Egypt one of the oldest in Christendom. When Christianity was adopted as the official religion of the Roman Empire, under Constantine, Christians were allowed to worship and evangelize freely. Coptic (meaning "Egyptian") Christians, over time, had adopted an understanding of Christ's nature that was at variance with that of the main church. The Copts consequently found themselves cast as heretics and persecuted. So when an invading Arab army appeared in A.D. 641 under the flag of Islam, it was welcomed by the predominantly Christian Egyptians. The Copts survived the rise of Islam and remain a strong religious entity today.

Ignoring Alexandria, the Arab army camped beside a Roman fortress on the Nile across from the old pharaonic capital of Memphis. This encampment, called Fustat, gradually took on a more permanent aspect and became a city in its own right. During these early years of Islam (founded by the Prophet Muhammad around A.D. 610), Egypt passed through the hands of several warring dynasties as the line of succession from Muhammad was disputed. With each dynasty the new Arab city was extended a little farther north. In A.D. 969, it was the turn of the Fatimids, a North African dynasty whose leaders claimed descent from the Prophet's daughter. Their extension to the city included palaces and mosques, plazas and thoroughfares, all wrapped around by high fortified walls. They gave this new city the name Al-Qahira, "the Victorious," later corrupted by European tongues to "Cairo."

Its walls were strengthened by the famous military leader Salah al-Din (better known in the West as Saladin), the successor to the Fatimids, who ruled as sultan (1171–1193) from the Citadel he built for himself. However, Cairo's greatest glories came during the 267-year rule of a strange warrior caste known as the Mamluks. The word *mamluk* means "one who is owned," and by origin they were slaves—mainly from the Caucasus region bridging Europe and Asia—purchased at a young age and brought to Egypt as palace guards. Their military service was rewarded by land and eventual freedom.

The Bible was first translated into the Coptic language in the 2nd century A.D. The term Coptic refers to the last stage of ancient Egyptian script as well as to Egyptian Christians.

Napoleon told his troops before defeating the Mamluks: "Forty centuries of history look down upon you from these Pyramids."

By the middle of the 13th century the Mamluks were the most powerful force in the land, and were able to dispossess the heirs of Saladin and claim Egypt for themselves. Raised as warriors, they were a fearsome caste and swept through Palestine and Syria, carving out an empire that extended northward as far as eastern Turkey.

This put the Mamluks in control of all East-West trade, and the profits from this made Cairo into one of the largest and richest cities in the world. It became a conduit for spices and silks from China, India, and Arabia, which then were traded on to Florence, Genoa, and Venice and through them to the rest of Europe. Incidentally, along with the precious goods, the Western world also imported essential vocabulary: so from the Arabic *ruzz* we have "rice"; from *kammun* we have "cumin"; from *zafaran*, "saffron"; from *qahwa*, "coffee"; from *sharbat*, "sherbet"; from *sukkar*, "sugar"; and from *makhzan*, the Arabic word for a place of storage, "magazine."

Writing in 1384, Italian merchant Leonardo Frescobaldi claimed that more people dwelled on a single street in Cairo than in all of the city of Florence. Precise figures are uncertain, but Cairo's population at the time may have been as large as half a million, making it twice the size of Europe's biggest city, Paris, and five times the size of Constantinople. Max Rodenbeck writes in his splendid *Cairo: The City Victorious* (1998), for sheer scale and density, enterprise and economic success, medieval Cairo was the New York of its day.

The bounty of the Mamluk era is reflected today in the buildings the Mamluks left behind, which represent a pinnacle of Islamic architecture in Egypt. Characterized by slender, multitiered minarets, exquisitely carved stone domes, and delicate inlays of marbles and other colored stone, Cairo retains some 200 Mamluk structures, ranging from mosques and palaces to fountains and even a hospital, founded 700 years ago and still in use today. This vivacious Mamluk legacy is largely unknown and unseen by most visitors to Egypt, but it is also one that is arguably every bit as impressive as the heritage of the pharaohs.

Yet, in addition to fostering wealth and beauty, this was an age of bloody violence and unimaginable cruelty. With no system of hereditary lineage, succession went to the strongest. To become sultan meant first eliminating all potential rivals. Once a ruler was in power, assassination lurked around every darkened corner. Rare was the Mamluk sultan who died of old age.

One sultan who died at least *in* old age, if not of it, was Qansuh al-Ghouri. When he assumed power in 1501 he became the 46th Mamluk sultan. He had begun his career as a slave and page boy to former sultans and had clawed his way up the ladder carefully and slowly, so that by the time he reached the summit he was already 60 years old. Though he is known to have been fond of the perfume of flowers, make no mistake: He would not have balked at having miscreants sawn in half alive—a favorite Mamluk punishment. In 1516, when he had already held power three times longer than the average reign of a sultan, he was obliged to ride out to meet the threat of the Ottoman Turkish Empire. His Mamluk army, for two and a half centuries the scourge of the Near East, was defeated in battle. In January of the following year the Turks entered Cairo.

During the late 15th century, two other events had taken place that would prove to critically affect the future of Cairo and of Egypt in general. In 1498 the Portuguese explorer Vasco da Gama successfully rounded the Cape of Good Hope and reached the coast of southwest India. Six years earlier, Genoese mariner Christopher Columbus had reached the Americas, opening up a whole new world of riches to Europeans, who no longer had any need of the Mamluk middlemen who had long controlled trade. From being the center of the world, Cairo was downgraded to a provincial capital, subject to Istanbul. Egypt shrank in on itself, and became ever more isolated.

Writing in 1384, Italian merchant Leonardo Frescobaldi claimed that more people dwelled on a single street in Cairo than in all of . . . Florence.

Egypt & Europe: Napoleon

Just as with Alexander the Great some 2,000 years previously, it took another exceptional and hugely ambitious young general to bring Egypt back to the world's attention at the end of the 18th century. Napoleon Bonaparte was looking for a way to hurt the English, with whom France was at war, and he concluded that the shrewdest answer was to capture Egypt. From there he could threaten British interests in India. His dreams went further, as he was later to write: "I saw myself founding a religion, marching into Asia, riding an elephant, a turban on my head, and in my hand the new Koran that I would have composed to suit my needs."

In the event, his campaign ended disastrously. Napoleon and his army landed in 1798 near Alexandria only to be stranded when the French fleet was blasted out of the water by the English admiral Horatio Nelson in an engagement remembered today as the Battle of the Nile. However, in a famous confrontation fought in the shadow of the Pyramids, the French did defeat Egypt's Mamluks, back in power in the absence of any real control from Istanbul, but the country remained hostile.

Unable to exert control, battered and humiliated, by the end of 1801 the expedition was over. But the military failure was counterbalanced by the achievements of Napoleon's other army, the 154 scientists, painters, physicists, anthropologists, and more, who spent three years investigating everything in and about Egypt. The results were gathered in 24 volumes as *Description de l'Egypte (Description of Egypt)*, and through its publication Europe rediscovered its interest in this ancient land.

Egypt & Europe: Muhammad Ali

Napoleon's defeat of the Mamluks also cleared the way for new blood. Into the power vacuum in Egypt stepped an Albanian mercenary named Muhammad Ali who, within five years of the French army's departure, had successfully maneuvered to become Ottoman viceroy of Egypt.

Muhammad Ali (R.1805–1848) was anxious to continue the affair begun between Egypt and Europe. He encouraged foreigners with talent to come to Cairo. One to take up the invitation was a French veteran of the Napoleonic Wars named Joseph Sèves, who trained the viceroy's armies. He later converted to Islam, becoming Suleyman Pasha, and his statue used to stand in downtown Cairo until the 1952 revolution relegated him to the Citadel.

Muhammad Ali also hired Western teachers and experts in all fields to help resurrect his adopted country. At the same time, Egyptian students and scholars were dispatched to Europe to learn Western ways. Politically Muhammad Ali supported the Ottoman sultan at first, but his own military victories in Greece, Arabia, and the Sudan gave him the confidence to challenge his masters. When Sèves's troops

Blue & Gray in Egypt

In the late 1860s, the Khedive Ismail was devoted to showing that his country could claim equal footing in world affairs with other powers. He desired to develop his armed forces and his defenses, and to extend by exploration his country's reach into Africa. Who better suited to these purposes than men trained at West Point and Annapolis in the United States, tested in battle and organization? So off they went, survivors of America's Civil War, both Northern and Southern, bound in Egypt to a common cause, for the money, or the adventure, or to try to make good a tarnished reputation. Dozens of American veterans trained the Khedive's army, built forts, and surveyed land.

Opened up to the West by Muhammad Ali and his successors, Egypt became an attraction for tourists from the mid-19th century onward.

decisively defeated an Ottoman army in 1839, Muhammad Ali was poised to attack Istanbul. In return for the hereditary right to rule Egypt, he backed down and gave up his gains in Syria.

Egypt & Europe: The Canal

Though not without its warts, Muhammad Ali's rule is generally viewed favorably for nurturing the seeds of the modern Egyptian state. However, the dynasty he founded (which he ruled with the title of "khedive") came to be increasingly reviled by the Egyptian people, who labored under heavy taxes to support new projects that seemed primarily to benefit European powers.

Egypt was seen as the fast overland route to the East. Under Abbas (*R.* 1848–1854) a railroad line was constructed by the British from Alexandria to Cairo; then under Said (*R.* 1854–1863) a concession was given to the ruler's friend, French engineer Ferdinand de Lesseps, for the cutting of a canal across the Isthmus of Suez. The work was completed in 1869. The French-educated and devoutly Francophile Ismail (*R.* 1863–1879), grandson of Muhammad Ali, orchestrated the lavish inaugural celebrations. The royalty of Europe and their retinues came in great numbers, all at Egypt's expense. Hotels and palaces were specially built: The result was bankruptcy.

Ismail was forced into exile, and financial advisers were appointed by Britain and France, Egypt's two main creditors. An Egyptian citizen did not have to be a passionate nationalist to conclude that the country was being run for, and by, foreigners. But when the people objected too loudly, with rioting in Alexandria in 1882, the British stepped in and assumed control of the country. The heirs of Muhammad Ali remained on the throne, but all real power was concentrated in the hands of the British consul general. Promises of Egyptian self-rule made in 1914 in return for help in World War I were not honored; in 1919 Egyptians vented their anger in rioting. By 1922 Britain was forced to proclaim the end of its protectorate and recognize Egypt as an independent state with a hereditary constitutional monarch, although British influence and soldiers remained.

A 1936 treaty formally ended British occupation, but that was all but negated by the outbreak of war in 1939, when Egypt became vital to British strategy. Battalions were barracked beside the Pyramids and on the banks of the Nile. While the fighting went on in the desert, Cairo and Alexandria became fleshpots for troops on leave. Militant Egyptian nationalists conspired with German spies. It was a time of turmoil and some danger, but also plenty of romance, the inspiration for a whole slew of literature.

Lost Gospel

The fact Judas betrayed Jesus to enemy soldiers was common belief until 2006, when a new gospel came to light. The Gospel of Judas, part of a 1,700-year-old papyrus book discovered in the 1970s near El Minya in Egypt, revealed an alternative story: that Judas was following Jesus' orders to betray him. Given the fact that it was in extremely poor condition, in nearly 1,000 broken fragments, the gospel's interpretation is ongoing. Learn more at www.nationalgeographic.com/lostgospel.

The Arab Republic of Egypt

By the end of the war, new forces were emerging in Egypt, impatient with both the king and existing political representations for having failed to secure the country's independence, and for having collaborated with the British. Then came the disaster of the 1948 Arab-Israeli conflict, in which the Egyptian army was defeated by the newly formed state of Israel. Egyptian anger at the humiliation found an outlet on a January 1952 weekend remembered as "Black Saturday." Clouds of acrid smoke swallowed the whole of central Cairo as some 700 stores, hotels, and premises in the European quarter were torched by rampaging mobs. Six months later, on July 23, a group calling itself the Free Officers, led by Gamal Abdel Nasser, occupied the ministries, palaces, and parliament in a bloodless coup. The last king of Egypt, Farouk, was forced to abdicate and was dispatched into exile, and in June 1953 the Republic of Egypt was proclaimed.

After the brief presidency of Sudenese-born Gen. Mohammed Naguib, Nasser became president the following year, the first native Egyptian to wield power in his own country since the last of the pharaohs. British and French nationals were sent packing, along with other colonials. Rich pashas had their land confiscated and parceled out among the *fellaheen,* the peasant classes. Nasser was a socialist hero, especially after the defiant stance adopted during the Suez Crisis in 1956 when he faced down the combined forces of Britain, France, and Israel after he nationalized the canal. Nasser came to symbolize social justice and anti-imperialism, as well as pan-Arabism. He was the John F. Kennedy of Egypt, until his magic rule was ended not by a single bullet, but by the Israeli air force's precision bombing on June 5, 1967. The scale and suddenness of Egypt's military defeat in the Six Day War, as its air forces were caught napping on the ground and Israeli troops advanced across Sinai, totally destroyed the aura of Nasser's new Egypt. He died three somber years later.

His successor, Anwar Sadat, took Israel by surprise in October 1973, when he initiated a new military campaign (see p. 138). The Egyptian army's initial successes, regardless of later reversals, were a boost for the country's morale. They opened the way for the peace talks that culminated in the signing of the American-brokered Camp David peace treaty on March 26, 1979. Sadat and Prime Minister of Israel Menachem Begin were awarded the Nobel Peace Prize for 1978 for their contribution to the two frame agreements on peace in the Middle East, and on peace between Egypt and Israel, signed on September 17, 1978.

Sadat was assassinated in 1981 by Islamic extremists. He was succeeded by his vice president, Hosni Mubarak. A pragmatic leader, lacking the charisma or flamboyance of his predecessors, Mubarak has proved solid. Egypt may no longer be the center of the Arab world, but regional relations are good, and international standing has been enhanced by Cairo's role in negotiating between the Palestinians and Israel.

> Schemes are afoot to reclaim more living space from the desert, ... and ever more areas are being opened up to tourism.

The threat of violence from religious extremists seems to have been met at the start of the 21st century, and the focus is on self-development. Schemes are afoot to reclaim more living space from the desert, privatization has given a shot in the arm to the moribund state economy, literacy is up, population growth is down, and ever more areas are being opened up to tourism. After 4,500 years of often tumultuous recorded history, if Egypt can't quite yet rest on its laurels, it is at least in a position to make a decent tourist buck off past achievements. ∎

Egypt's second president, the charismatic Gamal Abdel Nasser (1918–1970), was a hero to his own people and those of all developing nations.

Pharaonic Culture

For most people, the pharaonic culture of Ancient Egypt consists of little more than temples and gods, tombs and mummies. Although these things tend to give the impression that the ancient Egyptians were obsessed by death, theirs was a culture firmly rooted in the belief in eternal life, which they went to enormous lengths to ensure with help from their many gods.

Pharaonic Religion

Ancient Egyptian religion was a highly complex system of ritual and belief at the core of which lay the need to maintain cosmic order in a perfect balance of opposites. This was only possible with the help of the gods, who were honored with endless rituals designed to keep the universe in harmony.

Initially worshiped as representatives of the natural world, the Egyptians' many deities developed more complex personalities as the myths surrounding them became more numerous. Each myth also had its local variant, with even the story of creation preserved in at least three different forms. Although all creation myths were based on the belief that life first appeared from the waters of chaos on a mound of earth, a number of places claimed to be the original site of this mound. The life it supported was believed to have been created by the deities associated with that particular place, be they the nine gods of Heliopolis, the eight gods of Hermopolis, or the one god of Memphis.

> Ancient Egyptian religion was a . . . complex system of ritual and belief at the core of which lay the need to maintain cosmic order.

In the "solo" version of creation, the god Ptah simply thought the world into being before naming everything in it and creating life quite literally by "the word of god." Elsewhere, credit was given to Atum, the creator god of Heliopolis, who had produced his own children Shu and Tefnut by "sneezing out one and spitting out the other"—or simply by ejaculating them. These two gods then produced the earth god and sky goddess, whose own children in turn were Isis, Osiris, Seth, and Nephthys.

Others believed in more cataclysmic events, during which life was created by eight mysterious gods. Their combined energies sparked life into being and formed the primeval mound from which the sun burst forth in the earliest version of the big bang theory. Always at the center of Egyptian life, the sun was regarded as all powerful and was considered as capable of taking life as of creating it. The god most often associated with this power was the falcon-headed god Re, although at dawn the sun was also identified with the scarab beetle Khepri, with Horus as it rose in the east, and Atum as it sank in the west. Then as it entered the underworld, the sun once again became Re, traveling through the hours of the night to conquer the forces of darkness before returning victorious each dawn to begin the eternal cycle all over again.

As the sun god's representative on earth, the king ("pharaoh" from the Egyptian

The gilded wooden figure of Selket is one of the four protector goddesses of the dead who stand around the canopic shrine of Tutankhamun in Cairo's Egyptian Museum.

EXPERIENCE: Volunteer on an Archaeological Dig

For many people, the first thing they associate with Egypt is an archaeologist, either a real one like Howard Carter or fictional characters (Indiana Jones and Brendan Fraser in *The Mummy* series come to mind.) Ancient finds are still being made, including a new chamber, KV63, in the Valley of the Kings in early 2006. And as Egypt's chief archaeologist Zahi Hawass likes to point out, perhaps 70 percent of the artifacts buried under the sands have yet to be discovered.

Even if you don't have a background in ancient history, you can still participate in an ongoing dig in Egypt. Working on a dig can be both tedious and thrilling (often at the same time). But because of a past history of antiquities theft by foreigners, Egypt requires that anyone working on a mission be officially listed and approved by the project's director. Every director has to submit a list of his team, including volunteers, to Egypt's Supreme Council of Antiquities to get a security clearance before they start their work.

The best approach is to contact the American Research Center in Egypt, which funds and organizes archaeological missions. Take a look at current and upcoming expeditions on their website at www.arce.org and contact the project director directly about volunteering.

per-wer meaning "great house") was always acknowledged as the "Son of Re," and even when local god Amun became the national deity for political reasons, his status was assured by using Re's name to create Amun-Re, king of the Gods.

It was essential that male deities have female counterparts since Egyptian belief required complete balance between dualities, an idea embodied by the goddess Maat, who held the universe together. It was she who set the rules by which each king must govern, protected by an array of largely female deities.

Honored by massive cult temples to which only their priesthood had access, Egypt's numerous gods were also worshiped by the majority of the population in small domestic shrines, together with a whole range of protective household deities such as Bes, Taweret, and the spirits of each family's ancestors. Gods great and small were an essential part of daily life, and as protective funerary deities they accompanied the dead into the eternity of the afterlife.

Gods & Goddesses

The ancient Egyptians represented their deities in both human and animal form, and as a combination of both. Many of them shared characteristics, titles, and attributes creating an incredibly complicated pattern of religious belief. Here is a cast list of key players in the divine dramas.

Ammut This composite figure of a lion, hippopotamus, and crocodile ate the hearts of sinners after death.

Amun Local deity of Thebes whose name means "the hidden one," he became king of the gods when combined with Re as Amun-Re. His cult center was Karnak.

Anubis Jackal-headed god of embalmers and guardian of cemeteries.

Atum The great creator god known as "the one who came into being of himself"; like Re he was worshiped mainly at Heliopolis.

Bes Grotesque dwarflike god of the household; protector of women in childbirth.

Geb The son of Shu and Tefnut, Geb represents the earth and is shown as a green man.

Hathor Goddess of love, pleasure, and beauty, she is often represented as a cow. Her name means "the house of Horus" as protector of the god, the king, and all dead souls, and her cult center was Dendara.

Horus Usually represented as a falcon, the son of Isis and Osiris was conceived after his father's resurrection to avenge and succeed him (see "Isis & Osiris," p. 305) and was the god with whom all living kings were identified.

Isis The great goddess of magic who reassembled Osiris's dismembered body to create the first mummy and conceive Horus. Her name was written with a throne sign, and her cult center at Philae was the last outpost of the ancient religion.

Khepri The sun god appears at dawn in the form of a scarab beetle.

Maat Goddess of universal order and symbol of truth, identified by her feathered plume, against which the hearts of the dead were weighed for sin.

Nekhbet Vulture goddess of Upper Egypt whose out-stretched wings protect the king. Together Nekhbet and Wadjet were known as the "Mighty Ones."

Nephthys Sister of Isis. Together they were the protectors of the dead.

Nut The sky goddess is portrayed as a woman whose body forms heaven, arcing over that of her brother Geb, with the pair held apart by their father Shu, god of air.

Osiris Initially an earthly ruler and bringer of fertility, his name is also written with the throne sign; after his murder and resurrection as the first mummy he became savior of the dead and lord of the underworld. His cult center at Abydos was a place of pilgrimage.

Ptah Creator god and patron of craftsmen whose cult center was Memphis.

Re Preeminent form of the sun god whose name means "the sun," generally portrayed as a falcon-headed figure with the sun's disk on his head. His cult center, Heliopolis, is the area now partly beneath Cairo airport.

Sekhmet Fearsome lioness goddess of destruction whose name means "the powerful one," she directed the forces of aggression against all enemies of the state. The center of her cult was Memphis.

The goddess Nut stretches her body protectively over the dead as shown on the underside of the stone sarcophagus lid of King Merenptah.

Seth God of chaos and storms, murderer of his brother Osiris, he was repre-sented as a mythical animal.

Shu God of the air represented as a human figure wearing a feather on his head. He was created when Atum sneezed him into being.

Taweret Hippopotamus goddess of childbirth.

Tefnut Goddess of moisture and twin sister of Shu, she was created when her father Atum spat her out—her name is sometimes written with the hieroglyph sign of lips spitting.

Great entrance gateway
("pylons") flanked by huge
temple flagpoles

**Example of a classic
New Kingdom temple**

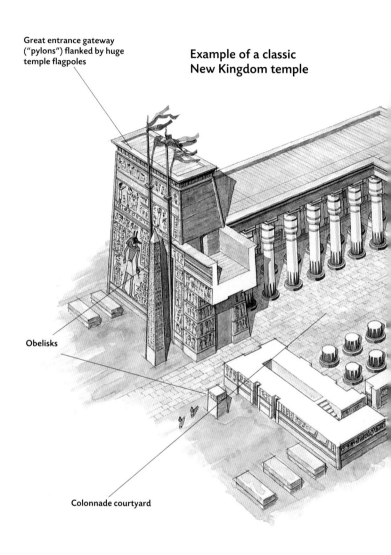

Obelisks

Colonnade courtyard

Thoth Ibis-headed god of wisdom and patron of scribes, he was worshiped at Hermopolis.

Wadjet Cobra goddess of Lower Egypt, represented by the protective serpent, or uraeus, on the brow of the king's headdress.

Pharaonic deities have many different aspects and there are lots of overlapping areas of their connotations and responsibilities, as you can see in the above list. Also, certain gods are particular to specific regions of Egypt, and they may fulfill roles that are filled by another god elsewhere in the country. With their wide-ranging duties and stories, Egyptian gods and goddesses provide a fascinating glimpse into ancient culture.

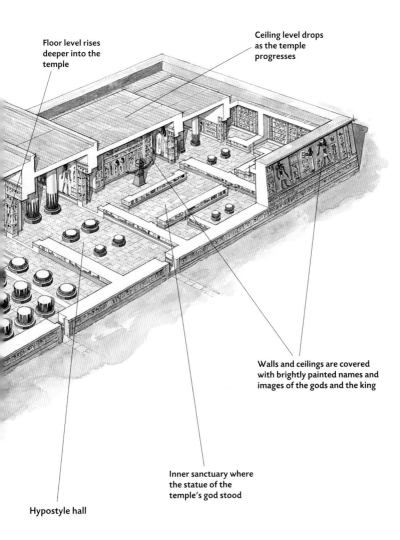

Floor level rises deeper into the temple

Ceiling level drops as the temple progresses

Walls and ceilings are covered with brightly painted names and images of the gods and the king

Inner sanctuary where the statue of the temple's god stood

Hypostyle hall

The Temple

The temple lay at the heart of Egyptian life and formed the focus of each settlement. It combined the roles of town hall, college, and medical center, as well as performing a religious function. But whereas the modern church or mosque has a congregation, only the priesthood were allowed inside the ancient temples, where their role was simply to serve the gods whose divine powers could then be harnessed for the benefit of all.

Each day in temples all over Egypt, the high priest, standing in for the king, acted as intermediary between the mortal and divine worlds. He used traditional rituals in which the gods were honored with a constant flow of offerings intended to encourage them down to inhabit their statues, housed inside small shrines to which only the king and high priest had access.

The clergy themselves ranged from the most highly educated priest to the man who tended the sacred cattle. They lived in their own small communities attached to the temple, often close to its sacred lake in which they were required to bathe twice each day and twice each night, since ritual proceedings required that they maintain total purity.

Although the priests' houses, storerooms, and subsidiary buildings were made of standard mud brick, the temples themselves were constructed of stone, their every

Repeated figures of Horemheb, in a striped headcloth presenting offerings to the gods, decorate a tomb in the Valley of the Kings.

surface covered in brightly painted images and texts. Scenes of warfare and destruction on the outside walls contrasted sharply with the calm scenes of devout worship inside, graphically illustrating the idea that the source of universal order could only be found within the temple walls.

Tomb Art

The distinctive style of ancient Egyptian art was established at the very beginning of the pharaonic period, about 3100 B.C., and remained largely unchanged for more than three millennia. Despite its instantly recognizable appearance to the modern viewer, the reasons why it was created are still very much misunderstood. Unlike art produced to be appreciated for its own sake, Egyptian sculpture and painting were meant to be functional rather than simply decorative.

The breathtaking beauty of the art is therefore all the more remarkable, given

that the paintings, reliefs, and sculpture were made mainly for religious and funerary purposes. Hidden away from public gaze, they were either in the darkness of temple interiors or buried with the dead to protect them in the afterlife. This explains the nature of painted and relief scenes in particular. Their deceptively simplistic appearance and lack of perspective have a functional purpose since it was vital that the subject be portrayed with every relevant feature shown as clearly as possible. Human figures are given a clear profile of nose and mouth, whereas the eye was shown as whole: It was thought that the correct rituals would reanimate the subjects and that only the clearest of representations would enable the senses to work efficiently on that reanimation.

Inanimate objects were also represented as clearly as possible, with the vast quantities of food and drink offered in temples and tombs duplicated on the walls to ensure a constant supply of sustenance for eternity. The offerings are shown piled up in distinct layers, often to the extent of "floating" in suspension, and the contents of boxes were portrayed in a similar fashion. Although working within strict stylistic conventions, the ancient artists still managed to capture the vitality of images inspired by the world around them. These images repeatedly emphasize the concept of life and rebirth and were thought capable of transmitting the very vitality they depicted. They include scarab beetles and tilapia fish, believed capable of self-generation, the animals and plants offered as food for the deceased and the gods, and the life-giving lotus flower (the heraldic symbol of Upper Egypt, as the papyrus reed was of Lower Egypt).

Art's functional nature was also enhanced by a careful use of bright primary colors. The land of Egypt, represented politically by the White Crown of Upper Egypt and the Red Crown of Lower Egypt, was also divided into the fertile black land and the red desert wastes. This distinction explains the choice of black and green in representations of Osiris, god of fertility and eternal life, in contrast to the redness associated with his murderous brother Seth, god of chaos. The ethereal blue of the sky also had divine associations and was used in representations of the gods in general, with the golden yellow of the sun employed for its protective qualities. Even humans were represented with different-colored skin tones, the red-brown of men contrasting with the paler, more yellowed tones of female figures.

Hieroglyphs & Cartouches

The beginnings of ancient Egyptian writing were thought to have emerged about 3100 B.C., until recent discoveries indicated that it was actually in use almost two centuries earlier, making it the world's oldest script, predating that of Mesopotamia. The Egyptians first developed writing as a means of organizing resources, using a pictorial script that came to be known as hieroglyphs from Greek words meaning "sacred carved letters." In continuous use for more than 3,500 years, hieroglyphs evolved from a simple script made up of a handful of signs to a highly

Hieroglyphs

Thanks to the translation of the Rosetta Stone by French scholar Jean-François Champollion (1790–1832), ancient Egyptian hieroglyphs are as comprehensible to modern Egyptologists as they were to priests in Cleopatra's day. Though some hieroglyphs represent individual sounds or letters, others are ideograms that represent whole words, or simply determine the meaning and context of the word immediately before them. To make things more complicated, they can be read either from right to left, from left to right, or from top to bottom.

One thing you'll notice is that the names of pharaohs always appear within a cartouche—the round-cornered rectangle around a name. For a handy overview of the various Egyptian divinities and their symbols, see Robert A. Armour's *Gods and Myths of Ancient Egypt*. An excellent introduction to reading hieroglyphs is Janice Kamrin's *Ancient Egyptian Hieroglyphs: A Practical Guide, A Step-by-Step Approach to Learning Ancient Egyptian Hieroglyphs*, which explains the hieroglyphic alphabet, common symbols, and how to read longer texts.

While you may not have the time to master the script and language of the pharaohs, here are a few recurring words and symbols that pop up frequently at ancient sites:

House

Son of Ra

Lord of the Two Lands

Anubis

Full name of Ramses II

Osiris

complex compendium of more than 6,000, each sign representing one, two, or three consonants, or simply acting as a determinative. The lack of vowels, punctuation, and spacing, together with the practice of writing hieroglyphs horizontally right to left and left to right—as well as vertically—only added to their cryptic nature.

Although a "shorthand" form (known as hieratic) soon developed for day-to-day transactions, hieroglyphs were retained for religious purposes. They were regarded as "the words of Thoth" after the ibis-headed god of writing, and their magical nature was enhanced by the fact that only one percent of the ancient population was literate, with those who had direct access to this "divine wisdom" forming an elite scribal class.

Their aesthetic appearance made hieroglyphs a perfect medium for both tomb and temple inscriptions in which they form

The royal cartouche punctuates funerary liturgy carved into the wall of a tomb.

an integral part of scenes, both words and pictures infused with divine power. The symbols of strength, prosperity, and above all life were regarded as especially potent, as were the names of the king and the gods, written again and again to preserve them for eternity.

The Egyptians sincerely believed that "to speak the name of the dead is to make them live," since the name is as essential to an individual's identity as his or her soul. The loss of either would result in permanent oblivion, the fate of those unfortunate enough to incur official censure, whether commoners, kings, or even the gods themselves. To counteract this, the names of the most powerful individuals were not only repeated, but protected with epithets such as *ankh, wedja, seneb* ("life, prosperity, health"). Parts of the royal name were also written inside a protective fortress wall *(serekh)*, which later developed into an oval-shaped cartouche (from the French for "cartridge"). The cartouche enclosed two of the five names given to each king, first the "King of Upper and Lower Egypt" name, which was written with a sedge plant and a bee and assumed at the coronation, followed by his "Son of Re" name, written with a sun disk and a goose; this name was given at birth.

As a good luck charm, names frequently incorporated those of the gods, such as Amenhotep, meaning "Amun is content," or Ramses, "born of Re." An individual could also be given a simple name such as Nefer, meaning "beautiful" or "happy," or Seneb, meaning "healthy," while some chose to name their children after aspects of the natural world, including Miwt ("Cat") or Seshen ("Lotus").

The last known hieroglyphic inscription is dated to A.D. 394, after which time the acceptance of Christianity led to the closure of the temples and all the knowledge they contained. Ancient Egypt had been lost and remained so until revealed once again with the decipherment of hieroglyphs in 1824 (see "The Key to Ancient Egypt," p. 167). ■

Timeline of the Pharaohs

The precise dates of the Egyptian dynasties and of individual reigns are still the subject of much heated scholarly debate. The following table, based on the chronology presented by the *British Museum Dictionary of Ancient Egypt* by Ian Shaw and Paul Nicholson, is also selective, including only the major kings and pharaohs, usually those who have left enduring monuments to their reign.

One of many statues of Ramses II carved by his subjects. He was the greatest builder of all ancient Egyptian pharaohs.

Early Dynastic Period
CA 3100–2686 B.C.

Formative period during which many major aspects of pharaonic culture and society emerge.

1st dynasty	3100–2890
Narmer/Menes	ca 3100
2nd dynasty	2890–2686

Old Kingdom
2686–2181 B.C.

Period marked by the rise of Memphis as Egypt's capital and the growth of absolute power of pharaohs who erect pyramids as monuments.

3rd dynasty	686–2613
Djoser	2667–2648
Sekhemkhet	2648–2640
4th dynasty	2613–2494
Sneferu	2613–2589
Khufu (Cheops)	2589–2566
Djedefra	2566–2558
Khafre (Chephren)	2558–2532
Menkaura (Mycerinus)	2532–2503
5th dynasty	2494–2345
Userkaf	2494–2487
Sahure	2487–2475
Neferirkare	2475–2455
Nyuserra	2445–2421
Unas	2375–2345

6th dynasty	*2345–2181*
Teti	2345–2323
Pepi	2321–2287
Pepi II	2278–2184

First Intermediate Period
2181–2055 B.C.

Unified rule gives way to rival principalities and civil war. The power of the pharaohs declines during this time.

7th–11th dynasties

Middle Kingdom
2055–1650 B.C.

Continued turmoil until Egypt is reunified under the rulers of Thebes, which now becomes increasingly important. Power shifts to Upper Egypt.

11th dynasty	*2055–1985*
Mentuhotep II	2055–2004
12th dynasty	*1985–1795*
Amenemhat I	1985–1955
Senusret I	1965–1920
Amenemhat II	1922–1878
Senusret II	1880–1874
Senusret III	1874–1855
Amenemhat III	1855–1808
Amenemhat IV	1808–1799
13th–14th dynasties	*1795–1650*

Second Intermediate Period
1650–1550 B.C.

Egypt is occupied by the Hyskos, foreign settlers from the north.

15th–17th dynasties

New Kingdom
1550–1069 B.C.

Golden age of the pharaohs as Egypt rises to unequaled greatness under a succession of powerful kings; Thebes is now the southern capital and Egypt's religious and funerary center.

18th dynasty	*1550–1295*
Ahmose I	1550–1525
Amenhotep I	1525–1504
Tuthmose I	1504–1492
Tuthmose II	1492–1479
Tuthmose III	1479–1425
Hatshepsut	1473–1458
Amenhotep II	1427–1400
Tuthmose IV	1400–1390
Amenhotep III	1390–1352
Akhenaten	1352–1336
Tutankhamun	1336–1327
Aye	1327–1323
Horemheb	1323–1295
19th dynasty	*1295–1186*
Ramses I	1295–1294
Seti I	1294–1279
Ramses II	1279–1213
Merenptah	1213–1203
Seti II	1200–1194
20th dynasty	*1186–1069*
Ramses III	1184–1153
Ramses IV	1153–1147
Ramses V–XI	1147–1069

Third Intermediate Period
1069–747 B.C.

Pharaonic rule breaks down. Tanis in the Delta supersedes Thebes. Libyans invade and rule.

21st–24th dynasties

Late Period
747–332 B.C.

Simultaneous dynasties of rival rulers in Thebes and the Delta. Egypt comes under both Kushite (a dynasty from the south) and Persian rule. However, the 26th dynasty (664–525 B.C.) saw native rule based at Sais.

25th–30th dynasties

Greco-Roman Period
332 B.C.–A.D. 395

Ptolemaic Period	332–30
Alexander the Great	332–323
Ptolemy I	305–285
Ptolemy II	285–247
Ptolemy III	246–221
Cleopatra	51–30

The Arts

For all that we in the West know about it, Egyptian culture might as well have died with the pharaohs. But to the Arab-speaking world, Cairo is their Hollywood and New York rolled into one, a powerhouse of film, television, music, theater, and literature.

Literature

Ancient Egyptian stories and legends have long made their mark on the psyche of Americans and Europeans via movies such as *Cleopatra, The Prince of Egypt,* and the countless undead risings of the *Mummy,* but probably the last time modern Egypt

Folk musicians and singers in Egypt's capital of Cairo entertain the faithful during the holy month of Ramadan.

and international culture crossed paths in any major way was when Omar Sharif wowed female audiences in David Lean's *Lawrence of Arabia* and *Doctor Zhivago*.

However, keen readers and news followers may have noted another Egyptian entry onto the international scene in 1988, when Cairo-born novelist Naguib Mahfouz was awarded that year's Nobel Prize for Literature, thus joining the ranks of the likes of Gabriel García Márquez, John Steinbeck, and Ernest Hemingway. Born in 1911, Mahfouz became the grand old man of Arabic letters. He started writing at age 17 and produced around 50 novels and collections of short stories before his death in 2006. He almost single-handedly shaped the nature of Egyptian literature in the 20th century, shepherding its transition from European imitation to a form with a distinct national voice of its own. The best of his work—which includes the novels *The Harafish* and *Children of the Alley*—harks back to the indigenous narrative arts of Arabic literature, drawing inspiration from medieval story cycles like *The Thousand and One Nights,* and those found in the Koran, the Muslim holy book. Many of his works have been translated into English, and they are, in the words of the *Washington Post,* "a marvelous read."

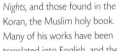

[Naguib Mahfouz] almost single-handedly shaped . . . Egyptian literature in the 20th century . . . with a distinct national voice of its own.

How much better it would be, however, if the stories were delivered by a master storyteller in person, instead of on the page. This is how it once was in Egypt: Tales such as those that make up *The Thousand and One Nights,* a bawdy collection of parables and entertainments, many of which are set in the Cairo of the Mamluks, were never meant to be read. Instead they were perpetuated by itinerant showmen, who carried the stories in their heads and related them in backstreet coffeehouses. Skillful manipulators of an attentive audience, they would end each tale on a note of high suspense, commanding a tribute of coins to reveal what happened next. Sadly, public storytelling is an art that has largely failed to survive the 20th century, supplanted in the coffeehouses first by radio, then by television. Only during the holy month of Ramadan does the storytelling recommence, revived by a new, young generation of raconteurs, who gather an audience each night in one of the old houses of Islamic Cairo to entrance with the tales of Sheherazade.

Part of the appeal of Mahfouz is that he transports his readers to a time before the advent of television. Ironic then that, despite his fame, Mahfouz is actually little read in his home country. Egyptians are not great readers of literary fiction; books on current events and religion find a bigger readership than novels, while poetry also retains a surprising popularity. Instead,

Mahfouz's fame at home comes from film and TV adaptations—even his own daughters confess to knowing their father's work through the screen rather than the printed word.

The Lady

Though she is virtually unknown in the West, one figure stands even taller than Naguib Mahfouz in the Egyptian cultural pantheon—a large woman with dark glasses and a handkerchief, often referred to with great reverence simply as Al-Sitt, "the Lady." She is Umm Kolthum, the 20th century's greatest Arabic singer. Born into poverty in a small Delta village, she gained early fame as a reciter of the Koran at weddings. She gave her debut radio broadcast in 1935 and rapidly became the voice of a nation. For almost 40 years until she retired in 1973, the first Thursday of every month became a celebrated occasion, eagerly anticipated by millions of Egyptians, as Umm Kolthum gave her monthly concert.

Kings, presidents, and princes would fly in from all over the Arab world to attend the show, while the streets of Egypt's towns and cities would become deserted as families stayed home to listen to the performance broadcast live on the radio. Her songs were great epics, with lyrics by famous poets set to tunes by contemporary composers. A single song could last an hour or more. Toward the end her voice would rise to an

A portrait of Umm Kolthum is carried aloft by mourners who thronged the streets at her funeral in 1975.

almost sobbing intensity, which would have her audiences shouting out of sheer ecstasy. It has been said that the whole country was enslaved to her voice.

The Lady's popularity was at its peak, in the heady days of the 1950s, when newly independent Egypt was a beacon of hope to the whole Arab world and the developing nations of Africa, still struggling to free themselves from colonial rule. Charismatic firebrand Gamal Abdel Nasser may have been the president, but Umm Kolthum represented the real embodiment of the Arabs' cultural renaissance. As critic Mustafa Mahmoud wrote, "Umm Kolthum is more effective in connecting the Arab world than thousands of airlines, more powerful than thousands of railways or telephone lines. Get in your car on the night of her concert and roam around the Arab countries, and you'll easily identify its borders."

Her male counterparts were Abdel Halim Hafez and Farid al-Atrash, Egypt's answers to Frank Sinatra and Elvis Presley. These crooners and movie stars had enormous popular appeal, but they never came close to attracting the adulation inspired by the Lady. When she died in 1975 her funeral was attended by a bevy of Arab leaders, and the streets of Cairo filled with over two million mourners.

In the decades since her death classical Arabic music has become much less popular. Egypt has experienced a population boom and the mean age has decreased. A new generation of singers has emerged. Egypt has its own take on pop, and rap, and other modern musical trends, and has its own homegrown hit parade of stars and starlets. For people of a certain age, however, the songs of Umm Kolthum remain as pinnacles, reminders of a great golden age of Arabic culture. They are constantly played on radio and TV, and a cheap cassette of *Inta Omri (You Are My Life)* or *Al-Atlal (The Ruins)*, two of the Lady's seminal works, is an essential part of any Cairo taxi-driver's kit.

Arab Music

Buying a CD of Egyptian music—such as a collection of standards by Umm Kolthum or Abdel Halim Hafez or an album of catchy Arab pop—is an easy way to re-create the soundtrack of your time in Egypt once you're home. You can hear the latest hits from pop stars like Tamr Hosny, Amr Diab, Ruby, and Nancy Ajram just about anywhere in Cairo. If you hear a catchy song you like on the radio or in a restaurant, ask someone who you're listening to.

Diwan (*159 26th of July St., Zamalek*) helpfully stocks its CDs in racks labeled in English. The **Mirage Megastore** (*71 Gamiat al-Duwal al-Arabiya, Mohandiseen*) has an even larger selection.

Hollywood on the Nile

During her lifetime Umm Kolthum appeared in six movies, including 1936's *Wedad*, the first long feature film to be made by Studio Misr, Egypt's equivalent to MGM. During the halcyon years of the 1940s and '50s, Cairo's film studios rolled out 50 to 100 movies annually, with many reaching technical standards that matched the best European and American productions. Egypt produced its own homegrown stable of square-jawed leading men and swooning starlets. Musicals, romances, and melodramas spread the Cairene dialect throughout the Arab-speaking world. Just as every kid in America at one time grew up familiar with the sights of New York via the big screen, so too children from Casablanca to Baghdad had their fantasies fueled with the glamorous settings of celluloid Cairo.

This is less the case today. Production has dropped and critics complain of a decline in quality. Egypt no longer has the cinematic cachet that it once did. However, within Egypt itself local product still has the edge over Hollywood imports and fills more of the country's screens. Walk around any town or city and large, lurid, hand-painted billboards advertise the latest movies, with their stars, standing many times larger than life-size, bearing down on the passersby below.

Unfortunately, the Egyptian product has never translated beyond its Arabic-speaking audience. In that sense, it is a little like the output of India's Bollywood—too firmly tailored to its home audience to appeal to non-natives. Typical fare is slapstick comedy, full of raised voices, exaggerated gestures, and high-pitched hysterics. There are some exceptions: Shadi Abdelsalam's *The Night of Counting the Years* (1969) is a beautiful and truly original film based on the story of the tomb-robbing Abdel Rassoul brothers (see "Guardians & Thieves," pp. 264–265). Among film critics it ranks as the finest Egyptian movie ever made.

Also highly regarded is the output of the late director Yousef Chahine, who has been called Egypt's Fellini and was honored with a lifetime achievement award at Cannes in 1997. Born in 1926, he directed around 40 films during a career that defies classification. Chahine's films were also some of the very few Egyptian productions that are subtitled into English or French, and they regularly made the rounds of international film festivals. It was Chahine who discovered the young Omar Sharif, casting him in three films in the early 1950s. Sharif acted only in Egyptian films until his role as Sharif Ali in *Lawrence of Arabia*. For anyone who was wondering what happened to Sharif, he is now back in Egypt making undistinguished made-for-television films and TV commercials.

EXPERIENCE: Learn to Belly Dance

Most people are happy to simply watch belly-dancing performances (see p. 382). But if you're a woman interested in trying out this sensual, challenging art form, it can be a wonderful introduction to a part of Egyptian culture—one often misunderstood or easily stereotyped. Belly dancing—more properly called *raqs sharqi*, or "Oriental dance" in Arabic—is also great exercise, and a number of health clubs in Egypt, such as the **Creative Dance and Fitness Center** (*13B Rd. 254, Digla, Maadi*), or the **Fitness & Dance Academy** (*8th floor, Yamama Center, 3 Taha Hussein St., Zamalek*) offer belly-dancing workout classes.

If you have time, consider taking lessons with a real belly-dancing teacher. Belly dancing has found growing popularity among dancers outside the Arab world, even as a growing religious conservatism has frowned upon it and discouraged some Egyptian women from taking it up.

One of Egypt's most famous dance teachers is the renowned **Raqia Hassan,** who offers private lessons as well as intensive lessons for more advanced students (*tel 02/27482338, www.raqiahassan.net*).

Fatiha Bouzidi (*tel 012/3282807*) teaches a "revisited form of Egyptian dance." She holds classes Mondays and Wednesdays in the Bowling Room of the Swiss Club (*90 El Gihad St., off Sudan St. from Kit Kat Sq., Imbaba*). Four classes cost 200LE, and a drop-in session is 70LE.

Some of the most devoted dancers and teachers are not, in fact, Egyptian: Australian-born Keti Sharif is a regular performer at Cairo hotels and also offers lessons and workshops at various points throughout the year (*www.ketisharif.com*).

Belly Dancing

One of the staple sights in the majority of Egyptian films is a wiggle of the belly. A truly indigenous art form, there is strong evidence from sources such as tomb paintings that the belly dance dates back to the time of the pharaohs. During medieval times dancing became institutionalized in the form of the *ghawazee*, a caste of dancers who traveled in groups and performed publicly or for hire. The female ghawazee, who according to 18th- and 19th-century descriptions danced in baggy pants and loose shirts sometimes open to the navel, were also often prostitutes.

Belly dancing began to gain credibility and popularity in Egypt with the advent of movies, when the dancers were lifted out of nightclubs and given roles on the big screen. Movies imbued belly dancing with glamour and made household names of a handful of dancers. Slinkiest of all was Tahiyya Carioca, who named herself after a Latin American dance, the *carioca*, popularized by Ginger Rogers and Fred Astaire. From the 1930s to the 1990s she appeared in more than 200 films and was married no fewer 12 times. Artists such as Carioca started the modern phenomenon of the belly dancer as superstar, someone who can command Hollywood-style fees for an appearance. Current dancers at the top of the league, including names such as Fifi Abdou, Lucy, and Dina, can expect as much as $10,000 for a single performance.

A superstar in the world of belly dancing, Fifi Abdou has also starred in television dramas.

Despite the celebrity and wealth of some of its practitioners, belly dancing is still not considered to be completely respectable, especially not by Egypt's Islamic fundamentalists. For a time in the early 1990s, pressure was successfully exerted on the dancers to cover up their midriffs, but today they are once again exposed.

Away from the glitz of the professional scene, dance in Egypt continues to thrive at a grassroots level. At the even the humblest of weddings the unmarried girls sway to the beat of the *tabla*, the Egyptian hand-held drum, hands clasped above their heads and pelvises gyrating in a blatant bid to attract male attention and a possible future groom of their own.

Belly dancing is an exclusively female pursuit, but there is also a male dance performed with wooden staves. It involves lots of stick-twirling and mock fighting and comes across as rather contrived, although the hotel nightclubs that present it in performances billed as "folkloric dancing" insist that it is an authentic rural tradition.

Wonderfully decorated walls at Gurna, near Luxor, are a popular art form. Designs often celebrate a pilgrimage to Mecca.

Art

The billboards advertising local films represent a wonderfully vibrant form of street art. This is at odds with the rather moribund mainstream art scene. Although in the past Egypt has produced fine artists of merit and originality, notably Abd al-Hady al-Gazzar (see p. 121) and Mahmoud Said, who has a museum devoted to his work in Alexandria (see p. 190), and the sculptor Mahmoud Mokhtar (1891–1934), the contemporary scene is straitjacketed by a state teaching system that continues to penalize originality and stifle experimentation.

Architecture for the Poor

Folk tradition unquestionably lies at the heart of the architecture of Hassan Fathy (1900–1989), one of the few Middle Eastern names in the field that is also known in the West. In fact, Fathy is reputedly the favorite architect of Britain's Prince Charles. He is, however, known for more than his work as an architect. Fathy was also a philosopher, artist, humanitarian, and even a visionary. From his base in Cairo (which, in his later years, was a house in the city's Islamic quarter, beside the Citadel), Fathy devoted himself to housing the poor in developing nations. Utilizing ancient design methods and materials, he integrated a knowledge of peasant economics with a mastery of age-old, common-sense, design techniques; for example, dense mud-brick walls to minimize heat transfer, so that rooms stay cool during the day and hold their warmth when the sun goes down at night, and natural air-conditioning achieved by carefully situated apertures.

Fathy's efforts, which were ahead of his time, did not always meet with success. His showpiece village of New Gurna (see p. 252) on the West Bank at Luxor remains empty to this day. However, his ideas on sustainability, an architectural way to deal with our dependence on dwindling natural resources, are coming of age, and posthumously Fathy is gaining in influence.

New hotels, such as the Adrere Amellal in Siwa (see p. 367), are being designed based on his principles. Not only are the results environmentally sound, but with their domed roofs, and myriad internal courtyards open to the stars, they are beautiful buildings to look at and inhabit.

Going Global

Naguib Mahfouz and Hassan Fathy have gained international recognition, and the belly dance has been exported worldwide, where it competes with aerobics and Pilates as a fun way to keep fit. Now there are signs that other aspects of Egypt's rich modern culture might finally be breaking through. In summer 2000, lawyers claimed that producer Timbaland and American rap artist Jay-Z had stolen the riff to one of his hit singles, "Big Pimpin'" from an old Abdel Halim Hafez song, "Khosara." Legal wrangling over the copyright continued for years.

In 2006, an English-language translation of the best-selling Egyptian novel *The Yacoubian Building* by Cairene Alaa Al Aswany was released to critical and popular acclaim in the United States. The practicing dentist's second novel, it was made into a hugely successful 2006 film that was a hit at the Berlin, Cannes, and Tribeca film festivals; Adel Imam won an international jury prize for best actor at the São Paulo International Film Festival. In 2007, the story was made into a television series. In 2008, the author was profiled in the *New York Times Magazine*.

Meanwhile, Cairo is still the center of Arabness, and worn as it is, the city still draws the best practitioners of Arab arts. As Abdel Halim might have sung had he lived longer, "If I can make it there, I'll make it anywhere...." ∎

Astonishing Artistry

The strength and power displayed on the outside of a mosque is often balanced by the delicacy and grace of the decoration inside. Proscribed from representational art by an interpretation of the Koran, Islamic craftsmen poured their ingenuity and skill into brilliant non-representational artistry. No material seemed too onerous to shape or carve into astonishing patterns; rich or poor, the faithful desired the interiors of their mosques to be works of inspiration.

Muslim artists plotted rich patterns on floors and walls. They embellished windows and lamps with colored glass. Metalworkers applied exuberance to geometry in hammering or casting their metals. The *minbar*, or pulpit, was often of the most delicately carved wood, inlaid with ivory or ebony. Craftsmen worked intricacies out of brick, marble, and terra-cotta to match the splendor of prayer rugs and carpets, also adorning the mosque interior.

Nothing was too astonishingly complex to be displayed where the faithful met for study and prayer. And to all of these patterns, the craftsmen added the calligraphy of Arabic script, itself a study in visual grace.

Food & Drink

Much of the food eaten in Egypt is not unique to the country, but is shared with other Middle Eastern neighbors and near neighbors. Most of the dishes Egyptians claim as their own are arguably Turkish, Lebanese, or Persian, but there are a few specialties that can truly be claimed as national dishes.

Chief of these national dishes is *fuul,* also known as *fuul medames,* which are small brown beans, soaked overnight, then boiled for eating. Considered something of a poor man's dish in a country where the greater part of the population lives on the breadline, it has become a national staple. In fact, fuul is claimed to have been eaten in Egypt as far back as the time of the pharaohs. In its most refined form the beans are sprinkled with olive oil, have a little lemon juice squeezed over them, and are seasoned with salt, pepper, and cumin, and maybe garnished with a chopped boiled egg. Much more common, though, is for them to be mashed to a paste and ladled into small pockets of flat pita bread as a sandwich. For many Egyptians a fuul sandwich serves for both breakfast and lunch.

Egyptians are also big consumers of *felafel* (called *taamiyya* in Cairo), patties made from dried white broad beans *(fuul nabeid),* spiced and flavored and deep-fried in oil.

Although felafel is ubiquitous throughout the Middle East (especially in Lebanon and Israel, where it is made with chickpeas), again it is claimed that the dish dates back to ancient Egypt. As part of a meal the felafel are served whole on a small plate, but they, too, are often eaten as a street snack, broken up and stuffed into a pita sandwich along with salad and small pieces of pickles known as *torshi.*

Stuffed vegetables are popular, particularly eggplant *(bedingan)* and peppers *(filfil).* These are eaten hot and cold. Eggplant is also grilled and mashed and seasoned with *tahina* (a sesame seed paste), olive oil, and garlic to make a purée known as *baba ghanoug.* Also common are stuffed grape leaves, a dish called *warak enab.* In addition to ground meat, a spicy mix of rice, chopped tomatoes, onion, mint, and cinnamon—or some similar variation—is also often used to stuff these leaves.

EXPERIENCE:
Foods to Try

While in Egypt, be sure to try some of the following local favorites:

basboosa: semolina cakes drenched in sugar syrup. As a super-sweet dessert, this pairs well with bitter Arabic coffee.
kushari: a bowl of macaroni, lentils, rice, vermicelli, and chickpeas, mixed with a vinegary tomato sauce. An inexpensive but delicious lunch for many Egyptians.
umm ali: pastry with nuts and raisins, soaked in cream and milk, then baked.
shurbat ads: a savory yellow lentil soup flavored with cumin, lemon, and dill.

Wheat is the staple cereal of the countryside, but rice is more often used as a base or side dish to most meals. It is given an unusual twist by the addition of small, very thin strands of noodles. Beans of all types, split peas, lentils, and chickpeas also form an important part of the diet. They are used in the many different soups and stews that Egyptian women are so fond of cooking—which, unfortunately, rarely find their way onto restaurant menus—and, in the case of chickpeas, are ground into a paste known as hummus, also often served as a side dish, to be eaten with bread.

With influences of Turkey, Lebanon, and Iran, Egyptian cuisine does have its own character.

A meal without bread is absolutely unthinkable, and in fact the Arabic word for it, *aish*, also means "life." Bread types are wide and varied, but the most common form is a round flat disk the size of a dinner plate, made from a coarsely ground flour.

When it comes to meat, lamb is the favorite and predominates. Beef is much less common, and, because of the dietary laws of Islam, no pork is ever eaten. Traditionally the cost of meat has been prohibitive and so it tends to be served in small chunks, flame grilled, known as kabobs, or stretched in a stew, or ground and used as part of a filling in vegetables. Chicken is common, as are pigeons, which are something of an Egyptian delicacy, especially when stuffed. In Alexandria it is also possible to find quail on the menu.

One dish to seek out is the infamous *molokhiyya*, made from the molokhiyya leaf, which looks a little like spinach. It is boiled up into a soup with an extraordinary glutinous texture that makes eating it a little like swallowing warm, savory Jell-O. It is a sensation that many find unpleasant. Nevertheless, the dish has acquired a symbolic, almost patriotic importance in Egypt and you ought to try it at least once.

Sweet Treats & Desserts

Given the Egyptian addiction to very sweet, sticky pastries, it is no wonder that dentistry is such a popular profession. The generic term for these sugar-loaded confections is baklava: layers of wafer-thin phyllo filled with crushed nuts and pistachios and drenched in syrup. It is baked in trays, then typically sliced into small diamond-shaped pieces sold by the kilogram. Another generic type, *konafa,* is made by straining liquid batter onto a hot metal sheet so it sets in strands, which are quickly swept off so they remain soft and piled on top of a soft cheese or cream base. Konafa is associated with feasts and is always eaten during Ramadan.

> **Given the Egyptian addiction to very sweet, sticky pastries, it is no wonder that dentistry is such a popular profession.**

Around the markets and bazaars, you may see vendors pushing small, wheeled glass cabinets filled with dishes of what looks like blancmange; this is *muhalabiyya,* a milk cream thickened by cornstarch or ground rice, often flavored with rose water, and with chopped almonds or coconut sprinkled on top. For the sake of your stomach, though, it is better to try it in a restaurant.

Drinks

Tea *(shai)* and coffee *(ahwa)* are an integral part of culture and hospitality in Egypt. Business meetings never begin and bargaining in the souq never finishes before all parties involved have sat and drunk at least one strong, sugary cup. Tea comes in a glass with the leaves swirling around in the bottom, while coffee Egyptian-style (also known as Turkish coffee) comes in tiny cups half full of grounds. It is often flavored with cardamom, but is still very bitter. "Of all the unchristian beverages that ever passed my lips," wrote grouchy American humorist and traveler Mark Twain, "Turkish coffee is the worst. The bottom of the cup has a muddy sediment in it half an inch deep. This goes down your throat, and portions of it lodge by the way, and produce a tickling aggravation that keeps you barking and coughing for an hour."

If you would prefer Western-style instant coffee, ask for "neskaf." A healthier option is to take advantage of Egypt's abundance of fresh fruit. A platter of fruit is usually served at the end of a meal, but on practically every street throughout Egypt there is also a juice stand at which you can get a drink squeezed out of just about any fruit in season. Most common are guava *(guafa),* mango *(manga),* orange *(bortuaan),* sugarcane *(asab),* and lemon *(limoon);* the latter drink is also offered in most cafés and restaurants.

In coffee shops, during the colder winter months, many patrons like to drink *sahlab,* a milky drink thickened with the powdered bulb of a type of orchid and flavored with chopped nuts and cinnamon. In summer, try *karkade,* made from boiled hibiscus leaves, which is a beautiful deep crimson color and drunk from a tall beaker filled with ice.

In this Islamic country, alcohol is not part of the culture, though hotels and restaurants catering to tourists will serve beer or wine if asked. Locally brewed Stella beer is good. Egypt also produces a number of wines, both red (usually Omar Khayyam) and white. ■

Beyond the Pyramids and Tutankhamun's treasures, the capital of Egypt—and the Arab world—a nonstop whirl of culture, arts, good humor, and hospitality

Cairo

Introduction & Map   66–67

Egyptian Museum   68–76

Feature: Collecting Ancient Egypt   77

Central Cairo   78–81

Downtown Cairo Walk   82–85

Islamic Cairo   86–102

Feature: The Coffeehouse   97

Experience: Take *Oud* Lessons
    in Islamic Cairo   98

Experience: Learn Arabic   103

Museum of Islamic Art   104–105

Experience: Order a Coffee   105

Sultan Hassan Mosque   106–107

The Citadel   108–110

Experience: Visit the City of the
    Dead   110

A theater poster in downtown Cairo

Al-Azhar Park   111

Ibn Tulun Mosque   112–113

Coptic Cairo   114–117

Nilometer   118–119

Gezira   120–121

Experience: Egyptian Weddings
    in Your Hotel Lobby   121

Zamalek Walk: Fine Living
    & Fine Art   122–124

Western Cairo   125–127

The Pyramids   128–135

Experience: Go Horseback Riding   129

Experience: Get in Touch with
    Your Inner Isis   132

Heliopolis   136

More Museums in Cairo   137–138

Experience: Football Madness   137

Hotels & Restaurants   357–363

Cairo

As skyscrapers are to New York City and parks to London, Cairo has its traffic. You hit it the moment you leave the airport, and it provides a wonderful introduction to the city. Cairo's traffic swirls with oddities and spectacles: Cars are dented and patched; passengers cling to the outside of buses; motorbikes carry whole families; and they all dart and weave to the frenetic chorus of beeping horns.

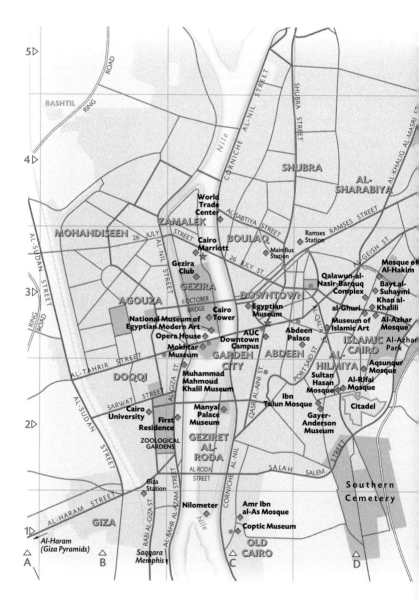

Driving rules appear nonexistent. Yet there is a system, one that relies on unwritten understandings backed by nods, and waves. Against all the odds it works, a bit like Cairo itself really. Half the cars in Egypt are in the capital because, in a sense, all roads lead here. Rarely is a country so completely dominated by a single city. Politics, finance, media, and popular culture scarcely exist beyond its boundaries. Only when it comes to tourism does any other city rate seriously. Tellingly, in the Egyptian language the word for Cairo and for Egypt is the same: *Masr.*

Cairo sprawls over roughly 175 square miles (450 sq km), about half the size of New York City, but with twice the residents. That number swells almost daily as *fellaheen,* or rural peasants, pour into the city looking to improve their lot. Incomes are, of course, better here, but Cairenes also are healthier than their country cousins.

Cairo has always absorbed outsiders in its role as Umm al-Dunya, or Mother of the World. In the 19th and early 20th centuries, it was a winter playground for Europeans and Americans. Now Gulf Arabs arrive each summer, fleeing the seasonal heat back home. To them, Cairo is familiar from countless movies, and its street talk is emulated throughout the Arab world. For Africans, too, here as students, economic migrants, or refugees , the Egyptian capital is the ultimate uptown experience.

Unfortunately, tour companies tend is to reduce the city to a two-day stopover en route to the pharaonic monuments of Upper Egypt or the beaches of Sinai. Wonderful as the Pyramids and Egyptian Museum are, there really is a lot more to Cairo. ∎

Quba Palace

Merryland

HELIOPOLIS

Nasser's Tomb

Airport

Cairo Stadium

Sadat's Tomb

AH SALEM STREET

Northern Cemetery

Cairo ✪

Area of map detail

MADINET AL-MUQATTAM

| 0 | | 2 kilometers |
| 0 | 1 mile | |

△ E

△ F

NOT TO BE MISSED:

Egyptian Museum   **68–76**

Khan al-Khalili: one of the Middle East's most famous *souqs*   **87**

People-watching at Fishawy's   **90**

Al-Azhar Mosque   **91**

The City of the Dead   **110**

Al-Azhar Park at sunset   **111**

The Gayer-Anderson Museum   **113**

The ancient Nilometer   **118**

The Giza Pyramids and Sphinx   **128–135**

Egyptian Museum

Though many Western museums contain impressive collections of ancient Egyptian antiquities, none begins to rival the riches on display at Cairo's Egyptian Museum. Devoted entirely to the legacy of the pharaohs, the museum has more than 120,000 items of antiquity on display, ranging from delicately crafted jewelry to towering granite colossi of kings.

The museum is not especially big, and the floor plan of both upper and lower floors is simple: rectangular, with a series of rooms around a central court linked by a perimeter corridor. The collection on the ground floor is organized chronologically. As you enter, bear left for the Old Kingdom and continue clockwise through the Middle and New Kingdoms, ending up in the Greco-Roman period. You can then take the

INSIDER TIP:

Don't try to see the whole museum in one visit: It is vast. Be selective, and go more than once.

—NEIL HEWISON
American University in Cairo Press

southeast staircase to the upper floor, where all the exhibits are arranged thematically.

Ideally, try to arrive as close to the 9 a.m. opening time as possible, as the museum gets very crowded toward the middle of the day.

Planning Your Visit

Once inside, you may not get lost, but you may become bewildered and possibly overwhelmed. There is simply too much to take in. Also, the

The famous gold mask of Tutankhamun—the exhibit that everyone wants to see

century-old museum is something of an antique piece itself, a product of the age when it was considered enough simply to catalog an artifact and pop it in a glass case. Labeling (in Arabic, English, and French) remains not just poor but frequently nonexistent. One good strategy to deal with this is to read a description of the museum before you go and identify pieces of interest, perhaps even noting their location on a map. If you have the time, plan for two visits, tackling one floor only on each occasion. If your itinerary is too tight for this, then you could at least take a time out in the museum garden. There is also a café of sorts on the ground floor, entered from the garden via the gift shop.

When considering what to see, most visitors would agree that the highlight has to be the treasures of Tutankhamun. His golden funerary mask and coffins are possibly the most stunning objects on display in any museum anywhere in the world. Save them until last because the dazzle eclipses everything that comes afterward. The museum's other big draw are the mummy rooms, which bring you face to face with several of the greatest of the pharaohs, including Seti I and Ramses II. The mummies and Tutankhamun are on the upper floor. On the ground floor, many of the best pieces are in the Old Kingdom rooms and include the statue of Khafre (see p. 72), the wooden statue of Ka-Aper (see p. 72), and the double statue of Rahotep and Nofret (see p. 72). Also impressive is the Amarna col-

lection of objects from the reign of Akhenaten, the "heretic king" (see p. 73).

The perpetually crowded bookshop at the entrance has plenty of further reading about the museum and ancient Egypt in general. The official guide is not

Egyptian Museum

Ⓜ 66 C3

✉ Tahrir Square

☎ 02/2575 4319

$ $$, extra fee ($$$) for Royal Mummy Room. Camera $, video camera $$$

Papyrus "Museums"

Passing through Giza on your way to the Pyramids, you will notice a string of "Papyrus Museum" storefronts en route. All of them are stores selling modern painted papyrus sheets to tourists. The paintings, usually in vivid colors, generally have pharaonic motifs or hieroglyphs, and vary in quality from well-drawn to crudely-done. Your taxi driver may try to steer you to one on your way back from the Pyramids. See p. 378 for more about buying papyrus.

---

particularly good as it does not provide locations for any of the objects that it catalogs. Far better is *Cairo: The Egyptian Museum & Pharaonic Sites* by Muhammad Salah, which describes 50 of the most important pieces accompanied by good color photographs.

Ground Floor

After passing through security you emerge beneath the museum's rotunda; the chronological sequence starts off to the left, but directly ahead is the **Central**

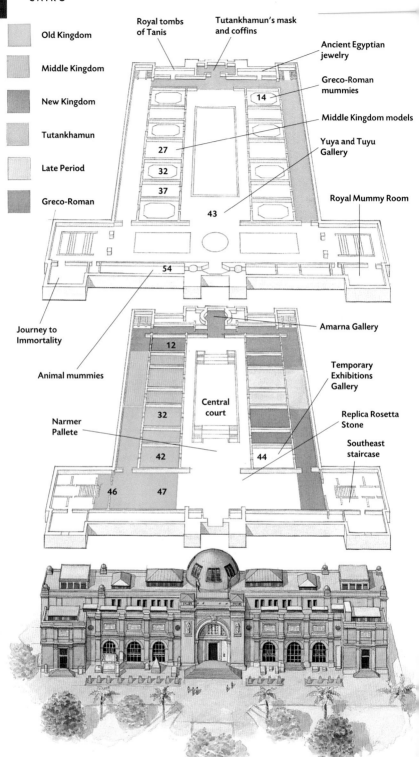

Old Kingdom

Middle Kingdom

New Kingdom

Tutankhamun

Late Period

Greco-Roman

Royal tombs of Tanis

Tutankhamun's mask and coffins

Ancient Egyptian jewelry

Greco-Roman mummies

Middle Kingdom models

Yuya and Tuyu Gallery

Royal Mummy Room

14

27

32

37

43

54

Journey to Immortality

Animal mummies

Amarna Gallery

Temporary Exhibitions Gallery

Replica Rosetta Stone

Southeast staircase

Narmer Pallete

Central court

12

32

42

44

46

47

Like some vast warehouse, the central court of the museum is filled with monumental antiquity.

Court, containing monumental sculpture from all ages. To the right, set into the wall, is a replica of the Rosetta Stone, which provided the key to unlocking the mystery of hieroglyphics (see pp. 50–51). The original is still in the British Museum in London, despite frequent requests from the Egyptian antiquities authorities for its return.

Moving into the court, you pass a free-standing glass case containing the Pallete of Narmer (see p. 26), one of the museum's key artifacts, and descend to a collection of sarcophaguses. The sarcophagus of Psusennes I (circa 1000 B.C.) has a relief figure of the sky goddess Nut on the underside of its lid, covering the pharaoh in a protective embrace (star-spangled Nut is often depicted across the ceilings of tombs).

The centerpiece of the court is a painted floor dating from the Amarna period (see pp. 214–217);

unusually for this museum, it has a good caption. Sitting in stately fashion at the end of the hall is an imposing group of colossi representing Amenhotep III, his wife Queen Tiye, and their daughters. These statues were discovered in fragments on the West Bank at Luxor and were painstakingly reassembled here.

Returning to the **Old Kingdom Galleries,** look for the crude limestone statue of King Djoser (or Zoser), which dates back to the 27th century B.C., making it one of the oldest pieces in the museum. It was discovered in 1924 within its *serdab* beside the Step Pyramid at Saqqara (see p. 145). In **Rooms 47** and **46** the most striking things are three slate triads—sets of three standing figures about 3 feet (1 m) high—depicting the pharaoh Menkaura (Mycerinus) flanked by the horned goddess Hathor on his right and the female personification of one of the territories under his jurisdiction on his left. Four of these triads were discovered at the pharaoh's temple beside his pyramid at Giza.

In **Room 42** another of the pyramid builders, Khafre (Chephren), is represented by a superb, larger-than-life-size black diorite statue that was also discovered on the Giza plateau, in the pharaoh's valley temple. The wings of the falcon god Horus protectively embrace his head. In the same room is the wooden statue of Ka-Aper, an amazingly lifelike figure with a potbelly, fleshy face, and lively eyes. Workers present at the discovery at Saqqara

pendant hung around his neck, that you are gazing on the face of someone who died more than 4,600 years ago. The royal couple were discovered in a tomb at Meidum in the Fayoum region, as were the friezes on the wall to the left, depicting with great skill a gaggle of feeding geese. To this day the lakes at Fayoum remain a popular spot with bird-watchers (see pp. 154–155).

The beginning of the **Middle Kingdom Galleries** is marked by the red-crowned seated figure of Mentuhotep II, the first pharaoh of this particular era. He came to light at Deir al-Bahri (see p. 269) when

Egyptian Treasures Overseas

After Cairo, the world's largest collection of pharaonic antiquities belongs to the Egyptian Museum in Turin, Italy. It includes some magnificent colossal statues removed from the Temple of Amun at Karnak, as well as the complete funeral paraphernalia from an intact 18th-dynasty tomb.

Berlin's Egyptian Museum, founded 13 years before the one in Cairo, houses some of the most valued treasures of Egyptology, including a striking 3,350-year-old painted head of Nefertiti. This piece, which was smuggled out of

Egypt by an archaeological expedition in 1912, is one that the Egyptian authorities would dearly love to see returned.

Another disputed item is the Rosetta Stone in London's British Museum, which also has a fine granite bust of Ramses II, as well as a series of important papyri and a great many mummies and coffins. Best of all, the Metropolitan Museum of Art in New York has a complete temple, a gift from Egypt in recognition of American efforts to save the monuments of Nubia from the rising waters of Aswan's High Dam during the 1970s.

nicknamed him Sheikh al-Balad (the head of the village) because of the statue's resemblance to their own chief.

Equally lifelike are the statues of Prince Rahotep and Princess Nofret, which take center stage in **Room 32.** It is hard to imagine as you look at Rahotep, with his neat mustache, well-groomed hair, and simple heart-shaped

a horse ridden by Howard Carter (finder of Tutankhamun's tomb) put its foot into a hole in the ground. This led to the discovery of an unsuspected burial chamber.

The central exhibit in **Room 22** is a complete example of a Middle Kingdom burial chamber, also from Deir al-Bahri, with its limestone sarcophagus. The ten surrounding statues of Senusret I have nothing to do with the burial chamber; they are from a slightly later period and were discovered in the Fayoum region.

A parade of shaggy, gray granite sphinxes from the Delta city of Tanis (see p. 165) introduces the transition to the **New Kingdom Galleries. Room 12** is devoted to some of the early New Kingdom pharaohs of the 18th dynasty. They include the great conqueror Tuthmose III, seated in a traditional pose with his enemies symbolically represented as nine bows under his feet, and Hatshepsut, ancient Egypt's only female pharaoh (see pp. 268–270). Hers is the pink granite statue with arms at its side; she wears a king's costume and false beard and has been given a masculine physique, but her face is noticeably feminine.

Midway along the northern wing is the **Amarna Gallery,** a room displaying finds from the era of the rebel pharaoh Akhenaten (see pp. 214–217). Artistic style took a strange new turn under his rule, evident in the four fragmented colossi of the pharaoh, showing him with bulbous belly, almost feminine hips and thighs, elongated skull, and sensuous facial features, notably heavy-lidded eyes and bee-stung lips.

Several stelae depicting Akhenaten and his family at rest and worshiping the sun disk, Aten, make the pharaoh look even more alien. However, a sculpted quartzite head of Akhenaten's wife Nefertiti shows her to have been anything but freakish, with high cheekbones and an exotic beauty that would not look

Small figurines called *ushabti* were put into the tomb with the deceased to carry out any labor in the afterlife.

out of place on the cover of *Vogue* magazine.

A colossal statue of Ramses II as a young child, sheltering beneath the breast of the falcon god Horus, marks the entrance of the museum's east wing, which continues with the **Late Period Galleries.** The rulers of this era were mostly foreign, and under their imported influence the archetypal sleek, hardened forms of pharaonic sculpture begin to loosen up. This shift culminates in a full-blown metamorphosis into classicism following the invasion of Alexander the Great and during the subsequent era of Greco-Roman rule.

Room 44 is used for temporary exhibitions. In recent times

A quartet of Tuts carved from alabaster serve as stoppers on jars containing the king's internal organs.

these have focused on the life and works of eminent historical Egyptologists. From here take the southeast staircase to reach the galleries on the upper floor.

Upper Floor

From the top of the southeast staircase the Tutankhamun Galleries begin off to your right. Leaving those for later, buy a combined ticket (sold at the top of the stairs) for the **Royal Mummy Room** and **Journey to Immortality** exhibition. Within these two darkened rooms, entombed in glass cases are the dessicated bodies of 21 ancient royals, including Seti I and his son Ramses II, Tuthmose II, and Queen Meret Amun (wife of Amenhotep I). Once you have seen the human mummies, you might want to head for **Room 54** to see the **Animal Mummies,** a bizarre collection that includes cats, monkeys, a falcon, and even a fish. (For information on the hows and whys of embalming see "Making Mummies" on pp. 238–239.)

From the mummies, walk straight ahead to **Room 43,** the **Yuya and Tuyu Gallery.** Before Carter discovered Tutankhamun's tomb, this cache of funerary furniture, found in 1905 intact in the tomb of these two nobles (parents of Queen Tiye, wife of Amenhotep III), had constituted the biggest find in Egyptian archaeology. Displayed in this gallery are a number of items for use in the afterlife, including beds, biers, a chariot, and several coffins. The two former occupants of the coffins are now among the inhabitants of the Royal Mummy Room.

Moving clockwise around the central atrium, **Rooms 37, 32, and 27** contain **Middle Kingdom models,** providing a fascinating glimpse of daily life circa 2000 B.C. The lovingly detailed scenes include a weaver's workshop, fishing boats, and a herd of cattle being counted by a master and his scribes. Though they may look like children's toys, these models were funerary offerings, and 25 of them were found sealed within the tomb of an official on the West Bank at Luxor. Part of the find is displayed at the Metropolitan Museum of Art in New York.

Room 14 contains **Greco-Roman mummies,** many adorned with what have come to be known as "Fayoum portraits" (see p. 153). Unfortunately, the mummies are not so much displayed as stashed—in stacks of grimy glass cabinets; this effectively makes it impossible to view the painted faces. Many rooms along this upper east wing are particularly badly presented, and although they contain objects of great interest, few visitors have the patience to investigate. You could be excused for hurrying on, back to the top of the southeast staircase and to the first of the rooms devoted to Tutankhamun.

Tutankhamun Galleries

Ironically, Tutankhamun was a relatively minor pharaoh who reigned for less than ten years (1336–1327 B.C.) before dying of unknown causes at the age of 18. He may have been murdered. The name of this son-in-law and heir to the heretic king Akhenaten was erased from all monuments, and he would have merited no more than a foot-note in ancient Egyptian history if it were not for the fact that his tomb survived intact to be discovered by Howard Carter in 1922 (see pp. 276–277). Of the unimaginable treasures found chaotically heaped inside—which took four years to catalog and remove—some 1,700 objects are displayed here.

INSIDER TIP:

Don't miss the museum's animal mummy room. It's in a small section around the corner from King Tut's treasures.

— ANN WILLIAMS
National Geographic
magazine writer

Entering the galleries you pass between two life-size, bitumen-coated wooden statues of the boy-king, which stood as guardians outside the antechamber where his body lay. Many of the objects in this first area are connected with hunting, such as leopard-skin shields and a wooden casket depicting the king hunting—a reminder that Egypt was once home to rich and varied wildlife. Glass cases lining the gallery are filled with small figurines, which include a series of gods placed in the tomb to protect Tutankhamun, and some of the 400-plus *ushabti:* miniature effigies of the king that would carry out any tasks or labors on his behalf

A queen anoints her king on Tut's golden "lion" throne.

in the afterlife. Also here is the royal "lion" throne, covered with sheet gold and inlaid with glass and semiprecious stones; on the backrest is a colorful tableau of Tutankhamun being anointed by his queen (see above).

Farther along are several delicately made alabaster jars, lamps, and a chalice as well as a number of intricately rigged model ships for the journey in the afterlife. The real crowd-pleasers begin in the north wing where the king's three animal-headed funerary couches stand. Beside the couches is an alabaster chest; during the embalming process the internal organs were removed from the body and placed in canopic jars or urns, four of which you see on page 74 with their stoppers fashioned in the likeness of Tutankhamun. The chest containing the canopic jars was then enclosed within the neighboring golden canopic shrine, protected at its corners by the four goddesses, Isis, Neith, Nephthys, and Serket.

The gilded wooden boxes that fill the remainder of the north wing fitted into each other like Russian dolls, and at their center were the sarcophagus and a series of inner coffins encasing the king. The outer, quartzite sarcophagus remains in the tomb at Thebes, but in a small guarded room are the inner coffins, one of gilded wood set with semiprecious gems and the innermost of solid gold weighing over 440 pounds (200 kg).

The body of Tutankhamun lay within this, the smallest and most precious of the coffins, wearing the fabulous death mask that takes center place in this room. Made of solid gold, it is an idealized portrait of the young king, with the eyes fashioned from obsidian and quartz, and the outlines of the eyes and the eyebrows delineated with lapis lazuli. If this was the treasure of only a minor pharaoh, one has to wonder what the looted tomb of a great pharaoh such as Ramses II might have held.

On either side of the main Tut room are two well-organized galleries; one contains finds from the **Royal Tombs of Tanis** (see p. 165), five intact New Kingdom tombs found in the Delta region in 1939. The objects include a dazzling silver anthropoid coffin of the pharaoh Psusennes I (1039–991 B.C.) with the head of a falcon. The other room displays some of the museum's finest pieces of **ancient Egyptian jewelry,** as well as items from the Greco-Roman era, found in the Western Oases. ■

Collecting Ancient Egypt

Egyptology is a very young science, with almost everything known about ancient Egypt's 5,000-year history discovered in the last two centuries. Enlightenment first came from the scholars who accompanied Napoleon Bonaparte's military expedition to Egypt in 1798; their resulting 24-volume work, *Description de l'Egypte* (*Description of Egypt*), has formed the cornerstone of all future research.

Members of the grandly titled Commission des Sciences et des Arts de l'Armée d'Orient survey antiquities for Napoleon.

Following Napoleon, in the first decades of the 19th century, Egypt was rediscovered by a flood of intrepid travelers. One unfortunate consequence of this Egyptomania was the wholesale looting of the country. With no law against removing antiquities, the *Description de l'Egypte* was used as a catalog by European agents in Egypt who systematically plundered the land of anything that could be carried off.

Among the treasure-hunting adventurers, one name in particular stands out: Giovanni Belzoni. Born in Padua, Italy, in 1778, he at one time earned a living in London on the music-hall stage with a strongman act that involved him carrying 12 people at once. In Egypt, Belzoni found employment with the British consul general and supplied the British Museum with some of its key items, including a massive head of Ramses II transported from the Ramesseum at Thebes. In such a way, from around 1810 to

1850, was the core of the Egyptian antiquity collections of the great European museums created.

Frenchman Auguste Mariette (1821–1881) put a stop to the pillaging. A former teacher from Boulogne, Mariette developed a passion for Egyptology, leaving his job for a menial position at the Louvre, then securing a small stipend to head out for the deserts to dig. In 1851, acting on a passage from Greek geographer Strabo (64 B.C.–A.D. 23), Mariette achieved success with the discovery of the Serapeum at Saqqara. The Egyptian viceroy Said Pasha invited Mariette to become the head of the newly founded Egyptian Antiquities Service with a remit to "collect stelae, statues, amulets, and any easily transportable objects...in order to secure them against the greed of the local peasants or the covetousness of Europeans."

To house the fruits of the service's excavations, in October 1863 Mariette inaugurated the first Egyptian Museum in the Cairo suburb of Boulaq. But the collection rapidly expanded to fill its initial warehouse premises and outgrew a second home, too, before moving in March 1902 into its present specially built, dusky pink premises on Tahrir Square. Mariette did not live to see the Tahrir Square museum, but he was reburied in its garden with an impressive monument erected to mark the resting place of the institute's founder and first director.

A century later, the number of finds made in the last hundred years and shut away in storage in the Egyptian Museum's basement has come to outnumber the artifacts on display. Consequently, a new antiquities museum, the Grand Egyptian Museum (GEM), is currently being built at a site near the Pyramids at Giza. It's expected to be completed in 2011 or 2012.

Central Cairo

No one would claim that the modern center of Cairo is beautiful. Certain streets do have a worn charm and there is the odd architectural gem. But for the most part the city center is under siege from neglect, unregulated planning, and the destructive demands of the automobile. Yet anyone who spends more than a little time here quickly realizes that what central Cairo lacks in initial appeal, it more than makes up for on further acquaintance.

Tahrir Square (Liberation Square) is the perpetually crowded center of modern Cairo.

Tahrir Square is to Cairo what Times Square is to New York: not a grand plaza with statues and fountains, but a clamorous crossroads, filled night and day with people and a great deal of traffic. For tens of thousands of Cairenes, Tahrir serves as a commuting hub; they arrive here each morning from the suburbs by cab, busy bus, or overcrowded subway. Many of these commuters file into the square's monolithic state office building, the Mugamma, workplace for 20,000 paper-swamped civil servants. The formerly elegant sweep of buildings on the east side of the square is home to travel agents, importers and exporters, and myriad other miscellaneous small businesses. On the sidewalk out front, traders sell anything from watches to a shoeshine. At dusk the square is lent a touch of glamor by a curve of neon signs along the building tops.

Every visitor spends time around Tahrir, if for no other

reason than this is where you will find the famous **Egyptian Museum** (see pp. 68–76). Conveniently sited beside the museum is the former **Nile Hilton,** the first modern five-star hotel to be built in Cairo (in 1959) and a distinctive city landmark. The glory days when the hotel welcomed the likes of Frank Sinatra are long past, but the courtyard coffee shop remains a popular meeting place for Cairo's moneyed classes. Yet new glory is on the horizon for this old favorite, as the hotel began its transformation into a Ritz Carlton in 2009.

Dominating the south side of the square is the monolithic bulk of the Mugamma, which is occupied by the teeming employees of the Ministry of the Interior. As the national home of intractable and unfathomable bureaucracy, the building is as much an icon of modern Egypt as the Pyramids are of Ancient Egypt. The idea of a visit to the Mugamma strikes a similar fear into the average Egyptian as a summons from the IRS would to someone in the U.S.

East of the Mugamma is the former campus of the **American University in Cairo,** where the wealthy pay big bucks to confer on their sons and daughters the prestige of a Western-style education. Although the University recently moved outside the city center, the historic downtown building will reopen in 2009 as a cultural center with performance spaces and art galleries, in addition to the revamped AUC Press bookstore, well-stocked with Egypt-related titles.

Following either Muhammad Mahmoud Street or Sheikh Rihan Street, east past the university leads to another large square, on the far side of which is **Abdeen Palace.** Designed by a French architect in a graceless neoclassical style, the palace was completed in 1874 as a residence for Egypt's khedival rulers. Since the 1952 revolution and the exile of the last king, Farouk, Abdeen has served as government offices; grander rooms are reserved for receiving visiting heads of state.

In 1998 part of the rear of the building was opened to the public as a museum. Unfortunately, the rooms that everyone really wants to see, like the Byzantine Hall with its art deco "pharaonic" frescoes, remain behind closed doors. Those halls that can be visited are plainly decorated and house an endless array of daggers, swords, pistols, and other firearms, plus medals, decorations, royal silverware, and ceramics. There is a certain

Abdeen Palace

🄰 66 D3
✉ Al-Gamaa St., Abdeen
☎ 02/2391 0130
🕐 Closed Fri.
💲 $. Camera $, video camera $$$

Cairo's Metro

The Cairo metro is still fairly new, and although it can be crowded, it is well-run, efficient, and fast. Fares are only 1LE and are paid at the ticket booth by the turnstiles. Fortunately, signs are in English, and with only two lines currently built, it is hard to get lost. (See the map on p. 388.) Usually the center car on a train is reserved for women only; male metro riders should look carefully to avoid getting into the wrong car.

Cairo's luxurious Manyal Palace, modeled in Arabesque style, now holds a museum that showcases an astounding collection of Ottoman art.

separate buildings, executed in pastiches of Islamic styles and set amid luxuriant banyans, palms, and rubber trees—all that remains of an extensive royal botanical garden that once covered the whole island. The palace was commissioned by Prince Muhammad Ali Tewfik (1875–1955), a monarch-in-waiting who never made it to the throne. This did not prevent him from building his own private Throne Hall, complete with red carpet, gilt furniture, and the ranked portraits of his illustrious forebears.

Another of the buildings is the prince's actual residence, or *haramlek*. Its overblown interiors include a Turkish room covered in Iznik tiles and a Syrian room with an exquisitely painted wood ceiling. Oriental paintings, ceramics, and carpets further decorate the salons. French composer Camille Saint-Saëns (1835–1921) was a sometime house guest here and entertained the prince's circle with private recitals. He is said to have composed his Piano Concerto No. 5, "The Egyptian," while in residence. Also within the grounds are a mosque with a Turkish-tiled interior and an adjacent, crudely fashioned Moorish tower.

Near the palace you'll find the Hunting Museum. In addition to a menagerie of shot and stuffed animals—including a hermaphroditic goat—this long hall contains an astounding testament to excess in the form of the mounted heads of more than 300 gazelle, all bagged by Farouk and his cronies.

The most convenient way to get to Manyal is to take a taxi, but a more pleasant alternative is to walk from Tahrir Square down

raised-eyebrow factor in items like a set of gold-plated machine guns presented by a Gulf Arab dignitary to President Hosni Mubarak. Another oddity is the small domed mausoleum of a 19th-century Muslim saint, which lies off one of the fountain courtyards. The mausoleum predates the palace and, rather than see it demolished, the architect incorporated it into the overall design.

In contrast to the austerity of the rooms at Abdeen is central Cairo's other remaining former royal residence, the wildly eccentric **Manyal Palace.** This is located on the island of Roda, about a mile (1.5 km) south of Tahrir Square. Inside a walled compound are five the Corniche, Cairo's extensive Nile-side boulevard. This is one of the city's main north-south traffic arteries, but with the cars and trucks partially screened from the sidewalk by trees, and cool breezes coming off the river, it is a popular place for strolling.

Located on the Corniche are the **Semiramis** (see p. 359) and **Shepheard's,** modern incarnations of hotels that, in their time, were as famous as the London Ritz and Singapore's Raffles Hotel, and attracted a similar class of international high society. The original Shepheard's, a vast Victorian edifice with Moorish halls, stood just north of Opera Square, and it was here, according to the hotel's historian, Nina Nelson, that "practically every world-renowned person has sat at one time or another on the famous terrace." Theodore Roosevelt was there in 1910, and T. E. Lawrence (of Arabia) stayed; Noel Coward, staying there in 1942, gave impromptu performances on the hotel piano. Sadly, the original hotel was burned down in the Black Saturday riots of 1952. Its concrete replacement has nothing to recommend

it and the only continuity is a dedication plaque in the entrance hall, rescued from the ashes.

From a landing opposite the hotels it is possible to rent a *felucca,* the graceful lateen-sailed boats that have been plying the Nile since antiquity. For a charge

of around U. S. five dollars an hour a captain will take a party out, tacking back and forth across the river. Watching the sun set over the city skyline while languidly drifting on the Nile makes for a stress-relieving end to a busy day of sightseeing. ■

Manyal Palace

🅰 66 C2

✉ Al-Saray St., Manyal

☎ 02/2368 7495

💲 $. Camera $, Video camera $$$

INSIDER TIP:

Go to Abu Tarek (40 Champollion St.) for the national dish of Egypt: *kushari.* **It is inexpensive and delicious, and the restaurant is filled with local Cairenes.**

—ELLEN MILLER
National Geographic field researcher

Getting Around Cairo's Railway Station

Cairo's Ramses Station (it still goes by that name, although the Ramses statue outside moved away a few years ago) is always crowded, but its layout is straightforward. It has only one entrance: If you're facing the station with the crowded traffic circle and overpass behind, it's the door on the left. Once inside, the tourist office is on your immediate left. Also on your left is the sleeping car office—head there if you

plan to take an overnight to Luxor or Aswan. First class tickets to Alexandria and elsewhere in the Delta are straight ahead. For second class to Alex, go out the large doorway at the far end on the left to the small annex a few feet away. Non-sleeper car tickets to points south (such as Middle Egypt) are on the other side of the train tracks; take the underground walkway to the opposite platform.

Downtown Cairo Walk

Determined to modernize Egypt along European lines, Khedive Ismail (R.1863–1879) planned a new Paris-on-the-Nile on the swampy floodplain between the old medieval city and the river. His dream was realized in the creation of a quarter with wide, tree-lined boulevards, grand squares, and public gardens, capped by an Italianate opera house. This walk revisits the past of Ismail's belle epoque Cairo.

Downtown Cairo is at its busiest once the sun goes down and the heat of the day is over.

Start at Tahrir Square and head north up Talaat Harb, the main street of *wust al-balad*, or downtown. If you have not yet eaten breakfast, you could drop in at the **Café Riche ❶** *(17 Talaat Harb St., tel 02/2392 9793)*, a haunt of artists and intellectuals since it opened in 1908. Allegedly Gamal Abdel Nasser and his co-plotters used to meet and talk revolution here. A little farther on, a portly statue presides over one of Ismail's Parisian-style *places*; the figure is Talaat Harb, a financier who gave money to

NOT TO BE MISSED:

Pastries at Al-Abd • Painted billboards at the Miami and Metro cinemas • Facade of the Shaar Hashamaim Synagogue

the nationalist cause and his name to this square. Fittingly, the statue has its back to **Groppi** *(Talaat Harb Sq., tel 02/2574 3244),* a Continental-style tearoom established in 1925 that was once a byword for glamor and excess. All that was extinguished by the nationalization that came as a consequence of Nasser's long afternoons in the Riche, but the beautiful floral mosaics around the entrance still have their sparkle.

Follow Talaat Harb's gaze and head down Qasr al-Nil Street, lined with boutiques and shoe shops with more bright, shiny color than a package of M&Ms. Take the second small street on the right to face the **Cosmopolitan**

Hotel (see p. 359), opened in 1902 as the Metropolitan, and a gorgeous example of some of the fine architecture hidden in the downtown backstreets. Next door to the hotel is the **Bourse ②,** or stock exchange. At the time it was built, in the early 20th century, Egypt's economy was booming and its stock exchange was rated among the world's top ten. Since the government initiated a program of privatization in the mid-1990s, share trading has become big business once again, meriting a face-lift for the Bourse, and for the surrounding streets.

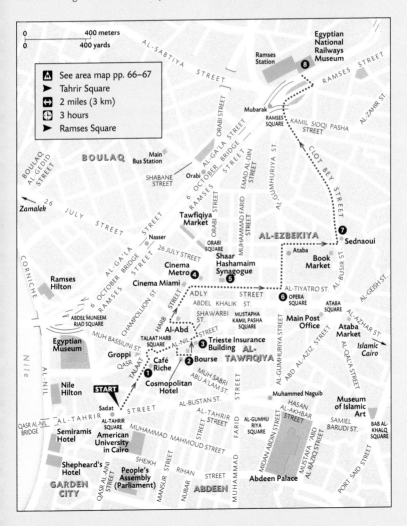

From the Bourse rejoin Qasr al-Nil Street beside the **Trieste Insurance Building** ❸ (*11 Sharifeen St.*), designed by one of the many European architects Ismail commissioned to help him create his new capital, a prolific Italian

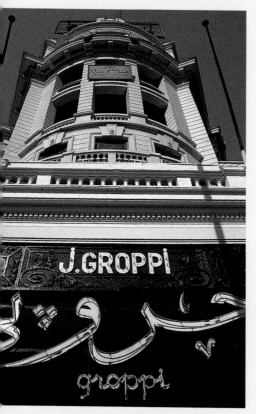

Founded by a Swiss confectioner, Groppi once supplied chocolates to the British royalty.

named Antoine Lasciac. Across from Lasciac's elegant building, modern Cairo reasserts itself on pedestrian-only Shawarby Street, full of shops selling jeans and jackets and loud with pop soundtracks emanating from half a dozen music cassette stores.

Halfway along on the left, a little alley leads back to Talaat Harb, emerging beside a popular bakery called **Al-Abd** (*19 Talaat Harb St.*). Perpetually packed right up until closing

at midnight, it serves Cairo's best baklava and other syrupy nut pastries, costing just a couple of dollars for a half pound (230 g) to take out.

This upper end of Talaat Harb marks the beginning of Cairo's entertainment district, with theaters and low-rent belly-dancing joints. Most of these advertise with huge, garish, often hand-painted billboards, as seen at the **Cinema Miami,** which screens Egyptian movies. Across the road, the jaggedly art deco **Cinema Metro** ❹ first opened in 1939 with a screening of *Gone With the Wind,* and it still shows mostly Hollywood fare.

Adly Street runs east off Talaat Harb beside the Metro building, and along here is what looks like a movie-set construction for a Babylonian epic but is in fact one of the few remaining monuments to Cairo's once substantial and influential Jewish community, the **Shaar Hashamaim Synagogue** ❺. Jews were founders of the national bank and were heavily involved in the development of the city during the early decades of the 20th century, but most left following the creation of the state of Israel in 1948. Numbers are now so low that although the synagogue still opens for Shabbat there are not enough people for a *minyan* (the minimum ten required for a service). Beyond the synagogue is the visitor **information office** (*5 Adly St., tel 02/2391 3454*), where the staff are friendly but poorly resourced.

Continuing on, Adly links with **Opera Square** ❻. It's hard to imagine now, but this large, open plaza was originally the center-piece of Ismail's Cairo. As the name suggests, it was once graced by an opera house, hastily built just in time for the celebrations accompanying the opening of the Suez Canal in 1869. It was to have been inaugurated with a performance of *Aida,* a new opera with an Egyptian theme specially commissioned for the occasion from Italian composer Giuseppe Verdi. In any case, *Aida* was not ready in time, so the first-night guests were entertained with Verdi's *Rigoletto* instead. Fire destroyed the Opera House in 1972 and it was replaced with a building far more suited to modern Cairo life: a multistory parking garage. The equestrian statue is of Ibrahim, father of Ismail, who ruled Egypt for just 40 days before his death in 1848.

Though the city was once rich in parks, today greenery is a rarity in central Cairo,

INSIDER TIP:

Crossing Cairo streets can be challenging. Look for locals and join a group; they cross all together, one lane at a time.

—ANN WILLIAMS
National Geographic *magazine writer*

an almost extinct phenomenon. The flat green patch on the north side of Opera Square is all that remains of what until not too long ago was a wooded park known as the Ezbekiya Garden, designed as a French pleasure garden with paths around a lake and pavilion cafés where bands played. It has the appearance of a site waiting for a building to happen. One paved corner is taken up by the cabins of a secondhand book market, beyond which is Khazinder Square, site of the **Sednaoui department store ❼**. Modeled on Galeries Lafayette in Paris and opened in 1913, it merits a look inside for the grandiose central atrium.

From Sednaoui head north along **Clot Bey Street**, named for a French physician to the 19th-century Egyptian court. You are now leaving European Cairo behind and entering an old residential quarter, little changed in character since the time of the good doctor. Streets become narrower and the architecture more ramshackle. During World War II, Clot Bey was more commonly known as the "Birka," and was a seamy red-light district. It would be wrong to suggest that Clot Bey has since become gentrified. Instead, it is prostitution

that has gone upscale.

At its northern end, Clot Bey joins numerous other streets in spilling into Ramses Square, the most chaotic spot in Cairo. All routes from the north of the city converge here, spewing cars, buses, and taxis into one great screeching, horn-honking melee. A colossus of Ramses II traditionally stood at the square, but it suffered from traffic vibration and pollution and was moved for eventual display in the Grand Egyptian Museum under construction near Giza.

North of the square is Cairo's main railroad terminal, Ramses Station. Part of the station building houses the **Egyptian National Railways Museum ❽** *(tel 02/2576 3793, closed Mon.),* which has a tiny royal locomotive with plush seating for four only. This fanciful machine was presented to Egypt by Empress Eugénie of France at the opening of the Suez Canal.

From Ramses Square it is a brief three-stop ride on the subway back to Tahrir Square (metro: Sadat), where this walk began.

English-language Bookstores in Cairo

A number of bookstores in Cairo cater to the English-language market (which includes Egyptians versed in English, as well as expats and tourists). The downtown campus of **American University in Cairo (AUC)** on Tahrir Square reopens in 2009 as a cultural center with an expanded bookstore, entered from Qasr al-Aini Street *(tel 02/2797-5929)*. In addition to new English titles, it stocks international best-sellers, newspapers, and magazines. Other fine resources for English-language books include **Diwan Bookstore** *(159 26th of July St., Zamalek);* and **Ezbekiyya Book Market** *(Ezbekiyya Gardens),* offering antiquarian as well as modern fare. For other bookstores, see p. 376.

Islamic Cairo

UNESCO, the cultural wing of the United Nations, includes Islamic Cairo on its select World Heritage list, which puts it on a par with the Pyramids, the Great Wall of China, and Venice. It is a historic area that contains the greatest concentration of medieval Islamic monuments to be found anywhere. The skyline is a spiky signature of minarets and domes, reflecting a time when Cairo was the wealthiest capital in the world.

Merchants and shopkeepers have been trading in the narrow alleys of Khan al-Khalili since the 14th century.

Islamic Cairo is the term for the part of the city that dates back to before the development of the new European quarters—modern-day central Cairo. Because the word "Islamic" is unfortunately at times associated with terrorism, the Egyptian authorities are now promoting the term "Fatimid" or "Historic Cairo." This is valid, given that the core of the area is the fortified city founded by the Fatimids in A.D. 969 (see pp. 92–98). Most of the walls that encircled the city are long gone, but hundreds of monuments still line the traditional historic thoroughfares. These range from modest streetside marble fountains to splendid stadium-size mosques, the equal of Europe's great cathedrals in scale and beauty. In age, they cover the spread of Islamic history from the 10th century to the 19th.

Unlike historic districts elsewhere in the world that have been preserved, sterilized, and pickled, Islamic Cairo makes few concessions to the visitor. It has not been able to afford to do so. Lying at the heart of the metropolitan area, it is home to a dense 21st-century population still living in what are essentially medieval quarters. Plumbing and sewer systems gave up long ago, and those who could afford it moved out. This is now one of the poorer areas of the city. When you encounter a printing shop cranking out flyers on hand-operated presses, this is not part of a heritage industry—the antique machinery survives because there is no money to replace it. The decay and neglect may be sad, but as a consequence, Islamic Cairo retains a vital human presence, making it something more than a mere open-air museum.

Planning Your Visit

Islamic Cairo covers an area of several square miles, and exploring it could occupy days, even weeks. Fortunately, there are several key clusters of buildings, all conveniently located along one linear route. This stretches about a mile and a half (2.5 km) and can be walked, but there is so much to see that it is better to pace yourself and, if time allows, make several visits.

Begin at Khan al-Khalili, the extensive bazaar at the heart of the area. With its miles of lanes, alleys, and cul-de-sacs, cruising the Khan requires a day in itself, though you could combine it with a visit to the neighboring Al-Azhar Mosque. Your next trip could take in the Northern Walls and include visits to Al-Hakim's Mosque, Bayt al-Suhaymi, and the three great Mamluk complexes on Bayn al-Qasreen. A third expedition might begin at the Al-Ghouriyya and involve a walk down to Bab Zuwayla and the Tentmakers' Market. Non-Muslims are welcome to visit any Islamic monument other than the Al-Hussein Mosque beside Khan al-Khalili. The only stipulation

Haggling in the Khan al-Khalili

Bargaining over the price of a souvenir in the Khan can seem intimidating at first, but it can be a great part of your experience in Egypt, if you get the hang of it. If you're interested in buying, make an offer on the low side: The merchant will counter with a price that is too high—perhaps one-third more than the price he will end up settling for. In general, never accept a merchant's first offer. The key is not to let yourself be guilt-tripped into buying something at a price you don't want. Feel free to walk away, or at least make a pretense of doing so, if you think a price is too high. You may be surprised by how much the price quickly comes down!

is that footwear must be removed. In some cases tie-on cloth covers are provided to slip over your shoes. To avoid giving offense, dress modestly. A head scarf is sometimes necessary, but women must not be dressed in shorts, short skirts, or sleeveless tops or dresses; men should wear long pants (see "Mosque Etiquette," p. 93).

Khan al-Khalili

To reach Islamic Cairo from downtown, you can walk the half mile (1 km) from Ataba Square along crowded Muski Street, or just take a taxi and be whisked along the Al-Azhar overpass.

Islamic Cairo's profusion of domes and minarets creates an impression of piety.

Either way, you end up near Al-Hussein Square, on the fringes of one of the world's oldest shopping districts, the bazaar of Khan al-Khalili. This is Cairo at its most frenetic and seductive: the Cairo of Ali Baba and Aladdin, loud with the sound of bargaining. Salesmen hiss and beckon. Boys glide about with trays of tea. Everything sparkles and glitters—at least until you get it home, where the luster quickly wears off.

Merchants have been trading on this site since at least the 14th century. In 1384 an emir named Al-Khalili built a great *khan* here, a three-story hostelry intended to accommodate traveling merchants and their wares. Buyers visited the khan for the goods brought in on the merchant caravans, and the selling and bartering spread

to the streets around. Al-Khalili's khan was demolished in the 16th century, but by then the area had become firmly established as the city's commercial center. The earliest surviving parts of the bazaar today are several great stone gateways that date back to the 1500s.

To an extent, the types of goods offered here have changed surprisingly little over the centuries. The slave market closed in 1870, and no longer do you find silk, jewels, or diamonds, but cloth remains important. The aroma of spices is very much present on Al-Muizz li-Din Allah Street, where stalls are heaped with variously colored powders and sacks of seeds and pods. Farther east on the same street, coppersmiths hammer out platters and tureens, and create coffeepots and enormous crescent-shaped

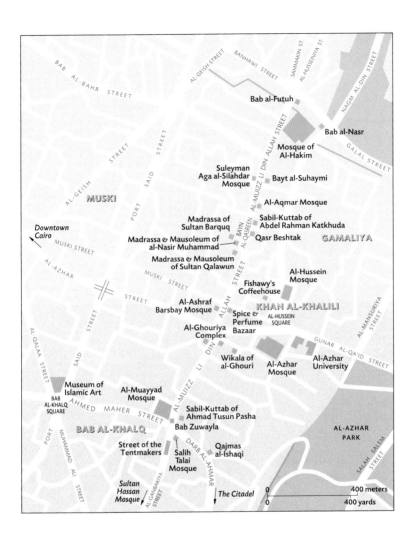

Map labels:

BAB AL-BAHR STREET
BANHAWI STREET
AL-GEISH STREET
SAMMAKIN ST
AL-HUSSENIYA ST
NAGM AL-DIN STREET
Bab al-Futuh
Bab al-Nasr
STREET
SAID STREET
GALAL STREET
Mosque of Al-Hakim
AL-GEISH
PORT SAID
MUSKI
Suleyman Aga al-Silahdar Mosque
Bayt al-Suhaymi
AL-MUIZZ LI DIN ALLAH STREET
Al-Aqmar Mosque
Downtown Cairo
MUSKI STREET
Madrassa of Sultan Barquq
Sabil-Kuttab of Abdel Rahman Katkhuda
Qasr Beshtak
GAMALIYA
AL-AZHAR
Madrassa & Mausoleum of al-Nasir Muhammad
BAYN AL-QASREEN
Madrassa & Mausoleum of Sultan Qalawun
MUSKI STREET
Fishawy's Coffeehouse
Al-Hussein Mosque
STREET
Al-Ashraf Barsbay Mosque
KHAN AL-KHALILI
AL-MANSURIYA STREET
AL-QALAA STREET
SAID
LI DIN ALLAH STREET
Spice & Perfume Bazaar
AL-HUSSEIN SQUARE
Al-Ghouriya Complex
GUNAR AL-QA'ID STREET
Wikala of al-Ghouri
Al-Azhar Mosque
Al-Azhar University
Museum of Islamic Art
Al-Muayyad Mosque
BAB AL-KHALQ SQUARE
AHMED MAHER STREET
AL-MUIZZ LI DIN
Sabil-Kuttab of Ahmad Tusun Pasha
AL-AZHAR PARK
PORT
MUHAMMAD ALI STREET
BAB AL-KHALQ
Bab Zuwayla
SALAH SALEM STREET
Street of the Tentmakers
Salih Talai Mosque
DARB AL-AHMAR
Qajmas al-Ishaqi
Sultan Hassan Mosque
AL-GANBAKIYA STREET
The Citadel
0   400 meters
0   400 yards

tops for minarets. However, it is unlikely that medieval citizens of Cairo would recognize the stuffed leather camels, alabaster pyramid paperweights, and their ilk that pile the stalls in the central section of the bazaar.

Whatever you are buying, expect to bargain (see "Haggling in the Khan al-Khalili," p. 87). It is a ritual of the bazaar, equally applicable to local Egyptian customers and foreign visitors. There are no hard-and-fast rules except one, which is that if you do not bargain, then you will certainly end up seriously overpaying for the item. One tip: If you see something you like, check the price of similar items at other stalls. Armed with an idea of relative values, you can go back and bargain more effectively. Keep your maximum price fixed in mind, and if the shop owner will not meet it, you can always walk away.

For a respite from the sales patter, retreat to **Fishawy's Café**, Cairo's oldest and most celebrated coffeehouse. Its rickety wooden chairs and tall, copper-topped tables line a narrow alley one block north of Al-Hussein Square. Huge, heavy-framed antique mirrors adorn the walls. It is open 24 hours and really comes to life late in the evening, when most visitors have left and the place returns to the locals. (For more on Cairo's coffeehouse culture see p. 97.) One famous regular here was Egypt's Nobel Prize-winning author Naguib Mahfouz (see p. 55). He grew up in the neighborhood and later held weekly literary gatherings in a back room heavy with the sweet smoke from the *sheeshas*, or water pipes, that many Egyptians smoke.

Around the corner is an upscale tourist café named after Mahfouz; its air-conditioned interior is a world away from all that he wrote about, but it is a good place for a lunchtime snack when sightseeing, and for freshening up. The Khan al-Khalili Restaurant in the same building is an atmospheric choice for dinner (see p. 361).

A tourist inspects the goods in the Carpet Bazaar, which is part of Khan al-Khalili.

To see what Al-Khalili's khan might have looked like in its original state, cross Al-Azhar Street via the pedestrian underpass at Al-Hussein Square and pay a visit to the **Wikala of al-Ghouri.** A *wikala* is essentially a larger version of a khan. At one time Cairo possessed more than 350 such structures, but of the handful left today this is in the best condition by far. Enter through a high, decorated gateway into the central courtyard where the caravans would have unloaded. Goods were stored and animals stabled on the ground floor, while the merchants took rooms above. Those rooms now serve as ateliers and workshops for local artists, some of them open to the public. Local handicrafts also are sold here.

As you leave the wikala, turn right and follow the road past a small open-air fruit and vegetable market, and then continue to the left. You are now walking in the shadow of the towering walls of one of Islamic Cairo's most important buildings.

Al-Azhar Mosque

Cairo has several hundred old mosques; if you visit only one, it probably should be the Al-Azhar Mosque. Founded in A.D. 970 as a place of worship and learning, the mosque remains one of the most important centers of Islamic theology more than a thousand years later, annually receiving a new intake of Muslim students from all over the world.

Throughout Cairo's history, the holy men in their precincts have been a channel of communication between the country's rulers and the ruled; sometimes

---

What to Buy in Cairo

Spices are inexpensive, as are perfume essences. You can get local blends as well as imitations of Western name brands, sold in small, delicately decorated bottles.

Despite the profusion of sellers, gold and silver work is not impressive unless you can find old pieces. Beware of claims of antiquity—most things come straight from the factory. Buy an item because you like it, not because it is "old."

Wood jewelry boxes and small chests inlaid with mother-of-pearl are attractive and cheap. For something more original, simple backgammon boxes resembling those used in coffeehouses are sold for a few U.S. dollars on Al-Muizz li-Din Allah Street, and there is a riotously glitzy belly-dancing costumer at Muski Street's eastern end. Remember to bargain hard.

Wikala of al-Ghouri

- 89
- Tablita St., off Al-Azhar St.
- 02/2511 0472
- $

Fishawy's Café

- 89
- Shariya al-Fishawy, Kahn al-Khalili

---

a force for moderation, other times a focus for discontent. When Napoleon invaded Egypt in 1798 one of his first actions was to try to win over Cairo's clerics. He failed, and resorted to ordering a cavalry charge into the mosque as the only way to subdue the rebellious city. The sheikh of Al-Azhar remains the highest religious authority in the land, and pronouncements from his office carry more weight than

Remodeled over the centuries, the prayer hall of Al-Azhar Mosque has been the spiritual heart of Egypt for over a thousand years.

governmental decrees. Al-Azhar is also a showpiece of Islamic-era Cairene architecture, as over the centuries a roll call of sultans and emirs added their imprint to the building.

You enter through the double-arched **Gate of the Barbers,** where freshmen students had their heads shaved. To the left and right, courts lead to two *madrassas*, or teaching schools; the one on the left, complete with its own dome and minaret, was added in 1340 and is worth entering for the glass-mosaic decoration in the prayer niche. Straight ahead is the central court, surrounded by an arcade of keel arches—so-called because the shape of the arches resembles a ship's keel turned upside down.

This is the oldest part of the building and dates back to Fatimid times. Across the court is the carpeted prayer hall, which used to extend only to where the prayer niche stands but was enlarged by a further four arcades in the mid-18th century. The courtyard also provides a good view of the three main minarets, which, from right to left, date from 1340, 1469, and 1510. The 1510 minaret, with its twin finials, was added by the last of the Mamluk sultans, Al-Ghouri, who was also responsible for the nearby wikala (see pp. 94–95) and Al-Ghouriyya complex (see p. 101).

Northern Walls

Once you have visited Khan al-Khalili and Al-Azhar Mosque,

the next must-do is to walk the length of the old medieval walled city, up to the northern gates and back down to the sole surviving southern gate. These are all that remain of what were once ten fortified gates of the Fatimid city.

Square-towered **Bab al-Nasr** and semicircular **Bab al-Futuh** are the two northern gates. First constructed in 969, then rebuilt in 1087, they are massively solid pieces of masonry. Their impact today is less than it formerly was, as the ground level has risen considerably over the centuries—originally ramps ran up from the street to the gates. You can visit the interiors and walk from one gate to the other along a corridor within the walls. As you do, look for fragments of hieroglyphic inscriptions and even a relief carving of a large hippopotamus, evidence that Cairo's early fortifications were built with stones quarried from the ruins of the ancient capital of Memphis. Further evocative detail comes in the form of French names carved above the tower doorways—echoes

of Napoleon Bonaparte's brief occupation of Egypt (1798–1801), when some of his troops were garrisoned in these towers.

The gates are entered via the roof terrace of the neighboring

Mosque of al-Hakim, another survivor of Fatimid times. The third caliph, or ruler, of the Fatimids, Al-Hakim (*R.*996–1021) was noted for his eccentricities. A lover of night, he banned

Mosque of al-Hakim & Northern Walls & Gates

⚑ 89

✉ Al-Muizz li-Din Allah St.

🕐 Closed to visitors Fri. noon prayers

💲 $$

Mosque Etiquette

Modesty and generally respectful behavior are the best things to keep in mind when visiting mosques. Egyptian Muslims are quite welcoming of visitors to their mosques (as Copts are to those visiting churches and monasteries), but remember that they are first and foremost places for worship.

Long pants or full-length skirts are appropriate (no shorts). Shoulders should be covered, but short-sleeved shirts and blouses are acceptable for both sexes. Women will often need to wear a head scarf inside mosques, so it's probably wise to keep a scarf in your bag if you plan to be visiting. You will almost always be asked to remove your shoes before entering, and there is often a pile of shoes by the door (or a shoe rack), with a doorkeeper keeping watch over them.

Mosques are fairly public places, and you will likely see locals sitting, praying, or quietly chatting along the perimeter. The only time you probably won't be able to enter a mosque is midday on Fridays, during the major weekly public prayer.

Al-Azhar Mosque

🅰 89

✉ Al-Muizz li-Din Allah St.

🕐 Closed to visitors Fri. noon prayers

💲 $$. Camera $, videocamera $$$

all business activity during the day; and a hater of women, he forbade the manufacture of women's shoes in order to keep them off the streets. Over the centuries his mosque has served as stables, a prison, a storehouse

for the objects that later made up the collection of the Museum of Islamic Art, and a school.

For much of its recent history it stood in ruins, but it was almost completely rebuilt in the 1980s. Only the strange minarets, look-

The Mosque of Al-Azhar

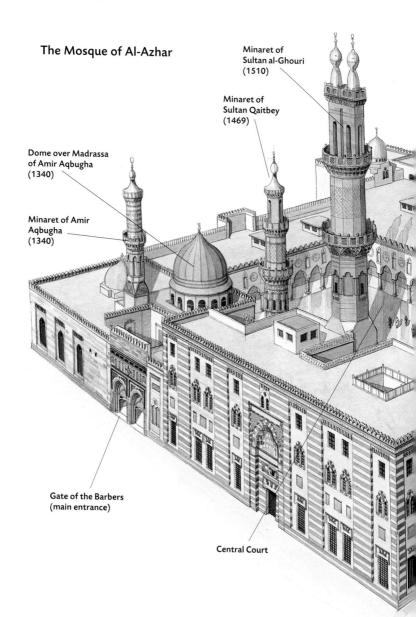

Minaret of Sultan al-Ghouri (1510)

Minaret of Sultan Qaitbey (1469)

Dome over Madrassa of Amir Aqbugha (1340)

Minaret of Amir Aqbugha (1340)

Gate of the Barbers (main entrance)

Central Court

ing like pepperpots on boxes, are original.

In front of the mosque, a widening of the street serves as a pungent open-air market for onions, garlic, and lemons, brought in from the surrounding coun-

tryside. The street in question is the former main thoroughfare of medieval Cairo, **Al-Muizz li-Din Allah Street,** named for the Fatimid caliph in whose name the city was founded. It runs a long stretch down to the southern

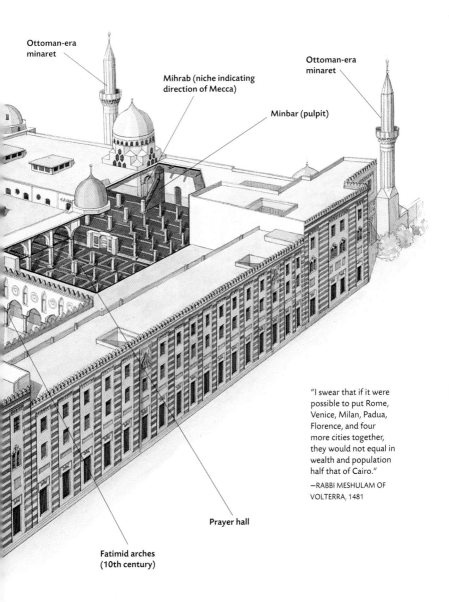

Ottoman-era minaret

Mihrab (niche indicating direction of Mecca)

Ottoman-era minaret

Minbar (pulpit)

"I swear that if it were possible to put Rome, Venice, Milan, Padua, Florence, and four more cities together, they would not equal in wealth and population half that of Cairo."
—RABBI MESHULAM OF VOLTERRA, 1481

Prayer hall

Fatimid arches (10th century)

gate of Bab Zuwayla and beyond to the Citadel, former seat of the city's rulers. Too narrow for modern conveyances, it is almost permanently congested with a low-tech jam of handcarts and donkeys that are almost invisible under their mountainous loads.

After 200 yards or so down Al-Muizz li-Din Allah, you come to a small alley off to the left, conspicuous for its blindingly whitewashed appearance, the result of a makeover by the Egyptian antiquities department. This is stage one of an ambitious project for the eventual restoration of the main spine of Islamic Cairo. The pilot work here has focused on the showpiece **Bayt al-Suhaymi,** Cairo's finest example of the traditional family mansion built throughout the city from Mamluk times to the 19th century. The *bayt* (meaning "house") presents a typically blank facade to the street, but once through the tunnel-like entryway the visitor emerges into a beautiful inner courtyard, overlooked by all the rooms. Guests were received in an impressive *qa'a,* or reception room, off the courtyard, graced with a polychrome marble fountain inset in the floor and a high, painted wood ceiling.

Upstairs are the family quarters, with the wood-lattice windows known as *mashrabiyya* that allowed the women to observe the goings-on below without being seen themselves. The rooms are kept cool by devices called *malqaf,* angled wind-catchers on the roof that direct the prevailing northerly breezes down into the building.

INSIDER TIP:

When negotiating for an item in an open-air market or tourist store, walk away at least once. When you return, the price will be lower.

—PEARCE CREASMAN
National Geographic field researcher

It is an amazingly effective system and, as far as both aesthetics and running costs go, it certainly beats mechanical air-conditioning.

Returning to **Al-Muizz li-Din Allah,** on the next left-hand corner is the neat little Al-Aqmar Mosque. Its name means "moonlit" and it is supposedly inspired by the luminous quality of the stone.

(continued on p. 98)

The Art of Taxi Fares

By common consent, Cairo taxi meters are never used, and riders are generally expected to know an appropriate fare. This makes it tricky for foreigners who don't know what the fares are, and although most drivers are honest, a few unscrupulous ones take advantage of this.

Fares are based on distance, not the number of passengers.
Some typical fares:
- Mohandiseen to Tahrir Square: 8–10LE
- Downtown to Islamic Cairo: 5–7LE
- Downtown to the airport: 60LE
- Zamalek to Tahrir Square: 5–6LE

The Coffeehouse

"Cairo, city of a thousand minarets." So says the old cliché, but if there is one institution found in more abundance than the mosque, it is the *ahwa*, or coffeehouse. A Turkish traveler to Cairo in the late 16th century wrote, "Also [remarkable] is the multitude of coffeehouses in the city of Cairo, the concentration of coffeehouses at every step." And that is still very much the case today. Not only is there virtually one on every corner, you will pass at least two in between.

Most men spend a part of every day at a coffeehouse, dropping in for morning tea, finishing the day with a *sheesha*, or both.

Coffee reached Cairo some time in the mid-15th century, some three centuries before it took hold in the West, and more than half a millennium before the first Starbucks. Initially the beans were viewed with distrust as an intoxicant, all forms of which were—and, of course, still are—forbidden by the Koran. Coffeehouses were associated with drug use, prostitution, and idleness—none of which prevented them from quickly becoming a keystone of Egyptian society. Today, most Egyptian men will drop into a coffeehouse almost daily. Arabic coffee is black and gritty, served in tiny cups holding no more than a half dozen sips. Occasionally it might be flavored with cardamom, nutmeg, or cloves. However, no one frequents a particular coffeehouse because of the quality of its brew.

Egyptian coffeehouses combine the functions of a bar, a social club, a street corner. They are a place to meet and talk, trade gossip, catch up on the news, read the paper, even watch TV. They are also almost exclusively male (women are welcome but may feel a little self-conscious). In Egypt, the house is the woman's domain; everything else belongs to the man. While wives visit with each other at home, husband and friends sit around in the coffeehouse.

It can be anything from a rag-covered bench served from a hole in the wall to a terrace with rattan chairs and menus, but typically a coffeehouse is a collection of cheap tin plate-topped tables and wood chairs in a sawdust-strewn room open to the street. Waiters shuffle around shouting orders to the boys at the water boilers and gas rings, while the *muwaalim*, the boss, sits at his desk, watching over proceedings and trading welcomes and backslaps with customers.

In Cairo especially, each coffeehouse fills its own niche. Some are frequented by writers and intellectuals, others by chess players, and a few known to keep particularly good tobacco are visited by connoisseurs of the *sheesha*, the burbling water pipe. In an alley off downtown's Tewfiqiyya market, theater musicians sometimes put on impromptu performances after work. Nearby, casting agents looking for movie extras patronize the Al-Shams Coffeehouse; many young travelers extend their stay by doing film work.

Perhaps in the 12th century, when the mosque was built, it did shine like the moon, but centuries of dust and grime have left it down at the heels and dulled. It is nevertheless notable for the exquisite carving on the facade.

Between the Palaces

At the center of the Fatimid city, two great palaces faced each other across a large public square. The palaces were long ago replaced by the monuments of later dynasties, but they are remembered in the name **Bayn al-Qasreen,** or Between the Palaces, still used for the stretch of Al-Muizz li-Din Allah south of the little Al-Aqmar Mosque. Of the royal residences themselves, only some finely carved wood friezes survive; these are displayed in the Museum of Islamic Art (see pp. 104–105).

Although credited with the founding of Islamic Cairo, it is not the Fatimids whose stamp is most dominant on the old city today. That distinction falls to the Mamluks (see pp. 35–38). Of the scores of domes and minarets that grace the skyline, the most magnificent and ornate were erected over the prayer halls and mausoleums of the soldier-slave dynasty that ruled from 1250 to 1517. The wealth of their conquests in Palestine, Syria, and Arabia went into these buildings. Since life was often short, and power was not hereditary, the Mamluk rulers were inclined to spend while they could. There was perhaps also an element of public relations involved: If the Mamluk warlords appealed enough to the glory of God, the people of Cairo might eventually forget their savage rule and sinful deeds.

EXPERIENCE: Take *Oud* Lessons in Islamic Cairo

Although its name simply means "stick" in Arabic, the *oud* is an elegant, multistringed wooden musical instrument, the precursor to the European lute (which took its name from the Arabic *al-oud*). Handsome new ouds are still manufactured and sold along Sharia Mohammed Ali in downtown Cairo, a street once famous for its musicians.

Under the assault of modern pop music, both Arab and Western, the traditional oud has fallen out of favor, although the Iraqi musician and composer Naseer Shamma, who has lived in Egypt for the past decade, has tirelessly worked to change that. A virtuoso player and an advocate for classical Arabic music, Shamma runs an oud academy, Beit al-Oud al-Arabi (House of the Arabic Oud),

in Islamic Cairo. The school is located in Beit al-Harrawi, a restored 18th-century private home in a square behind the Al-Azhar mosque.

Oud lessons are offered to both local and international students under the direction of Shamma himself or one of his senior students. Classes are generally held three times a week, on Saturdays, Mondays, and Wednesdays. (Shamma and his advanced students often hold concerts in Beit al-Harrawi as well.) To arrange some lessons before your arrival in Egypt, write to Shamma directly via his website (www.naseershamma.com).

Though the oud is a complex instrument to master, the rewards are great, and learning its intricacies in such an evocative setting is a rare treat.

Bayn al-Qasreen represents Mamluk Egypt at the zenith of its vigor and prosperity. Here three massive complexes stand shoulder to shoulder in a sequence of spectacular facades spanning 150 years. The northernmost is the **Madrassa of Sultan Barquq,** founded in 1386 as an Islamic teaching center. Most madrassas typically also functioned as mosques, and the terms are somewhat interchangeable, but if you enter the main courtyard you will find a door at each corner leading to four sets of classrooms, one for each of the four schools of Islamic law. Under the dome, reached via the prayer hall, is a highly decorated mausoleum, which contains not the sultan (he is buried elsewhere in Cairo) but his daughter Fatima.

Next door to the Barquq complex is the **Madrassa and Mausoleum of al-Nasir Muhammad,** erected by one of the most prolific builders in the history of Cairo. During his long reign from 1293 to 1340, Al-Nasir endowed the city with some 30 mosques, of which the best known is up at the Citadel (see pp. 108–110). His madrassa-and-mausoleum complex on Bayn al-Qasreen is squeezed between two giant neighbors but still manages to make an impact with its almost symmetrical facade. The white marble Gothic doorway came from a Crusader church in Acre (now in Israel), while the minaret, directly above, is covered in lacelike stucco patterning of North African influence. The interior is unfortunately in very poor condition and it is not usually open to visitors.

Mashrabiyya windows at Bayt al-Suhaymi allowed women to view the street scene below without themselves being seen.

The last, earliest, and most outstanding in the sequence is the **Madrassa and Mausoleum of Sultan Qalawun.** It is said to have been built in a single year in 1285, and that to achieve this feat the sultan's soldiers forced hapless passersby to join the labor gangs. The city's sheikhs were so outraged that they at first declared prayer there unlawful. However, such is the magnificence of Qalawun's legacy that his misdeeds are forgotten and he is praised as one of the greatest Mamluks—no doubt his intention.

Complexes of Barquq & Qalawun

🅰 89
✉ Bayn al-Qasreen
🕐 Closed to visitors Fri. noon prayers
💲 Both $

The wood-and-ivory-inlay ceiling at Qalawun's madrassa shows the Mamluk's mastery of geometric decoration.

Entrance to the complex is through an imposing bronze door. Immediately within, off to the left, is the madrassa, and to the right is the mausoleum, modeled on the Dome of the Rock in Jerusalem, which the Mamluks had recently recaptured from the Crusaders. The mausoleum's walls are faced from floor to ceiling with colored stone and decorative marble panels spelling out the name of Muhammad. Under a dome raised high on four massive pink-granite pharaonic columns is the cenotaph containing Qalawun.

As part of his complex, Sultan Qalawun also endowed a *maristan,* or hospital, which according to the Moroccan traveler and historian Ibn Battuta, visiting Cairo in 1325, contained "an innumerable quantity of appliances and medicaments." If such historical accounts are to be believed, the hospital treated up to 4,000 patients a day in its prime. Incredibly, an eye clinic still occupies a part of Qalawun's complex, maintaining an unbroken tradition of more than 700 years of medical care.

Southern City Gate

In the early 20th century, the creation of Al-Azhar Street broke the traditional spine of the old city. Previously all traffic had flowed north-south; now the main stream is east-west as cars thunder off the overpass, weave between the medieval mosques, and race on to link up with the road that encircles the city and runs out by the historic cemeteries. One solitary, shabby footbridge now links the two broken halves of Al-Muizz li-Din Allah Street to allow visitors to

INSIDER TIP:

If you're lost, pharmacies are a good place to ask for directions because pharmacists here do their degrees in English.

—RANDI DANFORTH
American University in Cairo Press

continue uninterruptedly along a route that has been in use for over a thousand years.

To the south of the bridge are the matching pink-striped blocks of the **Al-Ghouriyya,** another fine piece of Mamluk civic building. There is a mausoleum on one side and a madrassa on the other, but more than anything the complex stands as an architectural epitaph to the princely era when Cairo was more dazzling than Rome, Florence, and Venice put together. Little more than ten years after the Al-Ghouriyya was finished in 1504, the resplendent, 5,000-strong Mamluk army paraded past, accompanied by drums and trumpets and led by three caparisoned elephants, only to be slaughtered in battle by the Ottoman Turks. The sultan Al-Ghouri fell from his horse; his body was never recovered. In his mausoleum instead lies the body of Tumanbey,

who ruled for the time it took the Turks to march down and claim possession of Egypt.

The madrassa here has a square minaret with a strange five-bulbed top that is one of the tallest in the city. The dome covering the mausoleum was also once one of Cairo's biggest, but it collapsed three times and has been replaced with a flat wood roof. A wood canopy once stretched across the street between the two buildings, and in the covered space below was the silk market. Canopy and silk merchants are now gone, but the surrounding alleys are filled with narrow storefronts packing an abundance of textiles and rugs.

Cloth gives way to clothes as you move south, but before then, on the right-hand side, are the city's two sole remaining makers of the *tarboosh,* the little burgundy-

Whirling Dervishes

Every Wednesday and Saturday evening a group of Whirling Dervishes puts on a 90-minute display of Sufi dancing at the Al-Ghouriyya *(adm. free).* Sufism is a semi-mystical branch of Islam with a somewhat unorthodox approach to prayer. Urged on by the hypnotic pulse of drums and pipes, the dancers spin in a blur of multicolored skirts. Originally, the dance had the ideal of attaining a trancelike union with God. It may not now be wholly authentic, but it is a great spectacle.

Al-Hakim's unusual pepperpot minarets are some of the earliest structures in Islamic Cairo.

Al-Muayyad Mosque

🅐 89

✉ Al-Muizz li-Din Allah St..

🕐 Closed to visitors Fri. noon prayers

💲 $$

main standing. It's a fine example of early medieval architecture. The two minarets were added much later, in the 15th century, and belong to the neighboring Al-Muayyad Mosque. The gate is now open as a fascinating museum ($). From the minarets you'll enjoy some of the best views of the old city.

Outside the gate, which was closed each night until as recently as the 19th century, is an untidy and chaotic intersection of three streets. West leads to the Museum of Islamic Art (see pp. 104–105), which is no more than a five-minute walk away. To the east, the uneven road rambles past yet more mosques and madrassas before climbing up toward the Citadel (see pp. 108–110); a walk of maybe 15 minutes.

Straight ahead from the Zuwayla Gate is the **Street of the Tentmakers,** Cairo's only remaining medieval covered market. It takes its name from the bright, block-printed fabric traditionally sold here and still used today for the large street tents erected for funerals, weddings, shop openings, and feasts. This is also a center for appliqué panels and covers, sewn in nearby workshops and sold in the cell-like spaces that line the passage. Prices are reasonable and the beautiful calligraphic work makes an interesting alternative to the usual souvenirs.

From the market, you can either return the way you came or continue south, in which case a walk of 15 minutes will bring you to the great **Sultan Hassan Mosque** (see pp. 106–107). ■

colored "flowerpot" hat known elsewhere as a fez. Prerevolution, no *effendi*-about-town would be seen without one, but now the only buyers are hotels and tourist restaurants, for staff uniforms.

Past the clothes sellers, the street opens up, and you see on your left side the ornate **Sabil-Kuttab of Ahmad Tusun Pasha,** now a backdrop for fruit vendors' stalls. The hard sell and clamor continue for perhaps half a mile until they are brought up short by the towering **Bab Zuwayla,** built in 1092 and the third of the Fatimid gates that re-

EXPERIENCE: Learn Arabic

If you plan to spend any appreciable amount of time traveling in the Middle East, being able to converse—even haltingly—with the 200 million native speakers of Arabic in their own language will smooth your way immeasurably.

The good news is that Cairo is an ideal place to learn the language in a local environment. There are a number of established language schools and training centers that offer courses if you plan to stay longer than a few weeks. The bad news is that there is no one Arabic language to learn. Instead, there are several regional dialects as well as a formal "standard" language. You will need to decide which version you want to learn based on how you plan to use your Arabic.

If you're mainly interested in chatting with Egyptians, then learn Egyptian Colloquial Arabic (known as *ammeya*). Learning Egyptian *ammeya* has the added advantage of being the dialect most widely understood by other Arabic speakers, thanks to the widespread popularity of Egyptian films and television. On the other hand, if you are more interested in reading Arabic newspapers or understanding what they're saying on al-Jazeera, your best bet is to learn the more formal Modern Standard Arabic (MSA), known in Arabic as *fusha*.

In general, be careful of unaccredited "language schools" that may not have great teaching materials or qualified language teachers. Some tried-and-true standouts for learning Arabic

include the **American University in Cairo**'s School of Continuing Education, which offers both *ammeya* and *fusha* classes primarily for diplomats, businesspeople, and expats. It also has the advantage of being located downtown just off Tahrir Square (*113 Kasr El Aini St., Cairo, tel 02/2794 2964, www. aucegypt.edu/academics/ schools/sce*).

University students looking for courses for credit may be more interested in AUC's **Arabic Language**

4-week courses (*4 Mahmoud Azmi St., Medinat El Sahafyeen, tel 02/3346 3087, www. arabic egypt.com*). **Kalimat** (*22 Mohammed Mahmoud Shaaban St., Mohandiseen, Giza, tel 02/3761 8136, www. kalimategypt.com*), run by former Arabic teachers with the British Council, is nearby in Mohandiseen.

To really achieve fluency, though, you must combine your classroom work with conversation practice. Ask about private tutors at your language school or at one of

Arabic is not the easiest language in the world to learn.

Institute (*AUC, New Cairo, tel 02/2615 1000, www.aucegypt. edu/academics/ali*), which offers 20-hours-a-week courses on a semester basis. Another alternative is the **International Language Institute**, a well-established private academy that offers

the foreign cultural centers, or check out the bulletin boards at AUC. There is no substitute for regular conversation sessions with a native speaker (perhaps over tea and a sheesha) if you want to learn to speak like a local!

Museum of Islamic Art

The core of this collection comes from the loose bits and pieces of Cairo's mosques and monuments, gathered together in the late 19th century to prevent them from being carried off by European treasure hunters. Though the museum is currently closed for renovations, it is slated to reopen sometime in 2009: call or check local listings to confirm if it, in fact, has reopened.

The museum building belongs to a 19th-century revival of Mamluk architectural styles.

Museum of Islamic Art

- 🅰 89
- ✉ Port Said St.
- ☎ 02/2390 1520 or 02/2390 9930
- 🕐 Closed to visitors Fri. noon prayers
- 💲 $$. Camera $, video camera $$$

The museum is an imposing chocolate-and-buff-striped neo-Islamic block, easily spotted, though located off the tourist trail. It is only a 20-minute walk due east of Tahrir Square, but few visitors ever make it—which is a shame, because it really is worth the effort. Historically, the interpretation of a Koranic injunction against the representation of Allah (God) led Muslims to reject figurative forms; instead they developed exceptional skills in floral, geometric, and epigraphic forms, applying fantastic patterning to wood, glass, metal, stone, textiles, ceramics, bone, and paper, all of which are represented here. There are carved wood pulpits, panels, and doors; finely worked mosque lamps; and marble fountains from houses and palaces in the old Islamic city. Many items in the museum originated elsewhere, having found their way to medieval Cairo simply because it was one of the richest cities in the world. So the collection includes Armenian and Anatolian tiling, Persian manuscripts and carpets, and Moorish luster-painted dishes.

To better understand some of these objects, where they fitted, and how they were used, visit *after* a walk through Islamic Cairo, where you will see in situ many of the architectural objects represented in this museum.

Visiting the Museum

The collection numbers more than 10,000 artifacts. Among the masterpieces are examples of *mashrabiyya* screens. Made from thousands of small pieces of individually turned wood, such screens were a highly practical medieval alternative to glass. They filtered the harsh rays of the sun, while allowing ventilating breezes. In a society in which women were obliged to remain out of sight, the mashrabiyya made it possible for women to see without being seen. Until the 19th century, all the houses of Cairo's wealthier citizens had bay windows fashioned in this style, but few good examples remain today.

Other notable constructions include a coffered wood ceiling with stalactite carvings from the Ottoman Turkish period. There are also beautiful marble fountains that would have taken center place in the reception hall of a noble's house. You can see similar artistry in several of the preserved houses of Islamic Cairo such as Bayt al-Suhaymi (see p. 96) and the Gayer-Anderson Museum (see p. 113).

The museum holds beautiful Iranian and Turkish carpets. There is also a carved wooden *tabut* (casket) of Al Hussein from the Ayyubid Period (12th and 13th centuries). A fine example of a box made to hold a copy of the Koran is one once owned by Sultan Shaaban of the 14th century.

From the Mamluk era are enameled mosque lamps, stained-glass windows and another fountain, which the caretaker will sometimes switch on. There are also a series of unusual friezes—they are figurative. Carved into the wood are musicians, hunting scenes, and even men pouring wine. These are believed to be the work of the Fatimids, the North African dynasty that ruled Egypt from the mid-10th to the 12th century. Later, when the Fatimids were overthrown and their buildings torn down, these friezes were reused in the decoration of the Madrassa and Mausoleum of Sultan Qalawun (see pp. 99–100), but they were laid facing inward so as not to offend the pious. The Fatimids belonged to the minority Shiite branch of Islam, which had its greatest following in Iran, where a figurative tradition existed partly in the painting of miniatures, a few examples of which are brought out here for exhibition.

The museum holds a valuable display of woodwork and metalwork. There is also exquisite tiling, which is mainly of Armenian, Iranian, or Turkish origin because the Egyptians preferred using inlaid stone and marble from quarries south of Cairo. ■

EXPERIENCE:
Order a Coffee

If you get tired of drinking Nescafé, drink like the Egyptians do and order a strong, espresso-like Arabic *ahwa* (coffee) with your breakfast, or after dinner—the ideal antidote before or after extensive museum-going. Finely ground beans are brewed in a small pot. When the water begins boiling, the grounds float to the surface. The ahwa in the pot is then brought to you and poured into a demitasse. You'll know it's a perfect brew if the heavier grounds sink to the bottom and the lighter ones foam on top. Take care sipping, to avoid the grounds at the bottom (and if you don't like the foam, you can discreetly blow it aside). Remember, ahwa is never served with cream. Sugar is boiled with the water, so you will have to let the waiter know how sweet you want it:

ahwa saada	no sugar (black)
ahwa ariha	a little sweet
ahwa mazboot	moderately sweet (*mazboot* means "just right")
ahwa ziyada	very sweet

Sultan Hassan Mosque

Sultan Hassan's creation is regarded as one of the major monuments of the Islamic world. Its hulking size and brutal grandeur belie an inner simplicity and lightness, although given the mosque's turbulent history the real wonder is that it still stands at all.

Mamluk artisans' skill in marble inlay decoration is displayed in Sultan Hassan's prayer hall.

Sultan Hassan Mosque
- 66 D2
- Al-Qalaa Sq.
- Closed to visitors Fri. noon prayers
- $$

Al-Rifai Mosque
- 66 D2
- Al-Qalaa Sq.
- Closed to visitors Fri. noon prayers
- $$

Hassan became sultan in 1347, at the age of 13. Four years later, he was deposed in favor of an even younger brother, but was restored as sultan in 1354. Work on his mosque began two years later. The site was a prestigious one, overlooking the hippodrome at the foot of the royal Citadel (now predictably a traffic circle). Such a colossal project was expensive, but the population of Cairo had recently been decimated by the Black Death, and the properties of those who died intestate were used to bolster the royal treasury. Even with such funding, the construction of the mosque

nearly bankrupted the state. It continued for seven years, which proved to be too long for Hassan, who was assassinated in 1362.

Tragedy clung to the mosque. While under construction, a minaret collapsed, killing 300 onlookers. Once finished, the mosque's monumental scale and location opposite the Citadel proved a liability. During the frequent Mamluk skirmishes in pursuit of power it was used as a fortress, with soldiers armed with catapults firing at the sultan in his palaces. One canny ruler ripped out the staircase to prevent a repeat occurrence, while another began dismantling the mosque until public outrage forced him to stop.

Battle damage may have been responsible for the toppling of another minaret in 1659 (replaced by the smaller, less ambitious structure that survives today) and for the collapse of the dome just two years later (also rebuilt since, in a more modest form). The battering continued right up until the 19th century, when Napoleon turned his cannon on the mosque while quelling one of the frequent popular uprisings that were taking place against his occupation of the city. The facades still bear the scars.

Possibly the single most impressive element of the mosque is the towering, recessed entrance portal. Architectural historians identify strong similarities with portals in Anatolia in present-day Turkey, while some of the decoration is clearly inspired by Chinese flower motifs, evidence set in stone of the trading links between 14th-century Egypt and the world at large.

Inside, a dark passageway leads to the sudden brightness and humbling dimensions of the main courtyard. It has a central fountain for washing before prayers and four large, arched recesses known as *iwans,* where the Koran would have been taught—the mosque also served as a madrassa, or Islamic school. Each of the four doors off the courtyard leads to six stories of student cells. In all, this building provided free lodging for about 500 students, as well as a large staff that included professors, calligraphers, prayer-callers, and Koran readers. The many long, hanging chains in the iwans once held decorated glass

lamps—they are now displayed at the nearby Museum of Islamic Art (see pp. 104–105).

Beyond the prayer hall, with its fine marble *minbar,* or pulpit, is the domed mausoleum meant for Sultan Hassan. He never occupied it, as his murdered body mysteriously disappeared. Two of his sons are buried here instead.

Next to Sultan Hassan's mosque is a similarly monumental building that looks as though it could be a close relative. In fact, 600 years separate the two: The **Al-Rifai Mosque** was completed as recently as 1912. It was commissioned, in an imitation Mamluk style, by the mother of Khedive Ismail, to serve as a gran-

INSIDER TIP:

Combine a visit to Sultan Hassan with a long walk along Darb al-Ahmar to Bab Zuwayla. This old city street contains many fascinating sights.

—NEIL HEWISON
American University in Cairo Press

diose tomb for herself and her descendants. Royals buried here include Ismail, Farouk (Egypt's last king), and the last Shah of Iran. Chased out by Ayatollah Khomeini, the shah sought asylum in Egypt in 1979. When he died the next year, his casket was paraded through Cairo, with Egypt's President Sadat and former U.S. President Richard Nixon leading the cortege. ■

The Citadel

From its raised rocky platform on the city's edge, the Citadel dominates Cairo's eastern skyline. It was begun in 1176 by the famed Muslim general Saladin, who had its muscular walls and towers constructed with stones stripped from the Pyramids at Giza. The fortress served as Egypt's seat of power for the next 700 years, remodeled in the image of each successive dynasty.

Napoleon bombarded the city into submission from the Citadel's terraces, which today provide fine views.

The Citadel

- 66 D2 & 109
- Salah Salem St.
- 02/2512 1735
- $$$. Camera $, video camera $$$

Egypt's rulers moved from their medieval quarters to the newly built Abdeen Palace (see pp. 79–80) in the 1870s, but the Citadel retained its military role until the 1970s. Since soldiers still have a foothold, some areas are off-limits, but most of the complex is public. It is easy to spend half a day visiting the various mosques, museums, and other monuments enclosed within its walls.

By far the best reason to visit the Citadel is for the **views from its Western Terraces.** On a clear day you can pick out such vertical landmarks as the Ramses Hilton on the edge of the Nile, the Cairo Tower on Gezira, and—marking the city's westernmost edge—the distinctive zigzag of the Pyramids.

The Citadel's next biggest draw is the **Muhammad Ali Mosque,** a relatively late addition to the fortress that is the most visible monument in Cairo and symbolizes the Citadel in the minds of most visitors. Ironically, the mosque is designed wholly along Turkish lines and owes nothing to the architectural traditions of Egypt.

Muhammad Ali was the Albanian mercenary who, after a bloody contest with rival claimants, seized power in 1806 and ruled for 43 years, founding a dynasty that would last until it was removed by revolution in 1952. His mosque, begun in 1839, took 18 years to complete. Modeled on the great mosques of Istanbul, it sadly lacks their elegance and grace. Muhammad Ali lies in the marble tomb to the right as you enter. The iron clock in the courtyard was a gift from King Louis-Philippe of France in exchange for the obelisk that stands on the Place de la Concorde in Paris. Damaged during transit, the clock it has never worked.

To make room for his palaces and monuments, Muhammad Ali tore down a great many earlier buildings in the Citadel, but one structure that escaped demolition was the **Al-Nasir Muhammad Mosque,** completed in 1335. Considering it was spared for use as stables, it is still in good repair. The attractive courtyard has an arcade supported on a variety of pharaonic and Roman-era columns, and the minarets are unusual in that they are decorated with blue and green mosaics in a style more usually associated with Persia.

When you leave the mosque, across the plaza you'll see a pastiche Gothic gate that leads to another terrace with fine views and to the **Police Museum.** At the base of the museum's staircase is a frieze of carved stone lions, evidence of the 13th-century Lions Tower on top of which the museum is built. If you step across to the terrace wall from here, you look down on the Citadel's lower enclosure and a narrow defile of a roadway, which on March 1, 1811, was the site of one of the bloodiest episodes in Cairo's history.

The greatest challenge to Muhammad Ali's rule came from the Mamluks, former overlords of Egypt and still figures of influence. On the occasion of a celebration for his son, Muhammad Ali invited 500 of the leading Mamluk lords to the Citadel. They arrived with great pomp, feasted, and enjoyed the pasha's hospitality. As they departed in a mounted procession down toward the lower gate, the doors were slammed shut and Muhammad Ali's soldiers opened fire from the surrounding rooftops. Penned in and panicked, with no room for maneuver and no way to retreat, all 500 were slaughtered. Their heads were exhibited on stakes outside the city gates. According to an often recounted tale, a Mamluk by the name of Amin Bey survived by jumping his horse over the Citadel walls (a famous painting of the equestrian leap hangs in Manyal Palace). In fact, Amin Bey did survive the infamous massacre, but only because he failed to turn up for the feast that day.

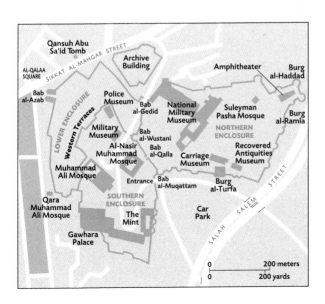

The buildings adjacent to the museum are part of the former **Military Prison,** established in the late 19th century by the British, whose forces were garrisoned here until the 1940s. The small cells were in use until 1983. An imposing gate opposite the north side of the Al-Nasir Muhammad Mosque leads to well-tended lawns. Directly ahead is the former Harem Palace, built in 1827 as the residence of Muhammad Ali and his family, and since 1949 home to the **National Military Museum.** Uniforms and ceremonial weaponry account for the bulk of the exhibits, but some of the rooms themselves are notable for their decorative excesses.

Two small museums in this part of the Citadel are devoted to ceremonial carriages and to recovered stolen antiquities. More worthwhile is the beautiful **Suleyman Pasha Mosque,** which, constructed in 1528, was the first mosque to be built in Cairo after the imposition of rule from Istanbul in 1517. Like Muhammad Ali's great mosque, this one is built along wholly Turkish lines, but with its graceful tumble of domes and half-domes it is far more successful. It's half-hidden behind a wall, with delicate decoration in the prayer hall and a leafy courtyard.

The solid walls around this part of the Citadel are the oldest elements in the complex—constructed under the command of Saladin himself around 1183 and strengthened 25 years later by his nephew Al-Kamil, using captured European Crusaders as labor. Walk across the concrete amphitheater to enter the twin half-round towers, the **Burg al-Haddad** (Blacksmith's Tower) and **Burg al-Ramla** (Sand Tower), which controlled the pass between the Citadel and the rocky hills behind. Al-Kamil felt they were too small, so he had them totally encased in new towers; Saladin's original window slits were broken open to serve as doorways into the new rooms. ■

EXPERIENCE: Visit the City of the Dead

Cairo's vast necropolis first took shape during the Mamluk period, outside the medieval city's walls. For centuries, wealthy families buried their dead here. Today, the tombs, with their stunning architecture, have become permanent abodes not only for the dead, but for the living. Several hundred thousand of the city's urban poor are permanent cemetery squatters.

A visit to this large area east of the Saleh Salim highway can be an eye-opening experience, revealing the city's architectural heritage as well as the resilience and ingenuity of its modern inhabitants (many have been there for generations, and electrical wiring and modern plumbing now running through the medieval buildings).

It is possible to visit the City of the Dead on your own, particularly if you plan to simply visit landmarks such as the Khanqah (a Sufi school) of Sultan Ibn Barquq or the Mosque of Qaitbey farther south. For the City itself, however, it is best have a guide, not least because you will be visiting a residential area without street markings.

A good contact is Italian anthropologist **Anna Tozzi,** who lived for several years among the City of the Dead's residents. She organizes private tours of the area using reliable local guides (e-mail: anna_tozzi@hotmail.com). Another licensed tour guide who regularly leads tours here is **Hany Halim Yousef** (tel 012/354 5968, www.hanyra.com).

Al-Azhar Park

For 500 years Cairenes tipped their garbage over the city walls creating a massive mound that eventually overshadowed the crumbling fortifications. That accumulation of debris has now been transformed into a recreational space and much-needed "green lung" opened in 2005.

The rolling hills and manicured gardens of Al-Azhar Park offer Cairenes much needed green space.

The 74-acre park stretches from just east of the Al-Azhar Mosque down toward the Citadel. It follows the old Ayyubid walls, built by the warrior sultan Salah ad-Din in the 12th century. While all around is dusty and dry, the park is dazzlingly green with lawns, orchards, and flower beds. It is bisected by a formal Persian-style garden with a central channel connecting shallow pools, and there's an artificial lake area—all fed by a pipeline from the Nile.

At the park's north end stands an impressive complex designed to emulate Cairo's grand Fatimid and Mamluk monuments. It houses the superb Citadel View restaurant (see p. 361), which boasts an open-air terrace and an equally fine café in

an outdoor, cushion-strewn salon. Elsewhere you'll find another lakeside café, a playground, and an amphitheater and stage. These will eventually be joined by a museum outlining Cairo's evolution. The park's western edge is delineated by the old walls, which were actually unearthed from centuries of compacted debris. The park will also prove a catalyst for renovation of the adjacent neighborhoods.

The elevated location on the fringes of Islamic Cairo affords a spellbinding panorama of minarets and domes with the towers of modern Cairo in the distance. The downside is that the park is only accessible by car. You need to take a taxi, then have the driver return at an agreed time. ■

Al-Azhar Park
🅰 66 D3
✉ Salah Salem St.
☎ 02/2510 3868
💲 $
www.alazharpark.com

Ibn Tulun Mosque

Ibn Tulun's is the oldest mosque in Egypt. This fact will excite an architectural historian, but for the casual visitor the main interest lies in its curious "open-air minaret" and in the adjacent Gayer-Anderson house, preserved as Cairo's most fascinating and quirkily individual museum. The mosque is a little awkward to get to from the city center and a taxi is the only option, but it is a mere half mile from the Citadel, and visits to the two can be combined in a half-day.

The mosque once served as the site of Friday prayers for the 9th-century court of Ibn Tulun.

Ibn Tulun Mosque

- 66 D2
- Saliba St.
- Closed to visitors Fri. noon prayers
- $$

Ahmed ibn Tulun (Ahmed son of Tulun) was sent to rule Cairo in the ninth century by the caliph of Baghdad. Ibn Tulun took advantage of his distance from court to turn his fief into an independent state and founded a mini-dynasty that ruled Egypt for three generations. With the tribute withheld from the caliph, the family built palaces, pleasure gardens and, according to legend, a pool filled with quicksilver where the ruler floated on an air bed. The Tulunid legacy largely perished after reconquest of Egypt by Baghdad, but, as a building dedicated to God, this mosque survived.

A commemorative plaque tells that it was opened for prayers in May 879. Its design is like nothing else found in Egypt and reflects Ibn Tulun's Iraqi origins. Architectural historians point out the similarities to the Great Mosque at Samarra, built around 30 years previously, especially the spiral minaret. The use of an outer enclosure is another Iraqi feature and is unique in Egypt. This is where today you buy your entry ticket, at a small wooden hut—although with so few visitors, the attendant has often wandered away and may have to be tracked down. The enclosure was meant to act as a buffer, keeping the surroundings at a respectful distance from the place of worship, but what worked in Iraq was not necessarily going to work in crowded, commercial medieval Cairo; for much of its history Ibn Tulun's outer enclosure was filled with a bazaar.

A flight of steps leads up into the mosque proper. Cloth coverings are provided for shoes (for which you will be expected to tip). This is to prevent soiling of the carpets on which the worshipers kneel to pray. In plan the mosque is almost square, with a vast central courtyard surrounded on four sides by shady arcades, two aisles deep on three sides but stretching back for five aisles on the side facing Mecca, which acts as the prayer hall. The decorative designs of the small windows that punctuate the back walls of the aisles are said to be all different with no repetition.

The minaret is reached from the outer enclosure, and from the tiny cockpit at the top a fine view of the mosque is laid out below. The panorama also takes in the minarets of Sultan Hassan's mosque and the distinctive silhouette of the mosque of Muhammad Ali at the Citadel to the east.

Equally if not more impressive than Ibn Tulun's mosque is the neighboring **Gayer-Anderson Museum,** which is off to the left, through a small entrance way, as you first enter the outer enclosure. It is a complete Orientalist fantasy: Two 16th-century houses joined by a covered bridge, with jasmine-scented courtyards, floor cushions and fountains, twisting passageways, and secret viewing galleries. All it lacks are its dark-eyed *houris,* although even they were briefly provided when Hollywood came

here to film the James Bond movie *The Spy Who Loved Me* (1977).

The Gayer-Anderson for whom the place is named was a British officer in Egypt, a keen collector of antiquities. Around 1930, he was allowed to occupy these houses—until that time family residences—in return for financing their upkeep and restoration. During the decade or more that he lived here he repaired and rebuilt, and added a vast miscellany of paintings, small pharaonic antiquities, and tribal artifacts to fill the maze of rooms. On his return to England he bequeathed his work and collections to the Egyptian

INSIDER TIP:

Egyptians are very hospitable to strangers. Stopping to talk could result in an invitation to tea. Repay the favor by carrying a few gifts to bestow on your enthusiastic host.

—GAYLE YOUNG
*Senior writer,
National Geographic Television*

government. Wonderful local legends attached to the houses include one concerning the courtyard well—said to be a passageway down to the domain of Sultan Watawit, Lord of the Bats.

Straight across the road from the museum and mosque as you leave is **Khan Misr Touloun,** an emporium stocked with pottery, handwoven textiles, and other beautiful objects made by Egyptian artists. ∎

Gayer-Anderson Museum

- 🅰 66 D2
- ✉ Saliba St.
- ☎ 02/2364 7822
- 🕐 Closed to visitors Fri. noon prayers
- 💲 \$\$. Camera \$, video camera \$\$\$

Coptic Cairo

Archaeological evidence suggests that Coptic Cairo is where the modern city began. But successive later conquerors shifted the urban center ever northward, so that Coptic Cairo now lies out on the southern fringes, well away from all the clamor and noise. Its high stone walls enclose a compound of silent narrow lanes, ancient holy places, and an important small museum.

For a few hundred years after the decline of the old pharaonic religions and before the arrival of Islam, Egypt was Christian. Alexandria was the seat of power and the country's only city of importance. Cairo-to-be existed as a modest port and river crossing in use since pharaonic times, and as a Roman fortress called Babylon-in-Egypt.

As you arrive by subway at Mar Girgis station, you have been traveling along the line of the banks of the Nile before the river changed its course 700 or more years ago. Steps down from the platform face the remains of two round Roman towers that formed the western gateway to the fortress, built in A.D. 98 by Emperor Trajan. As you pass between them, you are standing on top of the walls—centuries of mud and debris have raised the ground level by some 30 feet (10 m). Excavations down to the base of the right-hand tower have revealed traces of an ancient dock. Its twin on the left has been pressed into service as the foundations for the circular Greek Orthodox **Church of St. George.** George (in Arabic "Girgis") was an early Palestinian Christian martyr, executed by the Romans about A.D. 300. Returning Crusaders popularized his cult in Europe, and around the 13th century he was adopted by the English as their patron saint. His veneration in Cairo dates back earlier, and there has been a church dedicated to him in Coptic Cairo since the tenth century, although the present round basilica dates from the early 20th century.

Newly restored, the Church of the Virgin Mary is the spiritual home of Egypt's Coptic Christians.

Across a small garden is the **Coptic Museum.** Founded in 1908, the museum houses a fascinating collection representing a period of great change in world cultural history, when all around the eastern Mediterranean the old pagan gods—Greek, Roman, and Egyptian—were being usurped by the beliefs and icons of Christianity. Here you can see how Greek goddess motifs have become crosses, as have pharaonic *ankhs,* and the hawk-headed pharaonic deity Horus nestles at the corners of Coptic basket-weave capitals.

These objects are on the lower floor of the museum's **New Wing,** which is to the left on entering. On the upper floor are textiles, early Bibles, manuscripts, and painted prayer niches from early monasteries. The upper floor displays the bulk of the Nag Hammadi library (see p. 225) as well as the oldest Biblical text in Egypt, a complete Coptic psalter in its own gallery.

Exhibits are almost upstaged by the museum's beautifully painted wooden ceilings and mashrabiyya windows. The Old Wing galleries, reached via an upper floor passageway linking the two wings, are arranged by theme, such as the Nile or daily life in Roman and Byzantine Egypt. The Old Wing has a colorful collection of 18th- and 19th-century icons, and galleries displaying ceramics and metalwork (look for ornate keys from the White Monastery near Sohag.) The highlight of the final gallery, which leads to the courtyard, is an exquisite palanquin from the Ottoman period, inlaid with mother-of-pearl, bone, and ivory. The serene palm-lined courtyard includes column

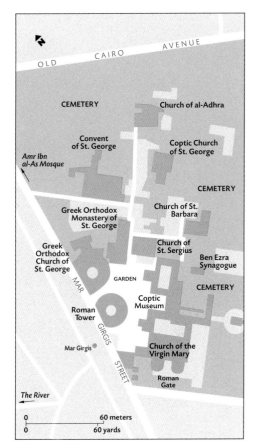

capitals from the ruined Monastery of St. Jeremiah in Saqqara.

Descend the staircase off the south side of the courtyard, which leads down into an area enclosed by the Water Gate, another two-towered portal from the Roman fortress. Built right on top of the gate is the **Church of the Virgin Mary,** also known as the Hanging Church (*Al-Muallaqa,* "the suspended" in Arabic) because it rests on top of, and literally hangs over, the Roman towers. It was probably founded in the ninth century, so it is not the oldest of

Coptic Museum

🅰 115

✉ Mar Girgis St.

☎ 02/2362 8766

💲 $$. Camera $, video camera $$$

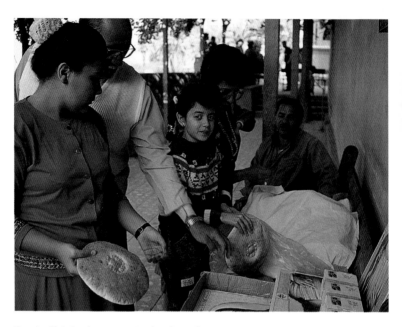

Egyptian Christians buy communion bread outside a Coptic Cairo church.

Coptic Cairo's half dozen ancient churches, but it is arguably the most beautiful. From the museum garden you enter the church up a steep staircase to a 19th-century portico. In an inner court, stalls do a good business in reproduction icons, taped liturgies, and videos of papal sermons. Inside, much of the decoration dates from the 13th century, including the bone-and-ivory screens shielding the altars. Mass is still celebrated here each Friday and Sunday morning.

On leaving the church, return to the main road and walk north beside the subway line to a flight of stairs that leads down, through a short tunnel, and back into the Coptic compound. Through a gate on the left in the high-walled alley is the **Convent of St. George,** closed to the public except for the main hall and chapel.

Farther on down, past several "antiques" emporiums and around the corner, is the **Church of St. Sergius,** also called Abu Serga. You have to descend another flight of stairs, which is an indication of the

INSIDER TIP:

Egyptian-style karaoke can be a way to meet the locals. Ask your hotel for suggestions of where to go.

—KORIN ANDERSON
National Geographic Television

building's age—around here, the lower you go the older things are. Historians dispute the age of this church; the likely consensus is fifth century. According to tradition, it is built over a crypt in which the Holy Family took shelter during their stay in Egypt (see pp. 218–219). In more recent times the crypt was flooded by groundwater but is now dewatered.

At the end of the lane, a left leads to the 11th-century **Church of St. Barbara,** while a right leads to a gate to **Ben Ezra Synagogue.** Venerated as the oldest synagogue in Cairo (it was founded in the 9th century and remodeled in the 12th by Abraham Ben Ezra, Rabbi of Jerusalem, though it is now a 19th-century structure), it is associated by tradition with the prophet Jeremiah, whose temple is said to have stood on this spot.

Another tradition says this is the place where the pharaoh's daughter found Moses in the bulrushes. The real find happened in the 19th century, however, with the discovery of the synagogue's intact *geniza,* or treasury. Since the 11th century, Cairo's Jewish community had been depositing documents in this chimney-like space in the synagogue because any paper bearing the name of God had to be preserved. The thousands of letters, promissory notes, deeds, accounts, contracts, and petitions recovered amounted to an account of medieval life comparable in completeness to the Domesday Book, William the Conqueror's 1086 survey of England. This priceless collection was rapidly spirited away to academic institutions abroad—most of it to Cambridge, England. Not one single bundle or sheaf remains in Cairo.

A short walk north of the walls of the Coptic compound is the **Amr ibn al-As Mosque,** established by the Arab general who captured Cairo in A.D. 640 and claimed Egypt for Islam. Today the mosque is a patchwork of countless rebuildings and restorations, but it holds a special place in the story of Cairo as the site where Islam

The Riverboat

You can ride the metro to Coptic Cairo; Mar Girgis station is four stops south of Tahrir Square's Sadat station, and a ticket costs the equivalent of just a few cents. But how much better to go by boat! Blue-and-white river buses depart from the Maspero Quay across from the Television and Radio Building, which is a few minutes' walk north of the Egyptian Museum. Broad and flat like water beetles, the boats take the greater part of an hour zigzagging leisurely up the Nile to finish the trip at Masr al-Qadima, or Old Cairo. From the boat landing, it is another walk of a few minutes directly inland to the subway tracks. Cross over the footbridge and you are in Coptic Cairo.

was introduced into Egypt. To get to the mosque, follow Mar Girgis Street, which runs beside the subway, north for 200 yards (180 m).

From Coptic Cairo it is just a brief walk to the Nilometer (see pp. 118–119): Cross the bridge over the subway tracks and go west until you reach the river, where a footbridge takes you across to the island of Roda. ■

Nilometer

From pharaonic times until the beginning of the 20th century, the cycle of Egyptian life was governed by the annual flooding of the Nile. Prosperity depended on inundation by the river's waters—but only by the right amount, as too much could be disastrous. Since it was necessary to be able to read the rising flood in order to know what to expect, a series of Nilometers was built along the Nile Valley, the most elaborate being this one on the island of Roda in Cairo.

The central column of the Nilometer was used to measure the rise and fall of the Nile.

Nilometer
- 66 C1
- Al-Malek al-Salah St., Roda
- $. Camera $, video camera $$$

Mummy-shaped Roda, which lies in the river off Old Cairo, has been inhabited since the era of the Pyramids. It was at various times a port and a shipbuilding center, and the Romans built a fortress here, the twin of that at Babylon (see p. 114). In the tales of *The Thousand and One Nights* the island is described as a garden paradise. It is no longer that, but the ranks of modern apartment blocks do at least stop short of the southern tip, which is an attractive vantage point.

Over half a mile (1 km) wide at this point, the river looks splendid and mighty, with reed beds lining the far banks. The Nile was wider still in ancient times, when a pontoon bridge of boats connected Roda to the mainland. These days, only a narrow channel separates the island and the Corniche, spanned by a wooden footbridge that gives access to the Nilometer from Coptic Cairo (see pp. 114–117).

Although there has been a Nilometer here since pharaonic times, the existing one dates only from A.D. 861, and the unusual little conical-capped kiosk over it is actually a modern re-creation of a Turkish building. The Nilometer takes the form of a great stone-lined pit that descends well below the level of the Nile. At the bottom is an octagonal column, measured off and marked. Water was let in by three tunnels at different heights, all now sealed. A good year was when the waters rose to the 16th of the column's graduated divisions, known as ells. This event was greeted by city-wide festivities and celebrations. Much more than 16 ells meant disastrous flooding; much less meant drought and famine. In the event of a shortfall, celebrations were canceled, their place taken by emergency prayers and fasting.

To improve the chances of just the right amount of flooding, Koranic verses carved on the walls of the Nilometer praise Allah and water as his blessing. Other decorations include four recesses with pointed arches resembling the Gothic arches seen in medieval European archi-tecture. However, these prefigure the Gothic style by several hun-dred years; it has been suggested that they may be the first pointed arches anywhere in the world. Although not particularly old, the elaborate carved and painted arabesques on the wooden ceil-ing are very impressive.

On leaving the Nilometer, turn left and follow the terrace path around the **Monasterli Palace,** built in 1851 on the site of the Nilometer Mosque, which had existed since the 11th century. For a time the headquarters of the Arab League (the organization is now in a grim

INSIDER TIP:

The Nilometer on the tip of Roda Island is a neat place. Everyone knows it's there, and everyone knows it's ancient and important, but few people actu-ally go to see it. It's a good off-the-beaten-path destination.

—ELLEN MILLER
National Geographic field researcher

building just off Tahrir Square), the palace is now used intermit-tently as an arts center.

An annex of the palace serves as the **Umm Kolthum Museum,** devoted to the greatest singer that the Arab world has ever known (see pp. 56–57). A vitrine at the entrance contains one of her trademark chiffon scarves and a pair of diamante-studded glasses. Inside, displays include several fabulous dresses that were once worn by the diva, plus there's a short film on her life (Arabic language only, un-fortunately) and an audio library where visitors can listen to some of her best-known recordings. ■

Gezira

Gezira is the Arabic word for "island," but if you hear it said in Cairo, chances are the speaker is referring to one particular island that lies midstream in the Nile between the city center and the west bank. Uninhabited until the 19th century, when it became a royal garden, Gezira these days is home to an arts complex, an exclusive sporting club, and Cairo's premier soccer team. But it also remains the greenest and leafiest part of the city.

Looking over Gezira Island, with the Opera House and Exhibition Grounds in the foreground

Mokhtar Museum

📍 66 C3
✉ Tahrir St.
☎ 02/2735 2519
🕐 Closed Mon.
💲 $

Cairo Opera House

📍 66 C3
✉ Tahrir St.
☎ 02/2739 8144 or 02/2739 8132
🕐 Only open for performances

From central Cairo's Tahrir Square, the elegant **Qasr al-Nil Bridge** forms a link to the southern end of Gezira. Originally built in 1871, it was completely overhauled in 1931 by Dorman Long & Co., the British firm responsible for Australia's famous Sydney Harbour Bridge. The splendid lions that stand guard, a pair at each end, belong to the original crossing.

At the Gezira end, the bridge leads into Saad Zaghloul Square,

named for an Egyptian nationalist leader of the early 20th century; that's him on top of the plinth in the traffic island. The statue is the work of Mahmoud Mokhtar (1891–1934), the preeminent Egyptian sculptor of modern times. The **Mokhtar Museum,** dedicated to his output, is due west along Tahrir Street. The work ranges widely in style, displaying warmth and humor, quite in contrast to the serious nationalistic pieces for which the artist is best known.

Southern Gezira is domi-nated by the **Cairo Opera House complex.** After fire destroyed the old downtown Opera House (see pp. 84–85), the city was left without a major concert venue until the Japanese stepped in during the late 1980s. They made a gift of the present building, which is a beautiful, cool white modernist update on Islamic architectural themes. It maintains a busy program of opera, ballet, theater, and music, and has a strict jacket-and-tie policy.

Adjacent to the opera is the **National Museum of Egyptian Modern Art.** Although they remain largely unknown on an international level, there are several outstanding Egyptian artists whose work deserves to reach a much wider audience. Chief of these are Mahmoud Said, who now has a museum devoted to him in Alexandria (see p. 190), and the surrealist Abd al-Hady al-Gazzar; both are represented here. Unfortunately, with its poor lighting and sparse collection, the museum does none of its artists justice. Two other major galleries within the Opera House grounds are used to host temporary exhibitions. Look for the larger-than-life statue of a woman on the lawn beside the main path; this is Umm Kolthum, the legendary Egyptian singer (see pp. 56–57).

Just a short distance north of the Opera House is another local icon, the **Cairo Tower.** It owes its conception to the Cold War of the 1950s, when Egypt was a part of the Middle Eastern chessboard pondered over by U.S. and Soviet policymakers. The story goes that in a bid to bring Egypt into the anti-Soviet camp, the U.S. State Department offered President Nasser a sweetener of one million dollars toward arms purchases. Furious at the assumption that he could be bought, Nasser took the money and used it to send a mes-sage back to Washington in the form of a great big raised finger. On a clear day from the top of the 614-foot (187 m) tower you can pick out the minarets of the Citadel to the east and the Pyra-mids to the west. Last admission is not until 11 p.m., and it is worth going late to view Cairo by night.

You also can look down over the swath of green in the island's center. This is the **Gezira Club,** founded by the British in the 1880s as an officers' club. It retains its exclusivity today, with a membership restricted to the elite who can afford the large annual subscription fee. ■

National Museum of Egyptian Modern Art
- ▲ 66 C3
- ✉ Opera House grounds, Tahrir St.
- ☎ 02/2736 6665
- 🕐 Closed p.m. & Mon.
- 💲 $

Cairo Tower
- ▲ 66 C3
- ✉ Hadayek al-Zuhreya St.
- ☎ 02/2735 7187
- 🕐 Last adm. 11 p.m.
- 💲 $$$. Video camera $

EXPERIENCE:
Egyptian Weddings in Your Hotel Lobby

If you're staying at one of the large interna-tional hotels in Cairo, such as the Ramses Hilton or the Semiramis, you might be lucky enough to spot an Egyptian wedding in the hotel lobby on a weekend night. The reception begins with a *zaffa*, a wedding procession for the bride and groom (often held on a hotel staircase) accompanied by a loud band of traditional musicians. Sometimes bridesmaids toss rose petals be-fore the bride's feet. The zaffa is loud and festive, and since it's being held in a public area, there's no reason you can't stand off to the side and watch!

Zamalek Walk: Fine Living & Fine Art

An island neighborhood on the north end of Gezira, Zamalek is Cairo's Manhattan, the city's most desirable address. Its well-to-do residents love it for its leafy streets and its vaguely European air, a legacy of the early 20th century when the neighborhood was the preserve of diplomats, colonial officials, and aristocracy.

Leafy Zamalek on the tip of Gezira Island has long been an appealing niche hidden away from Cairo's cacophony.

NOT TO BE MISSED:

The garden of the Cairo Marriott Hotel • Pizza at Maison Thomas • The view of houseboats from Zamalek Bridge

---

Zamalek's Origins

One of the first notable personages to grace the district with her presence was Empress Eugénie, wife of Napoleon III of France, who was accommodated on Gezira while visiting Egypt for the opening of the Suez Canal in 1869. A lavish palace was specially constructed for the occasion, with a striking facade of Islamic-style arches in cast iron. The Gezira Palace survives as the core of the **Cairo Marriott Hotel & Omar Khayyam Casino ❶** (*16 Saray al-Gezira St., tel 02/2735 8888, www.marriott.com; see p. 360*). Although modern wings have been added to the hotel, the central building is original and it remains regally opulent. If you are not able to enjoy the hotel as a guest, then it is well worth visiting for lunch or an evening drink in the garden, which spans six acres.

Royal overspending on extravagances such as the Gezira Palace led, predictably, to bankruptcy. By 1879 creditors were laying claim to the land and possessions of the khedive, including Gezira. They carved up the island and sold it off, triggering a real-estate boom, out of which was born Zamalek.

Rich Artistic Traditions

Leave the Marriott by the main drive. The apartments here on Saray al-Gezira Street overlooking the river are some of the most sought-after in town. They are a favorite with international correspondents, who no doubt appreciate being able to observe the goings-on at the towering white Foreign Ministry directly across the water. At No. 14,

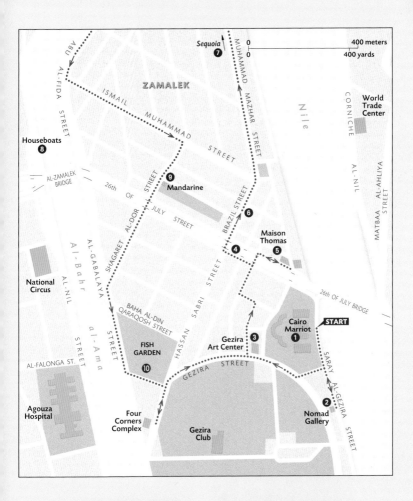

up on the second floor, is **Nomad Gallery**
❷ (tel 02/2736 1917), a beautiful little shop
specializing in Bedouin and traditional Egyptian jewelry and dress, as well as housewares.
It also has a small outpost at the Marriott.

From Nomad, backtrack slightly and walk
alongside the Marriott to come out opposite
the Gezira Club (see p. 124), and then follow
the road around. Opposite the club entrance is
a smart little 19th-century villa, once a private
residence, now the **Gezira Art Center** ❸
(1 Sheikh al-Marsafi St., tel 02/2737 3298, closed
Fri.). It contains a lovely collection of tiles,
bowls, pitchers, and vases, spanning ten centuries, and drawn not just from Egypt, but also

> ⛰ See area map pp. 66–67
> ▶ Cairo Marriott Hotel
> ⟷ 2 miles (3 km)
> ⏱ 2 hours
> ▶ Cairo Marriott Hotel

from Persia, Morocco, Turkey, and Andalusia
(southern Spain).

Hub of the Neighborhood

From here, head north across the small
square and then take a left and then a right
to come to **26th of July Street** ❹, the hub
of the neighborhood. If you are hungry,

then cross the road, and to the right you'll find **Maison Thomas** ⑤ (see p. 363), Cairo's only Continental-style deli, trading since 1930 and the source of the best pizza in town.

Head back the way you came on 26th of July and take a right onto the quieter backside of Yahya Ibrahim. Halfway up the street, you'll come across the **Fair Trade Egypt Center** (27 Yahya Ibrahim St., tel 02/2736 5123), a showcase of artisanal work from around Egypt run by a non-profit dedicated to preserving and encouraging traditional crafts.

Shop, Dine, & Relax

Running parallel to Yahya Ibrahim Street is **Brazil Street** ⑥, home to carpet-menders, butchers, and a great many small boutiques selling good-quality cotton Egyptian clothing, as well as a fair scattering of antique

stores and fine art galleries. Continue to the top of Brazil Street, where it bends slightly left to become Muhammad Mazhar Street. Follow it to the end and you will arrive at **Sequoia** (1–3 Abou Feda St., Zamalek, tel 02/735 0014) ⑦, an upscale open-air restaurant and bar that occupies the island's northern tip, overlooking the Nile. It serves a mix of Egyptian and Lebanese mezes, but also has an extensive pasta list.

After a Nileside drink and *meze,* continue your walk, heading down the island's west side on Abu al Fida Street. Lined up along the opposite bank of the river you can see a chain of old wooden double-decker **houseboats** ⑧. Turn left onto Ismail Muhammad Street, and after a few blocks, take a right onto Shagaret al-Dor Street, where you will pass **Mandarine** ⑨, one of Cairo's best patisseries.

Continuing south past 26th of July Street again will bring you to the **Fish Garden** ⑩, a small landscaped park with grottoes and aquariums that was once part of the Gezira Palace gardens. Recently restored, it was formerly known as the Gabalayia Garden or the Aquarium Grotto Garden.

From here turn inland along Gezira Street past the Gezira Club on your right and return to the Marriott on your left.

Cast-iron arcades originally part of a royal palace now provide an ornate frontage to the Marriott hotel.

Smoke a *Sheesha*

Perhaps as ubiquitous as camels in Egypt are *sheeshas*, or water pipes. If you order a sheesha at a café, you will be presented with a pipe and a plastic mouthpiece *(mabsim)* wrapped in cellophane for you to attach to the pipe end. Serious Egyptian smokers prefer a heavy honey-flavored tobacco, though most beginners will want to start with the sweet apple tobacco you can smell anywhere. A pipe-lighter *(walia)* will bring a brazier of hot coal around to your table and light the pipe for you. A few good huffs should start the air flowing through the water.

Western Cairo

As far as the visitor is concerned, Cairo is confined to one bank of the river. West of the Nile does not even appear on most tourist maps. That's because it is where a sizable proportion of Cairo lives, in an area dense with mid-rise apartment blocks and six-lane highways that fly past strips peppered with franchises of Arby's, Baskin Robbins, and KFC. While this is not somewhere to go strolling, there are several places worth flagging down a taxi for.

Visitors associate Giza with pyramids, but to Egyptians it is most famously home to Cairo University.

Though it's hard to imagine now, until well into the 20th century palm-decked farmland lay just over the river from central Cairo, bisected by a long, tree-lined road aimed straight at the Pyramids. A wealthy elite maintained "country homes" beside the Nile with gardens running to the water's edge. Population pressure has seen the majority of the villas give way to the more egalitarian high-rises, but there are some survivors. One such is a splendid, late 19th-century, Parisian-styled mansion, preserved as the **Muhammad Mahmoud Khalil Museum.** Khalil was a cabinet minister during the 1930s and a wealthy, compulsive collector of international, and particularly French, art. He bequeathed his house and acquisitions to the state, endowing Cairo with one of its best-kept secrets—a world-class collection of Impressionist paintings and other works by well-known European artists.

Muhammad Mahmoud Khalil Museum

🅰 66 C2

✉ 1 Kafour St., off Giza St.

☎ 02/3336 2358

🕐 Closed Mon.

💲 $$. Camera $, video camera $$$

www.mkm.gov.eg

Young men paint wall panels for a replica of a waterside Ptolemaic temple, an attraction at Dr. Ragab's Pharaonic Village.

Cairo Zoo

66 B2/C2

Giza St.

02/570 8895

$

The works on display in well-lit surroundings include sculptures by Rodin, several paintings by Corot, Pissarro, Sisley, Millet, and Renoir, works by Degas and Monet, two gorgeous Gauguins, a luminous Toulouse-Lautrec, and one of van Gogh's iris series. The house itself, which was well restored in the 1980s, is quite charming. As you gaze out of the back windows toward the Nile, note the nicely kept grassy lawn; 20 years ago that was a tarmac helicopter landing pad used by President Sadat, who commandeered the house as part of his residence.

Half a mile (1 km) south of the museum, along Giza Street, is **University Square,** a traffic circle with a striking monument at its center; this is "The Awakening of Egypt" (1928), the most lauded work of Egyptian sculptor Mah-

moud Mokhtar (see p. 120). Originally, the statue stood in Ramses Square until the present Ramses II colossus took its place. It is a little lost here, almost permanently cordoned off by fast-flowing traffic, but presumably its siting is intended to stimulate the students at nearby **Cairo University,** whose domed main building squats at the end of the avenue.

Across from the statue is the entrance to **Cairo Zoo,** which was established in 1894 on the grounds of the former royal Harem Gardens. The first animals came from the personal menagerie of Khedive Ismail, and the collection rapidly grew to make this one of the finest zoos in the world. Sadly, underfunding and neglect mean that today the place is a shadow of its former self, with little in the pens beyond lots of big birds, such as ostriches, emus, flamingos, and the like. This makes it fantastically popular with Cairo's roaming cat population. Nevertheless, as one of the city's largest green spaces, it continues to attract big crowds, especially on weekends and public holidays.

Although the zoo is no Central Park, it is overlooked by Cairo's most talked-about piece of real estate, the two towers of the **First Residence.** Apartments here start at 1.3 million dollars, while the penthouse is rumored to have gone for 14 million dollars. Back at ground level, the First Mall is a chichi air-conditioned shopping experience, with an atrium café that provides expensive respite from the heat outside.

Children will enjoy the **Pharaonic Village** *(3 Al-Bahr al-Azam St., tel 02/3572 2533, www.pharaonicvillage.com, $$$),* an ancient Egypt theme park on Jacob's Island, situated in the middle of the Nile, south of Giza. Visitors sail in small boats through the reed beds, viewing scenes of pharaonic daily life re-created by costumed actors. At the end of the boat journey they reach several small, lively museums.

INSIDER TIP:

Be sure to sit in a café drinking black tea and people watch. Nothing is quite like a three-camel traffic jam complete with horns beeping and riders yelling.

—KORIN ANDERSON
Associate producer,
National Geographic Television

One is devoted to early Egyptian history, including an absorbing mock-up of Tutankhamun's tomb as it was discovered by archaeologist Howard Carter, and another displays a new collection devoted to Alexander the Great and Hellenistic Egypt. ■

Buying Produce: Sampling Egypt's Justly Famous Fruits

The über fertile Nile Valley and Delta have blessed Egypt with a rich variety of fresh, flavorful fruits and vegetables, and no trip to the country would be complete without sampling some of the local produce. A bag of oranges makes a great snack when you're visiting an out-of-the-way site or don't want to stop for a sit-down meal.

As always, do your innards a favor and stay away from uncooked, unpeeled fruits. Peelable fruits such as oranges and bananas are fine, and if you have a knife, so are mangoes and kiwis. Egypt's delicious mangoes come in a number of varieties, with colorful names like Lady's Finger, Sugary, and Beautiful Cheek. They are available in markets between June and September. Dates are widely available year-round; Siwa Oasis produces some of the best, although Siwa dates can be purchased just about anywhere in Egypt.

You may be pleasantly surprised by the intense flavor of oranges, grapefruits, and other fresh produce here; American varieties are often bred for size, and as a result, can be watery in taste. What Egyptian fruits lack in size, they more than make up for in flavor.

The Pyramids

Trivia buffs, but perhaps no one else, know that the Seven Wonders of the Ancient World were the Pyramids of Egypt, the statue of Zeus at Olympia, the Colossus of Rhodes, the Temple of Artemis at Ephesus, the Mausoleum of Halicarnassus, the Pharos of Alexandria, and the Hanging Gardens of Babylon. But only the Pyramids are still with us. And modern visitors continue to find the Pyramids no less wondrous and mysterious than the ancients did.

The Pyramids have two fundamental characteristics: They are big and they are old. But despite these fairly straightforward concepts, exactly how big, and how old, is something that is still quite hard to grasp. Until as recently as the 19th century, the Great Pyramid of Khufu, built 4,400 years earlier, was the tallest building in the world. Napoleon, having conquered Egypt in 1798, calculated that it contained enough stone to build a wall 3 feet (1 m) high around the whole of France. The dashing young general also spent a night alone inside the Great Pyramid from which he reputedly emerged shaken, never to discuss the experience. As for their age, the Pyramids were already ancient at the time of the birth of Jesus Christ, year zero for much of the Western world. In fact, Christ's birth is closer in time to us than it is to the building of the Pyramids. As the world celebrated the arrival of the new millennium in 2000, the Pyramids were entering their fifth set of one thousand years. An ancient Arabic saying sums it up best: "Man fears time, but time fears the Pyramids."

Visiting the Pyramids

In spite of the awesome spectacle ("Like a thing of nature, a mountain...with something terrible about it, as though it were going to crush you," wrote French novelist Gustave

Time has not lessened the mystique of the world's oldest tourist attraction.

EXPERIENCE: Go Horseback Riding

There are a number of local stables around the main entrance to the Pyramids in Giza, renting camels and horses to tourists. Unfortunately, the quality of animals varies considerably from place to place, and Western standards of humane treatment are occasionally lacking.

Fortunately, a more humane alternative exists with the riding stable **Recoub al Sorat,** roughly translated as "Riding the Righteous Path" *(tel 012/3211 8386, www. alsorat.com)*. Based in Abu Sir (the site of the 5th Dynasty pyramids between Giza and Saqqara), Recoub al Sorat is run by Maryanne Stroud Gabbani, who ensures that her horses are well cared for and trained. Gabbani is an American who has lived in Egypt since the late 1980s, when she came here with her two children and her late Egyptian/Canadian husband.

In 2008, the Pyramids of Giza were enclosed in a 12-mile-long (19 km) fence to deter routine harassment of tourists from local touts. Sadly, it is no longer possible to ride a horse (or a camel, if you have a masochistic streak) up to the Pyramids themselves. However, Recoub al Sorat organizes rides through the Sahara to Saqqara, Dahshur, and Memphis, as well as evening rides and trail rides in the Nile Valley.

Flaubert of the Great Pyramid in 1849), a first visit can be disappointing. All the countless pictures and images—and the Pyramids must be the most photographed monuments in the world —show the Pyramids in the middle of the desert, but

INSIDER TIP:

For one of the best photo opportunities of the Pyramids, ask to eat on the roof of the Pizza Hut at sundown.

—LESLIE LYONS
National Geographic field researcher

suburban Cairo actually creeps right up almost to the paws of the Sphinx. Were hunger to strike the great beast now, it only need stretch out one of those paws to flag some service at the neighboring branch of an international pizza chain.

Of course, it wasn't always so. Giza Plateau, the rocky foundation on which the Pyramids and Sphinx rest, is 10 miles (16 km) southwest of central Cairo. It once took a horse ride through the fields to reach the monuments, where they stand on the edge of the desert. Then in the 19th century, a road was built and along it ran a tram. Now that road, Al-Haram, or Pyramids Road, is four lanes of horn-honking traffic, blocked solid night and day. The tram is gone, but in its place are buses, and there is a good air-conditioned service that runs between Tahrir Square in central Cairo and the Giza Plateau. Alternatively, a taxi costs about five dollars one way.

There are two approaches to the site: one through the village of Nazlet al-Samaan, the other up a curving slip road, an extension of Pyramids Road, passing the Mena House Hotel to the

The Pyramids

🗺 66 A1 & 141 C4

💲 $$, plus additional fee ($$ each) to enter Great Pyramid, Khafre's Pyramid, Menkaure's Pyramid, Solar Boat Museum. Sound-and-light show

☎ 02/3383 8823

right. Either way, entry tickets are purchased at a kiosk on the edge of the plateau. Separate tickets are necessary to go inside the Pyramids: Just 300 people per day are allowed to enter each one, with tickets sold on a first-come first-served basis. Ongoing restoration work means that usually only two out of the three Pyramids are open at any one time. Get there early. An early morning visit also means that you avoid the worst of the heat.

The **Great Pyramid of Khufu** is the first one to appear if you

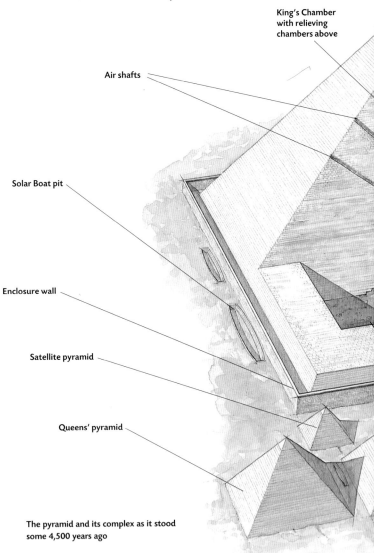

King's Chamber with relieving chambers above

Air shafts

Solar Boat pit

Enclosure wall

Satellite pyramid

Queens' pyramid

The pyramid and its complex as it stood some 4,500 years ago

approach from Pyramids Road, as most visitors do. Khufu (who is also known by his Greek name of Cheops) is thought to have ruled about 2589 to 2566 B.C., although these dates are far from undisputed. His pyramid is the oldest and the largest of the trio. It is estimated to contain about 2.3 million limestone blocks, each thought to weigh on average 2.5 tons (2.3 tonnes), although some of the stones at the base may weigh as much as 16.5 tons (15 tonnes). Originally 482 feet (147 m) high, it is now a little lower because of

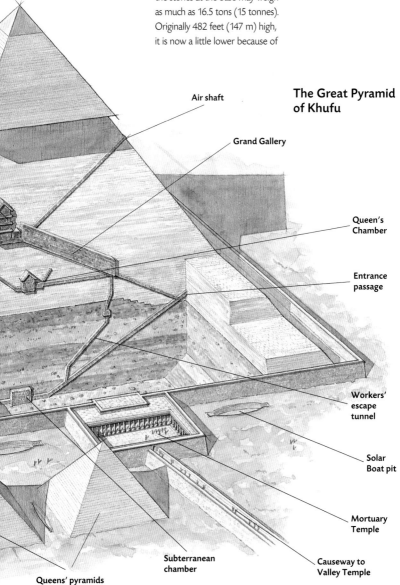

The Great Pyramid of Khufu

Air shaft

Grand Gallery

Queen's Chamber

Entrance passage

Workers' escape tunnel

Solar Boat pit

Mortuary Temple

Causeway to Valley Temple

Subterranean chamber

Queens' pyramids

EXPERIENCE: Get in Touch with Your Inner Isis

While not for everyone, "New Age" tourism—sometimes called "metaphysical tourism"—is a popular option for spiritual seekers looking to find enlightenment or out-of-body experiences in the land of the pharaohs. In some cases, Egypt's Supreme Council of Antiquities permits spiritual tour groups to enter the Great Pyramid of Giza in the early dawn, or hold ceremonies at ancient sites that they claim emanate spiritual energy. Some Egyptian travel companies specialize in this area and organize regular trips for large groups. **Luminati Egyptian Travel** *(tel 888-488-1151, www.luminati.net),* for example, is based in the United States,

but partners with a local travel agency in Cairo. **Guardian Travel** *(tel 757-422-5568, www.guardiantravel.net)* also offers metaphysical tours: look for tours on its website.

If you are not interested in a package tour, you can sign up for weekend events with a Maadi-based organization called **Insight Inside** *(tel 010/668 7203 or 02/2520 2945, e-mail: mail@insight-inside.com).* It's a holistic health center that offers workshops on spirituality. Insight Inside also sponsors spiritual trips such as the 6-day Egyptian Wisdom package and the 3-day Taba Incentive. Sign up for their e-newsletter to learn about upcoming events.

---

the removal of its outer limestone casing and capstone.

Visitors can climb a few feet of staircase purposely cut into the exterior face of the Great Pyramid and make their way inside through an opening, which was forced by the Egyptian ruler Caliph al-Mamun in A.D. 820. From the entrance a low, narrow corridor descends into an unfinished room, from which a second corridor ascends to another unfinished room, known as the **Queen's Chamber.** Visitors then go through the magnificent high **Grand Gallery** to the **main burial chamber,** right at the very center of the pyramid. In this chamber is an empty pink granite sarcophagus, all that was ever found. As the sarcophagus is too big to get through the door, Egyptologists deduce that the room and pyramid must have been built around the sarcophagus. Whether

it ever actually contained the body of Khufu, nobody can say for sure. Negotiating the steep slopes and confined spaces is arduous and not recommended for serious claustrophobes or for those with heart problems, but everything is clean and well lit, and there are hand rails and wooden ramps.

In its original form, the pyramid was the focal point of a small complex. It was surrounded by a high wall enclosing a limestone court. Entrance to the court was via a mortuary temple, itself reached by a long, sloping causeway. When the Greek historian Herodotus visited, somewhere between 449 and 430 B.C., Khufu's causeway was still intact with "polished stone blocks decorated with carvings of animals," and he described it as a work "of hardly less magnitude than the pyramid itself." At the bottom of the causeway was a second small "valley" temple below.

This lay beside a lake, which was fed by the Nile once a year during the annual flood. Both temples are gone, but the stone flagging of the causeway survives.

On either side of the causeway are large rectangular pits. In 1954, when covering slabs were lifted off one of these for the first time since antiquity, the dismantled planking of a boat was revealed. Its 1,224 separate cedarwood parts were painstakingly reassembled like a giant 3D jigsaw; the reconstructed boat is now displayed in its own specially built **Solar Boat Museum** on the south side of Khufu's pyramid. In 1985 a combined team from the National Geographic Society and the Egyptian Antiquities Authority explored a second pit, and that too was found to contain a disassembled boat. It has been left untouched beneath the sand.

The **Pyramid of Khafre** (or Chephren, as he is also known) is slightly smaller than that of Khufu, his father. It appears taller because it is built on higher ground. It is distinguished by a cap of smooth white stone—this is all that remains of a hard, polished outer limestone casing that once sheathed all three pyramids. It would have given them the appearance of pure, gleaming geometric prisms, but it was stripped away to build the palaces and mosques of Cairo.

Inside, the burial chamber lies just below ground level, incised into the bedrock. It is reached by a single descending passage, and the effort involved in a visit is much less than that required in the Great Pyramid.

The **Pyramid of Menkaura**

(Mycerinus) is the smallest of the group. It has a base area less than a quarter of that of the pyramids built by Khufu and Khafre. Archaeologists speculate that perhaps the Egyptians were running out of room. It may also be that the power of the pharaoh was waning, and it was no longer possible to raise the large workforce neces-

Pyramid Hassles

A visit to the Giza Pyramids used to mean that you passed through a gauntlet of insistent touts and hawkers offering camel rides, "special guides," and souvenirs on the way to the monuments. As of 2008, however, the Egyptian authorities have built a 12-mile-long (19 km) fence around the Giza plateau to keep out hawkers and make visiting the pyramids a slightly more serene experience and to better protect the sites themselves. Equipped with motion sensors and security cameras, the fence is part of a long-term project to modernize the site and make it more visitor friendly.

sary for another truly gigantic monument. The great vertical gash in the north face is from a 12th-century attempt made to dismantle the pyramid by Othman ibn Yousef, son of Saladin (see p. 35). But in eight months all his laborers had achieved was merely the creation of this large slot, so

The mighty Sphinx surveys Giza, with the Great Pyramid of Khufu rising beyond.

the sultan gave up the attempt.

From the entrance, also on the north side, a passage descends to an unfinished chamber with a series of panels carved with a stylized false door motif. A further passage leads down to the burial chamber, in which was found a beautiful basalt sarcophagus, subsequently lost when the ship carrying it to England foundered at sea and sank. The pyramid is flanked by three small queens' pyramids, two of which are unfinished, left stepped like Zoser's pyramid at Saqqara (see pp. 144–147).

The Sphinx—The Father of Terror

From the foot of Khafre's pyramid, another causeway descends to the east to the king's partially reconstructed valley

The Mystery of the Pyramids

The breathtaking accuracy and alignment of the Pyramids at Giza have given rise to much theorizing. Khufu's pyramid is laid out with its sides oriented to within just three degrees of true north. The pyramid's base, which has sides over 756 feet (230 m) long, is level to within 1 inch (2.6 cm), and the greatest difference in the length of the four sides is just 2 inches (5.2 cm)—a margin of error of less than 0.2 percent.

Another striking statistic: The southeast corners of the three main pyramids line up on an exact diagonal. Such phenomenal precision in such ancient structures inspires many pyramid enthusiasts to look for more alignments, hoping for hidden greater meanings and possible treasures.

temple. A striking diorite statue of Khafre that was found here is now exhibited in Room 42 of the Egyptian Museum (see pp. 68–76). The temple now serves as a viewing platform for audiences entranced by the Sphinx, the mysterious creature with a lion's body and a human face, known to the early Arabs as Abu al-Hol, or the Father of Terror. Although subject to much dispute—with one claim that it predates ancient Egypt and is an artifact of some older, vanished civilization—most archaeologists now agree that the Sphinx was carved during Khafre's reign (2558–2532 B.C.). It is thought that it represents the King, the lion being an archetype of royalty, and the King's head, framed by a flared nemes (the headdress worn by pharaohs), symbolizing power.

It was carved from a single outcrop of bedrock, with blocks used to build up the legs and paws, and it represents the earliest truly colossal piece of ancient Egyptian sculpture. Parts of the creature are gleaming white as a result of renovations undertaken in the 1990s, but repairs have been ongoing since at least as far back as the 18th dynasty, when a small temple was added between the forepaws, along with a stela describing how the pharaoh Tuthmose IV (R. 1400–1390 B.C.) rescued the Sphinx from the sands that covered it. More recently, it was an Italian, Giovanni Caviglia, who reexcavated the Sphinx in the 19th century, discovering as he did so the ashes of the last sacrificial fire burned there, probably late Roman. He also found Tuthmose's stela and fragments of the Sphinx's royal beard, part of which went to the British Museum in London. ∎

KEY TO SITE PLAN

The Pyramids

1 Ticket office
2 Site entrance
3 Office for tickets to enter inside the Pyramids
4 Solar Boat Museum
5 Solar Boat pits
6 Queens' pyramids
7 East cemetery
8 Sphinx
9 Site entrance
10 Ticket office
11 Sound-anwd-light pavilion
12 Tomb of Queen Khentawes
13 Khafre's Valley Temple
14 Causeway
15 Khafre's Mortuary Temple
16 Queens' pyramids
17 Pyramid of Menkaura
18 Enclosure walls
19 Pyramid of Khafre
20 Pyramid of Khufu
21 West cemetery

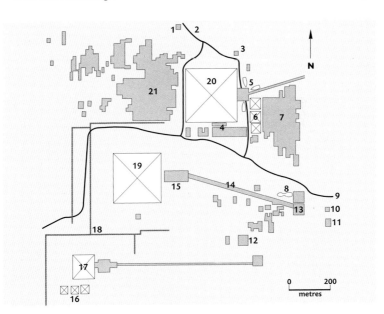

Heliopolis

Not to be confused with ancient Heliopolis, the pharaonic City of the Sun (of which nothing remains but a lone obelisk), the Heliopolis of today is an eccentric Cairo suburb with fantastical architecture and a relaxed, almost Mediterranean air.

Moorish colonnades bring a stage-set Orientalism to the northern suburb of Heliopolis.

Heliopolis

🄼 67 F4

Heliopolis is the creation of a wealthy Belgian industrialist, Baron Edouard Empain (1852–1929). In the early 20th century, he acquired a large tract of desert north of Cairo, where he constructed a satellite city of Moorish terraces and Oriental villas separated by green avenues.

Nearly a century later, though the ever expanding metropolis has swallowed up Empain's oasis, it still has a unique charm and quirky character. It also still has plenty of social cachet. President Hosni Mubarak resides here, close to his administration's headquarters, the **Uruba Palace** at Al-Ahram and Al-Mirghani Streets. Formerly the Heliopolis Palace Hotel, this was once Africa's most luxurious

accommodations. The only guests now are visiting foreign dignitaries.

A wide avenue (Al-Ahram Street) with central streetcar lines runs north from beside the palace to a squat neo-Byzantine **basilica,** where Empain lies in a black granite crypt *(not open to the public)*. His residence while he lived was even odder, exactly resembling a Hindu temple, with an exterior covered in carved temple dancers and gods. Known as the **Baron's Palace,** it stands newly renovated half a mile (1 km) east of the basilica on Airport Road.

It is worth walking around some of the streets crossing Al-Ahram for their wonderful whitewashed architecture of arcades, sculpted windows, and teardrop turrets. ∎

More Museums in Cairo

Ahmed Shawqi Museum

This elegant Giza museum was the former home of Egypt's early 20th-century poet Ahmed Shawqi, a major figure in nationalist and literary history. Shawqi, sometimes nicknamed "the Prince of Poets," lived here until his death in 1932. He named the house "Karmat Ibn Hani" (Ibn Hani's Vineyard), in a reference to the medieval Arabic poet Abu Nuwas. Set in an overgrown garden, the house offers a glimpse into upper-class life in pre-revolutionary Egypt. The museum houses a collection of his manuscripts, his bedroom, and his study, where his writing desk faces out on the Nile below.

✉ 6 Ahmed Shawqi St., Giza
☎ 02/3572 9479 🕐 Closed Mon. 💲 $$
🚇 Metro: Giza Square

Agricultural Museum

A badly neglected group of pavilions contains exhibits on early farming methods and ancient life in the Nile Valley. The highlight is a mummified bull from the Serapeum at Saqqara (see pp. 146–147); low points are the mounted animals which wear a somewhat moth-eaten appearance and the large jars full of stuffed birds. One of the pavilions houses the **Cotton Museum,** tracing the history of Egypt's main cash crop from its introduction to the country in the 19th century.

✉ Off Wizaret al-Ziraa St., Doqqi
☎ 02/3761 6785 🕐 Closed after 1 p.m.
& Mon. 💲 $ 🚇 Metro: Doqqi

The Child Museum

Located in a small wooded park just north of central Heliopolis (somewhat difficult to get to), this is an excellent place for keeping the children quiet for an hour or two. As a relative newcomer on the scene, the museum makes full use of multi-media technologies, and there are plenty of buttons to push that open up cross sections of pyramids, activate film clips of animals, and play music. In the

Arts Hall, children can paint and draw.
✉ 34 Abou Bakr al-Siddik St., Heliopolis
☎ 02/2639 9915 🕐 Closed after 2:30 p.m.
💲 $ 🚇 Metro: Darrasa

Dr. Ragab's Papyrus Institute

If you are considering buying decorated papyrus, then a visit here is not a bad idea. Housed on a boat moored a little south of the Cairo Sheraton, it is really a salesroom rather than an "institute." But the people here at least really do know about papyrus, and demonstrate the treatment necessary to turn the original reeds into sheet papyrus. They will be selling you the real thing, not banana leaves, which is what you may well be sold at Khan al-Khalili and from other disreputable sources.

✉ Corniche al-Nil, Doqqi ☎ 02/3571 8675
🕐 9 a.m.–9 p.m. 💲 $ 🚇 Metro: Doqqi

Entomological Society Museum

Dusty wood-and-glass cabinets, combined with the general appearance of a Victorian-era schoolroom, make this the museum that time forgot. Its collection of pinned insects and mounted birds dates from the British

---

EXPERIENCE:
Football Madness

The British introduced soccer to Egypt not long after they arrived in 1882 as part of a campaign to make Egyptians more like themselves. Today, Egyptians love soccer, and the professional clubs—Ahly, Zamalek, and Ismailia are three of the biggest—all have devotees. Ahly is the de facto national team; its fans (called Ahlawis) sometimes crowd outside the stadium, across from the entrance to the Opera complex in Gezira. Tickets are hard to come by; try asking at your hotel about upcoming matches.

occupation of Egypt at the turn of the 20th century, when colonial powers were collecting and cataloging the world. A real period piece, the museum itself deserves to be encased in clear plastic and preserved for posterity.
✉ 14 Ramses St., Downtown ☎ 02/2576 6683 🕐 Closed Thurs. & Fri. 💲 $
Ⓜ Metro: Orabi

National Postal Museum

Housed in an annex of Ataba Square's main post office (a nice old building with an attractive courtyard), this small but busy museum serves as a reminder that Egypt was one of the first countries to issue stamps (in 1866). Philatelists might also be interested in visiting the stamp shop on Sherif Street at the corner of Abdel Khalek Sarwat in downtown Cairo.
✉ 55 Abdel Khalek Sarwat St., Ataba Sq.
☎ 02/2575 4071 🕐 Closed Fri. 💲 $
Ⓜ Metro: Ataba

October War Museum

The series of 20th-century wars with Israel still looms large in the Egyptian national consciousness. Pride was wounded by the defeats in 1948 and 1967, but in 1973 some succor was provided by the success of an attack launched across the Suez Canal that took the Israeli army completely by surprise.

It is this breaching of the so-called Bar Lev Line, which took place on October 6, 1973, that is celebrated in this museum. Assorted military hardware fills the forecourt of the museum, while inside the purpose-built, circular exhibition hall a large model depicts the famous canal crossing. The museum is just off the airport road and is most easily reached by taxi.
✉ Al-Uruba St., Heliopolis 🕐 Closed Tues.
💲 $

Taha Hussein Museum

Taha Hussein (1889–1973), blind from the age of three, is one of the most celebrated figures of Arabic literature—as a scholar, novelist, and political writer. Trained at Al-Azhar University and the Sorbonne in Paris, he was a revolutionary thinker whose groundbreaking ideas occasionally brought him into conflict with the authorities. Hussein's novels display sympathy with the poor and oppressed and a desire for social justice. The museum occupies the white villa in which he spent the last 15 years of his life in the shadow of the Pyramids. Airy and elegant, it contains the writer's personal effects, including his 7,000-volume library.
✉ 11 Dr. Taha Hussein St., Haram
☎ 02/3585 2818 🕐 Closed Mon. 💲 $

An Egyptian Air Force fighter plane points its nose skyward outside the October War Museum.

Desert scenery, a lush oasis, and plenty of pyramids, all offering
a distinct antidote to the bustling urban experience

Around Cairo

Introduction & Map   140–141

Abu Sir   142–143

Saqqara   144–147

Feature: The Pyramid Builders   148–149

Memphis   150

Dahshur   151

Fayoum Oasis   152–153

Experience: Visit Pottery-makers
    in the Fayoum   153

Feature: Birdlife of Egypt   154–155

Experience: Go Bird-watching   155

Wadi al-Rayyan   156

Birqash Camel Market   157

More Places to Visit Around Cairo   158

Hotels & Restaurants   363

A man stops by the roadside at
Saqqara to read the Koran.

Around Cairo

The presence of the Pyramids often fools visitors into believing that Cairo must be a very ancient city. At heart, it is tenth century, founded by the Fatimids—modern by Egyptian standards. However, as the great and mysterious monuments at Giza attest, civilization in the immediate vicinity dates back far, far earlier. Within a short drive of Cairo's city limits are some of Egypt's oldest and most important ancient sites.

Long before the founding of Cairo proper, the mighty capital of the Old Kingdom of Egypt was Memphis, located not far southwest of the modern capital. The legendary King Menes, who first united the southern valley and north-ern delta (circa 3100 B.C.), laid the foundations here for the civilization of the pharaohs. Only a museum marks the site today, the rest is buried or vanished, but the ancient imperial city's glories are reflected in its vast necropolis at Saqqara, one of the finest archaeological sites in Egypt, if not the world. Dominated by its Step Pyramid—the prototype for all the pyramids to follow—Saqqara was in use as a burial ground for over 2,500 years. It covers a vast area and comprises so many separate tombs and tomb complexes that it is impos-sible to take it all in on a single visit. Much of the site still has to be excavated; archaeological discoveries are made on a regular basis.

North and south of Saqqara are the associated pyramid fields of Abu Sir and Dahshur. All of these monuments predate the better known temples of Luxor and Upper Egypt by several hundred years, and represent the formative steps of an architecture and art that would reach frui-tion at Karnak and in the Valley of the Kings.

NOT TO BE MISSED:

The Step Pyramid of Djoser in
    Saqqara **145**

The subterranean
    Serapeum **146–147**

The North Pyramid at Dahshur **151**

Watching the sunset over Lake
    Qarun in the Fayoum **152**

Strolling the pottery workshops in
    expat-laden Tunis **153**

Circling Fayoum's desert edge in
    Wadi al-Rayyan **156**

Seeing a camel auction at the weekly
    Birqash camel market **157**

A visit to these sites should arguably take third place on the itinerary of any visitor to Cairo, after the Pyramids of Giza and the Egyptian Museum. All four locations—Memphis, Saqqara, Abu Sir, and Dahshur—are connected by one highway, which runs south from Giza along the edge of the fields, where they sud-denly stop and the desert begins.

Driving a Car in Egypt: Rules of the Road

Driving a car yourself in Egypt is a real challenge, and not just because road signs (particularly outside Cairo) are sometimes only in Arabic. Traffic lanes on busy Cairo streets and highways are rarely observed, and behavior that would be considered highly aggressive and rude elsewhere, such as cutting off another driver, or turning without signaling (across several lanes of traffic), is common here. The good news is that once outside Cairo, highways to the Red Sea and North Coast are generally in excellent condition, and the chaos of city traffic mostly disappears.

The sites could be visited in a day, but that is inviting acute ancient Egypt overload. A better plan is to visit Saqqara and Memphis on one day, and Abu Sir and/or Dahshur on another. Most Cairo hotels organize excursions, as do many of the city's independent tour agencies, including companies like American Express and Thomas Cook. Failing that, you could hire your own taxi and driver, which costs around $25 to $30 for a full day. There is no public transportation that will take you to these sites.

It's striking how little time it takes to be free of the cement confines and in the countryside. Despite being home to between 13 million and 17 million people, Cairo does not sprawl. It ends abruptly, in luscious green fields to the north and south, lunar landscapes to the east, and endless sand to the west. One of the best ways to enjoy this contrast is to make a trip to Fayoum Oasis, Egypt's biggest oasis, just a 90-minute drive from central Cairo. It offers lakes and palm groves, tranquility and wildlife, all surrounded by spectacular sand hills. An easy excursion from the city, it is at the same time a whole other world. ■

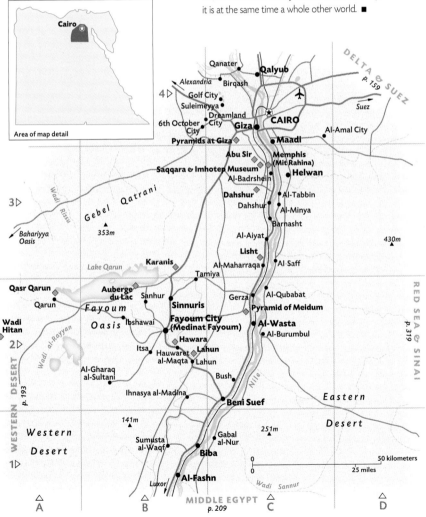

Abu Sir

Despite being open to the public only since the mid-1990s, Abu Sir has long been known to the most casual of Egyptologists as the place of discovery of a cache of important papyri unearthed in the last years of the 19th century. More recently, in February 1998, a team of archaeologists chanced upon the rare find of an undisturbed ancient Egyptian burial, putting Abu Sir back in the limelight once again.

The slumped pyramids of Abu Sir are near neighbors of the Pyramids of Giza.

Abu Sir
 141 C3
☎ 02/3383 8823

Located several miles south of Giza, Abu Sir is marked by a cluster of three pyramids belonging to little-known kings and queens from the 5th dynasty (2494–2345 B.C.). All are considerably smaller than even the smallest of the three Pyramids of Giza. They are also quite dilapidated, giving them a slumped appearance. The site's charm lies in its isolated setting on a sandy ridge, where the desert rises away from the palm groves of the Nile plain. Few visitors come here.

Abu Sir marks the continuation of a trend begun with the Pyramid of Menkaura at Giza; as the pyramids decrease in size, their accompanying temple complexes become proportionately larger, with a greater emphasis on decoration. At Abu Sir, the remains of the various mortuary and valley temples are by far the most interesting elements of the site.

Northernmost of the group, the **Pyramid of Sahure** (*R*.2487–2475) is the only one it is possible to enter—via a descending passage that is terrifyingly constricted and leads only to a single, small burial chamber. On the east side of the pyramid are the remains of Sahure's mortuary temple. Some of the walls have been reconstructed up to a height of about 18 inches (0.5 m), which is enough to give some indication of the floor plan. Reliefs decorated much of the wall surfaces and included scenes depicting the pharaoh's victories over a Libyan army. Most of these reliefs are now in the Egyptian Museum in Cairo, but a few fragments remain in situ, making the area worth exploring.

Sahure was succeeded by his brother **Neferirkare** (R.2475–2455 B.C.), whose pyramid is the southernmost and largest of the trio. Unfinished at the time of the pharaoh's death, its outer sheathing was hastily completed with perishable mud brick that has eroded, revealing a six-stepped stone inner core similar to Djoser's pyramid at Saqqara (see pp. 144–147). It is in Neferirkare's mortuary temple, on the east side of the pyramid, that a celebrated set of papyri was discovered. When deciphered, the expressive pictograms (written in hieratic, a shorthand form of hieroglyphics) revealed themselves to include priestly schedules, inventories of furniture and equipment, and accounts. Taken together, these offer a fascinating insight into the day-to-day administration of the Abu Sir temples of 4,000 years ago. Much is still to be learned from the papyri, which are being

INSIDER TIP:

For an inexpensive way to see sights, hire a taxi for the day, setting the price in advance. Drivers know the best non-tourist cafés and attractions.

—DR. JOEL D. IRISH
National Geographic field researcher

studied at the British Museum in London.

The third—and the most dilapidated—pyramid in this trio was built for Nyuserra (R.2445–2421), son of Neferirkare. His desire to nestle his monument between those of his father and his uncle limited the size of the pyramid. ■

Uncovering History

Abu Sir is also the site of a sixth-century B.C. cemetery of shaft tombs. In 1995 a team of Czech archaeologists began excavating one of these shafts. At 70 feet (21 m) below the surface, workers reached the burial chamber, located a small doorway, and removed the stones that sealed it. Inside, well-preserved inscriptions and reliefs covered the walls, identifying the occupant as Iufaa, a priestly palace administrator who lived about 500 B.C. Hundreds of artifacts lay intact, just as they had been left, but most of the chamber was taken up by a large, white limestone sarcophagus. Further examination was delayed by an earthquake that collapsed part of the shaft, and it was not until February 1998 that, using beams and jacks, the 24-ton (21,773 kg) lid was inched off to reveal a mummy-shaped sarcophagus of gray basalt covered with hieroglyphs. When the sarcophagus lid was hoisted off, it revealed a mummy covered with a magnificent shroud of ceramic beads. A once-in-a-lifetime find for the archaeologists involved, Iufaa's grave represents a wealth of new knowledge about ancient Egypt.

Saqqara

Only 15 miles (24 km) southeast of central Cairo, Saqqara is a vast desert necropolis built for the kings and nobles of the Old Kingdom, and among its highlights are the very first pyramid, some splendid tomb paintings, and one of the great oddities of Egyptology, the Serapeum, a haunting burial place of mummified sacred bulls.

A local tour guide addresses a group at the Step Pyramid.

Saqqara
🄰 141 C3
☎ 02/3383 8823

Saqqara was founded as the necropolis, or burial city, for Memphis, the Old Kingdom capital (see p. 150). Its earliest tombs date from the 1st dynasty (3100–2890 B.C.); its latest, from the Persian era (circa 500 B.C.). All this was unknown until a French former schoolteacher named Auguste Mariette (see p. 77) began excavating at Saqqara in 1850. He discovered a half-buried sphinx in the sand and remembered a passage from the first-century Greek geographer Strabo that mentioned a Serapeum at Memphis and sphinxes in the sand. Following this lead, Mariette began digging and succeeded in uncovering the avenue of sphinxes and, from that, the Serapeum. His discovery sparked the extensive and continuing excavation of the site. Much more has since been found, including the pyramid (and possibly the mummy) of Seshestet, mother of 6th-dynasty pharaoh Teti, unearthed in 2008 near her son's pyramid, and a burial chamber with more than 20 mummies found in 2009.

The First Pyramid

Centerpiece of Saqqara is the **Step Pyramid** and surrounding enclosure of Djoser (also spelled Zoser), king of Egypt from 2667 to 2648 B.C. It was built for the king by Imhotep, who was both high priest and the world's first big name in architecture. Though less than half the height of the two largest pyramids at Giza, and much less well known, Imhotep's monument represents a far greater achievement. Before Saqqara, the building material of choice had been mud brick, and the common building form was the *mastaba* (from the Arabic word for "bench"), a simple, rectangular, slablike structure covering a burial pit. Imhotep took the mastaba, constructed it in stone, and added to it five times, one on top of the other, each successive layer being smaller than those below to create a pyramidlike effect. The high priest surrounded his king's pyramid with a host of secondary structures and enclosed them all within a bastioned perimeter wall 32 feet (10 m) high.

Entrance was, as it is today, via a gate in the southeastern corner and along a corridor of 40 pillars, their design inspired by bundles of tied reeds. This leads into the **Great South Court,** an open area the size of a soccer field in front of the pyramid. Decoration is sparse, but in the southwest corner is a building projecting into the court that has a frieze of rearing cobras. This venomous reptile was a symbol of royalty, and it is here to protect the **Southern Tomb,** sunk deep below, where the king's

ka, or life force, was put to rest in the form of a statue. If you ascend the stairs to the top of the wall you can look down the shaft, but the tomb is closed to visitors.

On the east side of the court is the **Heb-sed Court,** linked to a ritual in which the king renewed his rule by reenacting his coronation. To the north are the remains of two pavilions, one dedicated to Upper Egypt, the other to Lower, the two kingdoms united under Djoser. In the first of these, protected under clear plastic, is the world's oldest known example of tourist graffiti (12th century B.C.), in which visitors from Thebes express their admiration for the king and his monuments.

A little farther north, the most intriguing aspect of the complex is usually indicated by a milling crowd in line to see Djoser himself. Here at the foot of the pyramid's north face is a stone kiosk, known

KEY TO SITE PLAN

Saqqara

1 Pyramid of Userkaf
2 Tomb of Mereruka
3 Tomb of Ankh-ma-Hor
4 Pyramid of Teti
5 Heb-sed Court
6 Causeway of Unas
7 Road to Cairo
8 Monastery of St. Jeremiah
9 Pyramid of Unas
10 Pyramid of Sekhemkhet
11 Southern Tomb
12 Great South Court
13 Step Pyramid
14 Mastaba of Akhti-Hotep and Ptah-Hotep
15 Serapeum
16 Mastaba of Ti
17 Philosophers' Circle

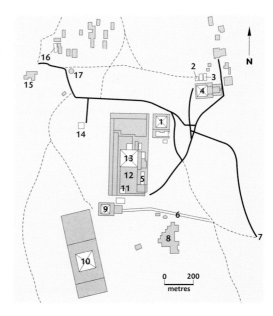

as a *serdab,* with a slot through which you look to meet the level stare of the king, enshrined in a life-size, painted statue. This arrangement enabled the king's *ka* to communicate with the outside world. The statue is a copy; the original is displayed in the Egyptian Museum in Cairo.

South of Djoser's enclosure, a misshapen mound represents the slumped remains of the **Pyramid of Unas,** resting place of the last king of the 5th dynasty (*R.2375–2345*). When the pyramid was entered in 1881, the walls were found to be covered in hieroglyphs, the earliest example of texts found in any ancient Egyptian burial. Unfortunately, because of the damage being caused by visitors, the pyramid is now closed to the public. Its causeway is flanked by a number of well-preserved tombs; several of these are usually open.

A worker in the Step Pyramid kneels beside a statue of a sacred bull that rests on the symbol for stability.

Tomb Paintings

Although the writings on the walls of the Pyramid of Unas are off-limits to visitors, similar early "pyramid texts" can be seen in the **Pyramid of Teti** (first king of the 6th dynasty, *R.2345–2323*). These vertical columns of script, which include hymns, litanies, and spells of protection, are the first flowerings of a tradition that would later blossom into the full-blown, full-color, floor-to-ceiling wall paintings seen in the tombs of the Valleys of the Kings and Queens in Luxor. Long before that time, however, tomb art had already become quite sophisticated, as can be seen in two later 6th-dynasty tombs adjacent to Teti's pyramid. Closest is the **Tomb of Ankh-ma-Hor**, also known as the Physician's Tomb because of its scenes depicting ancient operations, including surgery on a man's toe and a circumcision. Adjacent is the **Tomb of Mereruka,** a son-in-law of Teti—many of the large complex's 33 chambers bear magnificent reliefs. In the first chamber, Mereruka hunts from a boat among birds, fish, and hippo, scenes that have taught Egyptologists a great deal about the wildlife of Ancient Egypt.

The Serapeum

Mariette's Serapeum remains one of the great discoveries of Egyptology. It is a series of eerie catacombs created for the burial of sacred bulls, known as Apis bulls. Animals in ancient Egypt were often associated with gods, and bulls with particular markings—black with a white spot on the forehead and another near the tail—were regarded as the physical manifestations of the Memphite god Ptah, and later of the Greco-Roman deity Serapis. These creatures roamed the grounds of Ptah's Temple in Memphis, and when they died they were buried in the subterranean galleries of the Serapeum at Saqqara.

The catacombs date back to at least as early as the 18th dynasty (1550–1295 B.C.) and continued in use until the Ptolemaic period (332–30 B.C.). When Mariette entered in 1851, he discovered a series of passageways with side chambers containing 25 massive granite coffins, each weighing up to 80 tons (72 tonnes). All had been robbed in antiquity, save for one, in which was a solid gold statue of a bull (now in the Louvre in Paris) and an inner sarcophagus containing a mummified bull (now at Cairo's Agricultural Museum; see p. 137).

Near the Serapeum is the **Philosophers' Circle,** a collection of statues of Greek philosophers and poets, set in place by the Ptolemies. A short distance away is another of Mariette's discoveries, the **Mastaba of Ti,** the burial complex of a court official who served under three kings. Its wall paintings are unrivaled for the wealth of information they present on life in Old Kingdom Egypt.

Imhotep Museum

An addition to the ancient attractions is the modestly sized **Imhotep Museum,** opened in 2005. It's named for the architect of the Step Pyramid, but

The Proper Way to Ride a Camel

To the uninitiated, the camel's bouncing gait can be an unpleasant surprise. Before committing to an all-day camel ride, try a shorter trip and see how your bottom feels afterward. To get on a camel, swing your leg over the saddle while the camel is seated. When camels stand up, they get up on their front knees, then fully straighten their back legs. Remember to lean back and hold on to the saddle knob; otherwise, you might fall forward. The camel's owner will show you how to arrange your feet on the camel's neck; be prepared for a lot of swaying and bouncing. When sitting down, the camel drops to its front knees first, and then brings it back haunches down, at which point you can hop off.

contains all manner of artifacts, all of which were discovered at Saqqara. One of the few items to relate directly to the great builder is a reconstruction of the cobra frieze that runs around a part of the interior wall of the courtyard south of Djoser's pyramid. Also here are carved panels, wooden and limestone statues, and elaborately decorated sarcophaguses. The museum is beside the ticket office and a visit may help make sense of this bewilderingly large funerary site. ∎

The Pyramid Builders

In the space of about 500 years, Egypt's kings raised more than 80 pyramids in a strip between Giza and the oasis of Fayoum. But despite being perhaps the most famous monuments in the world, Egypt's pyramids still keep many secrets, even down to the very basics such as how they were built and why.

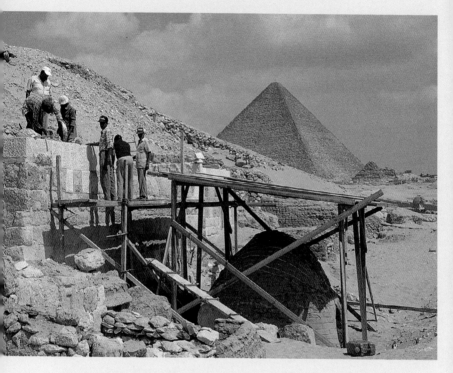

New theories dispel the popular perception of vast teams of slaves hauling up blocks under a fore-man's whip. Excavations are revealing housing that possibly accommodated a well-kept workforce.

Archaeologists, Egyptologists, and pyramid-ologists (for the study of the pyramids has become a science in its own right) have a great many theories, but there are a good deal fewer certainties. By the time of the Romans, the art of deciphering hieroglyphs was lost and real knowledge of the pyramid builders was drowned in a sea of myths and legends. The Greek historian Herodotus began the swell of misinformation with the story that Khufu forced his daughter into prostitution to pay for his pyramid. Three

centuries later, Roman Jewish historian Josephus Flavius included pyramid building among the hardships that the Jews had to endure during their years of labor in Egypt. In the 20th century, Hollywood director Cecil B. DeMille presented a panoramic vision of legions of whiplashed slaves toiling away to complete their king's work in his 1956 epic *The Ten Commandments*.

It is DeMille's vision that is the latest to be debunked. In 1993 archaeologists discovered fields of ancient graves at the Giza Plateau, which are most likely the burials of the actual builders of the pyramids. Bodies found in the graves showed evidence of the strains and stresses of physical labor, as well as of emergency medical treatment. They also discovered dwellings, which, while modest, are definitely not the abodes of slaves.

The prevailing belief now is that the pyramids were built by a willing labor force of peasants, employed perhaps in rotation, paid in foodstuffs, and led by a few thousand skilled craftsmen. Only during periods of

INSIDER TIP:

The much older and imperfect pyramids of Saqqara and Dahshur are far less frequented than those at Giza. If you want to go inside one, you will likely have it to yourself.

—TAYLOR KENNEDY
National Geographic photographer

great wealth and stability could the realm provide the authority and administration necessary for such an undertaking. Given this need, the age of the pyramids begins soon after Egypt was first unified and ends when centralized power broke down at the end of the 6th dynasty.

As to how the pyramids were built, we are still some way from a universally agreed-upon theory. The most common suggestion is that huge ascending ramps, either straight like causeways or spiraling around the structure, were laid and the massive stone blocks were hauled up these, but there is no hard evidence to either prove or disprove this idea.

Similarly, the mathematical precision of the pyramids' construction begs another question yet to be answered conclusively: What purpose do they serve? While most archaeologists agree that they were tombs, they disagree about what other functions these massively

proportioned monuments might have had. For example, the purpose of some of the internal chambers is not yet known, and the significance of the pyramids' alignment is hotly debated.

Our knowledge of the pyramids is still expanding. Everything we know could so easily be entirely rewritten by a single find. Investigating the pyramids now requires a team of scientists, including specialists in bone and plant remains and in radiocarbon dating, in addition to those who probe the structure of the pyramids themselves with remote-controlled robots. There is always the suspicion that the pyramids must hold more secrets.

King Khufu immortalized himself by building a huge pyramid at Giza, but why?

Memphis

Almost 4,000 years before the founding of Cairo, Memphis was Egypt's capital. One of the greatest cities of the ancient world, today it is marked solely by an open-air museum of meager finds, partially redeemed by its one outstanding exhibit, the remains of a mighty statue of Ramses II.

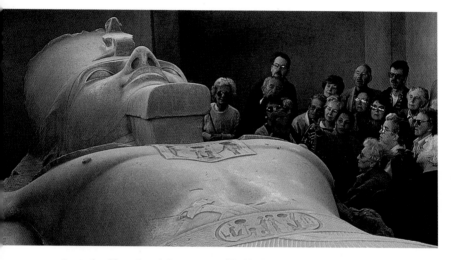

Larger than life as pharaoh, Ramses II spread his likeness across Egypt, including colossi at Memphis.

Memphis
 141 C3
☎ 02/3383 8823

The city itself lies buried beneath the modern village of Mit Rahina. It was already in decay when the Arab al-As armies conquered Egypt in A.D. 641. They, and their successors, used ancient Memphis as a quarry to provide building materials for their new capital—later known as Cairo. Silt deposits from the annual flood of the Nile gradually covered the pharaonic city, until Memphis became no more than a lumpy alluvial plain on which palms rooted and peasants founded their villages.

These villages, combined with a high water table (due to the damming of the Nile at Aswan), mean that archaeologists have never been able to excavate the site. However, over the decades, as a drainage

ditch or the foundations of a house were dug, a chink of spade against stone would signal the discovery of an ancient building block or statue fragment. Some of these finds are displayed at a small museum. Most striking is **a colossus of Ramses II** found in 1820. Missing his lower legs, the king lies on his back in a viewing pavilion; in its original state the statue would have stood as tall as a five-story building.

The garden contains more statues of Ramses II, indicating that the pharaoh built as prolifically here as he did in Upper Egypt. You have to wonder what has been lost, as with the sphinx here—at 80 tons the largest alabaster statue ever found. Was this just one in an avenue of sphinxes, as at Karnak? ∎

Dahshur

Dahshur is a small pyramid field in an isolated desert setting to the south of Saqqara. Only accessible to the public since the mid-1990s, it has yet to be added to the tour-bus trail. Visitors making the journey down here is likely to have the site completely to themselves.

In pyramid chronology, Dahshur comes after Saqqara but before Giza and Abu Sir. The two main pyramids here were both built for

INSIDER TIP:

The Red Pyramid loses its color in the midday sunlight. If you want to capture its tinge on camera, visit in the late afternoon or early morning.

—CHIP ROSSETTI
National Geographic contributor

the pharaoh Sneferu (R.2613–2589 B.C.), father of Khufu, builder of the Great Pyramid at Giza.

The **Bent Pyramid** was begun first. It can lay claim to being the first pyramid proper—all those that had come before were stepped. So it is perhaps understandable that the builders erred in their calculations: The pyramid started to rise at an angle of 55 degrees, but halfway up it must have become clear that the structure was becoming unstable, and it was completed with a less steep slope of around 44 degrees. The result is the distinctive "bent" look.

Uniquely, the Bent Pyramid retains much of its original white limestone casing. From nearby, you can appreciate how smooth

the surfaces of not just this one, but of all pyramids, would originally have been.

For reasons that remain unknown, in the 30th year of his reign, Sneferu abandoned his first pyramid and began a new one. Known as the **North Pyramid** (also called the Red Pyramid), this was constructed with a gentler slope of 43 degrees. A stair on the north face allows visitors access to the interior. From the entrance 100 feet (30 m) up, an excellent view to the south takes in the pyramids of Saqqara, Abu Sir, and Giza. A 70-yard (65 m) passage leads down to three chambers, the first two of which have high corbeled ceilings, foreshadowing the Grand Gallery of the Great Pyramid at Giza. ■

Dahshur
🗺 141 C3
☎ 02/3383 8823

The Bent Pyramid of Sneferu in Dahshur was a prototype of the Pyramids of Giza.

Fayoum Oasis

Fayoum, 60 miles (100 km) southwest of Cairo, is Egypt's largest oasis and a popular getaway for smog-choked city dwellers. While it has temples and archaeological sites and a history of settlement that goes back to pharaonic times, people are drawn to Fayoum's greenery and serenity.

The sun sets over Lake Qarun, a haven for migratory birdlife.

Fayoum Oasis
🅰 141 B2

Auberge du Lac
✉ Lake Qarun
   Fayoum
☎ 084/572 001
💲 $$$

Most visitors avoid **Fayoum City** itself (Medinat al-Fayoum) and head for the real heart of the area, **Lake Qarun.** Formed 70,000 years ago when the Nile overflowed into the Fayoum depression, the lake is fed by canals that connect it to the river. These channels were first dug during the reign of the 12th-dynasty pharaoh Amenemhat III (R. 1855–1808 B.C.). The ancients cultivated Fayoum and made it into a "garden of Egypt"—a role that it still plays, producing an abundance of fruits and vegetables. Unfortunately, the lake is becoming increasingly saline; the beaches have become encrusted with salt. Unsuitable for swimming, the lake is nonetheless beautiful from the vantage point of a rented rowboat. The views can also be enjoyed from the promenade café of the **Auberge du Lac,** a luxury hotel that was once King Farouk's hunting lodge, where King Ibn Saud and Winston Churchill held talks in February 1945.

Lake Qarun supports a huge number of birds (see pp. 154–155), most of which are migrants and winter visitors. We know that this was also the case in antiquity, as the ancient Egyptians recorded the wildlife of Fayoum in frescoes and friezes in local tombs and temples, most famously in the panels known as the Meidum Geese, displayed in the Egyptian Museum in Cairo.

Best preserved and most accessible of Fayoum's pharaonic remains is the small Ptolemaic temple of **Qasr Qarun,** at the very western end of the lake. It was dedicated to the crocodile god, Sobek, whose "offspring" flourished in the marshes and waters of the oasis in ancient times. The temple was heavily restored in 1956, and it is possible to descend into underground chambers (beware of snakes) and climb up to the roof for a view of the surrounding desert. Fayoum's other main ancient site is **Karanis** (known locally as Kom Oshim), a ruined third-century B.C. city, at the eastern end of the lake. There are two minor temples, plus a museum with pottery, glassware, and terracotta figures found on the site.

Pyramids

Fayoum has four **pyramid sites,** all lying just to the east of the oasis, in a desert strip between it and the Nile. Those at Hawara, Lahun, and Lisht are in bad shape and of interest mainly to keen pyramidologists, but Hawara is notable as the site of a great find of 146 **Fayoum Portraits** discovered in the early 19th century. Painted in the first to third centuries A.D. while their subjects were still alive, these hauntingly lifelike portraits were cut to life-size, and then at death they were laid over the mummified corpse's face.

Most of the portraits have been detached from their mummies, and are now displayed at Cairo's Egyptian Museum and other institutions worldwide, including the Metropolitan Museum of Art in New York. They provide a wealth of information about the clothing, hairstyles, adornment, and physical characteristics of Egypt's wealthier

inhabitants during Roman times.

The fourth Fayoum pyramid, the **Pyramid of Meidum,** if not conventional, is still impressive. It exists as a three-stepped tower rising above a mound of debris. This tower is the inner structural core,

INSIDER TIP:

Wadi Hitan, a World Heritage site west of Fayoum, is the best place to see early fossil whales and other marine life that lived in the sea covering Egypt 40 million years ago.

—PHILIP GINGERICH
National Geographic field researcher

exposed after the outer casing and packing around the steps collapsed. The failed pyramid is traditionally attributed to Sneferu, who went on to more successful endeavors at Dahshur (see p. 151). The famous painted wildfowl were found in a nearby building. ■

Wadi Hitan
🗺 141 A2

www.sis.gov.eg/En/Tourism/Egyptall/Enviormental/

EXPERIENCE: Visit Pottery-makers in the Fayoum

Though the Fayoum is mostly known for agriculture, the oasis is also home to a rich pottery-making tradition. Fayoum pottery can be bought at crafts shops in Cairo, but if you have your own transportation, you can visit some of the off-the-beaten-path workshops and schools where the ceramics are made. Alternatively, the Fayoum Ecotourism Project can arrange a guide for you from Cairo *(tel 02/2735-1045).*

The village of **al-Nazla,** on the road about 6 miles (10 km) southwest of

Ibshaway, is teeming with open-air potters' workshops (picturesquely sited along a cliff) and is a wonderful place to meet the artists at their work. **Tunis,** a village near the western end of Lake Qarun, has become almost an expat artists' colony in recent years. There, two Swiss potters, Evelyn Porret and Michel Pastore, have established a school for local children to learn the craft. Call to set up an appointment to visit the school and see its wares *(tel 084/682 0405 or 016/337 1604).*

Birdlife of Egypt

It is not just humans that take advantage of the incongruous fertility of the Fayoum. To other creatures, too, it is an oasis, and none are more obvious than the birds.

A spoonbill seeks out food among the reed beds.

Year-round, the Fayoum is home to a variety of species, reflecting not only the diversity of habitat from reed bed to desert but also Egypt's position at the junction of the African and Asian continents. Some, like the Senegal coucal, Senegal thick-knee, common bulbul, and little green bee-eater, are African at or near the northernmost limits of their range. Cattle egrets, kestrels, and palm doves are more widespread, while the little owl is a European species for which Egypt is a southerly outpost.

Olive groves play host to the incessant *zitzit* of the graceful warbler. The reed beds are full of clamorous reed warblers living up to their name, and you may be lucky enough to glimpse the elusive purple gallinule or crepuscular painted snipe. On the desert margins look for wheatears, especially the dapper white-crowned black wheatear. In winter these residents are joined by vast numbers of wildfowl and waders from more northerly breeding grounds.

The water regime of the Fayoum may be man-made and recent, but this gathering of the avian clans was well documented by the ancients. Some birds were worshiped. Thoth, the god of wisdom, for instance, is often portrayed as an ibis; sadly no longer found in Egypt, the species is still called the sacred ibis. Birds are depicted in tomb friezes throughout Egypt. The immaculately painted Meidum Geese, now in Cairo's Egyptian Museum, come from the site of Meidum, southeast of the Fayoum. At Saqqara, friezes of papyrus swamps, alive with many of the birds still found in the Nile Valley and Delta, cover the tombs of Ti and Mereruka.

But it is farther south, at Beni Hasan (see pp. 212–213), that the greatest of all pharaonic wildlife panoramas lies. Vividly colored and accurate paintings of birds still familiar, such as the resident hoopoe, with its head shaped like a hammer, and migrants like masked and red-backed shrikes and redstarts, enliven the walls of the Tomb of Khnumhotep III, who was a vizier in the 12th dynasty.

Many of Egypt's more than 400 recorded species are migrants, using Egypt as a staging post every spring and fall as they journey to and from their European breeding grounds. The smaller birds—the warblers, chats, flycatchers, buntings, and so on—pass through in millions. In autumn, Egypt's north coast is a bird-watcher's paradise, first landfall for birds from Europe crossing the Mediterranean, where anything from a willow warbler to a nightjar can be seen flying in off the sea at places such as the Zaranik Protectorate near Al-Arish in northern Sinai (see p. 333).

However, it is for the large birds—storks, raptors, cranes, and pelicans—that Egypt is of most importance. These birds channel down specific migration corridors since, because of their large size, they are dependent on thermals of rising warm air for prolonged flight. Since thermals

The god Horus is represented as a falcon on the tomb of Inkerhau at Deir al-Medina.

are weak over open water, these species bottleneck at each end of the Mediterranean to avoid the sea. Many have to come through Egypt, converging at key points such as Suez, Ain Suhkna, and Gebel Zeit, and providing one of the world's great wildlife spectacles.

EXPERIENCE: Go Bird-watching

If you're interested in getting to know Egypt's varied avian life, pick up a copy of Bertel Bruun and Sherif Baha el Din's *Common Birds of Egypt*—a good place to start for identifying local species. Bird-watching presents its own challenges in Egypt, where locals (and security guards) sometimes find foreigners with binoculars somewhat perplexing.

If you can't get out to the north coast in the fall, or to Zaranik Protectorate in northern Sinai, you can still see some of Egypt's 400 recorded species of birds by paying the 20LE entrance fee to get into the leafy **Gezira Club** (map p. 123, *tel 02/2735 6000*), a good spot for urban sightings of hoopoe, bulbul, cattle egret, and (at dusk) the Senegal thick-knee.

Farther afield, you can take a taxi to the bird-watching village known as **Gebel Asfar,** off the Ismailia Road east of Cairo. Gebel Asfar is the site of a sewage farm, which, unpleasant as that is, attracts birds such as the painted snipe and Smyrna kingfisher. **Lake Qarun, Suez,** and the **north coast** are all major locations for bird-watching, as is the area around **St. Catherine's** in the Sinai (officially the St. Catherine's Protectorate).

For guided birding tours, contact American conservationist Mindy Baha el Din (Sherif's wife), who is based in Cairo and arranges tours for independent travelers or small groups *(tel 02/2360 8160)*. You can also check with international travel agencies that specialize in birding tours such as **Wings: Birding Tours Worldwide** *(tel 888-293-6443, www.wing sbirds.com; see p. 379)* for information on their planned birding tours to Egypt.

Wadi al-Rayyan

Out in the desert west of Fayoum, Wadi al-Rayyan is a large depression among the dunes into which excess water from the oasis has been channeled to create three freshwater lakes and a shallow waterfall. Stocked with fish, the lakes are a major nesting ground for birds and a big draw for picnicking visitors.

Little more than an hour and a half's drive from Cairo stunning desert scenery awaits.

Wadi al-Rayyan
🅰 141 A2

Absolutely unspoiled by development—and with protected status to ensure that it stays that way—the scenery is intensely dramatic. Although the lakes are attractive, it is the desert surroundings that really impress. Aside from the single thread of black tarmac road, all else is just oceans of yellow sand, sculpted into great wavelike hills by the wind.

Today, wildlife is among the wadi's chief attractions. The desert environment is home to some 15 species of animals, including gazelle, sand foxes, wildcats, and wolves. An estimated 134 species of birds inhabit or visit the wetlands surrounding the lakes. Among them are rare species of hawks, as well as kestrels, kites, egrets, and herons. There are plans to establish an information and bird-watching center, funded by the tolls cars pay to enter the reserve. Most visitors, however, head straight for the water and the much vaunted "waterfalls." These falls, in reality, have been created by piping water into rock-based reed beds just a few feet above the level of the lake. Nevertheless, it is an idyllic spot for swimming and sunbathing; avoid weekends and public holidays, when families crowd the place.

Access is by car only, via Fayoum Oasis. A trip combining these two places makes for a great excursion from Cairo and is highly recommended for anyone who does not have the time to make the trip out to the Western Oases or Sinai and might otherwise miss the country's spectacular desert scenery. ∎

Birqash Camel Market

Not for the faint-hearted, Cairo's Friday camel market is dusty, smelly, and unbelievably loud. It is held 22 miles (35 km) to the northwest of the city at Birqash. Proceedings start at first light and most of the business is done by nine, so it is advisable to get an early start. Public transportation is tricky, with no direct buses, and the best option is to arrange a taxi for the whole morning.

Camels are not indigenous to Egypt. Their absence from pharaonic art (which frequently depicts animals) suggests that they were unknown in ancient Egypt. Historians believe the Persians introduced the animals around the sixth century B.C. Since that time they have become indispensable hard-working, low-maintenance beasts of burden.

Although camels are now bred in Egypt, hundreds are brought into the country each week from northern Sudan. First stop is Daraw, just north of Aswan, the largest camel market in Egypt, from where

herders keep the bawling animals in line. Each camel is sold with a booklet issued by Ministry of Agriculture officials, which includes its state of health, age, and place of origin. The latter can also be identified through tribal branding. Herders claim a good camel is characterized by a big hump and sturdy bones. Tests on teeth, gums, and eyesight usually are done on the bigger animals, which are sold for farming; the smaller beasts usually go to the slaughterhouse. ■

Birqash
🗺 141 C4

INSIDER TIP:

Karkade tea, made from boiling hibiscus leaves, is served hot or cold. It is a delicious drink and classically Egyptian.

—TAYLOR KENNEDY
National Geographic photographer

a great many of the beasts are sent on in trucks to Birqash.

There is a daily market here, but Friday attracts the largest number of traders and animals. Grand men in *galabiyyas* (gowns) and turbans huddle on straw mats around trays of tea and discuss prices, while

To Market, to Market

Ancient Egyptian town and village markets bustled with buyers and sellers of fruit, grains, and vegetables. A constant din of bartering, of laughter and gossip filled the air. Markets meant far more than buying and selling. Villagers met relatives or bartered for occasional luxuries like simple copper ornaments. Merchants and small-time traders went from market to market with exotic wares. But food then, as now, was paramount, especially staples—grains, peas, onions, cucumbers, and figs.

More Places to Visit Around Cairo

Oranges are gathered and crated in orchards around the Nile-side town of Qanater.

Dreamland City

On the Western Desert's edge, a ten-minute drive north of the Giza Plateau, is the mirage-like vision of **Dreamland City,** one of Cairo's new, slightly surreal suburban communities. It could be California—or at least, that is the hope. Designed to offer wealthy Cairenes an alternative to the cramped, congested, and creaky old city, projects such as this combine condominiums and villas with malls, hotels, luxury amenities, and mosques. Dreamland comes complete with a theme park of Disney-type rides and an 18-hole, par 72 golf course with fairway views of the Pyramids. www.dreamlandegypt.com

141 B4/C4

Golf City

Strange as it may seem, given the arid climate and scarcity of useable land, Egypt is seeking to market itself as an international golfing destination. Thirty minutes' drive north of Cairo on the Desert Road to Alexandria is **Golf City,** opened in 2000 with 90 holes available to play, and more to come. What was once scrub and sand has been transformed by imported turf—rumored to require 1.2 million gallons of water each day. This is just one of—at last count—eight world-class courses scattered through the country (see p. 381). Each comes with pro shops, caddies, power carts, clubhouses, health spas, and restaurants. The Mena House Hotel beside the Pyramids has had a course since the 19th century, on which players once rode donkeys between the tees.

141 C4

Qanater

Roughly 15 miles (24 km) downriver from Cairo, **Qanater** is a small town on the Nile at the point at which the river forks into eastern (Damietta) and western (Rosetta) branches. Its main attractions are the Nile barrages, a series of early 19th-century locks, decoratively arched and turreted, spanning both river branches, with wooded parkland between. The trip to Qanater is a joy in itself, along the Nile on a ferry, caught from a landing just north of the Ramses Hilton in central Cairo. The journey takes around two hours. Avoid Fridays and public holidays, when the boats become uncomfortably overcrowded.

141 C4

Egypt's breadbasket–a triangle of green–with historic sites and two interesting canalside towns on the east

The Delta & Suez

Introduction & Map   160–161

Wadi Natrun   162–163

Experience: Stay Overnight at a Coptic Monastery   163

Bubastis   164

Experience: Attend a Sufi *Moulid* in the Delta   164

Tanis   165

Rosetta   166–167

Feature: Suez Canal   168–169

Port Said   170–171

Ismailia   172

Hotels & Restaurants   363

A Coptic monk in distinctive embroidered hood

The Delta & Suez

A green fan and a blue line: Together the Nile Delta and the Suez Canal represent two of Egypt's greatest riches. The Delta is the triangular swath of fertile land between Cairo and the Mediterranean coast, and a vital source of agricultural wealth; Suez is the preeminent engineering feat of the 19th century, an international waterway whose revenues provide a significant portion of the country's national income.

Most visitors only see the Delta through the windows of a train, speeding on the way to Alexandria. Scenes flash by of brightly dressed *fellaheen* working the lush green fields, gray water buffalo driving wooden waterwheels, and feathery date palms waving in the wind. The Delta population centers barely register; provincial places such as Damanhur, Mansura, and Zagazig are hardworking farmers' towns,

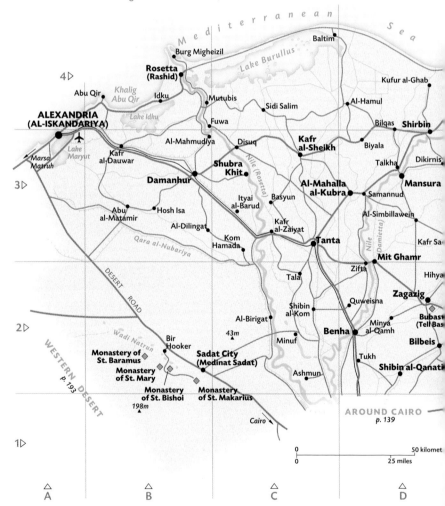

with little to offer visitors beyond hospitality. In antiquity, the Delta was a battleground and a strategic prize for victorious invaders. The Semitic Hyksos, the Libyans, and the Persians engaged the ancient Egyptians here, winning the right to settle, found cities, and reap the harvests. They have left their own riches in the form of the ruins of their civilizations. Archaeologists view the area as one of Egypt's richest remaining sites for excavation.

As the Delta nears the sea, a chain of salty lakes run parallel to the coast in a marshy transition zone between land and water. The need for fresh land has pushed the Egyptians to attempt to reclaim these seacoasts, in much the same

---

NOT TO BE MISSED:

The ancient desert monasteries of Wadi Natrun **162–163**

The ruins of the Late Period Delta capital city Tanis **165**

Rosetta and its unique brickwork architecture **166–167**

Crossing the Suez Canal on the Port Said to Port Fouad ferry **170–171**

The Ismailia Museum with its enormous Roman mosaic **172**

Strolling by Ferdinand de Lesseps's chalet in old Ismailia **172**

---

way as they are attempting to green the deserts. Historically, habitation in this region has been confined to the fertile zones where the two main branches of the Nile empty into the sea. Two estuary towns, Rosetta (see pp. 166–167) and Damietta, flourished while the Nile was a navigable route, but the 19th-century resurgence of Alexandria, along with the arrival of railroads, sentenced the pair to a gentle decline.

At about the same time, Egypt gained two new ports in Port Said (see pp. 170–171) and Suez, north and south gateways, respectively, to the Suez Canal. Both suffered badly in the wars with Israel in the mid-to-late 20th century, in which the canal was a vital strategic goal. From an aesthetic standpoint, Suez has not recovered, but Port Said is worth a visit for its harborside architecture. If you're interested in the canal and ships, a better spot is Ismailia (see p. 172). ∎

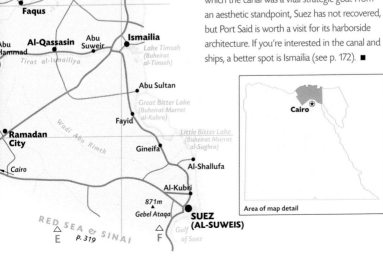

Area of map detail

Wadi Natrun

Egypt is regarded as the birthplace of Christian monasticism. St. Anthony from Upper Egypt is credited with being the first Christian monk, retreating into the desert in the latter part of the third century A.D. Wadi Natrun is not quite that old, but there has been a monastic presence here since the fourth century. A visit remains a trip back in time to the roots of the Christian faith.

The mud-brick building style of the desert monasteries has not changed in six centuries.

Wadi Natrun was known to the ancient Egyptians as a source of natron (from which it takes its name), a sodium carbonate deposit used in the mummification process (see "Making Mummies," pp. 238–239). After the advent of Christianity, the wadi (dry riverbed) attracted large numbers of Coptic followers of St. Anthony, who sought not only an ascetic existence but also an escape from Roman persecution. Numbers grew quickly, and in the fifth century the area was said to contain as many as 60 monasteries. Although only four survive,

monastic life is enjoying something of a resurgence, attracting plenty of recruits. Roughly 500 monks now live in the wadi.

Despite having chosen a life of seclusion, the monastic communities are exceptionally welcoming to visitors. The wadi is only an hour's drive from Cairo, just off the Alexandria Desert Road. Buses from Turgoman bus terminal in central Cairo run to the village of Bir Hooker, where you can rent a taxi to make the rounds of the monasteries, along roads that are more potholes than surface.

Most frequently visited of the four is the **Monastery of St. Bishoi** (Deir Anba Bishoi), the official residence of the Coptic Patriarch, Pope Shenouda. St. Bishoi was a fifth-century hermit who performed the act of kindness of washing the feet of a stranger, who revealed himself to be Jesus Christ. At the walled compound's heart is a church built around Bishoi's cell, where he used to tie his hair with a rope hooked to the ceiling to wake him if he fell asleep during his prayers. A sealed tube, kept at the church, is said to contain the saint's miraculously preserved body. Every July 17 the tube is carried in procession around the church, and the bearers are said to clearly feel the weight of a body within.

In addition to seclusion, these monasteries had to provide protection from Bedouin bandits. At the Monastery of St. Bishoi, the massive fortified keep, entered by a drawbridge, contained a well, kitchens, church, and storerooms

INSIDER TIP:

The monasteries own substantial farms and orchards. Consider buying a bottle of Wadi Natrun honey or olives before leaving.

—CHIP ROSSETTI
National Geographic contributor

to hold enough provisions for an entire year. Up on the roof, trapdoors open to small cells that acted as makeshift cemeteries for those who died while the tower was under siege, as it often was during the Middle Ages.

Equally popular with visitors is the adjacent **Monastery of the**

Syrians (Deir al-Suriani), so named because monks from that country occupied it for centuries. The central church here, dedicated to St. Mary, is famous for its wall paintings and icons, some of which date back to the seventh century. One of the monks takes visitors around the rest of the compound, including a look at a series of ninth-century cells. Apparently some of the monks use these cells to prepare for the life of a hermit; when they are ready, they move to desert cells where they pray in seclusion for six days of the week, joining the rest of the community over the Sabbath.

A little to the north, the **Monastery of St. Baramus** (Deir al-Baramus) contains no fewer than five churches. The **Monastery of St. Makarius** (Deir Abu Makar) is more secluded, lying 12 miles (20 km) to the southeast. Both are less visited than the other two because they do not accept tour groups. Individuals, however, are welcome. ∎

Wadi Natrun
⬛ 160 B2
🚌 Bus from Cairo to Bir Hooker, then taxi to monasteries

EXPERIENCE: Stay Overnight at a Coptic Monastery

During the Holy Week before Easter, monasteries are closed to outsiders. However, with advance notice, it is possible to get permission to stay at a centuries-old Coptic monastery as an overnight guest. Though accommodations can be spartan in these desert communities, they are very much a part of the modern world. Many Coptic monks are educated, and left behind more worldly academic or business careers before taking holy orders. Monasteries are not hotels, and some are only open to male overnight guests.

In any case, you will need to contact the monasteries' Cairo offices, located near St. Mark's Cathedral downtown, to request an overnight stay. You can call the monasteries' offices directly, or show up in person at the offices at 26 Al-Kineesa Al-Morqosia *(off of Clot Bey Street, south of Midan Ramses)* to request a permission letter. The three Wadi Natrun monasteries that accept visitors are **Deir Anba Bishoi** *(tel 02/2591 4448),* **Deir al-Baramus** *(tel 02/2592 2775),* and **Deir al-Suriani** *(tel 02/2592 9658).* If you plan to be on the Red Sea coast, you can request an overnight stay from the Cairo offices of **St. Paul's** *(tel 02/2590 0218)* or **St. Anthony's** *(tel 02/2590 6025).*

Bubastis

Around the tenth century B.C. Bubastis was the Lower Egyptian capital during a brief period of Libyan rule. Today it is a small archaeological site on the outskirts of the charmingly named town of Zagazig, 50 miles (80 km) from Cairo, with a famous temple to elegant cat goddess Bastet.

Bubastis

 160 D2

🚉 Train from Cairo's Ramses Station (or bus from Turgoman Station) to Zagazig, then walk

The former city, known locally as Tell Basta (Hill of Basta), is a modest, weed-covered mound strewn with huge blocks of carved granite, and packed with gaping archaeological pits. It enjoyed a long life span, flourishing from the 4th dynasty to the end of Roman rule (circa 2613 B.C. to A.D. 395). The city was renowned for its temple to Bastet, who was honored with licentious festivals.

During the fifth century B.C. Greek historian Herodotus visited Bubastis and wrote of hundreds of thousands of pilgrims gathering for the goddess's annual celebration, one of Egypt's greatest festivals. He described how revelers consumed more wine than during the whole of the rest of the year. Although a few papyrus-bud columns have been reerected, it is impossible to

get a sense of any structure today. Instead, most visitors' interest is taken by wandering the "cat cemetery," which lies 200 yards (182 m) away on the road to Zagazig. When these extensive underground earthen tombs were excavated in the mid-1900s, some 400 human mummies, as well as many mummified cats, were found.

Another Bubastis curiosity is a thousand-year-old holy well. Local Coptic Christians claim the Holy Family stopped here when they passed through on the journey to Egypt (see pp. 218–219). This may be why the well is still considered to have special fertility properties. Women hoping to conceive use clay pots to scoop up the water, pouring it over their heads before smashing the pots against a nearby weathered statue of Bastet. ∎

EXPERIENCE: Attend a Sufi *Moulid* in the Delta

Moulids, street fairs or carnivals marking the feast day of a local saint or holy man, are a lively tradition in Egypt, as crowds come for the open-air restaurants, music, sweets, and games. Each year, as many as 3,000 moulids, big and small, draw pilgrims from as far away as Sudan. Because moulids in commemoration of a local saint are determined by the Islamic calendar, their dates change year to year. (There are also Christian moulids and even a small heavily guarded Jewish moulid in the Delta.)

One of the biggest annual moulids is

held in the Delta city of Tanta, about 40 miles (65 km) northwest of Bubastis, in honor of Ahmed al-Badawi, the 13th-century mystic who founded the Badawiyya Sufi order. Al-Badawi's week-long moulid is always held in October, following the cotton harvest; ask around in Cairo about the dates if you are in Egypt then. Tanta is easily accessible by train from Cairo (it's on the Alexandria line), although because of the vast crowds of pilgrims it attracts, consider visiting it as a day trip from Cairo rather than trying to find a hotel there.

Tanis

Few visitors ever make it to Tanis, a capital of the Delta region during the Late Period (747–332 B.C.), when the pharaonic age was drawing to a close. Yet it was a major burial site, and it has yielded one of the most spectacular finds of Egyptology.

Tanis lies in the Delta's northeast corner, 42 miles (70 km) beyond the town of Zagazig, so the lack of visitors is not surprising. You need a car to reach it; from Cairo allow a day for the trip.

In its heyday, Tanis—known to the ancient Egyptians as Djanet—was a busy commercial city under the rule of pharaohs

INSIDER TIP:

Do not miss the fabulous gold and silver treasures found at Tanis in Room 2 on the upper floor of Cairo's Egyptian Museum.

—NEIL HEWISON
American University in Cairo Press

of the 11th and 12th dynasties. At its center was a large temple dedicated to Amun, surrounded by smaller shrines and temples, all enclosed within a mud-brick wall. All that remains is a large field with areas of weed-covered paving and a wealth of scattered blocks, column stubs, rubble, and broken statuary. Excavations were carried out as far back as the 1860s by Auguste Mariette (see p. 77), but the important find came in 1939, when French archaeologist Pierre Montet discovered intact

The shattered and fallen visage of pharaoh Ramses II in Tanis

royal tombs—the only untouched tombs yet found aside from Tutankhamun's. Gold death masks, solid silver coffins, and superb jewelry belonging to 11th dynasty pharaohs were brought to light after 3,000 years.

However, the find was over-shadowed by the advent of World War II, and the Tanis treasures have remained largely ignored by visitors to Cairo's Egyptian Museum (see pp. 68–76), who bypass them en route to the treasures of Tut. That may change, as Egypt's antiquities authorities have plans to invest heavily in Tanis. Someday, the names of its pharaohs—Psusennes, Osorkon, and Sheshonq—might be as well known as those of Tutankhamun and Ramses. ■

Tanis
Ⓜ 161 E3

Rosetta

If Rosetta is known at all today it is only because its name is attached to the famous black stela that provided the key to unlocking many of the mysteries of ancient Egypt. As the stone is now held by the British Museum in London, the small Nile-side town where it was found has become little more than a historical footnote. However, Rosetta (Arabic name Rashid) is actually a very attractive place; it can't be too long before it is rediscovered and put back on the tourist map.

Fishing contributes heavily to the north Delta economy.

Rosetta
🅰 160 B4

Rosetta Museum (Bayt al-Kili)
✉ Al-Geish St.
☎ 045/292 1733
🕐 Closed after 4 p.m.
💲 $$

Rosetta is located where the western branch of the Nile flows into the sea. During the Middle Ages it was Egypt's busiest port and a major city in the trade between Egypt and the Italian city-states. But the town's fortunes have always been inversely linked to those of Alexandria, and when that city experienced a rebirth in the 19th century, it was at the expense of Rosetta.

Today as you travel from Alexandria, the road is almost a causeway in parts, with the Mediterranean on one side and reedy lakes on the other, colored by great shoals of small, bright blue and green fishing boats. The lakes feed roadside canals, irrigating groves of palms bowed by the weight of massive clusters of dates. Between them, the boats and the palms constitute a thumbnail sketch of the local economy.

One reminder of Rosetta's wealthier past is roughly 20 fine Turkish-era houses, built by wealthy burghers and merchants and situated within a few minutes' walk of each other. Dating from the 17th and 18th centuries and built three or four stories high in a distinctive Delta style of flat bricks painted alternately red and black, these houses represent the finest legacy of domestic architecture in Egypt. Studded with *mashrabiyya* windows (see p. 96), many incorporate blocks and columns scavenged from ancient sites.

Restoration of some of the finest residences has been

see p. 96

INSIDER TIP:

Make sure you try the fruit bars all over Egypt—but bring your own glass as they're often reused without being washed.

–TAYLOR KENNEDY
National Geographic photographer

ongoing since the 1970s, and several are now open to the public. **Ramadan House,** just downhill from the square where the local minibuses congregate, has a typical and fascinating interior. Its first floor is given over to stabling and warehousing, the second floor was for the men, and the third floor for women. The uppermost floor, with its terrace areas open to breezes, was used in the hot summer months as sleeping quarters. Both the men's and women's areas have reception rooms adorned with intricate wooden paneling. Partway up the stairs between the two is a turntable at foot level that allowed the women to serve the men's food while remaining out of view.

Other houses are scattered on and just off the winding market street running north. The street emerges into a small square, across which is the **Rosetta Museum,** housing a collection of Ottoman weapons and documents from the Napoleonic era, including the locally famous marriage certificate between a Rosetta woman and a French general who converted to Islam.

Just east is the wide, broad river. Follow it north for 4 miles (6 km) to reach the restored Mamluk Fort of Qaitbey, also known as Fort Julien, where Napoleon's soldiers found the Rosetta Stone (see below). ∎

The Key to Ancient Egypt

Arguably the most significant find in Egyptology, the Rosetta Stone was unearthed in 1799 by Napoleon's soldiers while they were restoring an old fort. The irregularly shaped slab of black basalt is inscribed in three scripts: Egyptian hieroglyphs, Egyptian demotic (a cursive script derived from hieroglyphs), and Greek. Napoleon's savants were quick to realize that by comparing the demotic and the hieroglyphs with the Greek text, they could crack the previously baffling code of the pharaohs.

Linguists and academics applied themselves to the task with vigor, but it was not until 1824 that a Frenchman, Jean-François Champollion, was able to fathom the scripts. His achievement opened up many of the mysteries of ancient Egypt.

Suez Canal

Almost as startling and magnificent a sight as the Pyramids or temples of Upper Egypt is the vision of a giant oil tanker gliding between the dunes. Mirage or miracle? A miracle is exactly how the Suez Canal was hailed internationally when it first opened, but this verdict failed to recognize that the Egyptians had been digging enormous canals since the time of the pharaohs.

A procession of royal yachts makes the first voyage through the canal on November 17, 1869.

As early as the seventh century B.C., the 26th dynasty pharaoh Nekau II connected the Nile and Red Sea with an east-west canal. It was later renewed by Egypt's early Arab conquerors in order to tighten the tie between their new Nile territories and the homeland of Arabia. Appropriately, it was the canal-loving Venetians who, in the Middle Ages, first considered slicing a north-south waterway through the Isthmus of Suez to connect the Mediterranean Sea and the Red Sea. The project became a pre-occupation of colonialist Europe in the early 19th century, but progress was stalled because of a misguided belief, based on calculations by Napoleon's engineers, that the Mediterranean was 33 feet (10 m) higher than the Red Sea.

A later report set the seas on a level, and the idea of a canal was enthusiastically taken up by a young French vice-consul, Ferdinand de Lesseps (1805–1894). He doggedly pursued his dream for 20 years until, with the succession of Said Pasha, a personal friend, to the throne of Egypt, De Lesseps was finally granted permission to proceed. Ground was broken on April 25, 1859.

Rather than following the shortest route across the isthmus, which is only 75 miles (120 km) wide at its narrowest point, the canal utilized several lakes: Lake Manzala at its northern end, Lake Timsah and the Bitter Lakes farther south. By this route, the canal measures 101 miles (163 km) long. At the project's outset, the canal was largely dug by hand, but after five years the Egyptian government refused to continue providing the 20,000 necessary laborers, and work continued with mechanized diggers.

Finally, after almost ten years of excavating, in March 1869 Mediterranean waters flowed into the basins of the Bitter Lakes. On November 17, 1869, the Suez Canal was inaugurated with magnificently flamboyant festivities in the presence of guest-of-honor Empress Eugénie of France, wife of Napoleon III.

Ownership remained largely in French and British hands for the next 86 years. That changed when revolutionary leader Gamal Abdel Nasser nationalized the canal in 1956.

A view of the Suez Canal early in the 20th century from Port Said

Britain and France, in conjunction with Israel, invaded in an ungallant attempt to take it back by force, but had to retreat in the face of international condemnation of their actions.

Deepened and widened three times since it was completed, the canal is one of the world's most heavily used shipping lanes. An average of 60 vessels a day pass through in three convoys, in alternate directions. Shipping tolls bring the Egyptian treasury more than a billion dollars a year, making the canal one of the top three contributors to the economy.

Celebration Suez

Ismail, who ascended the throne in 1863, grasped the importance of the opening of the Suez Canal and wanted to take best advantage of the public relations triumphs the important event could lavish upon Egypt. Accordingly, he devoted huge amounts of time to the planning of this critical event. He traveled to Europe so he could personally deliver invitations to Europe's rulers and nobility. He invited the world's leading lights in science, business, and literature.

Much of Ismail's celebration he organized around Napoleon III's wife, the Empress Eugénie. He placed her on the first ship to navigate the canal, and threw a party for her in a palace erected for the occasion along the shore. Nearby he built a city of tents for thousands of visitors and fed them all for three days and nights. He produced pageants in Eugénie's honor, and showcased fireworks.

The whole affair was meant to impress the world with the wealth and importance of Egypt, once again the crossroads of commerce. Indeed, the celebration did, but the huge price addled the treasury and drew the ire of Ismail's nominal master, the Sultan in Istanbul, who made a public rebuke.

Port Said

Port Said was founded in 1859 as the Mediterranean gateway to the Suez Canal. It was the site of the inaugural celebrations in 1869, dubbed by the press as the "party of the century." Before long, though, Port Said's tag became the "wickedest town in the East," known for smutty postcards and brothels, pandering to the baser tastes of long-distance seafarers. A combination of a sobering revolution, devastation during the wars with Israel, and cheap air travel changed all that.

The white-painted frontage of Suez Canal House addresses the waterway it controls.

Port Said

🗺 161 F4 & 171

Visitor information

✉ 8 Palestine St.
☎ 066/323 5289
🕐 Closed Fri.

Today Port Said (Bur Said in Arabic) is a little-visited backwater, although it has enough pockets of charm to make it a worthwhile day trip from Cairo. The town grew out of shallow Lake Manzala, on land reclaimed with sand excavated from the canal. Ground zero was a single outcrop of rock just below water level, on which a landing dock was anchored to receive supply ships. This artificial islet is well buried by 150 years of development, but its site is marked by an empty plinth at the northern end of Palestine Street, on which for a long time stood a larger-than-life statue of Ferdinand de Lesseps, architect of the canal. It was very nearly something much grander. At the time of the canal's construction, French sculptor Frederic Auguste Bartholdi approached Khedive Ismail with the idea of a colossal torch-bearing statue to stand at the mouth of the canal; rejected for Port Said as too expensive, the proposed "Light of Asia" found a new home where it received a new name—the Statue of Liberty. De Lessep's statue was torn down in 1956 during the Suez Crisis, and the plinth has been vacant ever since.

Just south on Palestine Street find the **Port Said National Museum,** set in its own neat garden. Sadly, it has little about either the town or the canal and instead concentrates on local prehistory and the pharaonic, Islamic, and Coptic eras. Modern history gets a look at the **Military Museum,** with relics from the 1956 Suez Crisis, and the 1967 and 1973 wars with Israel; it is a mile west along 23rd of July Street. Close to the National Museum is the mooring place for boats that take tourists on 1.5-hour cruises on the canal, departing three times nightly from 5 p.m.

Alternatively, take a ride on one of the cross-canal ferries

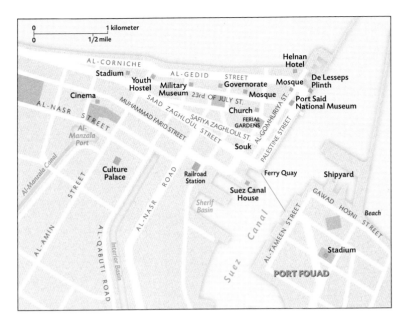

0   1 kilometer
0   1/2 mile

AL-CORNICHE
Stadium   AL-GEDID   STREET
        Youth   Helnan
        Hostel   Military   Governorate   Mosque   Hotel
Cinema   Museum 23rd OF JULY ST.   Mosque   De Lesseps
                                                     Plinth
AL-NASR STREET   Church   Port Said
                                          FERIAL   National Museum
Al-   GARDENS
Manzala
Port   Souk
                          Railroad   Ferry Quay
        Culture   Station   Shipyard
        Palace
                          Sherif   Suez Canal
                          Basin   House
                                                     GAWAD HOSNI Beach
                                                                  STREET
                                                     Stadium
                          Suez Canal   AL-TAMEEN STREET
Interior   PORT FOUAD
Basin

AL-NASR STREET · AL-QABUTI ROAD · AL-AMIN · Al-Manzala Canal · ROAD · PALESTINE STREET · AL-GOMHURIYA ST. · MUHAMMAD FARID STREET · SAAD ZAGHLOUL STREET · SAFIYA ZAGHLOUL ST.

shuttling over to the bedroom community of Port Fouad. From the deck you have a good view of the quayside **Suez Canal House,** the white colonnaded building with three green Byzantine domes.

INSIDER TIP:

Pack a lot of patience. The Egyptian sense of time often doesn't include a great sense of urgency.

—ANN WILLIAMS
National Geographic
magazine writer

Built in 1869 as the Canal Company Offices, it still plays a part in controlling the waterway and is off-limits to the public.

One block in from the ferry quay is Port Said's old commercial center, once a mix of Greek and Italian restaurants, French *patisseries,* Jewish stores, and Egyptian tailors, all of which would flicker to life, no matter what the hour, whenever a big liner docked. This cosmopolitan past survives only in a legacy of raffishly elegant buildings with wooden balconies that are more New Orleans than Mediterranean. Look for faded signs such as that of Simon Arzt, who arrived from New York in the late 19th century to found his fashionable department store, and Woolworth's, now a souvenir emporium.

In recent times Port Said has been blessed with a new lease on life as a free-trade zone. Its retailers are now kept busy by busloads of Egyptians on the hunt for discount clothing and electronics. Their main target is the souk, west of main Gomhuriyya Street, a clothes and household goods market occupying a grid of narrow lanes. ■

**Port Said
National
Museum**

✉ Palestine St.
☎ 066/323 7419
🕐 Closed Fri.
💲 $

**Military
Museum**

✉ 23rd of July St.
☎ 066/322 4657
🕐 Closed after
   3 p.m.
💲 $

Ismailia

Founded as the center of operations during the building of the Suez Canal, Ismailia is now better known as a popular day out for Cairenes, who each summer weekend flock to the beaches around Lake Timsah, just to the south of town.

The dome of a Coptic church, and its multifaceted supporting walls, rises above greenery in Ismailia.

Ismailia
161 F2

Visitor information
✉ Governorate Building, Al-Togari St.
☎ 064/332 1078
🕐 Closed after 3 p.m. & Fri.

Ismailia Museum
✉ Muhammad Ali Quay
☎ 064/391 2749
🕐 Closed after 4 p.m. & Fri.
💲 $

The day-trippers tend not to visit the town of Ismailia itself, which offers little in the way of things to see. Nevertheless, if you are looking for a place to spend a few hours away from crowds and traffic, then the old center of Ismailia is an attractive option. Low-rise and leafy, it has an appealingly out-of-time colonial air. It covers a few blocks between the railroad tracks and the small **Sweetwater Canal,** which runs through green parkland beside the lakeshore. Ferdinand de Lesseps, the founder of the Suez Canal, had his chalet-style residence on Muhammad Ali Street, across from the park, now used as a government guest house and closed to the public. North of

the De Lesseps's house is Sultan Hussein Street, which probably qualifies as the town's main thoroughfare.

Several blocks farther on, still heading along Muhammad Ali Street, is the **Ismailia Museum,** designed in pharaonic style. It houses objects from pharaonic and Greco-Roman times, the highlight of which is a beautiful fourth-century A.D. mosaic depicting characters from Greek mythology. A second museum devoted to the history of the Suez Canal had its cornerstone laid in summer 2000, but is still incomplete.

To see the **Suez Canal,** head out of town. Most Egyptian visitors favor the beaches to the south. These tend to be owned

INSIDER TIP:

Try traveling by bus. This is the best way to make friends, see the country, and really experience Egypt.

—PEARCE CREASMAN
National Geographic field researcher

by clubs and hotels, however, and they charge for access. If you simply wish to see the ships sailing by, it is possible to do so from the main road between Cairo and Ismailia, which runs parallel and close to the waterway to the south. ■

The European face of Egypt, with cool sea breezes, plenty of good seafood, and a cosmopolitan café culture

Alexandria

Introduction & Map   174–175

Greco-Roman Museum   176–177

Feature: Rediscovering Ancient Alexandria   178–179

Experience: Dive in Alexandria's Harbor   179

Catacombs of Kom al-Shuqafa 180–181

Fortress of Qaitbey   182–183

A Walk Through the Capital of Memory   184–186

Alexandria National Museum   187

Bibliotheca Alexandrina   188

Royal Jewelry Museum   189

Experience: Browse the Bookstalls on An-Nabi Daniel   189

Mahmoud Said Museum   190

Montazah Palace Gardens   191

More Places to Visit in Alexandria   192

Hotels & Restaurants   363–366

The catch of the day for sale at the fish market

Alexandria

With its key figures of Alexander the Great and Cleopatra, its famed ancient library, and the towering Pharos lighthouse—counted by the ancients as one of the Seven Wonders of the World—the Alexandria of old is a city of legend bordering on myth. For some, the modern-day reality comes as a disappointment: all that history and so little to show for it. Yet the lack of visible monuments only adds to the mystique.

After staking his claim to the land of the pharaohs in 331 B.C., Alexander the Great decided that Egypt should have a new capital on the Mediterranean, tying his conquest to Europe by sea. Over the next 300 years this spot became the crossroads of trade from Britain to China, growing rich on commerce and in culture. Alexandria's library, part of the great research center of science, philosophy, and the arts known as the Mouseion, reputedly contained the sum total of knowledge

available to the ancient world, earning the city the epithet the "most learned place on Earth." And just as New York celebrates its glories with the Statue of Liberty and Paris with the Eiffel Tower, the ancient Alexandrians erected an enormous beacon, the Pharos, which trumpeted the successes of the city while guiding ships into their busy harbor.

But for all its learning and wealth, ancient Alexandria all but completely vanished. Its great temples and centers of learning were burned to the ground through the intolerance of Christians, while neglect and natural disasters took care of the rest. Earthquakes tipped the royal quarters into the sea and toppled the Pharos. When, after centuries of obscurity, the city experienced a revival in the 19th century, the ruins of antiquity were simply built over. Today, as you walk the streets of Alexandria, the past

Area of map detail

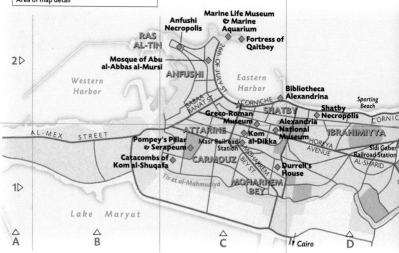

is quite literally under your feet. Some of the more portable remnants were carried off, like the two obelisks known as Cleopatra's Needles, which now grace Central Park in New York and the Thames Embankment in London.

Nevertheless, for a time Alexandria again burned bright. From the mid-19th to the mid-20th century it was a thriving, cosmopolitan Mediterranean port. "Five races, five languages, a dozen creeds," wrote English author Lawrence Durrell in *the Alexandria Quartet*, a four-novel study in decadence that further embroidered the myth of the city (see p. 184). Then quite abruptly, this particular vital chapter was brought to a close when Egypt's socialist revolution of 1952 led to the mass exodus of Alexandria's foreign communities and the dismantling of its sophisticated and multicultural society.

Twenty-first-century Alexandria

Since that time the population has exploded, reaching the five million mark. The Alexandria of the 21st century is a wholly Egyptian and largely modern city of high-rises, traffic jams, and fast food. Scratch away the surface, however, and antiquity pokes through. For instance, construction on a highway in 1997 had to halt when workers unearthed

a Roman necropolis. More recently, the waters of the Eastern Harbor have begun to give up some of their treasures, too (see pp. 178–179). Alexandria's young population is coming to terms with its own history, and perhaps recognizing that their city's past may well be its future. ■

NOT TO BE MISSED:

The Greco-Roman Museum 176–177

The Kom al-Shuqafa catacombs 180–181

Pompey's Pillar and the Serapeum 181

The picture-perfect Fortress of Qaitbey, built on the site of the fabled Lighthouse 182–183

The Cecil Hotel, a throwback to the city's cosmopolitan heyday 184

The Constantine Cavafy Museum 186

Bibliotheca Alexandrina 188

Coffee and a pastry at the century-old Athineos café 365

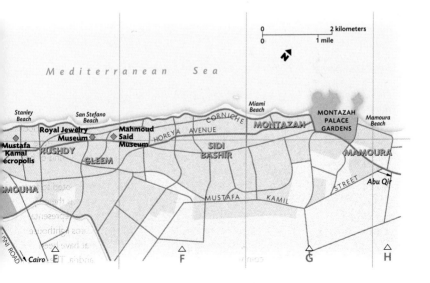

Greco-Roman Museum

One of the few places in Alexandria where it is possible to get any sense of the city as it was 2,000 years ago is this small but densely packed museum. Its exhibits illustrate a fascinating period in Egyptian history, when pharaonic traditions and gods were being wedded to those of the occupying Ptolemaic Greeks and the Romans who followed them.

Tourists walk down the aisles and on the stage of Alexandria's Roman theater.

Alexandria
🗺 174–175
Visitor information
✉ Saad Zaghloul Sq.
☎ 03/485 1556

You can meet more legendary figures from Alexandrian and world history elsewhere in the museum; there is a white marble head of an imperious Julius Caesar in **Room 14** and a supposed head of Marc Antony mounted on the wall of the museum's restful central garden. In **Room 24,** Cleopatra, lover of both men, is represented on a silver coin which was minted during her reign. Either the artist lacked skill, or Plutarch's remarks about the queen's looks (see p. 34) are indeed more truthful than the legend of her beguiling beauty.

Room 18 is devoted to terra-cotta pieces and has the only contemporaneous representations of the Pharos lighthouse (see p. 183) that have been found in Alexandria. These are in the form of three-tiered lanterns, with the squared base, octagonal middle, and circular top that the Pharos is said to have had. Neighboring cabinets are filled with terra-cotta figurines of women of Alexandria dressed in richly pleated robes and sporting a third-century B.C. fashion spread of hairstyles and hats. According to contemporary accounts, the city's women were famous for the artfulness of their dress, coiffures, and cosmetics. But these dolls were no ornaments; they were made to be placed beside the deceased and were found in the city's necropolises, in the tombs of women who had died young.

INSIDER TIP:

The museum's porphyry statue of Diocletian demonstrates imperial power: The purple stone is found only on one remote mountaintop of the Eastern Desert.

—NEIL HEWISON
American University in Cairo Press

Kom al-Dikka

Further evidence of ancient Alexandria lies southwest of the museum. Kom al-Dikka, which translates as "mound of rubble," is a large city-center excavation of the ancient Panion, or Park of Pan, a Greco-Roman-era pleasure garden. Pride of the archaeologists is a small but beautifully preserved **Roman theater,** the only one found in a city that once boasted 400 (according to the Arab general Amr ibn al-As in A.D. 642). Digging is ongoing, uncovering Roman baths and a villa where floor mosaics include a nine-panel masterpiece depicting a number of colorful birds. ∎

The Search for Alexander's Tomb

When Alexander died in 323 B.C. in Babylon (in modern-day Iraq), his body was carried back to Alexandria, placed in a gold coffin, and buried near the crossroads of the city. In the first century A.D., Emperor Augustus paid his respects at the tomb, as did Emperor Caracalla in A.D. 215. But after that there are no further records of the tomb. Perhaps it was pillaged in the riots that took place in the third and fourth centuries A.D., or maybe Alexander's remains were moved to a secret, safer place. No matter what, the lost tomb constantly inspires new theories and renewed searches for its location. The idea that Alexander may still lie entombed beneath the streets of Alexandria is an enchanting one, and one day—who knows— someone might just sink a spade in the right place.

Greco-Roman Museum

- 🅰 174 C1/C2
- ✉ 5 Al-Mathaf al-Romani St.
- ☎ 03/486 5820
- 🕐 Closed Fri. noon–2 p.m.
- 💲 $$. Camera $, video camera $$$

Kom al-Dikka

- 🅰 174 C1
- ✉ Al-Muhafza St.
- ☎ 03/486 5106
- 💲 $. Camera $, video camera $$$

Rediscovering Ancient Alexandria

Alexandria's classical glories were long thought lost, with Cleopatra's palace engulfed, the Pharos toppled into the sea, and the Mouseion and library burned down. In the 21st century, however, all three are reappearing, as two teams of archaeologists make fantastic discoveries on the seabed and a team of architects completes what has already been heralded as one of the seven wonders of the modern world.

An ancient sphinx is lifted from the waters near Alexandria.

Chief of the discoveries is what is being described as the palace of Cleopatra, venue of trysts with Marc Antony and setting for the dramatic finale of the queen's asp-assisted suicide (see p. 34)—that is, if such an event ever actually happened. Practically everything we know about Cleopatra is based on literature and myth, and the truth about her remains hidden. Other than coins bearing her image and a few stone busts, all

physical evidence of her reign disappeared during the fourth century A.D., when great cataclysms submerged a large part of the North African coast, including Alexandria's royal quarters.

However, a French-Egyptian team headed by explorer Franck Goddio has discovered ancient wooden piles, limestone paving, red granite columns, and a small temple to Isis on a sunken island in the Eastern Harbor. There is no conclusive proof that these are the remains of Cleopatra's palace, but Strabo (64 B.C.– A.D. 23), a Greek geographer visiting Alexandria about 27 B.C. (three years after the death of the queen), described the royal quarters as being on a small harbor island, known as Antirhodos. Anecdotal this evidence may be, but it has captured the world's imagination, particularly when in October 1998 a beautiful sphinx and statue of a priest of Osiris, unseen for one-and-a-half millennia, were raised out of the water before the assembled cameras of the world's media. Following the viewing and photo opportunity, the pieces were returned to the seabed until it is decided what to do with them.

Meanwhile, on the other side of the harbor, in the shadow of the Fortress of Qaitbey, another French-Egyptian team, led by archaeologist Jean Yves Empereur, has been diving an extensive field of over 2,000 large stone blocks lying 25 feet (8 m) below the water's surface. In all probability, these are the remains of the legendary Pharos lighthouse, shattered by its fall into the sea (see p. 183). The team has also found columns, fragments of obelisks, and a colossal statue in four parts which, reassembled, stands 41 feet (12.5 m) high. Empereur believes that the colossus, representing a Ptolemaic pharaoh, once stood at the foot of the lighthouse.

In addition to these investigations, underwater archaeologists have been probing two ancient cities up the coast to the northeast. Near the tip of the peninsula forming the western edge of Abu Qir Bay, the archaeologists have been excavating what they believe are the ports of Canopus and Herakleion, coastal settlements that predate Ptolemaic Alexandria. The divers have surfaced coins, jewelry, pottery and utensils as well as statues.

UNESCO is now gathering funds for an underwater archaeological museum incorporating the finds of both the Goddio and the Empereur explorations, where visitors would view objects in situ, from an offshore fiberglass dome reached by tunnels underneath the modern city.

Complementing all the activity beneath the waves, on a seafront site overlooking the harbor, is a different sort of revival of the past: a massively ambitious and architecturally exciting new library and study complex, a replacement for the lost Mouseion of old.

EXPERIENCE: Dive in Alexandria's Harbor

Underwater excavations continue to locate and recover statuary, stone blocks, and sphinxes at the bottom of Alexandria's Eastern Harbor. It is possible that archaeologists will someday have a clearer picture of the structure and position of the Pharos and Cleopatra's palace than we do now. In the meantime, diving in the harbor to see these ruins—located only a few yards from the modern city, but utterly forgotten until recently—is an amazing experience. Amid the stone structures and shipwrecks from Alexandria's Ptolemaic past, you can also spot an Italian fighter plane, shot down during an Axis raid on the city in World War II.

If you're used to Red Sea diving, however, you may be in for a disappointment: Alexandria's harbor waters are quite dark, with a visibility of only a few yards. The harbor is shallow, so objects are at most 30 feet (9 m) from the surface, although the surge is minimal. The local diving company **Alex Dive** handles harbor dives (tel 03/483 2042 or 016/666 6514, www.alexandria-dive.com). Its offices are located on the grounds of the large Fish Market restaurant that juts out into the harbor, halfway between Midan Saad Zaghloul and the Fortress of Qaitbey. They charge 650LE for two dives with lunch included.

Catacombs of Kom al-Shuqafa

Alexandria is riddled with underground passages and chambers belonging to catacombs, cisterns, and who knows what else. In the early years of the 20th century, the disappearance of a donkey into a hole that suddenly opened up in the ground resulted in the chance discovery of an elaborate and unique Roman burial complex.

Jackal-headed figures of Anubis, god of death, guard the main tomb.

Catacombs of Kom al-Shuqafa

- 🗺 174 C1
- ✉ Al-Nasseriyya St.
- ☎ 03/486 5800
- 🕐 Closed after 4 p.m.
- 💲 $$. Camera $, video camera $$$
- 🚃 Karmouz

A rackety tram ride away from the railroad station square, Kom al-Shuqafa appears as a baked-earth hillock surrounded by concrete mid-rises in one of the poorer quarters of the modern city. What lies beneath, however, is a different world altogether.

A descending stair spirals around a central shaft down which the bodies of the dead once were lowered. It leads to three levels of tombs, hollowed out of rock in the second century A.D., probably as a crypt for a wealthy family of nobles. On the upper level is a rotunda with a central well down to the lowest level's flooded, inaccessible chambers. To the left is the *triclinium*, the banqueting hall for funeral feasts. The broken remains of plates and dishes, perhaps from such feasts, give the locale of the catacombs its Arabic name, meaning "mound of potsherds."

Another staircase descends to the **central burial chamber**, the complex's showpiece, filled with a bizarre confusion of the iconography of death. On either side of the doorway are bearded Greco-Roman serpents, wearing the pharaonic double crown of Egypt. Above the door the snake-haired Medusa of Greek mythology is meant to turn would-be tomb robbers to stone. Inside the cramped tomb chamber is the usually fearsome jackal-headed god Anubis—with a pudgy body squeezed into a Roman legionary's uniform.

In keeping with the idea of all show and no sense, the lids of the chamber's three sarcophagi were never meant to open; instead the bodies were put in place from a passageway behind. Later, this passage was enlarged to create galleries lined with pigeonhole spaces, known as *loculi,* for several hundred more burials.

Pompey's Pillar & Serapeum

Another worthwhile site is a short walk from the catacombs, helpfully indicated by the distinctive landmark of Pompey's Pillar. The Crusaders mistakenly thought that this 100-foot (30 m) red Aswan granite column marked the burial site of Julius Caesar's rival, the Roman general Pompey, murdered in Egypt in 48 B.C. (see p. 33). In fact, it was erected in honor of Emperor Diocletian about A.D. 300, according to an inscription part-way up the shaft. However, the pillar is a red herring, because the far more significant ruins are those found around it.

What is now an archaeological park, with neatly kept shrubbery surrounding a somewhat pockmarked rocky hill, is all that remains of Alexandria's acropolis,

the **Serapeum.** Dedicated to the city's homemade god, Serapis (see p. 180), this had as its centerpiece a vast temple that, according to contemporaneous accounts, was reached by one hundred steps and had a marble exterior and interior walls plated with precious metals. A colossal statue of Serapis, also made from precious metals, inspired awe in the worshipers within. But pagan worship was anathema to the growing Christian movement and, in A.D. 391, a mob led by the patriarch Theophilus reduced the Serapeum to ruins.

During the past century, archaeologists have rediscovered some of the Serapeum's treasures, such as an impressive life-size black basalt Apis bull (see pp. 146–147) and a gold plaque commemorating the foundation of the Serapeum etched in both Greek and hieroglyphs; these

INSIDER TIP:

The catacombs are an eerie, twisting maze that takes you deep underground, but they are incredible to see.

—TIFFIN THOMPSON
National Geographic contributor

are displayed at the Greco-Roman Museum (see pp. 176–177). Visitors to the site have to be content with broken column shafts, some Ptolemaic sphinxes, and several pharaonic oddments moved up here from ancient Heliopolis. And, of course, Pompey's Pillar. ■

Pompey's Pillar & Serapeum

- 174 C1
- Amoud al-Sawari St.
- 03/486 5800 ext. 430
- Closed after 4 p.m.
- $
- Karmouz

Fortress of Qaitbey

This neat little fortress looks as though it was built for toy soldiers of days gone by. It has the most perfect location too, cast out on a spindly arm far into the Eastern Harbor. Long devoid of any military function, the place now serves as a small naval museum. But, this being Alexandria, it is what's not there that really excites, for the fortress occupies the site of the Pharos lighthouse, one of the ancient Seven Wonders of the World.

Now a spot for fishermen and courting couples, the tower that once stood here was a wonder of the ancient world.

Fortress of Qaitbey

🏛 174 C2
✉ Eastern Harbor
☎ 03/480 9144
🕐 Closed after 4 p.m.
💲 $. Extra fee ($) for Naval Museum

After enduring for more than 1,600 years, the lighthouse was rubble by the 14th century (see opposite). In 1480 Mamluk sultan Qaitbey (R. 1468–1498) made good use of the still solid foundations and fallen masonry to build a fortress as defense against the Turks, who were threatening Egypt. A prolific builder, Qaitbey has numerous monuments to his name in Cairo, including his mosque (depicted on the Egyptian one-pound note), but this is his only legacy to Alexandria. However, its current form is not as designed by the sultan; during a nationalist uprising in 1882, the fortress was targeted by a British naval bombardment, following which it was extensively rebuilt.

Today, the fortress is approached via a causeway with a sea wall that serves as a popular spot for anglers. A gatehouse provides access to the outer court, which has some passages and rooms to explore, but the main interest is the **keep.**

As you enter the keep, you pass through a doorway whose lintel and doorposts are formed from large granite slabs, in all likelihood salvaged pieces of the Pharos. Inside, three floors contain a variety of maritime artifacts and displays, including bits and pieces recovered from Napoleon's fleet, sunk off Alexandria by Admiral Horatio Nelson in 1798 (see p. 38). Part of the keep was built as a mosque, and for four centuries a minaret towered high above the ramparts until it was blown away by the British navy. The oldest surviving mosque in Alexandria, it is no longer used for worship. Its structure includes five monolithic, red-granite columns that are probably more survivors from the Pharos.

Even if you are not interested in the fortress and its contents, it's still worth a walk down here for the sweeping views of central Alexandria seen across the Eastern Harbor.

INSIDER TIP:

The nearby Greek Nautical Club is a good place for lunch, with a fabulous view of the harbor.

—NEIL HEWISON
American University in Cairo Press

On the peninsula leading to the fortress there is a **Marine Life Museum,** with kitschy dioramas and a few shabby, long-dead specimens of sea life. Across the street is the **Marine Aquarium,** where the fish, sea turtles, and Nile crocodiles, housed in small and dirty glass tanks, are barely more alive. ∎

Marine Life Museum & Marine Aquarium

- 🅰 174 C2
- ✉ Eastern Harbor
- ☎ 03/480 1553
- 🕐 Closed after 2:30 p.m.
- 💲 $

Greek Nautical Club

- ✉ Corniche, Anfushi
- ☎ 03/480 2690

Pharos Lighthouse

Inaugurated in 279 B.C. during the reign of Ptolemy II (R.285–247 B.C.), the Pharos was a massive stone beacon built to aid ships navigating the featureless coastline of Mediterranean Egypt. More than that, it was the physical embodiment of the learning of Alexandria's Mouseion and a statement of the city's great wealth. Images of the Pharos appear in Roman mosaics in Libya, on a vase dug up in Afghanistan, and even in St. Mark's Basilica in Venice. From these, historians describe a structure about 500 feet (150 m) high, with a square lower section set with rows of small windows, an octagonal middle section, and a conical top.

It is thought that the tower became a functioning lighthouse during the first century A.D., but its workings remain a mystery. One idea that sounds plausible is that there was an oil-fed flame with sheets of polished bronze as reflectors, but a classical account describes a "transparent stone" through which ships invisible to the naked eye could be seen; did the ancient Alexandrians discover the lens? However the light beam was achieved, it was lost to the world about A.D. 700 when the lantern top fell. More natural disasters further reduced the tower until, in 1303, an earthquake shook the eastern Mediterranean and the Pharos was destroyed.

A Walk Through the Capital of Memory

English novelist Lawrence Durrell (1912–1990), author of the *Alexandria Quartet,* called the city "the capital of memory." He and his characters inhabited an Alexandria heavily shaded by its past. The *Quartet*'s success added a whole new layer of myth. Ghosts of the classical age have been joined by the spirits of Durrell's Justine, Balthazar, Mountolive, and Clea—ciphers for a cosmopolitan city now largely gone.

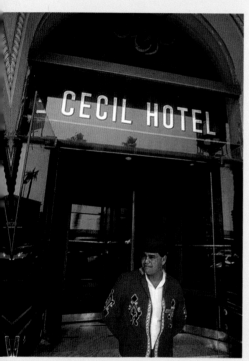

If you cannot afford a room at the Cecil, at least visit for a drink at Monty's Bar, named for Britain's General Montgomery.

NOT TO BE MISSED:

Cecil Hotel foyer • Lemon tea and pastries at Pastroudi's • The antique stores of Attarine Street

---

Durrell's book is almost an epitaph for the city of Alexandria. By the time the *Quartet* was published (the final volume, *Cleo,* came out in 1960), the city of which he wrote had ceased to exist. Cosmopolitan Alexandria was at its most boisterous in the 1920s and '30s. The city lived in a Babel of languages: It shopped in Greek, perused newspapers in French, skirted bureaucracy in English. Alexandrians, wrote historian Robert Ilbert, could have several nationalities, and they used them like credit cards. Foremost surviving symbol of this free-spirited age is the **Cecil Hotel** ❶ *(Saad Zaghloul Sq.; see p. 366),* which is a good place to begin a walk. Built in 1929 in a Moorish style, it was at the center of the city's dinner-and-dance scene, when guests included writers Somerset Maugham and Noel Coward. Durrell made it a haunt of the enigmatic Justine, eponymous heroine of the Quartet's first volume, published in 1957.

At the center of grassy Saad Zaghloul Square in front of the hotel is a **statue of Saad Zaghloul** (1860–1927), a nationalist leader who did much to pave the way for eventual Egyptian self-rule. At the southeast corner of the square is the city's **visitor information office** *(Saad Zaghloul Sq., tel 03/485 1556).* At its northeast corner, Saad Zaghloul Square links with one of the hubs of the city, **Ramla Square** ❷. From here trams run west to the Fortress of Qaitbey (see pp. 182–183) and east toward—though not as far as—Montazah (see p. 191). Around the tram station are several grand old patisseries, of which a favorite is the Trianon. Its dining hall is decorated with gorgeous Oriental murals, while the salon is a classy place for a Continental breakfast. Outside the Trianon's large picture windows, where the tram station is now, for almost two millennia stood two great obelisks. They were carved during the reign of Tuthmose III and originally adorned ancient Heliopolis. In the first century B.C. they were removed to Alexandria by Augustus Caesar. Nineteenth-century travelers dubbed them "Cleopatra's Needles." In the 1870s the British took one (it now stands beside the Thames in London), and then the Americans took the other; you can see it now in New York's Central Park.

On leaving the Trianon, bear right, then right again, so that you are now heading back west along Saad Zaghloul Street. Opposite

the Brazilian Coffee Store, turn left on narrow An-Nabi Daniel Street, lined with small stores. Just a few paces along is a large iron gate, almost rusted shut, which is a sad commentary on the fate of the city's **Great Synagogue ❸**. Jews have been living in Alexandria continuously since it was founded by Alexander the Great in the fourth century B.C. After their expulsion from Jerusalem in the second century A.D., Alexandria became for a time the world center of Judaism. At its peak the community numbered about 40,000, but tragically, its numbers are dwindling due to anti-Jewish sentiment over the founding of Israel. There is a side entrance, guarded by soldiers, but the synagogue is rarely open.

Take the next left on Sultan Hussein

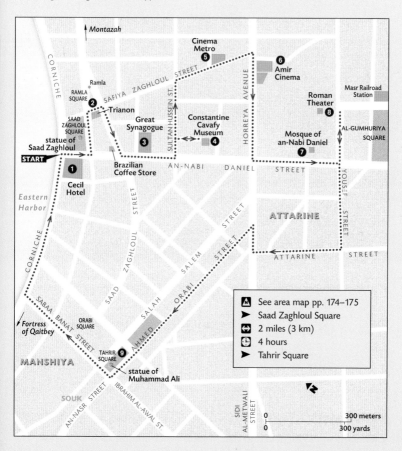

Street and then cross to head south down little Sharm al-Sheikh Street, entering No. 4. A creaky, sparsely furnished apartment on the second floor is preserved as the **Constantine Cavafy Museum ❹** (*4 Sharm al-Sheikh St.*). Cavafy (1863–1933) was a Greek poet, whose work, despite being widely translated, is too little known outside the Mediterranean world, though his poem, *Ithaca, was* read at the funeral of Jacqueline Kennedy Onasis in 1994. Alexandria, the city in which he lived all but a few of his 70 years, was his muse. In turn, it was Cavafy's verse that provided inspiration for Durrell, who immortalizes Cavafy throughout his *Quartet* stories as the "poet of the city."

Return to Sultan Hussein Street and walk to Safiyya Zaghloul Street, where you should turn right. Ahead is the **Cinema Metro ❺** (*26 Safiyya Zaghloul St., tel 03/487 0432*), inaugurated in 1950 by MGM and still splendidly maintained, with colored marble floors, mahogany panels,

---

Pick Your Fish

At seafood restaurants in Alexandria and other seaside cities, you'll often be brought to a tray of fish on ice and asked to select which one you want, then whether you want it fried (*ma'li*) or grilled (*meshwi*). Your meal's price will be determined by the fish's weight. Commonly offered fish include sole (*samak musa*), red mullet (*barbuuni*), gray mullet (*buuri*), bass ('*arus*), crab (*kaburia*), and shrimp (*gambari*).

---

and stylish geometric detailing. Beyond the Metro, turn right on Horreya Avenue, where you'll pass the **Amir Cinema ❻** (*42 Tariq-al-Horreyya, tel 03/491 7972*) with its great art deco foyer, opened in 1952 by 20th Century Fox. Still one of the city's major thoroughfares, Horreya Avenue is the modern incarnation of one of the two main streets originally laid out by Alexander. At that time it was known as the Canopic Way and stretched between the eastern Gate of the Sun and the Gate of the Moon. A fifth-century

bishop described how a row of columns went from one end of it to the other.

After a few minutes' walk you reach a busy intersection, where you turn left onto **An-Nabi Daniel Street,** once the other major thoroughfare of Alexander's city. This intersection was still impressive when Amr ibn al As saw it the 7th century. Today, the street is named for a local saint, and booksellers display their well-thumbed wares on sheets on the sidewalk flanking it. Partway along is the Mosque of an-Nabi Daniel ❼, which over the years has been a favorite site for hunters of Alexander's tomb (see p. 177). Some people are convinced that it lies beneath the foundations, but the religious authorities will not allow any digging here. Serious archaeologists dismiss this as a potential site, preferring a set of cemeteries to the east of the city center as a more likely location.

An-Nabi Daniel exits onto al-Gumhuriya Square, recently spruced up as part of a campaign to reverse the decline in the appearance of the city. After decades of neglect, wonders are now being achieved with cans of paint and brooms. If you haven't already visited the Roman theater ❽ (see p. 177), it is to the left, behind the high wall; otherwise bear right down Yousef Street for two blocks then right again on **Attarine Street,** the center of Alexandria's antiques trade. It is possible to spend hours rummaging through the stores in this warren of alleys, all filled with offcasts from the city's ornamented past.

At the far end of Attarine Street, turn right, then left to get to Ahmed Orabi Street, which you should follow to **Tahrir Square ❾.** Muhammad Ali (see pp. 39–40), whose equestrian statue rides high above the traffic, planned the square as the heart of his new Alexandria in 1830. It remains a grand space, although the vital institutions that once gave it life, such as the Bourse and law courts, are no longer present. Instead, it is better known now as the starting point for the city's main souq, which stretches west from here. To find your way back to the Cecil, head for the sea and stroll back along the **Corniche.**

Alexandria National Museum

A striking Italianate villa that formerly housed the U.S. Consulate in Alexandria has been reclaimed, renovated, and reopened as an attractive showcase of general Egyptian history.

When this museum opened in 2004, critics pointed to what they thought a missed opportunity. Though the history of Alexandria is the history of Western thought, philosophy, and culture, you wouldn't know it from visiting here. Absent are the Pharos and the ancient library, and even Alexander and Cleopatra barely get a mention. Instead, the city's newest museum offers little more than overflow from the far more engaging **Greco-Roman Museum** (see pp. 176–177) down the street and the Egyptian Museum in Cairo.

The lower floor is filled with a miscellany from the pharaonic era, including examples of alabaster statuary from Giza, a false door from Abydos, an early wooden statue from Saqqara, and a truly spooky sandstone of Akhenaten, with distinctive pinched face, pursed lips, and catlike eyes. Down a farther, narrow set of stairs is a chilled subterranean vault in which a statue of the jackal-headed Anubis guards two finely-painted sarcophagi from the Late Period. All of these exhibits predate the founding of Alexandria and are geographically distant.

The ground floor bears more relevance with the majority of the items on display originating in the Greco-Roman era and most of them unearthed in and around the city. Particularly worth seeking out is a large Roman mosaic with a

In an Italianate building, Alexandria's National Museum holds artifacts that narrate the city's history through the ages.

central panel of a Medusa's head, discovered during excavations in the city center. There are also representations of the Alexandrian gods Serapis and Harpocrates (the Greek version of Horus); the latter appears as a nude bronze statue with forefinger to mouth, in Pharaonic style, and curls and clothing of Greek inspiration.

The top floor is particularly sparse. It has two rooms devoted to Coptic Christian artifacts (including some carved tombstone panels that combine Roman-style figures with hieroglyphic-like symbols); two rooms of glass lamps, ivory-inlaid doors, and arms and armor from the Islamic era; and a small collection of black-and-white photographs of the "European" Alexandria of the 19th century. Labeling is generally informative; the presentation is uncluttered. ∎

Alexandria National Museum

🗺 174 C1
✉ 110 Horeyya Ave.
☎ 03/483 5519
🕐 Open 9 a.m.–4 p.m.
💲 $$

Bibliotheca Alexandrina

A striking piece of 21st-century architecture that is pure high-tech while simultaneously evoking the glory of the ancient Ptolemaic capital, the new Bibliotheca Alexandrina is the largest and most advanced library in the Arab world, and it has helped put the city back on the map.

Alexandria's spectacular new library strives to revive the educational brilliance of the ancient original.

**Bibliotheca
Alexandrina**

🅰 174 C2

✉ Al-Silsila,
Shatby

☎ 03/483 9999

💲 $

www.bibalex.org

The precedent for Bibliotheca Alexandrina, the Great Library, was founded in the third century B.C., shortly after the city itself. Perhaps Alexandria's finest achievement, it held as many as half a million texts; legend has it that every vessel entering the harbor had to hand over any manuscripts for copying. The library was part of a larger institution, the Mouseion (House of the Muses), forerunner of universities everywhere. Here in Alexandria scholars first accurately measured the Earth's circumference, mapped the stars and planets, and dissected bodies to discover the central nervous system. When the library was destroyed—no one knows how—much of this knowledge was lost.

This ancient wealth of learning is evoked on the new library's exterior walls, which are carved with giant letters, hieroglyphs, pictograms, and symbols from every known alphabet. The building itself, on the Corniche, close to the eastern promontory of Silsila, takes the form of a huge disk, tilted into the ground. Its near-circular roof is a mesh of interlocking glass panels that looks like an integrated circuit.

Separate entry fees get you into an excellently curated exhibit of ancient manuscripts, a planetarium, and an antiquities gallery on the lowest level, which includes recent finds from the harbor and elsewhere. A viewing gallery allows you to appreciate the reading hall, which has terraces cascading down ten levels. ■

Royal Jewelry Museum

Jewelry is less than half the story in this small but absorbing museum, which houses a glitzy collection of personal heirlooms and valuables formerly belonging to the family of Farouk, Egypt's last king. Closed for renovations for three years, this gorgeous museum is slated to reopen in 2009.

King Farouk was a notorious womanizer and gambler. It was said that when he crashed parties, hostesses rushed to hide their daughters. In 1951, on one night of his 13-week honeymoon with his second wife, Farouk blew a record $150,000 in a baccarat game. The hedonism ended when Egypt's rulers were unseated by the coup of 1952. Farouk was deposed, the royals were stripped of their properties, and most then departed for exile. Sequestered villas and palaces were converted, serving as everything from presidential residences to primary schools.

However, the Fatma al-Zahraa Palace, built by French and Italian architects in 1923 for the family of Farida, Farouk's first queen, has survived largely unscathed. This modestly sized mansion set on beautifully kept grounds has kept much of its wildly eclectic original decor, and this, rather than anything in the display cabinets, is the main attraction.

One hall has floor-to-ceiling painted-glass windows depicting a bright parade of waltzing courtesans. Ceilings are crowded with pink cherubs frolicking on cottony clouds. A "Greek" room has stylized mock-classical friezes and stenciled frescoes. Best of all in this feast of gaudy taste is the trio of bathrooms, each with tiled scenes adorning the walls: one has

a farmyard, one has fishing boats, and one has a beach scene.

Trinkets and follies make up most of the museum's collection. High points—or lows, depending on your humor—include a silver gardening trowel with ivory handle, a silver-plated shaving set, and—most impractical of all—an amber mouthpiece for a water pipe set with 204 diamonds. Considering this gratuitous squandering of Egypt's wealth (and at this time just 2 percent of the population owned more than 50 percent of the land), it is difficult to feel anything but empathy with the revolutionary leaders who kicked the royals out of their silk-sheeted beds.

To find the museum, alight from the tram at the Qasr al-Safa stop, beside the Faculty of Fine Arts, and look for the big white villa surrounded by a high wall. ■

Royal Jewelry Museum

- 🅰 175 E2
- ✉ 27 Ahmed Yehiya Pasha St., Gleem
- ☎ 03/586 8348
- 🕐 Closed Fri. during noon prayers
- 💲 $$. Camera $, video camera $$$
- 🚋 Tram No. 2 from Ramla Sq.

EXPERIENCE: Browse Books on An-Nabi Daniel

When Alexandria's foreign communities left the city in the 1950s, they left behind (among other things) their libraries. Today, on the stretch of An-Nabi Daniel Street, south of Horreya Avenue, there is a great stretch of open-air bookstalls selling books in English, French, and Arabic. If you're lucky, you might find a paperback that's been tossing around since pre-1957 Alexandria, marked with the imprint of a long-gone local bookstore.

Mahmoud Said Museum

A pioneer of Egyptian modern art, Mahmoud Said was honored in 2000 by the opening of a museum of his works in the eastern suburb of Gianaclis. The museum's setting, a beautiful Italianate villa in which the artist once lived, is also worth seeing. Said (1897–1964) was born into an aristocratic family, the son of a former prime minister, and trained in law. He painted only as a sideline while pursuing a career in law that culminated in his appointment as a judge.

Mahmoud Said Museum

- 🅰 175 E2
- ✉ 6 Mohammed Said Pasha St., Gianaclis
- ☎ 03/582 1688
- 🕐 Closed Mon.
- 🚃 Tram No. 2 from Ramla Sq.

Said is arguably the finest painter produced by Egypt in modern times. In tune with the renaissance of the 1920s and '30s, he and other artists strove to forge an Egyptian artistic identity by depicting scenes of rural life and by drawing on motifs and styles from the pharaonic and Greco-Roman traditions. This is seen most clearly in Said's soulful self-portraits, which resemble nothing so much as the famed Fayoum Portraits (see p. 153).

However, along with absorbing his country's heritage, Said was also taken with European and American influences. A canvas called "At the Ballroom" is pure Jazz Age. Best of all are the portraits in the nudes room—which, in a sad indictment of the current social climate, museum attendants usher visitors past. Not lewd or lecherous, these paintings are of honey-toned, earthy women depicted against richly colored landscapes. These wonderful works deserve to be far better known—they are something of a neglected national treasure.

Also of interest is a cartoonish panorama of the opening of the Suez Canal (see pp. 168–169), with Khedive Ismail and his distinguished guest, Empress Eugénie.

The restored building has been planned as an open university to celebrate Egypt's contribution to modern art. In addition to 54 paintings by Said, 115 works by the Wanli brothers are displayed and there are more than a hundred exhibits in the accompanying Modern Egyptian Art Museum.

To get here, take the No. 2 tram from Ramla Square to the Gianaclis stop, then walk on along the tracks and take the first right. ∎

Alexandria's Tram System

The focal point of Alexandria's tram system for most visitors is Ramla Station, the stop just east of Saad Zaghloul Square. Trams run east and west from Ramla, and travel parallel to the Eastern Harbor, a block from the Corniche, for part of the way. Tram destinations are printed in Arabic, so unless you can read Arabic letters, remember that blue trams waiting to depart at Ramla travel east, while yellow ones go west, heading to Anfushi and beyond (the #14 circles around to Masr Railroad Station). The tram is the best way to travel the city, and at 25 piastres, it is one of the cheapest. Buy tickets from a ticket seller on the tram itself.

Montazah Palace Gardens

Traditionally, Alexandria has always been the place that Cairo escaped to during the punishingly hot summer months. Vacation apartments line the seafront, blooming into life each July and August. Egypt's rulers valued the cooling sea breezes too, and at the far eastern end of the Corniche, at the point where the city stops 11 miles (18 km) east of the center, Khedive Abbas Hilmy II (*R.* 1892–1914) built Montazah as a royal summer residence.

Montazah Palace, built for royalty, now serves as the Egyptian president's summer retreat.

Montazah is not so exclusive since the abolition of the monarchy, and for a small fee you can go into the grounds. Within the walls are the khedive's former residences and extensive, well-tended gardens, heavily planted with pines and palms and with even the odd flower bed. There's an attractive sandy cove (the beach is private) with a bridge running out to a small island. It is probably the most appealing spot in all Alexandria for walking, and on Fridays and holidays the place is packed with picnicking locals.

Abbas Hilmy's palace, sited on a bluff overlooking the sea, is vaguely Moorish in style, with a definite Florentine twist–

particularly in the tower, which is a direct steal from Florence's Palazzo Vecchio. During World War I the palace was loaned to the British for use as a Red Cross hospital, and for a time one of the orderlies was English novelist E. M. Forster. Returned to the royals, the palace was seized by the state after the revolution and now serves as a presidential retreat.

A few minutes' walk away is a second royal residence. Known as the Salamlek, it was built in an Austrian style as a hunting lodge and has recently opened as a luxury hotel (see pp. 363–364). One of its two restaurants, Al-Farouk, once served as the study of the king of the same name. ∎

**Montazah
Palace Gardens**

🗺 175 G2

✉ Montazah St.

☎ 03/547 7152
   or 03/547
   7153

🕐 Open 9 a.m.–
   sunset

💲 $

More Places to Visit in Alexandria

Abu Qir

East of Alexandria proper is Abu Qir, a small coastal settlement notable for the naval battle fought just offshore in 1798. During the Battle of the Nile, Britain's Admiral Nelson surprised and destroyed Napoleon's French fleet at anchor in the bay. In 1994, divers discovered Napoleon's flagship *L'Orient* partially buried on the seafloor. More recently, the bay at Abu Qir has yielded further spectacular finds, notably the ancient cities of Canopus, Herakleion, and Menouthis, thriving cult centers in Greco-Roman times that subsequently vanished, perhaps due to an earthquake or tidal wave. Alexandrians flock here for seafood.

175 H1 minibus from train station

Anfushi

Anfushi is the one part of Alexandria that has a wholly Eastern feel. The district was developed during the Ottoman period, as people gradually abandoned the ruins of the Greco-Roman city to the south. It remains a warren of narrow alleys with listing buildings and time-worn, neighborhood mosques. At the quarter's heart is the modern, majestic **Mosque of Abu al-Abbas al-Mursi** (built in the 1930s). It occupies the site of a much earlier mosque founded by North African im-

migrants to honor a venerated 13th-century Andalusian saint, whose body lies in a tomb beneath one of the soaring domes. On feast days and during Ramadan, the piazza beside the mosque is the focus of festivities.

174 C1 ✉ 26th of July St. ☎ 03/480 1251 🕐 Closed Fri. during noon prayers

INSIDER TIP:

Check out some of the seafood restaurants in Abu Qir, east of Alexandria; Zephyrion *(Khaled Ibn el-Walid)* is a famous one.

—ANNA LOUIE SUSSMAN
National Geographic Traveler *magazine writer*

Durrell's House

Lawrence Durrell fans can see his Alexandrian home in the Moharrem Bay district, southeast of the train station. While occupying Villa Ambron's turret rooms for two and a half years in the early 1940s, he wrote poetry and his short novel *Prospero's Cell*. Sadly, the long-derelict house is under threat of demolition.

174 C2 ✉ 19 Maamoun St.

Necropolises

Northwest of the Mosque of Abu al-Abbas al-Mursi in Anfushi is the **Anfushi Necropolis** *(Ras al-Tin St., Ras al-Tin; map 174 C2)*, a five-tomb complex from the third century B.C. A limestone staircase descends to an open-air court, off of which are burial chambers with painted scenes of Egyptian gods and the underworld. Similar complexes have been found in the eastern suburbs, notably the **Shatby Necropolis** *(Port Said St., Shatby; map 174 D2)*, source of the Greco-Roman Museum's "death dolls" (see p. 177). At the **Mustafa Kamel Necropolis** *(Moaskar al-Romani St., Rushdy; map 174 E2)*, sphinxes guard Greek-style tombs.

The turret room in which Lawrence Durrell wrote while living in Alexandria

A country of sand but also with routes linking four lush areas, and a striking north coast along the blue Mediterranean Sea

Western Desert

Introduction & Map   194–195

Mediterranean Coast   196–197

Marsa Matruh   198

Siwa Oasis   199–201

Experience: Take a Sand Bath in Siwa   199

Bahariyya Oasis   202–203

White Desert   204

Experience: Take a Deep Desert Safari   205

Farafra Oasis   206

Dakhla Oasis   207

Kharga Oasis   208

Hotels & Restaurants   366–367

The preferred mode of transport in the oases

Western Desert

The Western Desert covers more than two-thirds of the territory of Egypt. It starts at the bank of the Nile and stretches west into Libya; to the south it is bordered by Sudan, while to the north it is halted by the Mediterranean. It is a vast world of beauty, solitude, and utter silence, one that has yet to be fully explored.

Although it appears desolate, the desert is actually not short of water. Though rain is infrequent, when it does rain, water is trapped in subterranean chambers, creating springs that support a scattering of oases dotted across the immense, empty expanse like a lonely constellation. Four of them—Bahariyya, Farafra, Dakhla, and Kharga—form a loop, connected by asphalt road to Cairo in the north and Luxor in the south. For the adventurous, a trip through the oases offers a chance of true discovery in a region still very little known, even to the Egyptians themselves.

The oases have surprisingly long and rich histories. They were occupied in ancient times and were known to Herodotus, who called them the Islands of the Blest (another name for the Elysian Fields of Greek mythology). During the Roman era they were thriving trade hubs on routes to the Libyan provinces. As a result, the Western Desert is now seen as Egypt's final archaeological frontier. Over the last couple of decades, hundreds of significant sites have been discovered, including the Valley of the Golden Mummies (see pp. 202–203), which brought camera crews from all over the world to a tiny village that, until recent years, had never even seen a television set.

High-profile finds like the mummies are attracting more and more travelers to the Western Desert, but there is one oasis that has long been a draw—Siwa. A place of legendary beauty, it also gains mystique through its relative inaccessibility. Lying way out of the oases loop, up in the northwest corner near the Libyan border, even today it requires tenacity to make the uncomfortable journey. The only way is via the northern coast,

sticking to the Mediterranean as far as Marsa Matruh, then striking south into the desert. Alexander the Great took this very same route in 331 B.C., probably only too aware that some 200 years earlier, in 524 B.C., the Persian general Cambyses had set out for Siwa from the south at the head of an army of 50,000 men, none of whom was ever to be seen again: All were lost to the desert.

In 2002, the Egyptian government made more than 1.9 million acres around Siwa a protected area. In 2007, archaeologists excavating near the oasis unearthed what may be the oldest human footprint ever discovered. ■

NOT TO BE MISSED:

Al-Alamein war museum and cemeteries 197

The Temple of the Oracle at Aghurmi in Siwa, where Alexander the Great found out whether he was the son of Zeus 200

Cleopatra's Bath (The Well of Jupiter) in Siwa 201

The Golden Mummies at Bahariyya's museum 202–203

The unearthly White and Black Deserts between Bahariyya and Farafra 204

Wandering the covered streets of medieval al-Qasr in Dakhla 207

The Necropolis of al-Bagawat in Kharga 208

The Roman fortress of Qasr al-Dush on the ancient caravan trail south of Al-Kharga 208

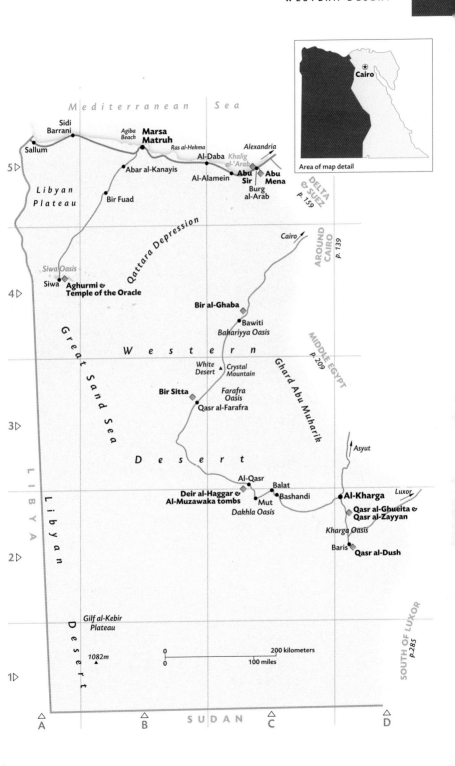

Mediterranean Sea

Sidi
Barrani

Sallum

*Agiba
Beach* **Marsa
Matruh** *Ras al-Hekma*

Abar al-Kanayis

Al-Daba Alexandria

*Khalig
al-'Arab*

Al-Alamein Abu
Sir Abu
Mena

Burg
al-Arab

*Libyan
Plateau*

Bir Fuad

5▷

Qattara Depression

Cairo

AROUND
CAIRO
p. 139

DELTA
& SUEZ
p. 159

Siwa Oasis

Siwa **Aghurmi &
Temple of the Oracle**

4▷

Bir al-Ghaba

Bawiti
Bahariyya Oasis

Western

MIDDLE EGYPT
p. 209

Great Sand Sea

White
Desert ▲ *Crystal
Mountain*

Bir Sitta *Farafra
Oasis*

Qasr al-Farafra

Ghard Abu Muharik

3▷

Desert

Asyut

Al-Qasr Balat

**Deir al-Haggar &
Al-Muzawaka tombs** Mut Bashandi

Dakhla Oasis

Al-Kharga

Luxor

**Qasr al-Ghueita &
Qasr al-Zayyan**

Kharga Oasis

Baris **Qasr al-Dush**

2▷

SOUTH OF LUXOR
p.285

*Gilf al-Kebir
Plateau*

Desert

▲ *1082m*

0   200 kilometers
0   100 miles

1▷

LIBYA

Libyan Desert

△   △   △   △
A   B   C   D

SUDAN

Area of map detail

⊛ **Cairo**

Mediterranean Coast

Throughout history the Egyptians have largely shunned their northern coast. Far removed from the life-sustaining Nile Valley, it involved too many days' travel across inhospitable desert. Instead, it has served as a lonely highway for traders and as a route for invading armies, from the Libyans in ancient times to Italians and Germans in World War II.

Foreign visitors flock to the beaches of Sinai and the Red Sea coast, but the Mediterranean is where Egyptians vacation.

That has all changed. As Egypt's population has boomed during the last several decades and more people have acquired cars and disposable income, developers have pounced on the long-uninhabited coastline. From the outskirts of Alexandria all the way west to Al-Alamein, the Mediterranean beaches have been barricaded off with an unbroken wall of vacation villages. Executed in a mishmash of architectural styles from neo-Moorish to neo-Disney, each village has a monumental roadside gateway, the modern-day equivalent of the pharaonic pylon.

However, there is a real pylon at **Abu Sir,** at Kilometer 47 on the coastal highway, part of the substantial remains of a Ptolemaic temple dedicated to Osiris. Beside it is a small, white stone tower, with a square base, octagonal midsection, and circular (partially collapsed) top story—a miniature version of its big brother, the Pharos (see p. 183). It was part of an ancient chain of lighthouses strung along this coast.

The tower played a role in a curious episode in American history, involving the first U.S. foreign intervention by land. In 1805, Gen. William Eaton (1764–1811), a U.S. Army officer and adventurer, led an expedition across the Western Desert to oust the government of Tripoli (present-day Libya) and put a halt to piracy against American ships in the Mediterranean. Eaton hoped to reinstate the exiled Pasha Hamet Karamanli, and a friendship treaty between the two men was signed in the Abu Sir tower.

Just past the tower, a road turns south, leading through the village of Burg al-Arab (Arab's Tower, the local name for the lighthouse) to the archaeological site of **Abu Mena.** One of Egypt's most revered Christian saints, Mena is believed to have been a conscript in the Roman army, martyred for his faith. Legend has it that the camel carrying his remains halted at this spot and refused to go any farther (hence, Mena is often depicted between two camels). Stories of miraculous events connected with the site turned it, from the fifth to seventh centuries, into a pilgrimage center supporting several churches, monasteries, bathhouses, shops, and inns. It lost its importance after the Arab conquest and eventually fell into ruin. Egypt's Coptic community is eager to resurrect the site's past glories, and monks from a new monastery, built in the 1970s, are usually happy to guide visitors through the ancient remains.

Back on the highway, the tourist villages peter out just short of the coastal village of **Al-Alamein,** which is famous as the northern end of one of the key battles of World War II. It pitted two master tacticians against each other: Field Marshal Erwin Rommel (1891–1944), the "Desert Fox," commanding German and Italian forces, and the British general Bernard Montgomery (1887–1976). In June 1942 the German army rolled across North Africa, threatening Alexandria and the Suez Canal. It was halted by a last-ditch line of defense at this remote desert spot. On October 23 of that same year, Montgomery's

The Battle of Alamein

British war leader Winston Churchill wrote of the battle of Al-Alamein, "Before Alamein we never had a victory. After Alamein we never had a defeat."

Eighth Army launched a devastating counter-offensive that drove the Germans back into Libya. Casualties on both sides were high, and Al-Alamein today is a place of cemeteries and somber memorials. Those of the Italians and Germans are just off the main highway, while the British and Commonwealth cemetery is south, opposite the **Al-Alamein Museum** displaying artifacts from the battle and leftover pieces of hardware. ∎

Al-Alamein Museum

- 🇦 195 C5
- ✉ Medinat al-Alamein
- ☎ 046/410 0021
- 🕐 Open 9 a.m.– 3 p.m.
- 💲 $$

Marsa Matruh

Marsa Matruh, 180 miles (290 km) west of Alexandria, is the only town of any size on the north coast. Yet it has just one main street, and half of its businesses slumber for two-thirds of the year. For the other third, Matruh is transformed into the most popular summer retreat for Egypt's middle classes—albeit a bargain-basement version of the Red Sea resorts.

If the shops are open it must be summer: Matruh is closed out of season.

Marsa Matruh
🔼 195 B5
Visitor information
✉ Omar Mukhtar St.
☎ 046/493 1841

Rommel Museum
✉ Rommel Beach, 2 miles (3 km) E of town
🕐 Closed after 3 p.m.
💲 $

The town wraps around a bay in use since classical times, when it was the port of Paraetonium. Shiploads of Greek pilgrims regularly disembarked here en route to consult the oracle of Amun at the oasis of Siwa. Legend has it that Cleopatra and Marc Antony came here shortly before doing battle with Rome (see p. 34).

During the North African campaigns of World War II, first Rommel, on the offensive, then Montgomery, giving chase, set up headquarters here. Rommel's was a cave, now turned into a small, half-hearted museum with a few photos and maps, and what is claimed to

be the field marshal's overcoat. The more urbane "Monty" took up residence at the stylish Hotel Lido (where in 1950 Rita Hayworth checked in on her honeymoon).

Since then, Matruh has gone decidedly downscale...and the Lido has gone, period. (For echoes of former grandeur, try the Beau Site Hotel; see p. 367.) In summer the beaches are thronged with vacationers. However, away from town unspoiled sandy sweeps border magnificent turquoise waters, notably at **Agiba Beach,** 15 miles (24 km) west. Beyond that, there is nearly nothing on the coastal highway until the Libyan border. ■

Siwa Oasis

The ultimate remote getaway, Siwa is a speck of life-sustaining greenery marooned far out in the Western Desert, almost nudging Libya on the map. Between it and Cairo is nothing but 340 miles (550 km) of sand. Famous in antiquity for its oracle, the oasis has been largely left alone ever since. It remains an appealing combination of tranquility, beauty, and inaccessibility.

Isolated throughout its long history from goings-on beside the Nile, the oasis has developed independently from the rest of Egypt. For instance, most Siwans speak Siwi, a Berber tongue, a reminder of their historic origins as wandering Bedouin. The community (pop. 15,000) also retains its traditional tribal structure, with the heads of the 11 tribes, the *sheikhs,* acting as the local council. Siwans are more conservative than other Egyptians: Alcohol is banned, and women are rarely seen unless swathed in a voluminous wrap known as a *milayah.*

Until as recently as the 1980s, Siwa had no television and no phones, and the donkey cart was the transportation of choice. But a new asphalt road linking the oasis to Marsa Matruh brought changes. The oasis is now firmly marked on the tourist map and is sprouting an increasing number of hotels and restaurants. It has logged on to the Internet with a free public-access cyber café, and an airport is on the drawing board.

None of this has yet affected significantly the splendor of the oasis, with its dense, green groves of date-bearing palms and olive trees watered by more than 300 freshwater springs and streams. At the heart is the modest market square, ringed by canvas-shaded stalls and dominated by the remains of the 13th-century, mud-brick enclave of **Shali.** This original oasis settlement was surrounded by high walls as protection against attacks by marauding Bedouin. Finding it too dangerous to build outside the walls, the Siwans instead built upward, with some of the houses rising four or five stories. Then, a freak three days of rain in 1926 was so damaging, dissolving the high salt content in the mud and causing the buildings to literally melt, that the inhabitants moved out. Looking like a canvas by Salvador Dalí, the abandoned Shali is a delight to explore; its upper vantage points offer excellent

Siwa Oasis

🅐 195 A4

Visitor information

✉ Town center

☎ 046/460 1338

🕐 Open until at least 5 p.m. every day including Fri.

EXPERIENCE:
Take a Sand Bath in Siwa

There are now a few doctor-run clinics in the Gebel Dakrur area of Siwa, southeast of the main town of Shali, that offer a sand cure, originally developed as a treatment for arthritis and rheumatism. Patients are covered in a hot sand "bath" for up to 30 minutes, then rehydrated with tea. The course of treatment can last up to a week, and the clinics draw large numbers of international clients each summer. The sand cure is offered only in summer. For more details, contact Siwa's main tourism office *(tel/fax 046/460 1338),* which is open Saturday to Thursday.

views over the oasis to the desert and tabletop bluffs beyond.

Down below Shali, just to the left of the main Mosque of Sidi Suleiman, is the **Siwan House Museum,** founded by a former Canadian ambassador to Egypt, who feared the complete demise of Siwa's mud-brick dwellings and associated way of life. It contains

once renowned throughout the Mediterranean world. In 331 B.C., Alexander the Great came here, trekking eight days across the desert from the coast, seeking confirmation from the Oracle of Amun that he was the son of Zeus, the Greek king of the gods. Nobody knows what the oracle's reply was (Alexander

Modern brick has replaced mud-brick; otherwise, isolation has prevented change in Siwa.

traditional dress, jewelry, and domestic implements.

Outside Town

Two miles (3 km) east of town is the ancient hilltop settlement of **Aghurmi,** which, aside from a restored mosque, is even more ruined than Shali. Signs lead to the remains of the sixth-century B.C. **Temple of the Oracle,**

never told), but afterward he asked his generals to bury him at the oasis. Though it is unlikely that they carried out his request— historians believe he was laid to rest in Alexandria (see p. 177)—of course, there are those who disagree. In 1995 two Greek amateur archaeologists announced that they had discovered the legendary lost tomb in Siwa; while they undoubtedly found a tomb, there is no evidence to suggest that it is Alexander's.

A short distance south lies the **Temple of Amun,** dedicated to the ram-headed Egyptian god of life. It is almost totally ruined, having been, unbelievably, dynamited for building materials in 1896.

Continuing south through the palms from the temple ruins is a well-marked track leading to **Cleopatra's Bath,** a stone-lined pool filled by a natural spring. It is a popular swimming hole for local men, but the water's scummy surface discourages most visitors. A much better spot for a soak is **Fatnas Spring,** a large, palm-shaded pool on an island in salty Lake Siwa, accessible by a narrow causeway. This is about 4 miles (6 km) west of central Siwa.

Just a mile (1.6 km) north of town, off the Marsa Matruh road, is **Gebel al-Mawta** (Hill of the Dead), a wind-eroded bluff honey-

INSIDER TIP:

If you can afford it, don't miss Adrere Amellal (see p. 367), the fancy eco-resort in the Siwa oasis. It's the most peaceful place I've ever been.

—ANNA LOUIE SUSSMAN
National Geographic Traveler
magazine writer

combed with tombs dating back to Ptolemaic and Roman times. Four of them are locked, but it's worth finding the guardian with the keys

to see some funerary paintings. In one tomb are colored reliefs of a Greek man and his family praying to Egyptian gods; another has a faded yellow crocodile, a representation of the god Sobek.

Desert trips are another popular Siwan activity. Lapping up against the oasis is the **Great Sand Sea,** the world's largest dune field, stretching west into Libya and for some 500 miles (800 km) to the south. Most hotels can organize a day's four-wheel-drive excursion into the dunes. ∎

Siwan Crafts

Siwan craftworks have become collectors' items to such an extent that, in the oasis itself, it is almost impossible to find the distinctive, finely embroidered dresses or heavy silver jewelry once produced here. All the best pieces have gone abroad, and with most of the original craftsmen dead, these reminders of oasis heritage are now lost even to the Siwans themselves. However, in local craft shops you can still get wonderful silver rings, shaped differently for each finger and inscribed with geometric patterns. Siwa is also known for its baskets, woven from date palm fronds, and its pottery (water jugs, beakers, and incense burners), made from local clays and colored reddish brown with a pigment made from local earth.

Bahariyya Oasis

At 205 miles (330 km) southwest of Cairo, Bahariyya is the closest of the four Western Desert oases to the capital. It was always regarded as the least interesting of the quartet until a series of significant archaeological discoveries in just the last decade put it on the map.

Carved into stone beneath the sands, this multi-layered tomb may have been used for centuries.

Bahariyya Oasis

🄰 195 C4

Visitor information

✉ Town council building, Bawiti

☎ 02/3847 3035 or 02/3847 3039

🕐 Closed 2–7 p.m. & Fri.

Museum Sharia al-Mathaf

✉ E of town center

💲 $

Several small villages are scattered throughout the Bahariyya oasis, but the main center is the town of **Bawiti** (population 30,000). With one main street of squat shanty buildings, the place has something of a frontier feel. At first acquaintance, there is no sign of the expected lush oasis greenery, but walk in almost any direction and paved roads give way to sandy trails lined with traditional mud-brick houses and palm groves.

Two thousand years ago, however, it was a very different story.

During the Greco-Roman period Bahariyya prospered as one of the greenest spots in all Egypt, sending its wheat and wine off to the Nile Valley. Archaeologists now estimate that the oasis may have had a population of up to half a million during this time. Evidence for this comes from a recent archaeological find of a vast and wealthy necropolis which may hold as many as 10,000 mummies.

Ten of the mummies are displayed in the new, bunkerlike **Sharia al-Mathaf museum.**

Valley of the Golden Mummies

In March 1999 a team of archaeologists began excavating a suspected desert burial site about 4 miles (6 km) away from Bawiti. They dug simultaneously in four spots, and each dig revealed a tomb literally piled with mummified corpses. Stacked in what were probably family vaults, a total of 142 bodies were found, surrounded by scarabs, necklaces, carnelian earrings, and silver bracelets, and accompanied by images of the fertility god Bes.

Further digging in May 2000, some of which took place in front of Fox TV cameras, revealed the tomb of Jed-Khenso-Iufankh. This 26th dynasty ruler of Bahariyya is well known to historians and archaeologists, who had been searching for the whereabouts of his final resting place for decades. At the same time, another seven tombs were opened containing one hundred mummies, some wearing golden masks. One mummified mother even carried an infant mummy on her chest.

The archaeologists estimate that there could be 10,000 more mummies awaiting discovery here. While the digging continues, the site is off-limits to the public, but there is talk of turning what has been dubbed the Valley of the Golden Mummies into an open-air museum.

Otherwise, Bahariyya has little to offer in the way of ancient sites. There are the partial remains of a 26th dynasty temple devoted to Amun-Re, and of another temple raised in honor of Alexander the Great, the only one of its kind in Egypt. There is also a series of ancient burial tunnels, known locally as Qarat al-Firekhi, or Ridge of the Chicken Merchant, because of the thousands of mummified birds discovered there. None of these places are easy to find; ask at the visitor information office for help in locating them.

Just over a half mile (about 1 km) east of the town center is the **Ethnographic Museum,** a grand title for a private house occupied by the owner's naive, life-size sculptures of oasis people.

Trips to Bahariyya usually focus on the hot springs. There are many of these, but most are inappropriate for soaking in because they are right beside tracks with a constant stream of local traffic.

An exception is **Bir al-Ghaba** (Well of the Forest), about 12 miles (20 km) northeast of Bawiti in a eucalyptus grove. On the way out, the road skirts a flat-topped mountain, known as the Mountain of the Englishman,

INSIDER TIP:

If you're doing an overnight in the desert, bring along a package of wet wipes: They're very handy for cleaning your face and hands when you're far from running water.

—CHIP ROSSETTI
National Geographic contributor

because during World War I the British manned a lookout post here, on the watch for Italian-sponsored raiding parties. ∎

White Desert

A place of surreal rock formations and patches of blinding white, the White Desert is fast becoming one of the most popular destinations in the Western Desert. It begins just north of the oasis of Farafra and continues for about 30 miles (50 km), stretching for about 12 miles (20 km) on each side of the road. It is best visited from Farafra Oasis (see p. 206).

Huge rock formations sculpted by the wind seem nothing less than a hallucination.

White Desert
△ 195 C3

Part of the 120-mile-long (200 km) Farafra Depression, the floor of the White Desert (in Arabic, Sahra al-Bayda) is a mixture of chalk and limestone, which gives the appearance of snow. The Bedouin call it Wadi Gazar, or Valley of Carrots, because in some areas the pinnacle-like rock stacks formed by wind erosion resemble, well...carrots. These weathered, odd rock formations give the area its distinctive character. You begin to see them just a few minutes outside Farafra on the Bahariyya road. Out of the desert floor rise strangely rounded shapes that resemble white sphinxes, weird birds, sunbathers, stone camels and so forth. As the sun shifts, the white rock takes on pink, orange, and even blue hues, adding to the already surreal aspect. Strewn across the ground are iron pyrites in fanciful shapes, and quartz crystals, used by Bedouin to promote salivation and quench thirst in the desert heat.

Another oddity of the White Desert are the springs, of which it has a number, including **Bir Makfi, Ain al-Sarru, and Ain al-Wadi.** They are marked by hillocks rather than depressions, formed when sand catches on the vegetation that flourishes around the water. The plants are forced to grow ever higher to avoid being smothered, and eventually a hill is formed.

In **Wadi Hennes,** at the northern end of the White Desert, there are some unexcavated Greco-Roman ruins, including a structure that is thought to be a watchtower, as well as some tombs. They lie along the ancient trade route that linked Farafra with the next oasis north of Bahariyya.

Although it is outside the White Desert proper, most excursions to the area include a stop at the **Crystal Mountain,** about 50 miles (80 km) from Farafra. It is less a mountain than a small outcrop of rock right beside the road, but a closer look shows the rock to be quartz crystal. ■

EXPERIENCE: Take a Deep Desert Safari

If you are touring the western oases, it is easy to arrange day-trips or overnights into the nearby desert through local tour companies, and sometimes through your hotel. While most trips are taken in 4x4s, some companies also offer camel safaris, and even desert hikes on foot.

But if you're up for a real challenge, you may wish to make an expedition into Egypt's Western Desert. The Great Sand Sea, which stretches south of Siwa, and the distant highlands of the Gilf al-Kebir and the Gebel Uweynat, remained unexplored until the 20th century. Expeditions to these remote sites can run anywhere from 12 to 28 days or more, and groups take along all the gas, food, and water they will need in the desert. Needless to say, these deep desert expeditions must be done with a professional guide; they also require a military escort. Companies will generally provide 4x4 transport, food and water, experienced guides, GPS navigation, and camping gear.

The pristine rippled landscape of the Great Sand Sea is stunningly beautiful. The Gilf al-Kebir plateau, in Egypt's southwest, is linked to early 20th-century explorers like Ralph Bagnold and Laszlo Almasy (the real-life *English Patient*) and contains a wealth of prehistoric rock art, such as Almasy's famous "Cave of the Swimmers." Desert travel companies will handle the military permissions back in Cairo for you, but be warned that security restrictions can change.

Because of the extreme summer heat, desert expeditions usually take place be-tween September and March. An excellent resource on the deep desert is the encyclopedic *The Western Desert of Egypt: An Explorer's Handbook*, by Cassandra Vivian.

A reliable company for desert safaris is **Badawiya Expedition Travel** *(42, Road 104, Maadi, tel 02/25260994, www.badawiya.com)*. It's run by the same three Bedouin brothers as the Badawiya Hotels in Farafra and Dakhla (see p. 368), and they have been organizing camel and jeep trips into the White Desert for years. They provide everything necessary for a night under the stars, including Bedouin musicians and a campfire. An expedition to the Gilf al-Kebir runs about $210 per person per day.

Other reliable companies include **Egypt Off-Road,** run by expat Peter Gaballa *(www.egyptoffroad.com)*. In addition to organizing expeditions, he offers desert driving courses for clients with their own desert-worthy vehicles.

Fliegel Jezernicky Expeditions is run by Andras Zboray and his wife *(tel 36-1-2744290 [Budapest], www.fjexpeditions.com)*. Zboray is an authority on desert rock art as well as his fellow Hungarian Saharophile Laszlo Almasy.

Another well-known guide is Amr Shannon, a Cairo-based explorer who has been traveling through Egypt's deserts for more than 20 years *(tel or fax 02/519 6894)*.

Siag Travel Egypt also has long experience organizing deep desert expeditions *(Siag Travel Hotel, Saqqara Rd., Giza, tel 02/23852626, www.siagtravel.com)*. For more possibilities, see pp. 379–380.

The White Desert's unearthly beauty is spurring interest in safaris.

Farafra Oasis

The small, isolated oasis of Farafra is famed for its picturesque scenery and tranquility. The main population center is Qasr al-Farafra, although it is more a village than a town, with only a few cafés, a small group of municipal buildings, and a couple of hotels. Surrounding it is some of the Western Desert's most beautiful scenery, including the White Desert (see p. 204).

Farafra's number-one celebrity is Badr, an artist who has filled his museum with representations of village life.

Farafra Oasis

🔼 195 C3

Badr's Museum

☎ 092/751 0091

💲 $

of the community belong to a few extended families. Orchards of dates, olives, and apricots are surrounded by old mud-brick walls. Traditional desert houses sit around the ruined qasr, or fort, up the hill, their single-story, windowless facades painted with images of pilgrimages to Mecca and topped with crenellations.

What is there to do in Qasr al-Farafra? You can just wander and relax; and you can visit **Badr's Museum,** a large, fantastical mud-brick house filled with the works of Farafra's most famous son, the artist Badr Abdel Moghny. Most of his paintings and sculptures portray village life.

Farafra's history stretches back to pharaonic times, but there are no monuments in the oasis, and what little knowledge we have of the area in that period comes from stelae found in the Nile Valley. The oasis sat on a strategic trade route to Libya and was an important watering point for caravans and armies. But the small number of wells here limited the permanent population and kept it poor until state investment in land reclamation over the last 20 years boosted its economy.

Until a road reached the oasis just two decades ago, Farafra's isolation helped to preserve its unique character. Most members

INSIDER TIP:

Whether male or female, dress conservatively; no bare legs, midriff, or shoulders. This also saves you from the inevitable sunburn.

—DR. JOEL D. IRISH
National Geographic field researcher

As with the other oases, there are several hot springs. The sulfurous waters at **Bir Sitta,** 4 miles (6 km) north of Qasr al-Farafra, are the most famous and are a wonderful place for a soak. ∎

Dakhla Oasis

Dakhla is actually a cluster of about 15 small settlements, strung east-west along the dusty highway. Also known as the Inner Oasis, it is perhaps the most attractive of all the Western Desert oases. Stretches of lush groves where dates, olives, and oranges grow are partitioned by sweeps of great white dunes.

The "capital" of the oasis is **Mut,** a sparse, small, low-rise town. While not particularly picturesque, it is friendly and has decent accommodations, a passable restaurant, and the visitor information office. There are hot sulfur pools dotted about, the most accessible being **Mut Talata,** 2 miles (3 km) west of the town center.

Of more interest is the medieval town of **Al-Qasr,** which is located some 20 miles (30 km) farther out in the same direction. The town's mud-walled alleys weave a complex pattern linking secluded courtyards and threading through mud tunnels supported by cross beams of roughly cut branches. Parts of it have been dated to the tenth century, and there is a 12th-century mosque complete with mud minaret. Some doorways have acacia beam lintels carved with the name of the house's owner, a date, and a verse from the Koran. There are 54 such lintels in the village: The earliest dates from A.D. 924.

Another 2 miles (3 km) beyond Al-Qasr, a track leads to the pharaonic era **Al-Muzawaka tombs.** Two main tombs still contain wall paintings, while a third contains four mummies. Farther west still is a turnoff to **Deir al-Haggar,** a recently restored temple dating from the reign of the Roman emperor Nero (A.D. 45–68).

Heading out of Mut toward Kharga, you come to two small settlements, **Balat** and **Bashandi;** both have wonderful old centers, with hardly a right-angle anywhere. Sadly, the lack of modern amenities means that the dwellings have largely been abandoned and are rapidly falling into disrepair. ∎

Dakhla Oasis

🔺 195 C2

Visitor information

✉ Al-Thawra al-Khadra St., Mut

☎ 092/782 1685

🕐 Closed after 3 p.m.

Al-Muzawaka tombs

💲 $$

Deir al-Haggar

💲 $$

Bounded by a high escarpment, Dakhla is a collection of green swaths interspersed with sand dunes.

Kharga Oasis

The largest of the Western Desert oases, Kharga stretches for 120 miles (200 km) along a flat, wide depression. Much of the depression has been used for land reclamation projects, making Kharga less picturesque than the oases to the north. However, some of the Western Desert's most impressive archaeological remains are here, and the surrounding desert with its undulating dunes is very beautiful.

Al-Kharga
🅰 195 D2
Visitor information
✉ Nasser Sq., Al-Kharga
☎ 092/792 1206
🕐 Closed after 2 p.m. & Fri.

Archaeological Museum
✉ Gamal Abdel Nasser St., Al-Kharga
🕐 Closed Fri.
💲 $$

Temple of Hibis
💲 $$

Necropolis of al-Bagawat
💲 $$

Qasr al-Ghueita
💲 $$

Qasr al-Zayyan
💲 $$

Qasr al-Dush
💲 $$

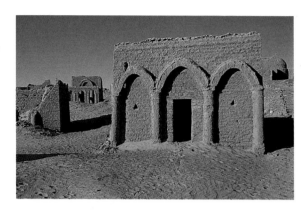

Christian-era tombs at Al-Bagawat are evidence that the oases were staging posts on an ancient trading route.

The chief town of the oasis is **Al-Kharga,** capital of the New Valley governorate. The town center has little to recommend it apart from a few hotels and the **Archaeological Museum,** with a collection of local artifacts. The highlight is a small display of prehistoric tools. At the northern end of the town is the sixth-century B.C. **Temple of Hibis,** dedicated to the Theban triad of Amun-Re, Mut, and Khonsu (see p. 242). Almost opposite the temple are the hilltop remains of the **Temple/Fortress of an-Nadura,** built by Roman emperor Antoninus Pius in A.D 138.

Farther north is the fascinating **Necropolis of al-Bagawat,** containing several hundred Christian-era mud-brick tombs dating from the fourth to sixth centuries. Up a track behind the necropolis stand the dramatic cliff-top ruins of **Deir al-Kashef,** an early Christian monastery that overlooked the crossroads of several trade routes. As you head south from Al-Kharga, two more ruined fortresses lie just east of the main road. **Qasr al-Ghueita** encompasses a well-preserved Ptolemaic temple; Roman **Qasr al-Zayyan** is close to a modern village.

Most worthwhile of the old remains is **Qasr al-Dush,** a Roman temple and fortress near the town of Baris, the gateway to Egypt for caravans from the south, 60 miles (96 km) south of Al-Kharga. Emperor Domitian built the well-preserved Temple of Osiris within its walls in the first century A.D. ■

A farming heartland around market towns, plus a wealth of ancient sites, including the short-lived capital of the "heretic pharaoh" Akhenaten

Middle Egypt

Introduction & Map 210–211

Minya & Around 212–213

Amarna 214–217

Feature: The Holy Family in Egypt 218–219

Experience: Travel in the Footsteps of the Holy Family 219

Asyut 220

Sohag 221

Abydos 222–223

Dendara 224–226

Hotels & Restaurants 367–368

A girl at Gurna chews on sugarcane.

Middle Egypt

Middle Egypt is that stretch of the country lying south of Cairo and north of Luxor, which virtually all visitors skip over by plane or sleep through on an overnight train. However, for anyone hankering to see the "real Egypt," this is the place to look.

The term "Middle Egypt" is an invention of 19th-century archaeologists. Egyptians themselves still only speak of Upper and Lower Egypt, terms in use since the time of the first ancient king, Menes (circa 3100 B.C.). But it is a useful handle to describe a region quite different in character from those areas to the north and south: the heartland of Egypt, largely untouched by either heavy industry or tourism. Not far south of Cairo the cliffs and rocky hills that hem in the Nile withdraw

Local village women come down to the banks of the Nile to do their washing.

to leave a wide and lushly green plain either side of the river. It is prime agricultural land, cultivated in age-old ways. Farmers still practice flood irrigation, and occasionally you can catch a glimpse of a waterwheel, or *sakia,* being turned by a blindfolded ox, or a *shadouf,* the ancient implement for lifting water. *Fellaheen,* the rural peasantry, work the land by hand, often using tools modeled on designs thousands of years old. Towns are provincial and conservative, to the extent that for all the connection it has with local affairs, Cairo has about as much to do with daily life in the countryside and towns as New York City does.

Unfortunately, this is not quite the rural idyll it might sound. Agricultural work fails to provide sufficient employment or income for the area's burgeoning population. The lack of income from industry or tourism results in economic hardship. Locals distrust the distant authorities in the capital, who are traditionally perceived as being neglectful of the region. These factors, and others, have meant that over the last two decades Middle Egypt has proved a fertile recruiting ground for extreme Islamic elements. In the early 1990s, when the extremists declared their intention to target Egypt's tourism industry, it was in the areas of Minya and Qena that most attacks on trains and Nile cruisers took place. Leaders of extremist Islamic groups have said that they are no longer threatening foreign visitors, and police have tightened up their protection, but the damage has been done and the area remains a no-go zone with tour groups, for whom anxiety overrides curiosity.

Even before the current troubles, however, Middle Egypt was a low priority with foreigners. Not only does it lack grand monuments, but there are also few hotels and little public trans-

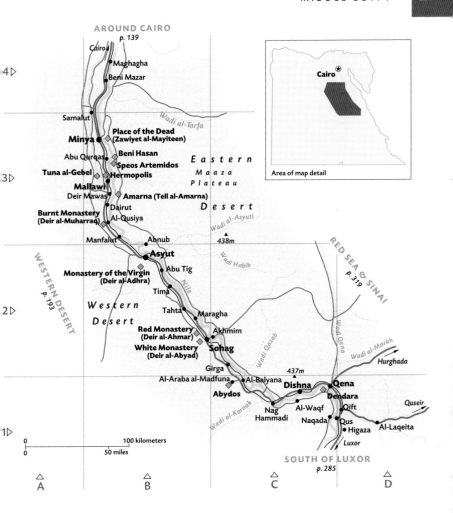

portation. That may change, however, because already there are initiatives afoot to make the area more visitor friendly. One of these efforts is the promotion of a Holy Family pilgrimage route (see p. 219), which would bring people to Asyut and other places.

Although at the moment travel in Middle Egypt can be difficult, the region's main sites are included here because the area may soon open up to foreign visitors. The two most appealing sites for ancient monuments are the Temple of Seti I at Abydos (see pp. 222–223) and the temple at Dendara (see pp. 224–226). Both of these can be visited from Luxor, a safer and more agreeable base. ■

NOT TO BE MISSED:

The Beni Hasan rock tombs   212–213

Amarna, Akhenaten and Nefertiti's royal city   214–217

Tuna al-Gebel, its catacombs, and the tomb of Petosiris   216–217

The Burnt Monastery, said to be visited by the Holy Family   219, 220

The Temple of Seti I   222–223

The Greco-Roman Temple of Hathor in Dendara   224–226

Minya & Around

A provincial capital 150 miles (240 km) south of Cairo, Minya has a relaxed atmosphere that belies its reputation as a center for extremist opposition to the government. The high-profile police presence aside, it is a pleasant Nile-side town with some fine, if badly neglected, architecture testifying to its former prosperity as a center of the cotton industry. It makes a good base from which to explore several important archaeological sites in the area.

Looking like eggs in cartons, the domes of Muslim tombs fill Minya's vast Place of the Dead.

Minya's small-town life centers on **Tahrir Square,** which is fringed by old colonial town houses built by Italian architects for local cotton magnates in the early years of the 20th century. Though shabby, the buildings retain a great deal of charm. The sidewalks out front are filled with coffeeshop tables and chairs, occupied by patrons puffing on waterpipes and playing games of dominoes and backgammon, games made surprisingly noisy by the Egyptian habit of slamming pieces down on the table. A new **Akhenaten Museum,** devoted to the heretic pharaoh, is slated to open in Minya some time in 2010. Closer toward the river, one block in from the attractive tree-lined Corniche, is a lively *souq* (street market), which, in season, is dominated by large mounds of watermelons.

Although there is little to see in Minya, there is plenty in the neighboring area. As public transportation to the ancient sites is limited, it is advisable to rent a taxi for the day. The local tourist office can help arrange this.

About 3 miles (5 km) south of town, on the other side of the river, is an immense cemetery known locally as Zawiyyet al-Mayyiteen, or **Place of the Dead.** Believed to be one of the largest burial grounds in the world, it contains thousands of mausoleums. Mud-brick domes mark the Muslim tombs, and crosses the Christian. Until the 1970s the dead were transported across to the cemetery by *felucca,* but a new bridge over the Nile has brought to an end that tradition.

A farther 10 miles (16 km) or so south are the rock tombs of **Beni Hasan,** burrowed into cliffs on the east bank of the Nile. Named for an Arab tribe that once inhabited the area, the tombs are pharaonic and date from the Middle Kingdom (2055–1650 B.C.). There are 39 tombs in total, all belonging to various nobles and regional governors, but only four are open to the public. Earlier and far less elaborate than the famed tombs in the Valley of the Kings (see pp. 271–284) at Luxor, they are nonetheless fascinating for their wall paintings, which vividly illustrate a wide variety of everyday activities of ancient Egyptian life.

Earliest of the four is the Tomb of Baqet, famous for its wrestlers, who are depicted in almost 200 different positions. Immediately south is the Tomb of Kheti, son of Baqet, with leisurely scenes of dancers, winemaking, and figures playing *senet,* a game similar to checkers. Kheti can be found seated beneath a sunshade attended by his dwarf and his fan bearers. The Tomb of Amenemhet displays a niche at the rear meant for statues, a later development. It still contains broken effigies of Amenemhet, along with his wife and mother.

Most impressive of the quartet is the Tomb of Khnumhotep, who lived around 1800 B.C. Beside the main entrance, paintings show acrobats dancing, but most of the scenes relate to the rites of officialdom, with peasants weighing grain, scribes recording its storage, and farmers working the fields. Most splendid of all, though, are the scenes on the back wall of hunting, fishing, and netting birds, which include depictions of a vast menagerie of animals such as hippos, crocodiles, and big cats. All must have been quite common in ancient Egypt, but they have long since been hunted to extinction.

From the tombs, the cliffside path goes south for 1.5 miles (2.5 km) to the **Speos Artemidos,** a rock-cut temple built by the queen-pharaoh Hatshepsut (see p. 268). It has the distinctive Hathor-headed columns also found at Hatshepsut's great temple on the West Bank at Luxor (see pp. 268–270), only in this case they are unfinished. Inside the pillared hall, painted scenes depict the queen with various deities.

Minya is also the best base for a visit to the revolutionary city of Amarna (see pp. 214–217). ∎

Minya

🅐 211 B3

Visitor information

✉ Corniche al-Nil

☎ 086/234 3500

🕐 Closed Fri.

Beni Hasan

✉ Abu Qirkus

💲 $$

You & Your Police Escort

In the mid-1990s, due to some high-profile terrorist incidents, Egyptian security cracked down on local extremists and upped security measures for tourists. Today, although the threats have mostly disappeared, some regions still insist on police escorts for foreign tourists. This only comes up in the Fayoum and Middle Egypt, where visitors are few on the ground. While it can be frustrating to have a junior policeman tagging along in these areas, remember that it's done only out of an overly cautious concern for your safety. Your personal security guard can be a good source of local information, too, and be a pleasant companion on your walk around town.

Amarna

The Egyptian empire was still in its golden age in the 14th century B.C. when, barely out of his teens, the pharaoh Amenhotep IV (R. 1352–1336 B.C.) swept aside the age-old order of gods, temples, and priests of Karnak at Thebes. In their place he elevated the Aten, the sun disk, as the sole deity, renamed himself Akhenaten (He Who Serves the Aten), and founded a new capital Akhetaten (The Horizon of the Aten).

Akhenaten ruled from Amarna (above) during Egypt's golden age in the 14th century B.C.

Amarna

🗺 211 B3

✉ Tell al-Amarna

💲 $$

Amarna, also known as Tell al-Amarna, is the site of this revolutionary city. A visit is best made from Minya, which is about 30 miles (50 km) north. Renting a taxi for the day is by far the best way to go, as transportation is also needed to get around the extensive site of Amarna. En route, you will pass through the town of Mallawi, where a small museum contains artifacts found in the region. In recent times, however, Mallawi

has been a hot spot for unrest, and as a result the local police do not permit visitors to make a stop in town. Your driver may drop you off at the el-Till ferry on the west bank, and you will continue your trip on the other side, where a now-empty new building will eventually hold a visitor's center.

The reasons Akhenaten chose this particular site are unclear, but at 240 miles (384 km) down the Nile from Karnak, it could well be that he was looking to put some distance between himself and the enraged establishment. With astonishing speed he erected his new city, complete with palaces, public buildings, and a great temple, on the east bank of the Nile on a crescent-shaped plain bounded by an arc of high cliffs.

However, Amarna served as the capital of Egypt for less than 15 years. It was abandoned shortly after Akhenaten's death, when the priests of Karnak managed to regain religious control. They desecrated the temple and did their best to obliterate all record of the heretic pharaoh and his wayward religion. Akhetaten city not only fell into ruin but was dismantled.

Unfortunately, the drama and mystery of the "rebel pharaoh" (and of his almost equally famed wife, Nefertiti) are of far greater interest than the site of his city. What remains today is only the faintest outline, delineated by low mounds of earth and trenches. There are no standing structures, and any finds, such as pottery and statues, have been removed to various museums. Almost all that there is to be seen at the site of the city are two sets of cliff tombs cut in the rock, one at each end of the former city. These feature colorful wall paintings of life during the Aten revolution.

Of the six northern tombs, the most rewarding are the **Tomb of Huya** (No. 1) and the **Tomb of Mery-Re I** (No. 4). In the latter, on the right-hand wall behind

INSIDER TIP:

On Amarna's main Nile-side road you'll pass plenty of *qasab* (sugar cane). If it's being harvested, ask your guide to stop and fetch you a piece— they're fun to gnaw on.

—CHIP ROSSETTI
National Geographic contributor

the two pillars, a painting depicts Akhenaten and his temple, which has helped archaeologists visualize what this city might have looked like. Notice also, down in the bottom corner, the relief of blind beggars awaiting alms; a distinctive characteristic of Amarna art was that it focused on nature and human life rather concentrating on the netherworld. The previously formalized and rigid court

The Strange Face of Akhenaten

One of the most striking aspects of Amarna art is the appearance of the pharaoh himself. In contrast to the sleek, muscled kings of before, Akhenaten is typically portrayed with a bulging cranium and a thin, feline face with protruding lips. His belly is rounded, and his pelvis and buttocks are matronly, almost voluptuous. Scholars speculated for decades that the pharaoh had a deforming disease. But now many believe that the apparent bisexuality of Akhenaten might in fact be rooted in the new religion, because Aten had both male and female aspects.

Hermopolis

◾ 211 B3

✉ Al-Ashmunein

$ $$

Tuna al-Gebel

◾ 211 B3

✉ Tuna al-Gebel

$ $$

style is replaced by something approaching naturalism.

A second set of tombs far to the south is grouped in two clusters. Of these, the ones to look for are the **Tomb of Mahu** (No. 9), burial place of Akhenaten's chief of police, and the **Tomb of Ay** (No. 25), finest of all the tombs at Amarna. Wall paintings here show palace scenes and the street life of

---

Leading to God?

American Egyptologist James H. Breasted called Akhenaten "the world's first idealist...the earliest monotheist, and the first prophet of international-ism." His elevation of the Aten—previously just one aspect of the sun god Re—to supreme status, subsuming all attributes of other gods, foreshad-ows the one God of Jews, Christians, and Muslims. Yet although Akhenaten insisted on one supreme god, he perceived himself and Nefertiti as extensions of that god, and therefore also deserving of worship.

---

the city, including gossiping neighbors, soldiers, and prostitutes.

All these tombs are of nobles and officials. Where Akhenaten himself was buried remains a great mystery. One possibility is in an unidentified tomb, known as the **Royal Tomb,** hidden in a valley 3 miles (5 km) east of the river. Its wall paintings and texts were virtually obliterated by the priests of Amun, but a few surviv-

ing scenes relate to Meketaten, daughter of Akhenaten and Nefertiti. It could be that this was a royal family tomb and the final resting place of the contentious pharaoh himself. Certainly no other tomb bearing his name has ever been found.

Where the World Was Made from Chaos

Visitors with their own transportation can include two other sites in a trip to Amarna, both with strong mythical associations. Five miles (8 km) northwest of Mallawi are the remains of the famed city of **Hermopolis.**

According to one ancient Egyptian tradition, Creation began here, with a primordial mound from which the eight creator gods first emerged to fashion the world out of chaos. From early dynastic times, the site became a center for the cult of Thoth, the ibis-headed god of wisdom, healing, and writing. He also assumed the form of a baboon, often endowed with an enormous erect penis. A pair of giant sandstone baboons now mark the entry to the site, but they are minus their phalluses, which were probably hacked off by early Christians. The Ptolemies identified Thoth with the Greek god Hermes, hence the name Hermopolis. Beyond the baboons, the only real monument here is a fifth-century Christian basilica built with slender granite columns from an earlier Ptolemaic temple.

Rather more remains of the city's necropolis, known as **Tuna al-Gebel,** after the small nearby village. Midway between village and site is the area's oldest monument, one of a series of stelae (inscribed stones) that marked the boundary of the royal city of Akhetaten. It depicts Akhenaten and Nefertiti with their daughters, adoring the sun. Highlight of the necropolis is the catacombs, the galleries of which were once filled with thousands of mummified baboons and ibises—both being sacred to Thoth. Although only a few main corridors are accessible, Egyptologists suspect this subterranean cemetery may extend all the way to Hermopolis, over 4 miles (7 km) distant.

Back above ground is a small "city of the dead" with streets of mausoleums. Grandest of these is the **Tomb of Petosiris,** dedicated to a high priest of Thoth and designed like a temple. Paintings inside show a mixture of two cultures: typical Egyptian scenes, but with all the figures wearing Greek dress. A small hall behind the tomb

INSIDER TIP:

Collect small bills. If you use 50 and 100 LE notes, you depend on someone else having change, which is not always the case.

—PEARCE CREASMAN
National Geographic field researcher

displays a well-preserved "mummy" of a young woman who drowned in the Nile in about 120 B.C. In fact, there are no indications of embalming—the dry desert air has preserved the corpse. ∎

The stubs of slender columns mark the site where, according to ancient Egyptian tradition, Creation began.

The Holy Family in Egypt

According to Scripture, the Holy Family of Joseph, Mary, and the infant Jesus came from Bethlehem to Egypt to escape Herod's "massacre of the firstborn." They remained for roughly four years. What they did and where they went during that time, the Bible does not say, but Coptic traditions link a surprising number of sites with the visit.

The genesis of many of these links lies with Theophilus, patriarch of the Coptic Church some time about A.D. 500. Theophilus had a dream in which the places where the Holy Family stayed in Egypt were revealed to him. Historical common sense supports at least the first of these sites, Farma in northern Sinai (see p. 332), formerly Pelusium, a Roman seaport, which was the gateway to Egypt on a well-trodden caravan route from Judea (now

Dating from 500 A.D., the White Monastery represents Christianity's long-standing tradition in Egypt.

Israel). From here the holy itinerants are said to have journeyed across the Delta region. Local tradition connects them with numerous places including Sakha near the town of Kafr al-Sheikh, where a church has a stone reputed to bear the footprint of Jesus, and the Virgin Mary Church in Mostorod, near Bilbeis. Thousands of pilgrims come to this church every August because they believe the Holy Family stayed there.

At Matariyya, a northeastern suburb of Cairo, is the Virgin's Tree. A gnarled sycamore, this is supposedly descended from a tree that shaded Mary during a rest stop. The tree is now enclosed within a walled garden, and a visit to this ancient pilgrimage site makes for a pleasant afternoon respite from Cairo's crowds.

According to tradition, the Holy Family then passed through the settlement of Babylon, now known as Coptic Cairo (see pp. 114–117), sheltering in a cave that is now a part of the Church of St. Sergius. Another Cairo church, in the southern suburb of Maadi and easily accessible by subway, hosts the next link in the journey south. This fourth-century church claims to occupy the site of a Jewish synagogue on the banks of the Nile from where the family took a boat for Upper Egypt. Copts believe that the stairway from the courtyard of the Church of the Blessed Virgin down to the river is the original, which the Holy Family descended.

The southernmost point associated with the holy route is the town of Asyut (see p. 220), 230 miles (370 km) south of Cairo. Between Maadi and Asyut, countless more villages and churches lay claim to being host to the travelers, boasting ancient churches, holy wells and trees, and myriad tales of miracles. What is undeniable is that Middle Egypt has a great density of

EXPERIENCE:
Travel in the Footsteps of the Holy Family

Only officially promoted as a tourism option since 2000, a pilgrimage to the major sites associated with the Holy Family is still a relatively new way to visit Egypt (at least for modern travelers—Christian pilgrims have been visiting these religious sites for centuries). Traveling the "holy route" is also a unique way to encounter an Egypt often overlooked by travelers. Between Egypt's awe-inspiring ancient past and its central role in Islamic history and civilization, it is easy to forget that the country has also played a major part in the history of Christianity. Many of the sites along this route are rarely visited by non-Egyptians, and chances are good you won't find yourself among a sea of tour buses when you arrive.

It is possible to organize your own trip, ideally starting from Sinai and working your way down to the Burnt Monastery (see p. 220). Some monasteries and churches along the way have guesthouses, but they tend to be basic, and may only accept male visitors; book ahead from Cairo if you want to stay in a hotel en route.

Given the numerous sites linked to the Holy Family's time in Egypt, it will only be possible to see a fraction of them. Your self-guided tour could cover the most important sites, beginning with the ruins of **Pelusium** in northern Sinai, about 11 miles (18 km) east of the Mubarak Peace Bridge at Qantara. You can reach Pelusium by private transport or long-distance taxi from Ismailia or Port Said. A car or public bus can also get you to Delta destinations such as **Tell Basta** (see p. 164), **Bilbeis, Sammanud,** or **Sakha** (just outside of Kafr el-Sheikh.) The three major Cairo sites—**Matariyya, St. Sergius** in Coptic Cairo, and the **Church of the Blessed Virgin in Maadi**—are all accessible by metro or taxi. **Gebel al-Teir** is an easy taxi ride from Minya (see pp. 212–213), and the **Burnt Monastery**—officially the farthest point south the Holy Family reached—is reachable by taxi from either Minya or Asyut.

A guided tour, however, will make your itinerary less taxing. An excellent guide is **Dr. Cornelis (Kees) Hulsman,** a Dutch academic who is an authority on the Coptic church and has lived in Egypt since 1994. Information about his tours can be found on his website (*www.holyfamilyegypt. com*). Though his tours are for large groups, he encourages independent travelers to contact him with the dates they plan to be in Egypt and he will try to link them to a planned group tour (*$150 per day*). Additionally, the **Biblical Vacations** travel agency (*tel 010/615 3331, www.bible vacations.com*) organizes visits to Holy Family sites on its "In the Footsteps of Jesus" itinerary, and it has an outstanding guide in Ramez Salama, who has been leading Christian-themed tours in Egypt for almost a decade.

---

ancient churches and monasteries, evidence of a long-standing Christian tradition.

Since 2000 the Egyptian tourism ministry has been working hard to package and market this "holy route," angling to attract some of the pilgrimage trade down from Jerusalem. June 1 has been unofficially designated Holy Family Day, this being the date that Theophilus dreamed that Joseph, Mary, and Jesus made their entry into Egypt. Hopes are that modern-day pilgrims from around the world can be persuaded to do likewise, joining a proposed annual anniversary procession beginning in Farma and moving on to explore some of the other associated sites, many renovated in anticipation of the hoped-for influx of visitors. It is a scheme that offers the chance for little-known places, which have lain well off most visitors' maps, to forge a valuable relationship with the lucrative tourist industry.

Asyut

Even before the troubles began in Middle Egypt, Asyut was never a major tourist stop. It is the region's largest and least pleasant town and has few sights. However, believed to be the southernmost point reached by the Holy Family, and reputedly the place in which they stayed the longest, Asyut is now being promoted by Egypt's tourist authorities as a venue for Christian pilgrims.

Middle Egypt is extremely fertile and towns like Asyut are major agricultural centers.

Asyut
🗺 211 B2

NOTE: Access to the monasteries is only possible by taxi or private vehicle, as there is no public transportation. Asyut can be reached by daily flights from Cairo or by bus. There are accommodations, although their quality is poor.

The town's history stretches back to the pharaonic era. Evidence of this remains at **Al-Qusiya,** the present name for the ancient settlement of Meir, where 17 tombs of ancient Egyptian princes and rulers of the region are open to the public. Wall reliefs include delightful scenes of daily life, sports, papyrus manufacture, viticulture, and hunting. Finds from the site are displayed at a **museum** on Gomhuriyya Street in central Asyut. In the 19th century, the town was famous for its slave market, the biggest in Egypt, with "merchandise" brought up from Nubia and Sudan. Goods at the *souq* are more conventional these days, but a few old *khans* (merchants' hostels) remain.

The two monasteries associated with the Holy Family are a short way out of town. The **Monastery of the Virgin** (Deir al-Adhra), 6 miles (10 km) to the north, is built around the caves of Dirunka, where the family is reputed to have sheltered. It resembles a great fortified campus, large enough to accommodate up to 50,000 pilgrims who attend the Feast of the Virgin (Moulid al-Adhra) in August each year. The **Burnt Monastery** (Deir al-Muharraq) is a farther 20 miles (32 km) north, near the desert's edge. It, too, is built around a cave sanctuary that is supposed to have been home to the Holy Family and is now the core of a church. This monastery also has an annual feast, in the last week of June. ■

Sohag

Sohag, 80 miles (130 km) south of Asyut, is an attractive rural town, with a large Christian community that is doing its best to woo visitors. Claims to fame include two of Egypt's most celebrated monasteries and a weaving center that produces Egypt's finest textiles, a craft that goes back to the pharaonic era.

Sohag's monasteries, which lie about 6 miles (10 km) south of town, are far smaller and more modest than those at Asyut, but

INSIDER TIP:

Bring several cheap writing pens. Egyptian children will often ask you for your pen; I have never been able to resist.

—PEARCE CREASMAN
National Geographic field researcher

also far more evocative. From a distance, the limestone **White Monastery** (Deir al-Abyad) resembles an Egyptian temple with pylon-like walls. Parts of the building are actually purloined from older structures, and some of the stone blocks on the wall of the monastery's church bear pharaonic hieroglyphs. In its heyday 2,000 monks lived here; today there are only a handful. Each year during the week of July 14, thousands of pilgrims come for the Feast of Shenouda, honoring the monastery's fifth-century founding saint. The nearby **Red Monastery** (Deir al-Ahmar), built of red brick, was founded by St. Bishoi, a reformed robber and follower of St. Shenouda.

Just across the Nile from Sohag is the small town of **Akhmim,** center of an ancient weaving tradition. Legend has it that pharaohs were buried in shrouds of Akhmim silk. The lustrous vestments of early Coptic Christians (seen in the Coptic Museum in Cairo; see p. 115) also came from here. Still produced, Akhmim cloth remains highly prized and extremely expensive when it can be found. It is best to acquire it directly from the weavers' workshops. The exquisite material makes for one of the most splendid buys in Egypt.

Akhmim also has a small **open-air museum** with a 34-foot-high (10 m) standing statue of Merit-Amun, daughter of Ramses II. ∎

Sohag
◬ 211 B2

Local children receive a Christian education at the ancient Coptic White Monastery.

Abydos

As modern Muslims all aspire to visit Mecca at least once in their lifetime, so ancient Egyptians tried to make a pilgrimage to Abydos, cult center of the god Osiris. Those who couldn't make it while living were often brought here posthumously for burial, because the Egyptians believed that the entrance to the underworld lay in the desert hills just west of this site.

Carved deities decorate the entrances to the seven shrines in the Temple of Seti I.

Abydos

🔺 211 C1

✉ Al-Araba al-Madfuna

💲 $$

Many Egyptian pharaohs constructed cenotaphs at Abydos because of its associations with the afterlife. It once covered a huge area, with various temple complexes, necropolises, and a town centered upon the great Temple of Osiris, built by Seti I. Though it is seldom visited since the troubles began in the early 1990s, Abydos can easily be seen in a day trip from Luxor, perhaps with a visit to Dendara temple (see pp. 224–226) on the way. A taxi for the whole day should cost about $30 to $40, and the tourist office in Luxor can help with the arrangements.

The site of Abydos is 6 miles (10 km) west of the village of Al-Balyana, which lies on the main Nile-side highway. From here a well-surfaced road leads through fields of sugarcane to another small hamlet on the edge of the ruins, Al-Araba al-Madfuna, .

Although there are the remains of several complexes, the most complete, and the one that everyone has been coming to see since its discovery about 1830, is the **Temple of Seti I.** The second pharaoh of the 19th dynasty, Seti I (*R.*1294–1279 B.C.) came to power about 30 years after the collapse of Akhenaten's

Amarna regime (see pp. 214–217). Seti was eager to erase all traces of this heretical interlude, and his reign was characterized by a return to Old Kingdom styles of art, while politically he strove to restore stability and recover lost territories. In all this, he was largely successful, laying the foundations for a new pharaonic golden age presided over by his son and successor, Ramses II. In fact, it was Ramses who largely completed the Abydos temple.

As the structure survives today, the entrance pylon and first and second forecourts are almost entirely gone, and the temple is entered via a portico leading straight into the hypostyle hall. The first part of this hall was completed following Seti's death, as most of the reliefs depict Ramses II in the presence of various gods and goddesses. As you penetrate deeper within the inner hypostyle hall, the sunken reliefs are noticeably finer—in fact, they are regarded as some of the most remarkable to be found in Egypt. These were executed during the reign of Seti and, again, depict the pharaoh in the presence of deities, notably Osiris, lord of the underworld, and Horus.

Beyond the column-filled halls are seven shrines devoted, from left to right, to Seti himself, Ptah, Re-Harakhte, Amun-Re, Osiris, Isis, and Horus. It is unusual to have so many gods and goddesses honored in one temple, but it is thought that the aim was to reconfirm faith in the pre-Amarna gods. More fine reliefs cover the walls of the shrines, many retaining much of their original coloring. False doors are painted on the back wall of each shrine, apart from that of Osiris, which has a real door leading through to a suite of inner sanctuaries.

From the inner hypostyle hall, a corridor goes to a southern wing. On one side of this corridor the walls have a particularly fine relief of Seti and his son—Ramses II—lassoing a bull, while opposite is what is known as the "kings' list." Beginning with Menes, the traditional founder of Egypt, reliefs list 34 pharaohs in roughly chronological order, ending with Seti. Editing deleted undesirables such as Hatshepsut (see pp. 268–270) and Akhenaten and his heirs (see pp. 214–217).

INSIDER TIP:

Consider visiting some of the ancient temples after dark. You escape the heat of the day that way, there are fewer people, and photos of the buildings after sundown are more dramatic.

—TAYLOR KENNEDY
National Geographic photographer

Behind the temple proper is an unusual structure known as the Osireion, a cenotaph constructed by Seti I. Unfortunately, the Osireion is half buried and mostly inaccessible, as it is surrounded by stagnant water. However, the sloping entrance tunnel has a splendid, spooky atmosphere. ∎

Dendara

Although it belongs to a time long after the era of the great pharaohs had passed, the Greco-Roman Temple of Hathor at Dendara offers a fantastic ancient Egyptian experience. It is one of the very few temples that remains almost completely intact, with a massive stone roof, dark chambers, underground passages, and towering columns topped by Hathor-headed capitals.

Despite lacking a main entrance pylon, the facade of the Temple of Hathor at Dendara is still impressive.

Dendara

 211 C1

✉ 3 miles (5 km) W of Qena

💲 $$

The temple stands just outside the town of Qena, a small agricultural center with the dubious distinction of possessing an air base that acted as a staging post for the abortive mission to rescue the U.S. hostages from Iran in 1980. The easiest way to visit is a day trip from Luxor, just over 35 miles (56 km) to the south. If you get an early start, you can also squeeze in a few hours at Abydos (see pp. 222–223).

Hathor, the goddess of pleasure and love, is usually represented as a cow, or as a woman with a cow's head or ears, or as a woman whose headdress is a sun disk fixed between the horns of a cow. According to mythology, she first suckled Horus, then later became his wife, and their union produced the minor god Ihy. She was identified by the Greeks with Aphrodite.

Shrines to Hathor were built on this site as early as Old Kingdom times (2686–2181 B.C.), but the existing temple is Greco-Roman and dates from between

125 B.C. and A.D. 60. As foreign rulers, the Greco-Romans were eager to emphasize dedication to Egypt's gods and hence a legitimacy to the throne, so the design of this place emulates exactly that of temples gone before.

INSIDER TIP:

Look out for figures of Cleopatra and Caesarion, her son by Julius Caesar, on the temple's exterior back wall.

—NEIL HEWISON
American University in Cairo Press

Visiting the Temple

As at Abydos, the temple lacks its entry pylons, and instead entry is directly into the **hypostyle hall.** Dating from the first century A.D. and raised by the Roman emperor Tiberius, the hall has 24 columns, each with a four-sided capital carved with the face of the cow-eared goddess. The ceiling of the hall has kept much of its original coloring and represents a chart of the heavens, including the signs of the zodiac (which were introduced by the Romans) and the sky-goddess Nut and other deities sailing their solar boats across the cosmos. Reliefs on the walls show Roman emperors making offerings to Egyptian gods.

This great hall leads through to the smaller, and earlier, **Hall of Appearances,** so called because it is here that the statue of the goddess "appeared" for religious ceremonies and processions. Beyond is the **Hall of Offerings,** with a list of offerings depicted on one of the walls. Straight ahead is the enclosed area of the **Sanctuary,** the most sacred part of the temple, into which only the pharaoh and high priests could enter. It housed Hathor's statue and ceremonial bark (boat). Once a year these were carried in procession to the river, placed on a boat, and sailed up to the temple at Edfu (see pp. 289–290) for a conjugal reunion with Horus. Ancient Egyptians celebrated in a two-week festival by imitating the gods and getting drunk.

Around the sanctuary is a series of dimly lit side chapels (it is a good idea to bring a flashlight),

Nag Hammadi & the Gnostic Gospels

In 1945, one of the most important collections of manuscripts from the early Christian period was discovered in Nag Hammadi, 30 miles (48 km) west of Dendara. The collection was a group of 50 Gnostic texts from the 2nd century A.D. Gnosticism, an offshoot of early Christianity that emphasized mysticism and esoteric knowledge, had been suppressed early on. But the discovery and translation of these texts, including the Gospel of Thomas and the Gospel of Philip, paint a different vision of creation and salvation. There isn't much to see in Nag Hammadi town now, but its impact on the study of early Christianity has been enormous.

The columns at Dendara were badly damaged by early Christians who attempted to obliterate the faces of the goddess Hathor.

some of which are home to colonies of bats. After exploring the ground level of the temple, go up to the roof—stairways ascend on either side of the Hall of Offerings. Reliefs on the stairs illustrate the New Year procession, when Hathor's statue was carried up to the roof at dawn. On the north are twin chapels, one of which contains a plaster cast of the famous Dendara ceiling; the original was removed by Napoleon's expedition in the early 19th century and now graces the Louvre in Paris. Views of the surrounding countryside from the roof are magnificent.

It is also worth walking around the outside of the temple. On the rear wall, two defaced reliefs of Cleopatra and her son, Caesarion (the outermost figures), feature in a procession of deities. There are also several buildings, now largely ruined. Closest to the main gate is a Roman birth house, or *mammisi,* dedicated to the god Horus. It has beautiful carvings on the wall facing the temple, with tiny figures of Bes, the dwarf god of fertility, on the capitals of the columns. ■

Boasting the greatest concentration of pharaonic monuments anywhere in Egypt, most notably the temple complex at Karnak, one of the most awe-inspiring pieces of architecture ever built

Luxor

Introduction & Map   228–229

Luxor Town   230–241

Experience: Sailing to Luxor's Banana Island   233

Feature: Making Mummies   238–239

Karnak   242–249

Exploring the West Bank   250–270

Cycling the West Bank   252–253

Feature: Guardians & Thieves   264–265

Experience: Take a Hot-Air Balloon Ride over Luxor   268

Valley of the Kings   271–284

Feature: Building a Royal Tomb   274–275

Feature: Bringing Egyptology Up To Date   278–279

Hotels & Restaurants in Luxor   368–370

The face of Queen Nefertari

Luxor

The modern town exists as little more than a support system for the millions of visitors who descend each year, drawn by the fabulous array of antiquities. Tourism accounts for about 85 percent of the local economy, so present-day inhabitants of Luxor are just as much in thrall to the temples and tombs as their ancient ancestors were.

At the height of its power, Thebes had a population of nearly one million. Vast manpower, combined with immense wealth brought in by foreign conquests, allowed the Thebans to build elaborate places of worship for their local god Amun, whom they united with the sun god Re to worship as Amun-Re. Built on the east bank of the Nile, these temples greeted the rising sun each day. The west bank was the land of the dead, where the sun set and the pharaohs, deified by their subjects as living gods, built funerary monuments.

Thebes was preeminent for 500 glorious years until the end of the New Kingdom and the last of the Ramses (1069 B.C.), after which power returned to Memphis in the north. The city persisted during Greco-Roman times, but by the time the Arabs conquered Egypt in the seventh century, it had been forgotten. Not until Napoleon's 18th-century expedition to Egypt

NOT TO BE MISSED:

Winter Palace Hotel, Luxor's elegant grand hotel   **230**

Luxor Temple   **233–237**

Luxor Museum, possibly the best museum in the country   **240–241**

Karnak   **242–249**

The Colossi of Memnon   **251**

Medinat Habu   **254–256**

Ramesseum, the mortuary temple of Ramses II   **262–263**

Temple of Hatshepsut   **268–270**

Valley of the Kings   **271–284**

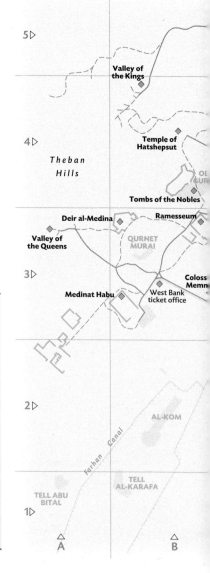

were the temples rediscovered and identified as the ancient city of Thebes, known through classical accounts. Arab villagers who lived among the sand-covered ruins called this Al-Uqsor (the Palaces), a name Europeans corrupted to Luxor.

By the mid-19th century, the first cruisers were already on the Nile, as Luxor became a must for adventurous travelers. "[Luxor] is a place where one could stay a very long time and in a perpetual state of astonishment," wrote Gustave Flaubert, French author, in 1850 in a letter home. Published accounts spread the word, and from the 1860s onward Luxor has welcomed eager tourists. ∎

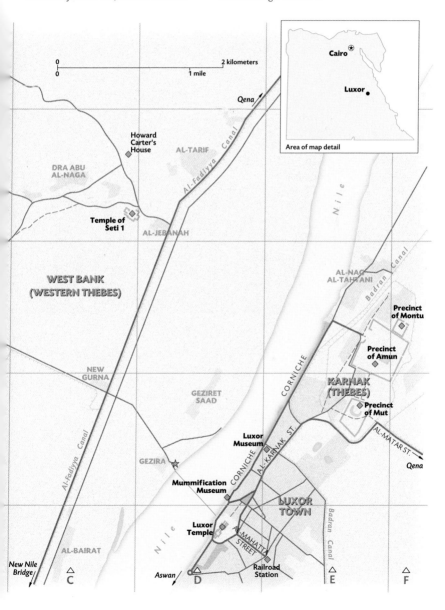

Luxor Town

Once the terrific heat of the day has passed, Luxor's Nile-side boulevard, the Corniche, is the perfect place for an evening stroll. Horse-drawn carriages canter by on one side, riverboats churn the water on the other, and as the sun drops spectacularly behind the Theban Hills to the west, lights sparkle in the trees.

Luxor's fabled Winter Palace, built in 1886, evokes British Colonial charm on the Nile.

Luxor
- 📍 211 E1/E2/ D1/D2

Visitor information
- ✉ Tourist Bazaar, Al-Karnak St.
- ☎ 095/237 2215
- 🕑 Closed Fri p.m.

It all has a very Victorian air, one that is majestically reinforced by the **Winter Palace Hotel** (see p. 368). Built in the 1880s, when long-distance travel was the preserve of the wealthy, this appropriately named establishment provided a palatial retreat for aristocrats and royalty sitting out harsh northern European winters in the balmy climes of southern Egypt. In 1922 the hotel's guests were the first to learn of Howard Carter's discovery of the tomb of Tutankhamun via a posting on the bulletin board. If you want to read up on Carter's find, then **Aboudi's Bookshop** in the Tourist Bazaar, a two-minute walk north of the Winter Palace, has an unsurpassed selection of titles on all things Egypt-related. Luxor's tourist office is housed in the same complex.

Continue up the Corniche and you reach **Luxor Temple** (see pp. 233–237). Across the road from the temple ticket office is the wharf for the local ferry over to the West Bank. Curving inland of the temple is Al-Karnak Street, the town's main thoroughfare. At its southern end is the **Luxor Wena Hotel,** another of the town's grand old places (in fact, Luxor's oldest hotel), but now sadly run down and dilapidated.

The intersection of Al-Karnak Street and Al-Mahatta Street (Station Street, because of the railroad station at its eastern end) marks the center of town. Most of the stores are devoted to souvenirs, but there is nothing here that

INSIDER TIP:

Take the overnight train from Cairo to Luxor. It's fun and a great experience. You pay in U.S. dollars.

—PEARCE CREASMAN
National Geographic field researcher

can't be found cheaper in Cairo. The same goes for the disappointing *souq,* or bazaar, just north of the mosque on Karnak Street. There is another mosque just a short walk farther north, beside a small green triangle of parkland, and standing next to it you can look right along the length of the **Avenue of Sphinxes** to the main pylon of Luxor Temple.

Immediately to the west is a narrow side street with a curbside canopy offering shelter from the sun for the horses that draw the tourist carriages. The canopy has been erected by the Brooke Animal Hospital *(tel 02/364 9312),* an offshoot of a clinic begun by an English woman, Dorothy Brooke, in Cairo in 1934 called

the Hospital for Old Warhorses. There are now several of these Brooke hospitals throughout Egypt providing free veterinary treatment for the country's much abused horses and donkeys.

At the point where this side street joins the Corniche is the **Mummification Museum** (see p. 239). You can continue north up the Corniche past a series of modern hotels, which are low-rise enough not to cause offense. One or two have gardens out front where it is possible for non-residents to sit and have a cold drink. Farther along is the **Luxor Museum** (see pp. 240–241), and on beyond that Chicago House *(tel 095/237 2525),* the Egyptian

Mummification Museum

🅰 229 D2
& 232
✉ The Corniche, opposite Mina Palace Hotel
☎ 095/238 1501
🕐 Closed 1–4 p.m.
💲 $$

A Word on Antiquities

Anyone claiming to sell you an antiquity in Luxor is almost certainly trying to pull a fast one on you. Salesmen on the West Bank may claim that a stone figurine they're trying to sell you is ancient, but most likely it's just painted plaster (which will break when dropped). There is a long tradition of tomb-looting in Luxor—it was a major source of income for some local families in the 19th century—but the Egyptian government takes a very dim view of antiquities smuggling. Please do your part by not encouraging a market for ancient objects—real or fake.

Luxor Temple

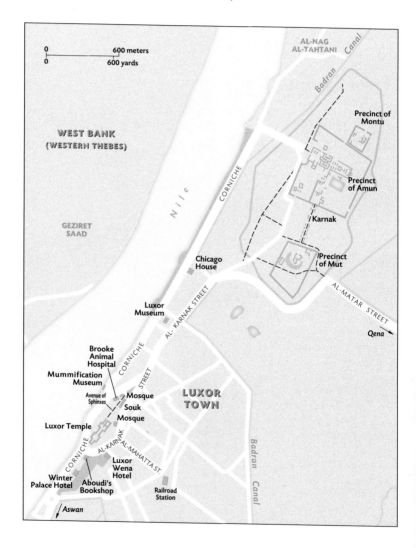

229 D1
& 232

✉ The Corniche

💲 $$ by day, $ by
night

base of the highly respected Oriental Institute of the University of Chicago, which has been working on the pharaonic sites here since 1924.

From Chicago House, it is only a walk of perhaps another five minutes or so, north along the Corniche alongside the Nile, to reach the entrance to the vast temple complex of **Karnak** (see pp. 242–249), the greatest of all the pharaonic temples.

An attractive alternative to walking around town is to ride in a horse-drawn carriage (known locally as a calèche). Dozens of these cruise the main streets of town beginning in the early hours of morning. Make sure you agree a price with the driver before you start the ride.

0 | 600 meters
0 | 600 yards

AL-NAG
AL-TAHTANI   Canal

Badran

Precinct of
Montu

WEST BANK
(WESTERN THEBES)

CORNICHE

Nile

Precinct
of Amun

GEZIRET
SAAD

Karnak

Chicago
House

Precinct
of Mut

AL-MATAR STREET

Luxor
Museum

AL-KARNAK STREET

Qena

Brooke
Animal
Hospital

CORNICHE

Mummification
Museum

STREET

Avenue of
Sphinxes

Mosque

LUXOR
TOWN

Souk

Mosque

Luxor Temple

CORNICHE

AL-KARNAK

AL-MAHATTA ST.

Luxor
Wena
Hotel

Badran Canal

Winter
Palace Hotel

Aboudi's
Bookshop

Railroad
Station

Aswan

A guardian leans against a sphinx, part of the avenue leading to the temple.

Luxor Temple

Set beside the Nile and surrounded by the modern town, Luxor Temple is one of the most beguiling of all Egypt's pharaonic monuments. Compact and simple in plan, it can be visited in an hour, but the wealth of reliefs and serenity of the site make it worth spending far longer. To catch it at its most atmospheric, visit at night when dramatic lighting brings the place to life.

Just as the temple today lies at the center of the modern town of Luxor, in pharaonic times it sat at the heart of the capital Thebes. Built on the site of earlier places of worship, it was raised by Amenhotep III (*R.*1390–1352 B.C.), the 18th dynasty "sun king," whose lengthy reign represented the zenith of ancient Egypt's power and prestige. Later he would build an even greater temple on the West Bank, possibly the greatest ever built in Egypt, but that has vanished apart from two lone guardians: enormous seated statues of Amenhotep himself (see p. 251).

Luxor Temple owes its excellent state of preservation to two factors: It was covered by sand,

---

EXPERIENCE:
Sailing to Luxor's Banana Island

If you have a free afternoon in Luxor, hire a felucca and sail to Banana Island (Gezirat al-Mawz), about 3 miles (5 km) south of the city. Depending on your willingness to haggle with the captain, a felucca trip usually costs between 40LE and 60LE per hour.

Banana Island is, in fact, a peninsula located on the west side of the Nile. The area is covered both in orange trees and, unsurprisingly, with shady banana groves, which makes it a pleasant place to stroll and sample the produce before heading back to town.

and the village of Luxor was built on top of it. Vacationing French writer Gustave Flaubert, visiting in 1850, described houses built among the capitals (the columns buried below) and chickens and pigeons nesting in the great stone lotus leaves. Excavation work, begun in 1885 and still ongoing, removed the sand and the village and revealed the temple.

It is approached by an **Avenue of Sphinxes,** which originally went all the way to Karnak, 2 miles (3 km) to the north. Traveling around Luxor today, you keep finding the groove of this avenue between modern buildings, along with bits of half-forgotten, stray statuary. In the temple, the sphinxes come to a halt before the enormous **first pylon.** This is the

work of Ramses II, ancient Egypt's other great builder-pharaoh.

Temples were constantly built and rebuilt (Karnak being the prime example), and a hundred years after the death of Amenhotep III, his monument was expanded—and virtually usurped

INSIDER TIP:

After making your way to the temple's central sanctuary at the far end, head out one of the west-side doorways and walk back north along the exterior, decorated with battle scenes of Ramses II.

—CHIP ROSSETTI
National Geographic contributor

in the process—by his distant successor. It is Ramses II who is depicted on the pylon's reliefs, slaying Hittite foes at the Battle of Kaddesh. The pylon was originally fronted by six colossal statues of Ramses II, two seated and four standing, and two obelisks. Two statues and one obelisk were carried off to Paris, where the latter now stands in the Place de la Concorde. "How bored it must be.... How it must miss its Nile," commented Flaubert.

Beyond the pylon is another addition, the **Great Court of Ramses II,** surrounded by two rows of papyrus-bud columns. Perched high in one corner, on top of the bricked-up colonnade, is the 13th-century A.D. **Mosque of**

KEY TO SITE PLAN

Luxor

1 Avenue of Sphinxes
2 Bark Shrine
3 First pylon
4 Mosque of Abu al-Haggag
5 Great Court of Ramses II
6 Grand processional colonnade
7 Sun Court of Amenhotep III
8 Hypostyle hall
9 Bark Shrine
10 Central sanctuary

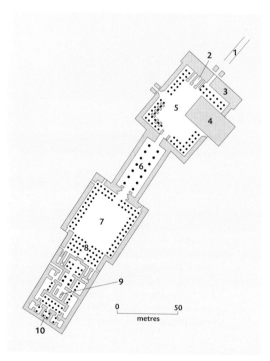

0   50
metres

The Temple of Luxor is made more dramatic at night by floodlighting.

Abu al-Haggag, which the people of Luxor demanded be left intact when archaeologists cleared their village from the temple precincts. Dedicated to a local holy man, the mosque still plays an important role in local life, maintaining an unbroken tradition of worship on this site that stretches back more than 3,000 years.

If you happen to be in Egypt at the right time, it is well worth aiming to be in Luxor for the *moulid* (festival) of Abu al-Haggag, which is one of the biggest local events of the year. During the raucous festivities, gigantic floats move through the densely packed streets, while the crowds are entertained by musicians, dancers, and horse racing. A giant boat is also paraded around town in a curious echo across the ages of the pharaonic Opet Festival (see p. 236). The exact date of the moulid, which lasts two days, varies from year to year, but it is usually held around two weeks before the beginning of Ramadan.

In the western corner of the

Opet Festival

Amun, one of the gods of creation, was the most important deity of Thebes. Once each year, the priests of his great temple at Karnak carried the images of Amun and the other two gods in the local triad—Amun's wife, the war goddess Mut, and their son, the moon god Khonsu—in the gods' portable barks to Luxor Temple for the Opet Festival, a celebration marking the annual flooding of the Nile. On arrival, the gods were placed in their special shrine and the celebrations began. Later, the entourage traveled back on the river, escorted by the elaborate barge of the pharaoh himself.

court is a small bark shrine with triple chapels dedicated to Amun, Mut, and Khonsu for use in the Opet Festival celebrations. Also look for the diminutive statue of a shapely woman in a diaphanous gown at the foot of one of the colossal statues of Ramses; this is his wife, Nefertari, whose exquisitely decorated tomb is one of the highlights of a visit to the West Bank (see pp. 260–262).

The temple as built by Amenhotep III begins with his **grand processional colonnade.** Its 14 columns are almost 65 feet (20 m) high and probably inspired the even more imposing Great Hypostyle Hall at Karnak (see p. 246). Unfinished at the time of the pharaoh's death, the hall was completed by his grandson Tutankhamun, who added the outer walls, with their scenes of the Opet Festival. On the right-hand side is the floating procession from Karnak to Luxor (look for the fattened sacrificial bulls that are being led by shaven-headed priests), while on the left-hand side is the better-preserved return to Karnak.

Highlight of the temple is the paved open-air **Sun Court of Amenhotep III,** enclosed on three sides by colonnades of perfectly proportioned lotus columns. The Corniche passes close by at this point, and the traffic is visible through the columns as flashes of color, with an added soundtrack of horn beeps and engine noise. It has the effect of making the court seem part of the modern town, like some small Italian piazza.

Evenings are an especially beautiful time to be here, when the columns may be lit orange against deep turquoise skies, and bats flit past overhead.

The fantastic cache of statuary, now displayed at the Luxor Museum (see pp. 240–241), was discovered in 1989 in a pit under the court. On the south side of the court is the **hypostyle hall,** with four rows of eight columns, leading through to an antechamber and the temple's roofed inner sanctuaries. Roman legionaries sealed the entrance to the inner temple and enclosed the whole complex in a fortified encampment sometime between the fourth and sixth centuries A.D. It is the remains of this fortress—

in the form of furrows and the foundations of walls—that you see scarring the grassy area around the perimeter of the temple. The Ro-

INSIDER TIP:

Luxor was a living temple, full of life and ceremony. Think of it as bustling with the energy of the pharaoh's cosmos.

—KEN GARRETT
National Geographic photographer

mans also transformed the entrance to the inner temple into a niche, flanked by Corinthian columns, that served as a shrine to the imperial cult. Here, local Christians were offered a choice between obeisance or martyrdom. Worn paintings of Roman emperors are still visible near the top of the wall.

The niche-shrine is now punctured by an off-center doorway opening to a small, square, second antechamber. This leads through to the **Bark Shrine,** rebuilt by Alexander the Great, who is depicted on the walls of the chamber (he is the one with the bare chest and angular skirt) before the god Amun (with raised flail and towering crown).

The final chamber is the "holy of holies," the oldest part of the temple, the **central sanctuary** where the image of Amun was kept. However, the statue of the god is long gone and only the base remains here.

(continued on p. 240)

Luxor Temple, the ancient site of Thebes. A portion of the Mosque of Abu al-Haggag is visible beyond the colonnade near the entrance pylon.

Making Mummies

Originally the ancient Egyptians buried their dead directly into the sand, where the hot, dry conditions allowed the fluids responsible for decomposition to drain away, at the same time preserving the soft tissue of skin, hair, and nails. As burial practices became more elaborate for the wealthy, the simple hollow in the sand was replaced with a bench-shaped superstructure, a *mastaba*, over a brick-lined burial chamber. Here the body lay in a wooden coffin, so the natural preservation once achieved by the dry sand had to be replaced with artificial techniques.

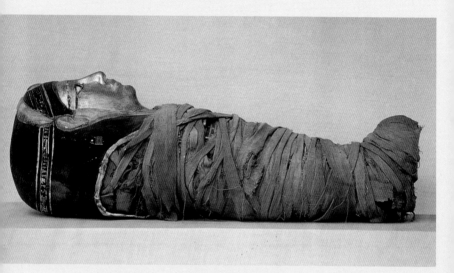

As well as royalty, nobles and their children were mummified.

Mummification practices became increasingly sophisticated over time, with recent excavations indicating that certain techniques were in use as early as 3400 B.C. These gradually developed during the Old Kingdom period (2686–2181 B.C.), and although initially restricted to royalty, mummification was gradually extended through all ranks of nobles.

Mummification developed into a major industry, employing embalmers, funerary priests, and purveyors of the necessary materials. Once the body had been handed over by the family, it would be washed and placed on a large embalming table. The embalmers would loosen the brain with a fine metal probe inserted through the back of the nose. Then they made

an incision on the lower left side of the body with an obsidian blade and all internal organs were removed and treated separately prior to burial inside the four canopic jars. Only the heart—considered the seat of wisdom—and the difficult-to-reach kidneys were left intact.

The eviscerated body was then covered with a great pile of dry natron salt for 40 days in order to dry it out. It was then washed and the skin anointed with a range of oils, spices, and resins. The embalmers wrapped the mummified body in layers of linen, and priests recited the incantations needed to activate the amulets placed within the wrappings.

The standard mummification process took 70 days; the linen-wrapped mummy

Mummification Museum

This small riverside museum is devoted to Egyptian burial practices, although the emphasis is not on the actual bodies. Below street level in the Corniche embankment, the museum is a little difficult to spot; it is opposite the Mina Palace Hotel *(tel 095/238 1502, closed 1 p.m.–4 p.m.).* Inside the dimly lit hall, a series of explanatory wall charts lead into the exhibits. While nicely designed, they are pretty skimpy on information, leaving out all the gruesome bits that everybody really wants to know about.

There is one mummy on display, that of Masaharti, a high priest of Amun-Re of the 21st dynasty (tenth century B.C.). Perhaps chosen because of his remarkable state of preservation, Masaharti has hair and a beard, and peacefully composed features that give the impression of sleep. The museum also has a cache of mummified animals (including a ram, cat, fish, and baboon), but otherwise the exhibits concentrate on the implements and materials used in the mummification process. No pictures are needed to cause unease at the sight of the instruments used to scrape the brain out of the skull and for the disemboweling of the body. Another cabinet contains many of the materials necessary for mummification, such as natron salts, bitumen, sawdust, and linen. There are also canopic jars, some beautiful painted coffin lids, and a statue of the jackal-headed god, Anubis, who was patron of embalmers and the guardian of cemeteries.

It is a modest collection, and probably takes no more than half an hour to visit. Afterward, visit the museum café with an open-air Nile-side terrace offering uninterrupted views across to the West Bank.

---

placed inside its wooden coffin was then ready for the funeral. Priests, ceremonial dancers, mourners, and servants carrying the funerary equipment went in procession to the tomb. Setting the coffin upright by the tomb, the priest performed the "Opening of the Mouth" ceremony in order to reawaken the soul and restore the senses, which were then sated with offerings of incense, flowers, choice cuts of meat, and wine. The mummy was finally laid to rest in its tomb, surrounded by items ranging from those used in daily life to those made specifically for burial.

Mummification ended with the spread of Christianity in the fourth century A.D., although some mummies have been found clutching crosses. Most of the mummies in museum collections today originated in the Luxor area and the royal necropolises centered on the Valley of the Kings (see pp. 271–284). The other major burial ground was Saqqara (see pp. 144–147), where caches of mummies are still being discovered.

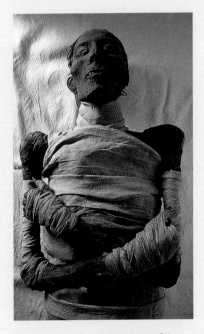

A mummy in the Egyptian Museum at Cairo

Luxor Museum

This is arguably the best museum in Egypt, with its collection of ancient Egyptian funerary items and statues found in and around Luxor. It contains just a fraction of the antiquities displayed at Cairo's Egyptian Museum (see pp. 68–76), but that is to its advantage. The treasures here are thoughtfully displayed in an attractively lit and air-conditioned environment, and—for a change—everything on display is well labeled.

Entrance is via an annex, added in 2004 and dedicated to the great warrior pharaohs of the 18th and 19th dynasties (see p. 53). Chronologically, the exhibition begins with the reign of Kahmose, the last king of the 17th dynasty, who recorded a famous victory over northern invaders, the Hyskos. This set the stage for a golden age of Ancient Egyptian history that commenced with the reign of Ahmose I, whose mummy is displayed here in a side room, wrapped in its linen shroud and surrounded by personal weapons. In another side room is a mummy thought to be that of Ramses I, recently returned by the U.S. city of Atlanta, Georgia, after years of languishing unnoticed in a provincial museum. An informative film provides background context to the period and exhibits.

The rest of the museum is a collection of prize finds from all different eras. A highlight is the gallery containing 16 of 24 mostly life-size statues discovered by chance while archaeologists were collecting earth samples at Luxor Temple in 1989. Pride of the find is an 8-foot-tall (2.5 m) red quartzite statue of the temple's builder, Amenhotep III, which, according to eminent Egyptologist George Hart

Something of a rarity in Egypt, the exhibits at Luxor Museum are beautifully lit and displayed, and well labeled.

of the British Museum, "for its serene beauty is unrivaled among the thousands of sculptures surviving from ancient Egypt." Beside the entrance to this gallery is an impressively massive head of the same pharaoh, part of a colossus that belonged to his lost funerary temple on the West Bank (see p. 251).

Around the corner in the main hall is a touching life-size calcite dyad of the crocodile god Sobek, with his arm resting paternally around a young Amenhotep III's shoulders. Two fat crocodiles contentedly basking on the block behind are pure Disney. Anyone who has previously found ancient Egyptian sculpture rigid and obsessed with death has some pleasant reevaluating to do.

The upper floor houses the museum's smaller pieces. There are a few items from the tomb of Tutankhamun, including sandals, arrows, bronze rosettes that were attached to the pall that covered the sarcophagus, and two model funerary barks, but this is just small fry—all the good stuff from this historic haul is to be found at the Egyptian Museum in Cairo.

Instead, the stand-out items on the upper floor are all related to the rule of **Akhenaten** (here called Amenhotep IV), second son and successor of Amenhotep III, who turned the world of ancient Egypt on its head (see pp. 214–217). His distinctive, almost alien features are immediately identifiable in three sandstone heads hung around the gallery. But most impressive of all is a reconstructed wall of painted sandstone blocks (talatat), which comes from one

Sa'idis

Upper Egypt (the Sa'id in Arabic) is home to the Sa'idis, the rural inhabitants along the Nile, far from the sophisticated big city of Cairo and the rich agricultural land of the Delta. In Egypt, they have the reputation of being proud and aloof. They also are often (unfairly) portrayed as country rubes. There are occasional news reports of Hatfield-and-McCoy-style family feuds between Sa'idi clans, which only reinforce stereotypes about them in Cairo. By any account, however, Sa'idis face significant challenges, such as poverty and the lack of jobs, which causes many of them to move to Cairo in search of work.

of the temples erected at Karnak by Akhenaten. These blocks, along with thousands of others, were discovered dismantled and buried away as infill within one of the great pylons—an attempt by a later pharaoh to obliterate evidence of Akhenaten and his heretical ways. Pieced together like some giant jigsaw by archaeologists, the blocks formed a wall, the greater part of which depicts in brightly colored relief incidents of ancient Egyptian daily life. Toward the left are scenes involving the king worshiping the sun god, Aten, standing beneath its rays, each of which ends in a tiny hand holding an *ankh* (the ancient Egyptian symbol of life). ∎

Luxor Museum

- 🄰 229 E2
- & 232
- ✉ The Corniche
- ☎ 095/237 0569
- 🕐 Open 9 a.m.– 9 p.m. (winter); 9 a.m.–1 p.m., 5 p.m.–10 p.m. (summer)
- 💲 $$. Camera $, video camera $$$

Karnak

To the ancient Egyptians, Karnak was known as Ipet-Isut, The Most Perfect of Places, and you can see why. Despite being in ruins, it remains spectacular. Possibly the largest temple complex ever built anywhere, it grew in stages over 1,500 years, added to by successive generations of pharaohs, and the resulting collection of sanctuaries, kiosks, pylons, and obelisks acts as a vast open-air archive of history set in stone.

During the New Kingdom period of glory from 1550 to 1069 B.C., Thebes was the all-powerful capital of Egypt, and Karnak was its heart. More than just a place of worship, it was the residence of the pharaohs, the center of administration, a vastly wealthy treasury, and the keystone of the economy, owning vast tracts of land and employing tens of thousands of workers. Ordinary folk were not allowed in its precincts, only the priests and royal retinue entered it.

The Karnak complex had three compounds. The main precinct, dedicated to Amun, lay at the center, dominated by the Great Temple of Amun and containing a large sacred lake. This was the main place of worship of the Theban triad of gods (Amun-Re, Mut, and Khonsu). Directly to the south was the precinct of Amun's consort, Mut, linked to the main temple by an avenue of ram-headed sphinxes. To the north was the precinct of the old Theban falcon god, Montu.

Although most of this vast complex was the work of New Kingdom rulers, including notably Hatshepsut, Tuthmose III, Seti I, and Ramses II, the original sanctuary of the Great Temple of Amun was built during the Middle Kingdom period (circa 1900 B.C.). Successive pharaohs expanded out from this core, with the first pylon—the present imposing

Stripped of its color, Karnak's Great Hypostyle Hall still feels like a hall of the gods.

Practicalities

The site of Karnak lies about a mile and a half (2.4 km) south of the modern center of Luxor. It is quite possible to walk there down the Corniche, but as you will be on your feet exploring over the next few hours, it may be preferable to make the trip in a taxi or a calèche. The site covers 247 acres (100 ha), so you need at least half a day just to walk around the many precincts. Visitors are first admitted at 6 a.m., and an early start beats the heat; from about 7 a.m. on the place gets very busy with tour groups. It is much quieter in the afternoon, but the downside is the intense heat, and there is little shade. If you have the time, consider visiting during the day, then returning in the evening for the sound-and-light show (see p. 246).

entrance to the site—dating from as late as circa 370 B.C. In the post-pharaonic age the Ptolemies, Romans, and early Christians all also left their mark. When visiting today, the deeper into the complex you venture, the farther back in time you go.

Since Egyptology became a science, Karnak has been subject

INSIDER TIP:

Consider visiting the temples in the early afternoon. You avoid groups from the morning bus convoys and, in the late afternoon, Nile cruise ships.

—DR. JOEL D. IRISH
National Geographic field researcher

to numerous excavations, and various projects are still ongoing. There have been major finds here, including an impressive haul of royal statuary (most now in the Egyptian Museum in Cairo; see pp. 68–76) uncovered in 1903, but today most of the efforts of the archaeologists are concentrated on conserving and systematically restoring the standing monuments.

Precinct of Amun

For most visitors, the Precinct of Amun *is* Karnak. Even without the neighboring complexes devoted to Mut and Montu, it completely dwarfs anything else in Egypt. The precinct has a complicated plan, combining two axes: north-south and east-west. East-west is the main axis, and the easiest way to explore is to stick to this. If you still feel able to take in more once you have reached the far end, you can walk back via the Sacred Lake and explore north-south.

A canal once connected the Amun precinct with the Nile, to allow for the passage of the sacred barks (see p. 236). Ramses II built a quay beside the canal, and it is this quay—flanked by a short processional avenue of ram-headed sphinxes, each with a statue of the king between its paws—that forms the impressive approach to the **first pylon** and entrance. Massive as it is, the pylon is unfinished,

Karnak

- 229 E2 & 232
- The Corniche
- $$. Open-air museum $ (ticket must be bought outside). Sound-and-light show $$$

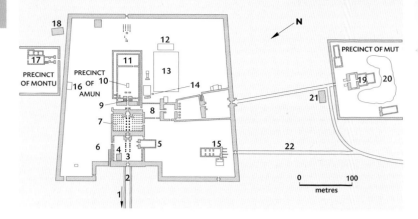

N

PRECINCT OF MUT

PRECINCT OF MONTU

PRECINCT OF AMUN

0   100
metres

KEY TO SITE PLAN

Karnak

1 To ticket office
2 Avenue of Sphinxes
3 Great Court
4 Shrine of Seti II
5 Temple of Ramses III
6 Open-air museum
7 Great Hypostyle Hall
8 Cachette Court
9 Obelisks of Hatshepsut
10 Sacred Bark Shrine
11 Festival Temple of Tuthmose III
12 Sound-and-light grandstand
13 Sacred Lake
14 Café
15 Temple of Khonsu
16 Temple of Ptah
17 Temple of Montu
18 Temple of Tuthmose 1
19 Temple of Mut
20 Sacred Lake
21 Bark station of Tuthmose III and Hatshepsut
22 Route of Avenue of Sphinxes to Luxor Temple

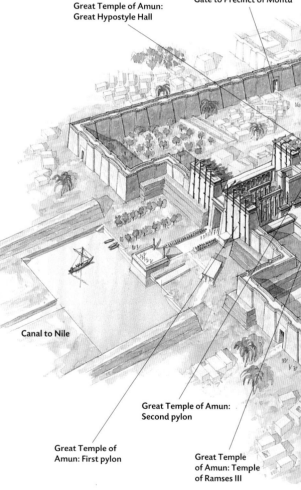

Great Temple of Amun: Great Hypostyle Hall

Gate to Precinct of Montu

Canal to Nile

Great Temple of Amun: Second pylon

Great Temple of Amun: First pylon

Great Temple of Amun: Temple of Ramses III

as you can see by the unequal heights of the two sides. If you stand close to the gate, you can make out an inscription left by Napoleon's expedition (see p. 38) high up on the right-hand jamb of the gate.

Beyond is the **Great Court** (everything at Karnak is "great")

of the Amun Temple, which contains a real grab-bag of ancient remains. To the left is the **Shrine of Seti II,** composed of a trio of small chapels for the sacred barks of Amun, Mut, and Khonsu. If you have already visited Luxor Temple, you will have seen similar chapels in the great court there.

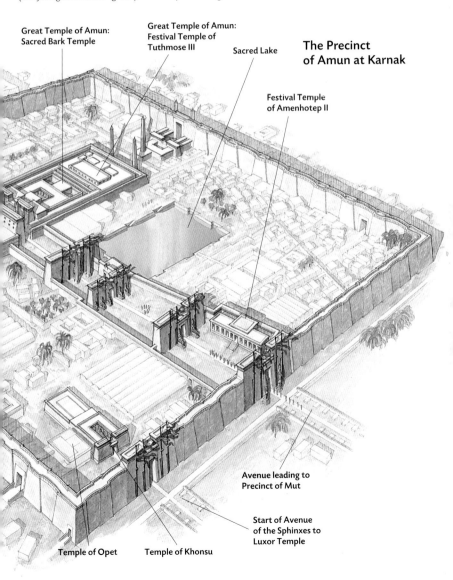

Great Temple of Amun: Sacred Bark Temple

Great Temple of Amun: Festival Temple of Tuthmose III

Sacred Lake

Festival Temple of Amenhotep II

The Precinct of Amun at Karnak

Avenue leading to Precinct of Mut

Start of Avenue of the Sphinxes to Luxor Temple

Temple of Opet

Temple of Khonsu

Sound & Light Show

Three times every evening, Karnak puts on a 90-minute, Hollywood-style sound-and-light show. The action starts at the avenue of ram-headed sphinxes, and then the audience follows as the narrative moves through the Great Court and Great Hypostyle Hall to a finale at the Sacred Lake. The commentary is pure bathos, but it is worth enduring for the opportunity to take a starlit walk through the temple. Obtain your ticket from the temple ticket office; times are posted there.

Opposite the shrine is a sphinx with the features of Tutankhamun. To the right is a small Temple of Ramses III, a miniature version of his temple at Medinat Habu (see pp. 254–256), and older than the court, which explains the odd way it crashes through the wall. One lone papyrid column stands near the center of the court, all that is left of a kiosk built by Taharqa, a 25th dynasty Nubian pharaoh. He ruled more than 600 years after Ramses II, whose pink-granite colossi stand just behind, fronting the **second pylon.**

Ramses II himself did not actually build the pylon (credit for that goes to Horemheb), but he was in the habit of adding his cartouche and likeness to the monuments of his predecessors. Pause for breath here, because after passing through the second pylon you are greeted by one of the most magnificent of spectacles, the dizzying **Great Hypostyle Hall.** To describe it, as many guidebooks do, as a forest of columns is to undersell it. Tree trunks are rarely this massive, nor are they usually so hypnotically regimented. It is hard to think of a space in any other building, ancient or modern, that so imbues the viewer with a sense of his or her mortality.

To state the facts: The hall is filled with 134 columns, which are roughly 50 feet (15 m) high, except for the center 12, which are 69 feet (21 m) tall. It takes six adults to stretch their arms around a column's girth, and it has been calculated that a crowd of 50 people could comfortably stand on one of the splayed column tops. Originally they supported a roof, so that the whole hall would have been enclosed and only dimly illuminated by sparse shafts of light admitted through small clerestory windows. Between the columns would have stood statues of the pharaohs. The whole effect would have been terrifying, and any visitors must have felt that they were trespassing in the hall of the gods themselves.

You leave through the **third pylon,** raised by Amenhotep III (R. 1390–1352 B.C.), the pharaoh responsible for Luxor Temple. Beyond it is a narrow court that also lies on the temple's secondary axis. Four obelisks once marked this juncture, erected by Tuthmose I and III, but only one remains standing. Sections of the other three lie in ruins.

Continuing to the east on the main axis, you'll come to the **fourth pylon,** built by Tuthmose I (R. 1504–1492 B.C.), which serves as the entrance to the earliest part of the temple. Immediately beyond, a small hypostyle hall contains later additions in the form of the **Obelisks of Hatshepsut.** Only one still stands (a second lies beside the nearby Sacred Lake). At almost 100 feet (30 m) high, it is the tallest obelisk in Egypt and although shaped from a single piece of granite, it appears to be made of two stones of different colors. The story behind this is that when Tuthmose III finally came to power (see "Family Feud," pp. 260), he had a wall built around the obelisks to hide the hieroglyphs that glorified his regent stepmother Hatshepsut. He could not cover the top portion, as it carried dedications to Amun, so for centuries that part was more exposed to the elements and has taken a lighter tone because of weathering.

From this point on, the temple is in a much more ruined state and it becomes increasingly hard to understand what all the elements are. Little remains of the fifth and sixth pylons, which stand close together, but just beyond them is a small court with two granite pillars carved with giant floral emblems representing Upper Egypt (the lily) and Lower Egypt (the papyrus). The boxlike structure ahead is the **Sacred Bark Shrine,** which still contains the plinth on which would have rested the bark of Amun. These barks were scale-model boats representing the vessels on which the gods traveled the heavens. Priests would have carried them aloft on poles during festivals and processions, including the local Opet Festival. The inner walls of the shrine are decorated with depictions of offering rites, while the outer walls show festival scenes, parts of which still have their original coloring.

The very earliest temples at this site stood where the central

A 3,200-year-old sentinel: One of two colossi of Ramses II fronting the temple's second pylon

Filled by groundwater, the Sacred Lake provided water for the priests' ablutions.

court now is. Across the open area, you reach the **Festival Temple of Tuthmose III,** built by the pharaoh as a memorial to himself. Curiously, the columns around the perimeter are square in section, while those in the center are round and larger at the top than at the base. Egyptologists speculate that they may represent tent poles, symbolic of the kind of military pavilion that might have been familiar to this pharaoh, who led his army on numerous campaigns. In the early Christian era this hall was used as a church, and you can still make out haloed saints painted on the columns. On the east side of the temple is a small roofless vestibule famed as the Botanical Room because of the fine painted reliefs of plants and animals.

From here you can walk back around the south side of the temple beside the **Sacred Lake,** which once supplied the temple with water. A modern café is perched beside the lake, and beyond is the first court of the precinct's north-south axis.

INSIDER TIP:

Hotel buffets can be really good, serving up a variety of European and Middle Eastern dishes. Look for plump dates for breakfast.

—ANN WILLIAMS
National Geographic
magazine writer

Precincts of Mut & Montu

This subsidiary axis is basically a processional way between the various precincts of Karnak. The first court, by the café, is known as the **Cachette Court** because a haul of some 900 stone statues and statuettes was unearthed here in a deep pit in the early 20th century. It is thought that these were surplus statues. The priests of Karnak no longer had room for all of them, but at the same time could not discard them because of their hallowed nature. Instead, they buried them, so they stayed within the temple precincts, but were out of the way. A similar cache was found buried beneath a court at Luxor Temple. Several of Karnak's statues now stand in front of the pylon to the south, the first of a series of four that ends with an avenue of sphinxes leading to the largely destroyed **Precinct of Mut.** The centerpiece is the ruined Temple of Mut, built by Amenhotep III, partly surrounded by another sacred lake. Throughout the precinct are granite statues of the lion goddess Sekhmet, the "Spreader of Terror."

As you return to the main Amun precinct, on your left is a monumental gateway covered with reliefs and with a winged sun-disk beneath a curving cornice. This belongs to the **Temple of Khonsu** and marks the original start of the Avenue of Sphinxes that joined Karnak to Luxor Temple a mile and a half (2.5 km) to the south.

Backtracking across the Amun temple, exit on the north side and to the left is an open-air museum with a collection of statuary found throughout the temple complexes. A separate ticket is required; buy it before entering Karnak.

Against the northern enclosure wall of the Amun precinct, inside the gate leading to the Montu precinct, is the small **Temple of Ptah.** Ptah is the creator god who thought the world into being, and whose cult center was the ancient capital of Memphis. The temple was begun during the reign of Tuthmose III and expanded under the Ptolemies.

The nearby gate leads into the **Precinct of Montu,** smallest of Karnak's three walled compounds. Montu was the falcon-headed warrior god, the original deity of Thebes, and the enclosure contains his ruined temple as well as a sacred lake. The area is very dilapidated and is often closed to the public. ■

The Nubian Pharaohs: Heirs to the Middle Kingdom

By the middle of the 8th century B.C., Egypt had undergone three centuries of political instability and weakness, and pharaohs were no longer fully in control of the entire country. Into this political chaos came invaders from the Nubian kingdom of Kush, in what is now northern Sudan. Between 747 and 656 B.C., the 25th Dynasty, known as the Nubian Dynasty, ruled Egypt, restoring its political unity and stability, and rebuilding many of its institutions. Their rule also ushered in a revival of ancient statuary traditions, resulting in a wealth of royal and private statues from this period.

Exploring the West Bank

Across the Nile from Luxor town lie the temples and tombs of the West Bank. Whether you explore them by air-conditioned tour bus, rented taxi, or by bicycle (see pp. 252–253), there are a few ground rules to bear in mind.

Twin figures of Amenhotep III greet the dawn.

The first and most crucial rule is to set off early in the morning. By noon the sun is ferocious. It saps away the energy, and all appreciation of the monuments is then reduced to how much shade they offer. Second, do not attempt too much. Ancient Egypt overload sets in quickly in the heat, and about two or three sights is the limit before most visitors' eyes begin to glaze over. Don't feel guilty about retreating to the hotel during the afternoon for a siesta or relaxation beside the pool. About the time you have recovered, the temperature will have dropped slightly, and you can then visit the museums in town, Luxor Temple by night, or Karnak for the sound-and-light show.

Unfortunately, everybody else is likely to have had similar advice, so the West Bank is at its busiest in the early morning. The Valley of the Kings and the Temple of Hatshepsut are perpetually crowded, but some sights—including Deir al-Medina, Medinat Habu, and the Tombs of the Nobles, which are no less interesting—are only visited by the tour groups if they have time after they have worked through the A-list. Heading to these places first means a good chance of having them to yourself.

Individual tickets are required for each temple, tomb, or group of tombs. These have to be bought at the **West Bank ticket office** (tel 095/231 1662; see maps pp. 228 & 253). As tickets are valid only for the day of purchase, you have to decide your day's itinerary in advance. A large board lists all the sights and admission fees, which average at about $3.50 per site. If you want to see everything here, you would end up spending just short of $100 on entrance fees alone (but you'd probably need to allow at least a week). The office opens at 6 a.m. If you are hoping to secure a ticket for the Tomb of Nefertari (see p. 260), you need to be in the line by at least 5:30 a.m., as the number of people allowed into the tomb each day is restricted to the first 150 visitors.

Colossi of Memnon

Beside the road to the West Bank monuments, in a dusty clearing among the sugarcane fields, these celebrated statues are virtually all that remain of one of Egypt's greatest temples.

Each carved from a single piece of stone, the colossi are 59 feet (18 m) high and were famous in antiquity for a bell-like tone emitted each sunrise by the more northerly of the two. This mysterious sound led the Greeks to believe the statues were of the immortal Memnon, who each morning was greeting his mother, the dawn goddess Eos.

Archaeologists think the noise could have resulted from the passage of air through the pores of the stone, caused by the warming of the sun's first rays. The noise ceased following a restoration of the statue by Roman emperor Septimius Severus in A.D. 170.

We now know that the giant seated figures represent the New Kingdom pharaoh Amenhotep III. The smaller carved figures at his feet are his wife, Tiye, and mother, Mutemuia. They stood here before the entrance pylon of the king's mortuary temple, just as Ramses II stands before the first pylon at Luxor Temple. However, it is believed that this temple was much larger. Archaeologists have calculated that it surpassed even Karnak in size, but it has almost completely vanished. Repeated

INSIDER TIP:

Visit the Colossi at dawn. If you are lucky, the dew drying in the cracks will make eerie noises, famous even in Greek times.

—TIFFIN THOMPSON
National Geographic contributor

plundering and ancient earthquake damage reduced it to rubble, which was then eroded away to nothing by the annual flooding of the Nile. This temple was unique in that it stood on a low-lying plain. Each year the rising waters flooded the outer halls and courts, leaving the raised inner sanctuary dry.

(continued on p. 254)

Colossi of Memnon

228 B3

Cycling the West Bank

The numerous temples and dozens of tombs of the West Bank spread over several miles, making it impractical to explore on foot. Tour buses and rented taxis are the usual options, but if you are in reasonably good shape, then there is no better way to get around than by bicycle.

Bicycles are ideal for stop-start sightseeing, but be prepared for long inclines and the heat.

Bicycles can be rented for just a few dollars at several places along Al-Mahatta Street in Luxor town (see p. 230). You can transport them to the West Bank on the local ferry, which departs every ten minutes from a dock in front of Luxor Temple. You also can rent a bicycle on the West Bank from the **village shops** just up the hill from the ferry landing. Try the bike out to make sure that it is road-worthy. Remember to take bottled water—it is essential to drink plenty to avoid dehydration.

The road to the monuments runs almost perfectly straight through fields watered by a network of small irrigation canals. After crossing a combination of a particularly large canal and a major road intersection, you'll see off to the right the domed mud-brick structures of **New Gurna ❶**, a model village designed in 1946 by Egypt's "architect of the people," Hassan Fathy (1900–1989). Made with traditional materials, it was constructed to rehouse the inhabitants of Old Gurna, but in the end they refused to move (see p. 265).

A mile farther on, you spot the first of the West Bank monuments, the **Colossi of Memnon ❷**, a lone pair of statues standing sentinel in the fields (see p. 251). Just a few hundred yards beyond, a small, single-story building off to the left houses the **West Bank ticket office ❸** (tel 095/231 1662), the only place you can purchase tickets for the sights (see p. 251). Past the ticket office the cultivation ends abruptly as the land begins to climb up to the Theban Hills. Go right at the big junction and cycle parallel to the edge of the fields, soon passing the **Ramesseum ❹** (see pp. 262–263) on your right. Huddled on the slopes to the left are the brightly colored houses of **Old Gurna ❺**, many painted with pharaonic motifs and the aircraft,

---

NOT TO BE MISSED:

Colossi of Memnon • Valley of the Kings • Ramesseum

---

ships, and black-cubed *Qaaba* that indicates the occupant has made a pilgrimage to Mecca. In such villages you may see children leading goats, women making bread, and farmers with water buffalo—sights familiar from the scenes painted on the walls of the ancient tombs.

About a mile farther you come to a T-junction; turn left. As you begin to cycle up a rise, **Howard Carter's House** ❻, recognizable by its dome, is off to the right. The Egyptologist lived

here during his search for an unrobbed tomb, which ended in success at that of Tutankhamun. For years there has been talk of turning the place into a museum. Go straight for another mile and a half (2.5 km) through rocky landscape to the **Valley of the Kings** ❼ (see pp. 271–284).

Return via the same route, possibly stopping off on the way back for lunch at the excellent **Tutankhamun Restaurant** ❽ (see p. 371), just south of the ferry landing.

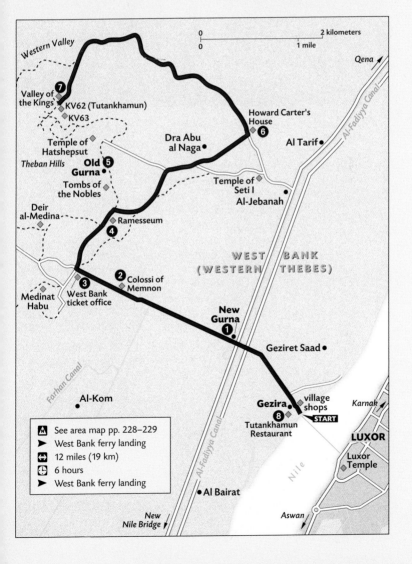

Ramses III is depicted on the massive entrance pylon with raised flail and gripping the hair of his vanquished foes.

Medinat Habu

Medinat Habu

🗺 228 B3

💲 $$. Tickets from West Bank ticket office only (see p. 251)

Aside from the colossi, all that remains of the temple are a carved reerected stela and some column bases. Luxor Museum (see pp. 240–241) and Cairo's Egyptian Museum (see pp. 68–76) display pieces of statuary from the site.

Medinat Habu

Often bypassed by tourists heading straight for the more famous Valley of the Kings and Ramesseum, this magnificent complex, dominated by the Temple of Ramses III, is the best-preserved monument on the West Bank. It contains more than 2,700 square miles (7,000 sq km) of decorated surfaces, and to explore the place properly can take up to half a day.

No one is quite sure where the complex's name (City of Habu) comes from, although there was a temple to a Hapu, son of Amenhotep, just to the north of here.

Built as a power base for Ramses III (R.1184–1153 B.C.), the last of the great pharaohs of Egypt, at its height Medinat Habu certainly re-

INSIDER TIP:

In the first court of Medinat Habu, look behind you at the back of the entrance pylon, which depicts the famous (infamous?) scene of a pile of severed enemy genitalia being counted by Ramses III's officials.

—CHIP ROSSETTI
National Geographic contributor

sembled a walled city, with temples, palaces, chapels, and accommodations for the priests and officials.

It was the administrative center for the region, and its great fortified walls offered refuge to the area's inhabitants in times of trouble. Later, during the Christian era, a Coptic town of churches and dwellings was built on and around the site, only to be abandoned in the ninth century A.D. after an outbreak of plague. As you approach today, you can still make out the ancient mud-brick houses built on top of the even more ancient enclosure walls.

Entrance is via the **High Gate,** a very unpharaonic, three-story structure designed along the lines of a Syrian fortress and commissioned to commemorate a Middle Eastern victory. Upstairs were the king's private apartments, decorated with reliefs of him being entertained by lithe dancers. Unfortunately, the staircase is in such a dilapidated condition that it is no longer possible to go up.

Through the gate is the great court and the approach to the massive main temple. Before that, off to the left, are the **Chapels of the Divine Adoratrices,** a series of small 25th-dynasty mortuary chapels contained in one well-preserved block dedicated to the priestesses of Amun. To the right is the **Small Temple,** begun in the 18th dynasty under Hatshepsut and constantly expanded until Roman times. It is hard to pay too much attention, though, when you are being visually mugged by the fantastic spectacle of the **Temple of Ramses III.**

Looking like an extension of the mountains behind, the **entrance pylon** is immense. Hyperbolic scenes of the king

defeating the Libyans and Sea Peoples, both of whom attacked Egypt during Ramses III's reign, decorate the pylon. Similar scenes are depicted in the **first court,** including scribes counting piles of severed hands and tongues and, over on the wall to the left, Ramses standing on the carved heads of captives, which protrude from the walls like medieval gargoyles. Elsewhere, figures and hieroglyphs are incised so deeply into the stone that they provide nesting places for birds.

What is especially fine about this temple is that parts of the wall reliefs, ceilings, and columns remain in their original painted state, colored with vivid primary blues, yellows, and reds, giving some idea of how riotously bright these places must once have been. This is particularly so in

KEY TO SITE PLAN
Medinat Habu

1 Ticket office
2 Entrance
3 Ptolemaic pylon
4 High Gate
5 Sacred Lake
6 Small Temple
7 Chapels of the Divine Adoratrices
8 Entrance pylon
9 First court
10 Royal Palace
11 Second court
12 Hypostyle hall
13 Side chapels

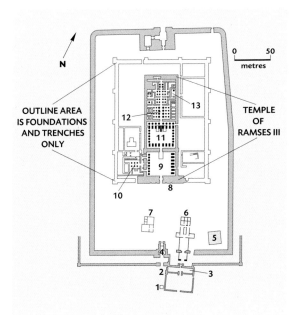

N

0   50
metres

OUTLINE AREA IS FOUNDATIONS AND TRENCHES ONLY

13
12
11
9
10
8

7   6
5
4
2   3
1

TEMPLE OF RAMSES III

the **second court,** which is in an excellent state of preservation, apart from the damage done by early Christians, who hacked away the giant figures of Ramses when they converted the court into a church; look for crosses carved into pillars. The **hypostyle hall** is in a worse condition, with only stubs of columns to indicate the presence of the courts, but there are a number of **side chapels,** with walls covered with reliefs depicting feasting and worship.

West of the temple are the remains of the **Royal Palace,** although these are no more than traces and outlines, while in the right-hand corner nearest the road is the fetid black **Sacred Lake.** Once the site of Osiris worship, the lake is still reputed by local villagers to have magical properties able to bring fertility to the barren.

Deir al-Medina

All those magnificent temples and tombs on the West Bank dedicated to the glory of ancient Egypt's kings, royals, and nobles—somebody had to build them. Traces of these largely unsung artisans and craftsmen are usually few, but Deir al-Medina provides a fascinating exception, because it was here that the workers engaged in the building and decoration of the monuments lived and were buried.

Excavations at this site have revealed a **Workers' Village** of about 70 dwellings enclosed within a protective wall. The ruins, while only a few bricks high, clearly show the layout of the houses, each with an entrance opening off the narrow streets, leading to three or four rooms, with stairs down to cellar spaces and up to what must have been roof terraces. In places the stone floors still bear the marks made by opening and closing doors. Remnants of foodstuffs discovered here by archaeologists show that the workers existed on a diet of fish

---

"Ozymandias"

English poet Percy Bysshe Shelley (1792–1822) never visited Egypt. His verse is fantasy, inspired by a visit to London's British Museum, where he may have seen the head of Ramses II, known to the Greeks as Ozymandias.

I met a traveller from an antique land
Who said: Two vast and trunkless legs
  of stone
Stand in the desert....Near them, on
  the sand,
Half sunk, a shattered visage lies,
  whose frown,
And wrinkled lip, and sneer of cold
  command,
Tell that its sculptor well those
  passions read

Which yet survive, stamped on these
  lifeless things,
The hand that mocked them, and the heart
  that fed:
And on the pedestal these words appear:
"My name is Ozymandias, king of kings:
Look on my works, ye Mighty, and despair!"
Nothing beside remains. Round the decay
Of that colossal wreck, boundless
  and bare
The lone and level sands stretch far away.

Stone walls at Deir al-Medina mark dwellings and streets where laborers and craftsmen lived.

and cereals, supplemented by fruit, honey, and occasionally meat. They brewed and drank beer.

Much of our knowledge of these people comes from limestone fragments called *ostraca* inscribed with accounts, records, and personal reminders. Archaeologists have found thousands of these ancient Post-It notes amid the houses. They tell us who lived here and where exactly, their names, what their work was, even how much they earned (payment being in grain and food). More than any other site in Egypt, here you feel the presence of the ancient Egyptians.

Nestled right beside the village is its small **necropolis.** Tombs here took the form of a walled courtyard with a chapel, beneath which was the burial chamber. Often the chapel was surmounted by a brick pyramidion (mini-pyramid), and some of these have been restored to their original state. Farther west, climbing up the valley side, you'll find a few more simple tombs, hewn out of the rock. Three of these are open to visitors and are well worth a look inside for the beautiful wall paintings, rendered predominantly in warm tones of yellows, ochers, and golds.

Closest to the parking lot is the **Tomb of Inherkhau,** a foreman who lived during the reigns of both Ramses III and Ramses IV. Inherkhau is depicted frequently, in some instances bald-headed and in other places with black curly locks. However, the scene in this tomb everybody remembers is that of a stylized long-eared cat killing the serpent Apophis under a holy tree.

Next along is the **Tomb of**

Deir al-Medina

🗺 228 B3

💲 $$. Tickets from West Bank ticket office only (see p. 251)

Valley of the Queens

🅰 228 A3

💲 $$. Tickets from the West Bank ticket office only (see p. 251)

Sennedjem, described in hieroglyphs as a "servant in the Place of Truth," which is the ancients' name for the Valley of Kings, where most of the inhabitants of Deir al-Medina were employed. Although today it is a distance of several miles by road between the two sites, they are actually almost adjacent, lying on either side of a rocky hill. It is possible to walk from one to the other in half an hour. When Sennedjem's tomb was first opened in 1886, it contained a rich cache of funerary equipment, now exhibited at the Egyptian Museum in Cairo (see pp. 68–76). The tomb is still worth visiting for the beautiful paintings found there.

A little farther up the slope is the **Tomb of Peshedu,** another servant in the Place of Truth. To enter his tomb you pass between two symmetrical representations of Anubis, the jackal-headed god, but the most famous scene is immediately to the right in the burial chamber; it shows Peshedu crouching by a stream under a palm tree.

Up the valley from the Workers' Village and necropolis, along

In the tomb of Nefertari, a tomb guardian ensures no touching and no lingering, with only ten minutes allowed per visit.

a rough path, is a small **Ptolemaic temple** dedicated to Hathor and built in the third century B.C. It is a very modest affair—a mud-brick wall around a compound—but painted bas-reliefs inside have kept some of their color. In the early Christian period it was taken over for use by the Copts, which is where the name of this whole site comes from: Deir al-Medina, Monastery of the City.

Valley of the Queens

A wide wadi in the southernmost part of the Theban necropolis, the Valley of the Queens is where royal brides, princes, princesses, and members of the royal court were buried. At least 75 tombs are burrowed into the rock, of which only a handful are ever open to the public—that may or may not include what for many is the highlight of the West Bank, the beautiful Tomb of Nefertari.

If you have already visited the Valley of the Kings, then you know what to expect here: a craggy, sun-blasted landscape pocked with the small black openings of tunnel-like entrances. Of the tombs that can be visited, three are of sons of Ramses III, builder of the great temple at Medinat Habu (see pp. 254–256). These are all fairly modest endeavors, tunneled straight and level into the rock face with few steps or slopes and consisting of a single, fairly short corridor with one or two small side rooms. When discovered by an Italian expedition early in the 20th century, all had been completely looted in antiquity, but the wall

---

Tipping the Guard/Caretaker

In the more isolated ancient sites, such as in Middle Egypt and on the Isle of Philae, you may be asked for a tip (baksheesh) from the ticket-taker, and sometimes from a uniformed guard who will be happy to snap your photo in exchange for some cash. Unfortunately, this is because soldiers, most of them draftees doing their national service, receive pitifully low salaries. But don't feel compelled to tip anyone unless you want to do so. If you do tip, it should be no more than a few Egyptian pounds.

---

decoration was remarkably well preserved and constitutes a great treasure in itself. Colored reliefs cover every surface of the tombs. These depict a ritual journey of the souls of the princes, beginning in the company of their father, who introduces them to various deities in the afterlife. Deeper into the tomb the princes are left alone in front of the gods.

The **Tomb of Khaemwaset** belongs to the eldest son. He is easy to pick out in the reliefs because of his distinctive hairstyle, collected in a braid and falling sideways over his ear—look for him in the second chamber, on the right, following behind his father, shown wearing the classic blue-and-gold pharaoh's headdress. In the final chamber is the prince alone making offerings to a seated Osiris, lord of the afterlife, whose face is painted green, the color of regeneration.

The Tomb of Amunherkhepshep is that of the designated heir to throne, who died at about age 15 (of what we don't know). As in his brother's tomb, the scenes on the walls show his father, Ramses III, introducing him to the gods and guardians of the afterlife. In the farthest chamber a glass cabinet contains the skeleton of a fetus wrapped in bandages. Guides will tell you how Amunherkhepshep's mother was pregnant at the time of his death, and in her grief she aborted the child and entombed it with her dead son. In reality, the fetus was discovered elsewhere in the valley and has no proven connection with this tomb.

On the way to the tomb of Amunherkhepshep you can usually also enter the **Tomb of Titi,** wife of a pharaoh from the 20th dynasty. The tomb is simple, but lavishly decorated. There are scenes depict-

ing guardians of the underworld, and Hathor is shown pouring Nile water to rejuvenate the queen.

All the above, while certainly worth visiting, pale before the **Tomb of Nefertari,** which is by far the most stunning tomb in all Egypt. So fabulous is it that it even

INSIDER TIP:

Ramses II referred to Nefertari as the Beautiful One, and her tomb surely survives as the most beautiful of the artisan's craft.

—KEN GARRETT
National Geographic photographer

justifies the extraordinary entrance fee of 100LE ($30) when it is open. As breathing increases humidity which in turn causes the salt crystalization so damaging to plaster, visitors to the tomb are limited. In fact, at the time of writing the tomb is closed. When it reopens, no more than 150 people per day are admitted, with a maximum of ten in the tomb at any one time. Each visitor is also limited to only ten minutes in the tomb. Despite the cost, demand for tickets is high. To have any chance of getting one, you need to be at the West Bank ticket office well before it opens (see p. 251).

Nefertari (whose name means "the most beautiful") was the favorite wife of Ramses II, the New Kingdom pharaoh known for his monuments of self-celebration, such as the Ramesseum and Abu Simbel (see pp. 262–263). But it

Family Feud

History has viewed Queen Hatshepsut (see p. 268) an envious regent who usurped her stepson, Thutmose III, who then after her death defaced her images as pharaoh. However, it is likely he did not start this campaign against his stepmother for 20 years, indicating that revenge may not have been his motivation. Instead, it may have been an attempt to legitimize his own heir.

At the Tomb of Nefertari, the goddess Isis presents Nefertari to the god Khepri.

is a mark of the pharaoh's respect for his wife that at Abu Simbel he dedicated a temple to her, where the queen is represented in large statues equal in size to those of the king—most queens in pharaonic art only come up to their husband's knees. Similarly, Nefertari's tomb appears as an exquisite labor of love.

Entered via a steep stairway, the tomb consists of an antechamber with annex, and then a second stairway leading down to the burial chamber. Every surface is adorned with scenes of the queen, usually wearing a flowing, partially transparent white gown and a vulture headdress, in the company of the gods. The blaze of color is, quite literally, breathtaking.

In the antechamber, to the left of the entrance stair, Nefertari plays *sennet*, a checkers-like game, while

to the right the roll call of gods starts with a seated Osiris holding a flail, followed by jackal-headed Anubis. On the inside of the arch is the goddess Neith, and then Harsiesis leads Nefertari before seated figures of Re-Harakhty and Hathor. Some of the best scenes in the tomb are in the annex, including the queen facing the ibis-headed god of wisdom, Thoth, and consecrating tables of offerings in front of Osiris (left) and Re (right).

Scenes down the second staircase show (on the left) Nefertari making offerings to the goddesses Isis and Nephthys, while opposite she does likewise with Hathor and Selkis. As in the upper chambers, the burial chamber has an astronomical ceiling of gold stars on blue. The queen's pink granite sarcophagus was originally located at the center of the hall, between

Ramesseum

 228 B3

$$. Tickets from the West Bank ticket office only (see p. 251)

KEY TO SITE PLAN

Ramesseum

1 **First pylon**
2 **First court**
3 **Second pylon**
4 **Fallen colossus of Ramses II**
5 **Entrance**
6 **Second court**
7 **Hypostyle hall**
8 **Astronomical Room**

the four pillars, but only a few fragments were found when the tomb was rediscovered by archaeologists in 1904, plunderers having got there first, way back in antiquity.

Ramesseum

As it exists today, the Ramesseum is no more than three small tableaus of ruins, with a field of ridges, holes, and bases to indicate where the rest of the complex once stood. But its reputation far outstrips its physical presence. Famed Egyptologist Jean-François Champollion called it the "most noble and pure in Thebes as far as great monuments are concerned," while the English poet Percy Bysshe Shelley immortalized it in verse (see "Ozymandias," p. 256).

Its reputation rests with its creator, pharaoh Ramses II (R.1279–1213 B.C.) of the 19th

dynasty, mightiest ruler of all, who wore the double crown of Egypt for 67 years. Construction of the Ramesseum began soon after Ramses II took the throne, and it was probably only finished around the 22nd year of his reign. Intended as his grand and immortalizing mortuary complex, in its completed state the Ramesseum had a central main temple flanked by small temples to his mother, Tuya, and favored wife, Nefertari, palaces, administrative buildings, and vast areas of storehouses. No effort was spared to make this the greatest of all monuments, but later dynasties dismantled the Ramesseum to use the stone in building their own temples. Early Christians took over what was left and converted the remains to a church, further damaging the ancient statues and reliefs.

What remains today are parts of Ramses II's main temple. Its layout inspired Medinat Habu (see pp. 254–256), which was built by Ramses III, and it may be a good idea to visit there first to help understand what you are looking at here.

Whereas at Medinat Habu visitors experience the building as intended—approaching the first pylon, passing through into the first court, the second, and then the hypostyle hall—at the Ramesseum visitors enter from the side, directly into the **second court.** This was originally enclosed by a double row of columns, of which just the bases remain.

On the left is a part of the **second pylon,** with four colossi of Ramses II in the form of a mummy, his arms crossed

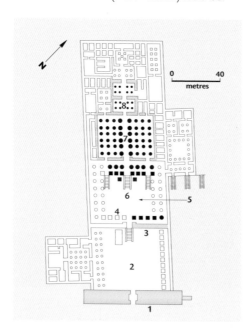

0   40
metres

Columns at Ramesseum portray the pharaoh in the guise of Osiris, Lord of the Underworld.

holding a flail and a scepter in the manner of the god Osiris. Beside them are the head and shoulders of a freestanding **colossus of Ramses II,** now toppled and smashed. The king's cartouche is plainly visible on his right shoulder. Estimated to have stood over six stories high, this is not only the largest freestanding statue ever made in Egypt, but also possibly one of the most titanic works of sculpture achieved in human history. What makes the task even more astounding is that the stone block for the statue came from the quarries at Aswan and had to be shipped some 150 miles (240 km) to the north. The feet of the colossus are planted in the first court of the temple, where the statue originally stood.

Across the second court are four more Osiride pillars, and before them a black granite head of the pharaoh that belonged to one of two statues that stood here. Its twin was removed by Giovanni Belzoni (see p. 77) in 1816 and is now displayed at the British Museum in London, although the lower half remains here in place, to the left of what was the main stairway up to the **hypostyle hall.**

Only 29 of the original 48 papyrus columns of the hall still stand, but they all have beautifully decorated and colored capitals. The surrounding walls show scenes of Ramses II's military victories, while on the far wall, on the right-hand side of the doorway, is a bit of historical graffiti—the inscribed and dated name BELZONI.

On the far side of the hall is the **Astronomical Room,** so called because of its ceiling, which depicts a celestial calendar of the constellations. This ceiling probably had a practical use in helping to determine the timing of religious ceremonies.

(continued on p. 266)

Guardians & Thieves

The mud-brick houses of Gurna have lined the mountainside above the magnificent temple remains of Thebes for generations. Prior to that, if 18th-century travelers' accounts are to be believed, the Gurnawis, as they are known, lived in the tombs themselves, many of which are little more than caves.

Gurna's colorfully painted, mud-brick buildings stand at the center of age-old controversies involving plundered pharaonic tombs and debates about further excavations.

On any given day, groups of tourists can be seen talking to the villagers and taking pictures of the brightly colored houses. The fact that people still live in and among the ancient monuments provides a continuity between ancient and modern that visitors find as fascinating as the pharaonic tombs and temples they have come to see. Many sit and have tea in the villagers' homes, often the only chance they have to interact with ordinary Egyptians during their stay in the country. Some of the villagers earn a living making small reproductions of pharaonic statues or little dolls that they sell to tourists. A few have set up small kiosks selling soft drinks or have opened "alabaster factories" making carved reproductions of pieces of famous pharaonic statuary. However, a century ago it was a very different kind of cottage industry that made the Gurnawis infamous.

About 1875, valuable antiquities began showing up in the marketplace, prompting the Egyptian authorities to suspect someone had found, and was plundering, an unknown tomb. Inquiries led to the village of Gurna, specifically to the Abdel Rassoul brothers. Initially they protested their innocence until, in the spring of 1881, a disagreement caused a disgruntled family member to blow the whistle and lead government officials to the stash. A crevice high up on a cliff face near the Temple of Hatshepsut was revealed as the opening of a massive shaft leading down into the mountainside. By the faint light of candles, officials were able to make out piles of sarcophagi inscribed with the names of some of the most famous pharaohs of the New Kingdom, including Tuthmose III, Seti I, and Ramses II. In all, the mummies of 40 pharaohs, queens, and nobles were found there.

It seems that the New Kingdom priests realized that the bodies of their kings would never be safe from violation in their own tombs, no matter what precautions were taken against grave robbers, so they moved them to this communal grave. When the cache was found by the authorities, the mummies were immediately removed to Cairo, where many of them are now on display at the Egyptian Museum (see pp. 68–76).

Ever since, the Egyptian government has been eager to get rid of the village of Gurna. In the 1940s it sponsored architect Hassan Fathy to create a new village, known as New Gurna (see p. 252), on agricultural land nearer to the river, but the Gurnawis refused to be tempted down from their traditional hillside homes. The Gurnawis insist that whatever tomb-robbing did occur in the past is now long over.

However, the authorities also contend that the houses of Gurna prevent the excavation of other, as-yet-undiscovered tombs in the hillside. Moreover, they say, the presence of the village destroys the "panorama" of the area. Most visitors would disagree and contend that the colorful village is a spectacle in itself. Nonetheless, the government has recently begun heavy-handed efforts to move Gurnawis to a new desert settlement some miles distant.

Brightly decorated Gurnawi houses add a welcome splash of color in the otherwise dusty, barren landscape, though proponents of a more natural landscape do not agree.

**Tombs of
the Nobles**

🅰 228 B4

🆂 $$. Tickets from
the West Bank
ticket office only
(see p. 251)

Tombs of the Nobles

Ancient Egypt overload means
that after visiting all the must-
sees, most visitors are too weary
to take on yet more tombs. But
the burial chambers that riddle
the hillside between the Rames-
seum and Hatshepsut's temple
are very different. Belonging
to nonroyals, like governors,
mayors, and scribes, these
modest little burial complexes
offer a glimpse of a more hu-
man side of ancient Egypt.

Set among the painted houses
and yards of the hillside village of
Gurna, the tombs are not always
easy to find. Signs are few and you
have to watch carefully for the
modern, bunker-like entrances.
Some 14 are open to visitors;
divided into five groups, each
requires its own ticket (bought
in advance from the West Bank
ticket office; see p. 251). All of the
tombs are heavily decorated, but
unlike those of the kings and
queens, where the images are
of a divine nature related to the
afterlife, scenes in the Tombs of
the Nobles depict the living, with
the day-to-day activities of life as it
was 4,500 years ago.

**Tombs of Ramose (no. 55),
Userhet (no. 56), &
Khaemhet (no. 57):** Lying
immediately north of the
Ramesseum, behind an alabaster
factory, this trio is just off
the main road. Ramose was a
governor of Thebes during the
reigns of Amenhotep III and
Akhenaten. His tomb is larger
than most, with a hypostyle hall
supported by a forest of col-
umns. Only one wall is painted;
it depicts the deceased's
funeral, with a procession
carrying the funerary furniture
and a crowd of wailing women.
Other surfaces are decorated
with sculpted reliefs that are
masterful in their definition and
texture and ability to convey life.
Khaemhet's tomb, which would
have been crafted at the same
time (he was Amenhotep III's

The depiction of the three musicians at the Tombs of Nakht
is one of the most famous of ancient Egyptian wall paintings.

court scribe and overseer of granaries), shares the same high quality of workmanship. On the left-hand wall of the first vestibule is a particularly fine depiction of Khaemhet making food offerings in the form of bread and geese.

Tombs of Khonsu (no. 31), Userhat (no. 51), & Benia (no. 343):

This cluster of tombs lies 100 yards (90 m) east of the previous group. Khonsu was an adviser to Tuthmose III, and unlike the ones described above, his tomb is covered with colorful reliefs, although many are badly damaged. On the right-hand wall of the first vestibule, down near the bottom, is a funeral procession beside a pyramidal tomb, very much like those at nearby Deir al-Medina. The tombs of Userhat (not to be confused with Userhet, No. 56) and Benia are also highly decorated. The last one has three painted limestone statues in a niche, representing Benia sitting between his mother and father.

Tombs of Nakht (no. 52) & Menna (no. 69):

Egyptologists speculate that these two tombs, dating from the reign of Amenhotep III, were the work of the same artist. Both are covered in images of rural life, depicting the plowing, sowing, and harvesting of crops; hunting and fishing; and, in the tomb of Nakht, winemaking—figures pick the grapes off vines, while others trample the fruit. In the same tomb is one of the most famous pieces of pharaonic

art, reproduced on posters and tourist bazaar papyri—three female musicians, one playing the lute, one a harp, and one a wind instrument.

Tombs of Nefer-Ronpet (no. 178), Dhutmosi (no. 295), & Nefer-Sekheru (no. 296):

About 100 yards (90 m) west of the tomb of Menna, this grouping of three is probably the least essential of all the Tombs of the Nobles, although two of them have ceilings with attractive geometric designs.

INSIDER TIP:

Pharaohs were required to dedicate their tombs to the sacred texts, but nobles could decorate with scenes of the good life, such as music and dance.

—KEN GARRETT
National Geographic photographer

Tombs of Sennefer (no. 96) & Rekhmire (no. 100):

These two tombs are the highlights of the area. Sennefer was a senior official at the time of Amenhotep II, and a man obviously very much in love with his wife. On the four pillars that support the deeply subterranean burial chamber, the couple are shown no fewer than 14 times, always touching and holding. The ceiling is wonderfully informal—the artist exploited the unevenness of the rock to give

Temple of Hatshepsut

 228 B4

$$. Tickets from the West Band ticket office only (see p. 251)

an almost three-dimensional quality to a spread of vines snaking across the chamber and hung with bunches of grapes.

Although roughly of the same age, the Tomb of Rekhmire is completely different in character. Where that of Sennefer suggested intimacy, this one is almost bureaucratic in its fastidiousness. It is also quite wonderful. Rekhmire was a governor under Tuthmose III and Amenhotep II, a time when the Egyptian empire was expanding, so one wall (left on entering the vestibule) shows tributes extracted from foreign countries, including baboons, monkeys, and a giraffe from Nubia; weapons, carts, horses, and a bear from Syria; and pots, perhaps from Crete. In the narrow chapel, in which the height of the ceiling climbs sharply from the entrance, the walls serve as huge storyboards. One side depicts the funerary banquet, while the other has scenes of temple-building, with laborers making mud bricks, sculptors working on two colossi, and the setting up of an obelisk.

Temple of Hatshepsut

A firm favorite with the tour buses, Hatshepsut's temple is a showpiece of the West Bank. Its setting is superb—the temple rises in a series of broad terraces that at the topmost level join with a great bay of limestone cliffs. Close up, though, there is far less to be seen than at many other sites, and crowds often obscure what there is to see here.

Much of the mystique of the temple has to do with the personality of Hatshepsut herself, ancient Egypt's only woman pharaoh. As a daughter of Tuthmose I she had been married off to her half-brother and heir to the throne. He duly succeeded to the throne as Tuthmose II, but died in his early thirties, leaving one young son—of a minor wife—whom he named as his successor, Tuthmose III. At first, stepmother Hatshepsut acted as regent for the young king, but later usurped him altogether and declared herself pharaoh. To legitimize her position she was portrayed in statues and reliefs with all the regalia of kingship, including the royal false beard. She held the throne until her death—

EXPERIENCE:
Take a Hot-Air Balloon Ride over Luxor

Some of the most stunning vistas of Luxor and the Valley of the Kings can be seen from the air. Not a few first-time visitors have found themselves staring open-mouthed at the sight of hot-air balloons floating over Luxor's West Bank. Balloon flights take place early in the morning, when the sun's light is ideal for taking photographs.

From a few hundred feet in the air, the Nile is at its most beautiful, and you can easily see the stark contrast between the green fields that line the river and the tawny desert beyond. There are currently three balloon companies in Luxor: **Balloons over Egypt** (tel 095/2370638); **Hod Hod** (tel 095/2370116); and **Magic Horizon Balloons** (tel 095/2365060, www. magic-horizon.com). All three leave from a field near the Ramesseum, and are priced around $250 per person per flight, which can include a champagne breakfast.

though there is some speculation that Tuthmose III might have had a hand in this, after being kept so long in waiting.

The site of her temple is often referred to as Deir al-Bahri, after a Coptic monastery *(deir)* that once stood here. The original ancient Egyptian name was the far more evocative Djeser-djeseru, Sacred of Sacreds. Three temples stood side by side, but the two neighbors have not survived. Hatshepsut's temple very nearly didn't make it either. Her successor, Tuthmose III, vandalized the place after she died (see "Family Feud," p. 260). When discovered in the mid-19th century the temple was in ruins, and its present appearance is largely due to massive reconstruction by a Polish-Egyptian team that has been working on site since 1961. It is debatable how successful this rebuild is–from a distance the temple has a modernist feel to it, almost non-pharaonic. But don't be fooled; there is interesting columnar and wall art beyond the clean lines of the exterior.

Only the core of the temple has been re-created; missing is the sphinx-lined causeway and the monumental entrance pylon that it would have led up to. Beyond the pylon would have been the first court, now a dusty flat area where the lower ramp begins. Most people pass straight on up, but first take time to look around the **lower colonnade,** which depicts scenes of fishing and birds being caught in nets (right-hand side), and the transportation of the queen's great obelisks from the Aswan quarries to Karnak (left-hand side).

A hot-air balloon drifts over Hatshepsut's terraces, offering its passengers a bird's-eye view.

Ascend to the second court and you can view the carved reliefs around the **second-level colonnade,** which on the right-hand side show the queen's divine "birth" (more propaganda to emphasize her right to reign as pharaoh), and on the left-hand side tell the story of an expedition to the land of Punt. Nobody is quite sure where this Punt was, but the best guess is that it equates to what is now Ethiopia or northern Somalia. There is a detailed scene of ships being loaded up with sacks and animals, and myrrh trees being carried in baskets. Look, too, for the reception of the Egyptian embassy by the king of Punt and his queen, who is almost elephantine in appearance.

Temple of Seti I

 229 C4

$ $$. Tickets from the West Bank ticket office only (see p. 251)

Beyond the Punt scenes is the small **Chapel of Hathor,** which was originally approached by its own separate ramp up from the first court. It is crowded with columns, with capitals in the form of the features of the cow goddess. At the very back of the chapel, just to the left of the entrance to the sanctuary (which is usually off-limits to visitors), you will find a carved relief of Hathor in the

INSIDER TIP:

Before visiting, look at pictures of the Temple of Hatshepsut from the 1950s. Once here, you'll see how it is slowly re-gathering the glory it once possessed.

—CHIP BROWN
National Geographic
magazine writer

form of a cow licking the hand of Queen Hatshepsut.

The third and uppermost terrace has been recently opened to the public. At its rear is a granite doorway leading to the Temple of Amun, carved out of the cliff.

Temple of Seti I

In ancient times, the Temple of Seti I (also known as Sethos I) was one of the major monuments of Western Thebes. But lacking the infamy of Hatshepsut or the ego of his son Ramses II, Seti I's fame has waned, and as a consequence his temple is one of the less-visited sights. This is a case of poor judgment, though, because

it is certainly worth seeing.

The reign of Seti I (R. 1294–1279 B.C.) was something of a high point. His first success was in restoring order to the country after the instability of the Amarna kings (see pp. 214–217). That accomplished, he expanded the Egyptian empire to include Cyprus and parts of Mesopotamia (modern-day Iraq).

His military achievements were matched by those he made in the arts. Under Seti's patronage some magnificent buildings were undertaken, including the Great Hypostyle Hall at Karnak (see p. 246), a structure later completed by Ramses II, and the king's temple at Abydos (see pp. 222–223) in Middle Egypt. The tomb created for Seti I is perhaps the most splendid of all those in the Valley of the Kings, and it has some of the finest wall paintings.

Unfortunately, the pylons and courts of his mortuary temple here on the West Bank have largely been destroyed, making it seem less significant than it was. Dedicated to Amun, it was originally meant as a place of worship for the king's own cult, and also served as a treasure house for some of the spoils of his military ventures. Only the central part of the building is preserved, including a portico of eight papyriform pillars and, beyond, a hypostyle hall, considerably less grand than the one at Karnak. However, the bas-reliefs adorning the temple walls are particularly elegant and constitute some of the finest examples of New Kingdom art.

The temple is just off the Valley of the Kings road, but heading in the direction of the river. ■

Valley of the Kings

This arid valley between rocky hills is one of the richest archaeological sites on Earth. During the greatest period in ancient Egyptian history, practically every pharaoh was buried here, in deep tombs of extraordinary beauty, decorated with images of the afterlife. These chambers were filled with vast treasures. Although almost everything was looted in antiquity, it is impossible not to entertain the thought that a magnificent cache remains secreted away, awaiting discovery.

So many tombs riddle the Valley of the Kings that Egyptologists have been kept busy here for nearly two centuries.

Mortuary temples, lined up along the edge of the floodplain, where the cultivation ended and the dry slopes of the Theban Hills began, kept alive the memory of the dead pharaohs. But the actual bodies were hidden away in this secluded valley, with only one easily guarded entrance. The secret tombs were intended to preserve the pharaoh's mummies for eternity.

It is sad that they should have so completely failed, but ancient tomb robbers got there long before archaeologists did.

Each tomb was designed to resemble the underworld, with a long, inclined corridor descending into either an antechamber or a series of pillared halls, and ending in a burial chamber. No two tombs are exactly the same, although they all share common features.

Valley of the Kings

⚠ 228 B4

$ $$. Tickets from the West Bank ticket office only (see p. 251)

Early tombs have a right-angled plan, later tombs have one straight axis. In the earliest tombs only the burial chamber received decoration, but beginning with the 19th dynasty (Ramses I in 1295 B.C.) the wall paintings were carried through into all parts. These scenes were copied from the books of the afterlife such as the Amduat, Litany of Re, and Book of the Dead, and act as a guide to the afterlife. They depict the protocol the king must carry out, presenting himself to the various gods and goddesses. So that the deceased could live as they had on Earth, the tombs were provided with furniture, papyrus scrolls, amulets, jewelry, ritual objects, statues of gods, and *ushabti*, miniature effigies of the king that would carry out any tasks or labors on his behalf in the afterlife.

Despite the ancient architects' best efforts, they were repeatedly thwarted by robbers who despoiled most of the royal mummies and carted away the treasures buried with them. Before the era of the pharaohs was over, most of the tombs had been emptied. A further two-and-a-half millennia of looting and scavenging meant that by the time the archaeologists began excavating here in the early 19th century, anything that could possibly be carried away had been. Almost. Howard Carter's amazing find (see pp. 276–277) proved that the robbers had not gotten everything.

In 2007, the chamber known as KV63 was discovered—the first in the Valley since Tutankhamun's—although it turned out to be a storage chamber rather than a tomb. Few serious archaeologists believe that there are more royal tombs to be found, and the priority is now to study the finds already at hand..

KEY TO SITE PLAN
Valley of the Kings

The numbers below are KV tomb numbers and are only those referred to in the text.

- 2 Ramses IV
- 5 "The lost tomb"
- 6 Ramses IX
- 8 Merenptah
- 9 Ramses VI
- 10 Ameemesses
- 11 Ramses III
- 17 Seti I
- 34 Tuthmose III
- 35 Amenhotep II
- 43 Tuthmose IV
- 57 Horemheb
- 62 Tutankhamun

INSIDER TIP:

Take small currency to the Valley of the Kings and stimulate tomb guides to point out very interesting but overlooked artwork.

—LESLIE LYONS
National Geographic field researcher

Visiting the Valley

Be aware that tickets for the Valley of the Kings cannot be bought at the site. They can only be purchased from the

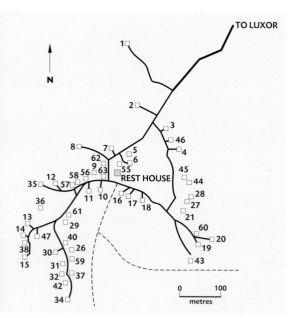

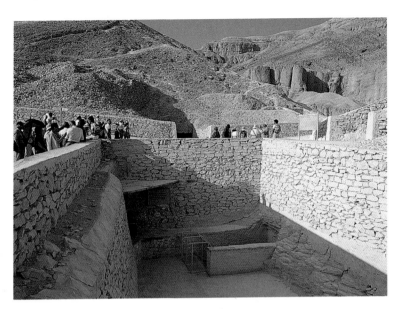

A tour group braves the heat to listen to their guide before descending into Tutankhamun's tomb.

West Bank ticket office (see p. 251), located near the Colossi of Memnon. One ticket is good for any three tombs, excluding Tutankhamun's, which has its own separate ticket. If you want to visit more than three tombs, then you need more than one ticket. There is a rest house at the entrance to the valley where you can buy over-priced bottled water and soft drinks, and beyond that a *tuf-tuf*—a noisy tractor inappropriately dressed up to look like a train—ferries visitors up to the first tombs.

To date, 63 tombs have been discovered here, although not all of them belong to pharaohs. Each one is assigned a KV, or Kings' Valley, number, usually in the sequence in which it was found. Not all the tombs are accessible to the public, and some of those that are open at the time of writing may well be closed when you visit, as part of an ongoing program of renovation. At the most popular tombs (which include those of Tutankhamun and Ramses VI) be prepared to line up. Be prepared also to sweat: Most tombs involve the descent of two long, steep staircases with the air getting steadily hotter and clammier the deeper you get.

Tutankhamun: The tomb that everyone rushes to is Tutankhamun's. It is not really deserving of the clamor; it is small and for the most part undecorated, and all the treasures have been removed to the Egyptian Museum in Cairo (see pp. 68–76). All that remains is the large granite sarcophagus. The story of his discovery is far more interesting than the now empty chambers.

(continued on p. 276)

Building a Royal Tomb

No sooner did Seti I ascend the throne of Egypt in 1294 B.C. than he began planning and building his royal tomb. First, stonecutters quarried away at the valley's limestone and shale, carving out hallways and chambers (shown below). Other craftsmen soon followed, transforming this crude cave into an intricately ornamented grave.

The insets depict the multiple stages involved in crafting an ageless portrait, as the stonecutters first chisel out a chamber, leaving behind raw rock walls (1). A coat of plaster then creates a smooth surface (2) on which an artist renders his subject in rough outline (3). Next, a master painter makes corrections to this draft portrait and adds

details (4) to help guide the hand of the bas-relief sculptor who follows (5). Finally, another artisan gives the portrait its royal finish (6), filling in the colors and adding the final details.

When building a royal tomb, the size of the workforce varied from a few laborers to more than a hundred. Breathing must have become difficult as workers inhaled air laden with plaster and stone dust. To deal with the darkness deep in the tomb, burrowing away hundreds of feet into the hillside, they burned pottery lamps fitted with linen wicks and fueled with oil or fat mixed with a bit of salt to inhibit smoke.

When their building and decorative work was nearly complete, laborers then set about hauling a large stone sarcophagus (top right) down to the burial chamber.

Seti I died in 1279 B.C., and the craftsmen building his grave had just 70 days—while the priests mummified his body—to finish readying the extensive royal tomb to receive the pharaoh's remains.

Lavishly decorated, the tomb of Seti I is the longest and deepest of all those discovered in the Valley of the Kings.

Arcing across the ceiling of Ramses VI's tomb, dual images of the sky goddess Nut bracket scenes from sacred texts.

Born in 1874, Howard Carter came to Egypt from Britain as a teenager and began as a humble junior draftsman responsible for copying wall paintings. He joined the Egyptian Antiquities Service in 1899 and was appointed inspector for Upper Egypt. Intrigued by the Valley of the Kings and convinced that a number of royal tombs lay undiscovered there, he teamed up with a wealthy English aristocrat, Lord Carnarvon, and began patient excavations.

Together the two explored the valley for ten disappointing years without success. Finally losing heart, Carnarvon announced he was not prepared to finance any more exploration

when, on November 4, 1922, workmen discovered a flight of steps. Uncovered, they led down to a walled-up entrance whose plaster face bore the seals of a little-known pharaoh, Tutankhamun. Carter resealed the tomb and telegraphed Carnarvon, who arrived on the 23rd. It took a another few days to reclear the door and the sloping corridor beyond it. On November 26 they stood before a second intact door, from which Carter removed a few stones and looked in. Asked by Carnarvon if he could see anything, Carter replied, "Yes, wonderful things." What he might more accurately have said was, "The most magnificent and unimaginable cache of glittering art and treasures ever discovered."

So much was stashed in three small chambers that, looking at photographs of the find, you would think the two men had discovered a badly kept junk store. It was to take Carter ten solid years to record, remove, and catalog all the items.

In the meantime, the discovery of these "wonderful things," which had lain undisturbed and unseen for thousands of years, took not just archaeology but the whole world by storm. As Carter labored to conserve the treasures, at the same time he was obliged to satisfy VIP visitors and the world's press. Tutmania became the craze of the 1920s. The Folies Bergère in Paris added "Tutankhamun's Follies" to its showgirl review, London seriously considered calling the latest extension to its subway system Tutancamden (it passed through Tooting and Camden Town), while in Russia Tutankhamun's chambers inspired the mausoleum in Red Square, and its occupant, the corpse of Lenin, was said to be embalmed with a fluid based on one used by the

INSIDER TIP:

Each tomb is unique to its creator. Choose a selection of tombs to visit that reflect the evolution of time through design.

—KEN GARRETT
National Geographic photographer

ancient Egyptians. So immense was the impact of Tutankhamun on all aspects of life that Pope Pius XI was led to comment of the find, "It's not an exhumation, it is a resurrection."

For all that, Carnarvon and (continued on p. 280)

The Lost Tomb

In 1995 archaeologist Kent Weeks was directing a mapping project in the Valley of the Kings and wanted to relocate KV 5, an ancient tomb entered in 1825, dismissed as unimportant, and subsequently forgotten. The roadway at the valley's entrance was being widened and he feared it might damage any tombs in its path, and that path, he suspected, lay above KV 5.

It took only a week of digging to locate the tomb's entrance. The plans for the road were changed, and Weeks and his team continued clearing debris from the tomb. In doing so, they uncovered an unknown doorway, beyond which a long corridor stretched out ahead. What had previously been thought an unimportant small tomb instead turned out to be a massive complex of 59 chambers. Even more exciting, inscriptions in two of the chambers indicated that this was the burial place of a number of sons of Ramses II, otherwise known as Ramses the Great.

KV 5 became the biggest and most newsworthy find since Tutankhamun. Not that there is any treasure involved this time around; ancient grave robbers had taken care of that. However, excavations have since yielded another 44 chambers, bringing the total in the complex so far to 110, making this by far the largest tomb ever discovered in Egypt.

Bringing Egyptology Up To Date

In the early years of the 20th century, scientific excavation in Egypt began to overtake treasure hunting. Individual enthusiasts backed by wealthy patrons gave way to officially accredited teams of foreign and local archaeologists sifting the sands of Egypt and attempting to make sense of its ancient past.

Zahi Hawass (in light blue shirt), Secretary General of the Egyptian Supreme Council of Antiquities, talks with fellow team members at a tomb in Abu Sir.

The opening of the tomb of Tutankhamun in 1922 is the defining moment in the history of Egyptology. Inevitably the discovery generated something of a political storm, the outcome being that any antiquities found in Egypt—including the entire contents of Tutankhamun's tomb—had to remain there.

Archaeology in Egypt became subject to much more stringent rules—but this did not mean a halt to the discoveries.

Less than 20 years after the Tutankhamun find, in 1939, yet more intact royal tombs were revealed when French archaeologist Pierre Montet made his staggering discoveries at the northern Delta site of Tanis (see p. 165). American discoveries at the pyramid site of Dahshur (see p. 151) uncovered the golden jewels of Queen Weret in 1995, the same year in which fellow American Kent Weeks discovered a whole network of chambers in KV 5, the massive tomb built for Ramses II's children in the Valley of the Kings (see "The Lost Tomb," p. 277). It is the largest tomb yet found and

(see p. 165)

(see p. 151)

(see "The Lost Tomb," p. 277)

INSIDER TIP:

If you're interested in books about Egypt, look for volumes published by the American University in Cairo. They're quite good, and many are not available outside Egypt.

—ANN WILLIAMS
National Geographic *magazine* writer

it will take many years' work to examine fully, together with several more of the valley's royal tombs, which are currently being studied by international teams of archaeologists.

Barely a year goes by without the report of another significant find. In early 2007, an entirely new chamber, KV 63, was discovered in the Valley of the Kings. In 2008, the pyramid of Queen Sesheshet, mother of the 6th dynasty pharaoh Teti, was uncovered in Saqqara beneath 23 feet of sand; two months later came news of the discovery of a mummy (likely Sesheshet herself) inside the pyramid.

In January 2009 Saqqara yielded another notable find: a so-called storeroom for mummies believed to date to the 26th dynasty. Amid the 20 or so mummies simply buried in sand were eight sarcophagi, materials for some of which are thought to have come from Thebes.

Though an old-fashioned hunch led to the chance discovery of the Valley of the Golden Mummies (see p. 203) in 1999, these days advances in Egyptology are less likely to come from headline-grabbing tomb openings than

(see p. 203)

from meticulous scientific examinations. With new methods of study out in the field there are philologists, epigraphists, engineers, forensic scientists, and geologists analyzing soil, reading striations in stone, and autopsying corpses that are several thousand years old. In the 200 years since the decipherment of hieroglyphics, the techniques available to Egyptologists have developed at an amazing rate: Tiny robot-propelled cameras can investigate deep inside the Great Pyramid, while extraction of DNA samples from mummies lets scientists study them in a virtually nondestructive way.

Egyptologists are now digging for information, not things. Which is not to say there are no more spectacular finds to be made. In the opinion of Dr. Zahi Hawass, Secretary General of the Egyptian Supreme Council of Antiquities and Egypt's leading archaeologist, there are many more finds to be made: "I still say all the time that you never know what the sands of Egypt might hold. And that's why I believe until today we have discovered only 30 percent of our monuments. Still 70 percent is buried underneath the ground." The rediscovery of ancient Egypt is a story still being told.

A statue of Cesarion awaits transfer to Paris.

Carter's prize was the burial of a very minor king, and it can only be wondered what the intact tomb of a Ramses II or Amenhotep III might have held. We can be sure that it would have put Tutankhamun's haul to shame.

Other Tombs

There are too many tombs to see to describe them all, but the following are some of the more interesting. They are listed in chronological sequence, which is

the ideal way to visit to witness the evolution of tomb design and wall paintings.

Tomb of Tuthmose III

(KV 34): Kept off the throne by Hatshepsut (see p. 268), when he eventually did attain power Tuthmose III (1479– 1425 B.C.) established himself as one of Egypt's greatest pharaohs. It was during his reign that the Valley of the Kings assumed the character of a royal necropolis, and he was one of the first to be buried in it. His tomb is one

of the most difficult to reach, at the far end of the valley, with the entrance in a narrow defile some 100 feet (30 m) above ground. It is necessary to ascend a steep wooden staircase to the entrance, then to make an equally steep descent down the rock-hewn corridor. Just before the bottom is a shaft, now traversed by a narrow gangway; similar shafts appear in other tombs and they are the source of much debate. One theory has it they were to protect the burial hall from flooding by torrential rains, another that they were traps for unwary thieves. Alternatively they may have some yet unrevealed ritual meaning. The burial chamber, which is oval-shaped like a cartouche, has peculiar stick figures rather than the fuller characters of later tombs, and script in a style used for writing on a papyrus.

Tomb of Amenhotep II

(KV 35): It is no surprise that the tomb of Amenhotep II (*R.*1427–1400 B.C.) is very similar to that of Tuthmose III, whom he succeeded on the throne. It has much the same plan, only on a considerably larger scale, and the same "prototype-style" wall paintings. When French archaeologists discovered the tomb in 1898, the quartzite sarcophagus still contained the body of the pharaoh, with a garland of mimosas around his neck. The mummy was left in peace until 1928, when it was removed to the Egyptian Museum in Cairo. In one of the small annexes off the burial chamber, walled up in antiquity, the archaeologists also made the surprising find of nine other mummies of royal blood, including Tuthmose IV, Seti II, Amenhotep III, and his wife, Queen Tiye. The bodies of kings and queens were often moved the tomb before it was required for use. Those figures that do appear, though—in the well shaft and antechamber—now have the fuller-bodied look that most people associate with pharaonic art. The scenes depict various

Decorations like these in the tomb of Seti I were a guidebook to help the dead pharaoh from this world to the next.

and hidden to foil robbers, who would rip them apart in their search for treasure, but nobody quite knows why or exactly when they were hidden in this tomb.

gods, such as Osiris and Hathor, presenting the pharaoh with the key of life, the *ankh*.

Tomb of Tuthmose IV
(KV 43): Tuthmose IV *(R. 1400–1390 B.C.)*, son of Amenhotep II, enjoyed a peaceful if brief reign. His death would seem to have come prematurely—the artists had no time to finish decorating

Tomb of Horemheb
(KV 57): Horemheb *(R. 1323–1295 B.C.)* had been commander in chief of the Egyptian army before becoming pharaoh. He was a prolific builder who greatly enlarged the temple at Karnak. His tomb displays a change in style from previous ones in that

it runs almost straight, with no right-angled bend. It also introduces bas-reliefs, where the figures and symbols are carved out before painting, as opposed to the earlier method of just applying the paint straight to the wall. What is also interesting

INSIDER TIP:

Don't be surprised if the Valley of the Kings looks like a construction zone. A number of archaeological missions are conducting excavations there, creating long trenches.

—ANN WILLIAMS
National Geographic
magazine writer

is that many of the figures are unfinished and left at different stages: Some are just roughly sketched out; some then display corrections by the chief artist; others are partially incised into the rock by a sculptor prior to painting. It gives a fascinating insight into how the tombs were created and gives the enterprise a human slant.

Tomb of Seti I (KV 17):

This is the longest, deepest, and most lavishly decorated tomb in the Valley of the Kings. It was discovered in 1817 by the famous Belzoni, one of the more colorful characters in the history of Egyptology (see p. 77). The tomb burrows some 390 feet

(120 m) down into the hillside in a series of descending corridors and chambers. The upper passages and first four-pillared room all exhibit scenes from the Litany of Re and Amduat. The lower passageway depicts the Opening of the Mouth ceremony in which the king's soul is reawakened and his senses restored. At the bottom is a six-pillared burial chamber with a vaulted heavenly ceiling showing the constellations, and a lineup of deities. In here Belzoni found an empty alabaster sarcophagus of such delicacy it is almost translucent. It now lies at the heart of the eccentric and wonderful Sir John Soane Museum in London.

Tomb of Merenptah
(KV 8): Merenptah (*R.*1213–1203 B.C.) was one of the many sons of Ramses II. Given the extraordinarily long reign of his father, he was probably already in his fifties when he came to the throne. His tomb sees an increase in the height of the corridors and chambers, and it is the first in which the axis is dead straight, ironing out the sideways jog present in all those that came before. The decoration is very similar to that in the tomb of Seti I: The upper passages contain the Litany of Re, followed by scenes from the Amduat; the lower passages have depictions of the Opening of the Mouth ceremony, although much was destroyed by flooding in antiquity. In the eight-pillared burial chamber is Merenptah's magnificent granite

sarcophagus, carved in the shape of a cartouche on which the dead king is depicted with his arms crossed in an Osiride position. Surrounding him is the *uroboros*, the serpent that encircles the world.

Tomb of Ramses III (KV 11):

Ramses III (*R.*1184–1153 B.C.), the builder of the glorious temple at Medinat Habu (see pp. 254–256), was the last of the truly great pharaohs. Not all of his tomb is open to the public because excavation work is ongoing in the lowest levels, including the burial chamber, but it is worth visiting for the wall paintings in the upper chambers and passageways. Expert opinion is that technically the reliefs here are poor, but the variety and unusual nature of the subjects portrayed are interesting. In ten small cells off the upper passages are paintings of jugs, pots, and amphorae; of the preparation of food; and of the furniture and weapons of the king. It is the ancient ancestor of *Better Homes & Gardens*. Most famous of all, in the last cell on the left, is a pair of musicians, from which the tomb gets its alternative name, the Tomb of the Harpists. Just beyond this cell is a stubby dead-end and a new parallel corridor starting to the right; this is where the workmen ran into another tomb (KV 10, belonging to Ameemesses) and had to switch direction. Visitors can follow the new corridor down to a pillared hall, which contains paintings of the known human races.

Tomb of Ramses IV (KV 2):

A very shallow and bright tomb

Osiris and the pharaoh at the Tomb of Seti I. After his death, Osiris (left), the Egyptian god of vegetation and civilization, became ruler of the dead and god of the underworld.

Archaeologists work at a newly discovered pharaonic-era tomb in the Valley of the Kings, the first uncovered there since Tut's discovery in 1922.

(*R.*1143–1136 B.C.). The earlier Ramses began the tomb and was first interred here, but then it was later extended by his brother and successor. Egyptologists still puzzle why Ramses VI did not build his own tomb, as was customary, and the best guess is that it was down to simple economics; at this period in history, ancient Egypt was in a weakened and bankrupt state. Little is known about Ramses VI, but his tomb, though very simple in plan, has perhaps the most sophisticated decoration of any. Its walls contain a vast encyclopedia of texts and images detailing the nightly journey of the sun-god Re through the underworld, and his victorious emergence each morning. This rebirth occurs at the center of the east wall of the burial chamber, with the sun disk being raised by the elongated arms of Nut, the "Lady of the Sky and Stars, Mother of the Sun." The same goddess also stretches along the ceiling, swallowing the sun, which travels through her elongated form to be reborn.

with no stairs, and with only one wide, reasonably airy, short passage to descend, this tomb has none of the claustrophobic air of its predecessors. It has been open since antiquity and carries the graffiti to prove it. Exposure to centuries of visitors has led to the deterioration of the wall paintings, but a vibrant depiction of the goddess Nut stretches across the blue ceiling.

Tomb of Ramses VI (KV 9): Strictly speaking, this is the tomb of Ramses V (*R.*1147–1143 B.C.) *and* of Ramses VI

Tomb of Ramses IX (KV 6): The closest open tomb to the site entrance, this is also one of the last to be dug in the valley (just as the tomb of Tuthmose III, one of the earliest, is right at the far end). Again, characteristic of these later Ramessid tombs, it has a simple plan of one relatively short, wide sloping corridor with few steps. The decoration is very similar to that in the tomb of Ramses VI. ∎

Looking more like the rest of Africa, with pharaonic monuments at magnificent settings beside the Nile

South of Luxor

Introduction & Map   286–287

Esna   288

Edfu   289–290

Kom Ombo   291

Feature: Nubian Culture   292–293

Aswan   294–301

Experience: Make Your Own *Karkadeh*   297

Experience: Hire a Felucca in Aswan or Luxor   301

Feature: Crusing the Nile   302–303

Philae   304–307

High Dam   308–309

Lake Nasser   310–311

Experience: Fish on Lake Nasser   311

Feature: Saving the Monuments   312–313

Abu Simbel   314–318

Hotels & Restaurants   370–372

Boats crowd a harbor on the Nile near Aswan.

South of Luxor

If Alexandria is Egypt's European face, and Cairo embodies the Arab Middle East, then south of Luxor is African Egypt. The banks of the Nile, here broad and dramatic, are heavy with lush vegetation. Urban centers are few, and even the capital of the region, Aswan, has a languorous air, stifled into inactivity by the heat.

NOT TO BE MISSED:

Edfu's Temple of Horus 289–290

Kom Ombo's unusual double temple sited by the Nile 291

Sunset drinks on the terrace of the Old Cataract Hotel 295

Nubian Museum 296–297

Sailing to the Botanical Gardens on Kitchener's Island in Aswan 299

The island of Philae 304–307

Cruising on Lake Nasser 310

Mountainside Abu Simbel 314–318

Since the time of the pharaohs, this area has always been the southernmost province of Egypt, and Aswan (population 150,000) the southernmost Egyptian town. For centuries, the cataract at Aswan, where rocks churn up the river and make it impassable by boat, marked the dividing line between ancient Egypt and its equally ancient neighbor to the south, Nubia. One of history's discarded empires, Nubia vanished under the onslaught of the Muslims, but it once encompassed the lands from beyond Aswan all the way down to what is now Khartoum in Sudan.

In times of strength, the Egyptians would undertake military expeditions to the south, erecting great monuments such as the imposing Abu Simbel to mark out their territorial gains. When Egypt wavered under weak dynasties, the Nubians (also known as Kushites) would, in turn, forge north. In 715 B.C. they succeeded in taking control of all Egypt and briefly establishing a new ruling dynasty in Memphis. Later, from

their base in Alexandria, the Greco-Romans managed to maintain a firm grip on this frontier territory, pursuing a politically sensible policy of assimilation rather than subjugation. Almost all the surviving monuments south of Luxor date from this era, notably the riverside temples at Esna, Edfu, Kom Ombo, and Philae—the latter two are striking as much for their location as for their architecture. The finest way to visit these sights is in the time-honored way, by boat, cruising from Luxor upriver to Aswan, or vice versa (see pp. 302–303).

Viewed from a cruise ship, the riverbanks are lined with forests of palm trees, banana plantations, and rows of crops. Signs of life are few, largely because villages have traditionally been built back from the water's edge to avoid being inundated during the annual floods. Villagers usually appear at sunset, coming down to the Nile to wash their dishes, water the animals, and socialize. The women are often carrying pots or water jugs balanced amazingly on their heads.

The influence of Nubia is still felt greatly. Even though no country or political entity called Nubia exists, there is still a Nubian people. Until the 20th century, many of them lived along the Nile south of Aswan, their ancient homeland. But following the completion of the first Aswan Dam in 1902, villages had to be abandoned in the face of rising waters. When the High Dam was built in the 1960s, the whole region was inundated. Many moved north, and now a large proportion of the inhabitants of Aswan and surrounding villages are Nubians, distinguished from the rest of the Egyptians by being taller and having darker skin. They speak their own language and also have their own traditional culture (see pp. 292–293). ∎

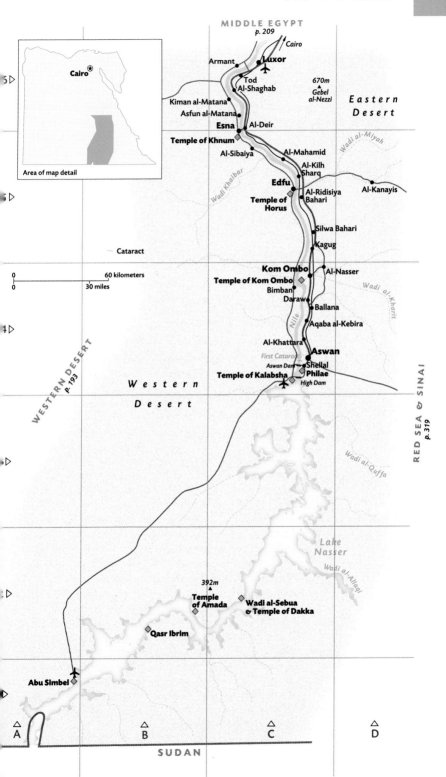

MIDDLE EGYPT
p. 209

Cairo

Armant
Luxor

Tod
Al-Shaghab

Kiman al-Matana

Asfun al-Matana

670m
▲
*Gebel
al-Nezzi*

*Eastern
Desert*

Esna   Al-Deir

Temple of Khnum

Al-Sibaiya   Al-Mahamid

Wadi al-Miyah

Al-Kilh
Sharq

Edfu   Al-Ridisiya
Bahari

Al-Kanayis

**Temple of
Horus**

Silwa Bahari

Kagug

Kom Ombo   Al-Nasser

Temple of Kom Ombo

Bimban   *Wadi al-Kharit*

Darawe

Ballana

Aqaba al-Kebira

Al-Khattara

Aswan

First Cataract

Aswan Dam   **Shellal**
Philae

Temple of Kalabsha   *High Dam*

Cataract

0 ———————— 60 kilometers
0 ———————— 30 miles

Nile

Cairo ✪

Area of map detail

WESTERN DESERT
p. 193

*Western
Desert*

RED SEA & SINAI
p. 319

Wadi al-Quffa

*Lake
Nasser*

Wadi al-Allaqi

392m
▲
**Temple
of Amada**   **Wadi al-Sebua
& Temple of Dakka**

Qasr Ibrim

Abu Simbel

△   △   △   △
A   B   C   D

SUDAN

Esna

Easily visited as a day trip from Luxor, Esna (Isna), 30 miles (48 km) to the south, is a busy little agricultural center on the west bank of the Nile. Its prime attraction, and the reason that many cruise ships stop here, is the Temple of Khnum.

Temple of Khnum
🗺 287 C5
✉ Tourist bazaar
💲 $$

The temple is buried in the middle of the modern town, sunk in a pit almost 30 feet (9 m) below the level of the surrounding buildings. Constructed in Ptolemaic and Roman times,

INSIDER TIP:

When you are at a site with large columns— or similar structures —don't try to photograph all of it to show how large it is. Rather, zoom in on a person standing next to it to get a sense of scale.

—TAYLOR KENNEDY
National Geographic photographer

it was dedicated to Khnum, the ram-headed god who created humankind on his potter's wheel, using clay from the Nile.

It was one of the last great temples to be built in Egypt. Even so, it has not lasted as well as some of the monuments built centuries earlier, and all that remains today is the columned **hypostyle hall.** This is the work of the Roman emperor Claudius and dates from the third century A.D. Twenty-four columns with lotus-flower capitals support the roof of the hall. An astronomical theme decorates the ceiling, showcasing a large zodiac, and the wall reliefs include a scene depicting a king netting wildfowl. Some walls have hymns to Khnum, one written almost entirely with hieroglyphs of rams, another written with crocodiles.

Originally, a ceremonial way linked the temple to the Nile, which is just a short distance to the east. Remains of the **ancient quay,** with cartouches of Roman emperor Marcus Aurelius, lie just south of the place where the modern cruise ships dock.

Nowadays a covered tourist bazaar connects the temple and river, and visitors are required to run a gauntlet of pushy salesmen offering thin cotton scarves, *galabiyyas* (the long robe commonly worn by rural Egyptians), and the handwoven baskets for which the area is known. Bargain hard if you are going to buy. Each Saturday morning the town also hosts a busy **camel market.**

The region around Esna, on the Kom Ombo plain, has been a good site for archeologists studying peoples inhabiting the river area in pre-pharaonic times. Ancient tools and bones have been found here.

Just to the north of Esna, two barrages, one with a hydroelectric generator, also act as bridges over the Nile. Both have locks that the cruise ships have to pass through as they travel from Luxor to Aswan and back. ∎

Edfu

Easily the most splendid of the Nile-side monuments between Luxor and Aswan, Edfu's Temple of Horus is the most complete of its kind. Though built by the Greco-Romans long after the true era of the pharaohs, it conforms exactly to the principles of ancient Egyptian architecture.

Unusually, the two towers of Edfu's great entrance pylon are perfect mirror images of each other.

If you want to see what virtually every other temple in Egypt would have looked like in its original form, visit Edfu (Idfu). A small, dusty regional center for the sugarcane trade, the town of Edfu lies about halfway between Luxor and Aswan, roughly 70 miles (112 km) from each. It's an easy day trip by bus from either, and all cruise ships stop off here. The **Temple of Horus** is some distance inland from the river moorings, and there is a thriving local trade in horse-drawn *calèches* ferrying visitors from one to the other. The ride costs no more than a couple of dollars. The approach to the temple is via the obligatory tourist bazaar, with streetside stalls peddling goods that are easily resisted.

Until the mid-19th century, as a commonly reproduced drawing by Scottish artist David Roberts (1796–1864) shows, the temple was almost completely buried, with sand filling the interior practically to the ceiling. A part of the village of Edfu stood on its roof. Auguste Mariette, the founder of Cairo's Egyptian Museum (see p. 77), began excavation in the 1860s. Today the whole of the temple has been revealed, and the village is pushed back so that the mud-brick houses line the top of

Temple of Horus
▲ 287 C5
✉ Tourist bazaar
$ $$

the compound walls overlooking the cleared forecourt below.

Unfortunately for visitors, the impact of the temple is lessened somewhat by having to approach from the rear and walk along the entire length of the side wall to view the splendor of the main **entrance pylon.** This massive structure was erected by Ptolemy XII (*R.*80–51 B.C.), father

INSIDER TIP:

Descendants of the pharaohs' cats are found all over Egypt, and they appreciate little snacks.

—LESLIE LYONS
National Geographic field researcher

of Cleopatra, and is decorated with twin scenes of the pharaoh grasping the hair of his enemies, with a staff raised about to smite them. The deities Horus and Hathor look on. Ptolemy XII was the ninth of his dynasty to add to this temple, which Ptolemy III began 180 years earlier, in 237 B.C.

Flanking the entrance gate are **two statues of Horus** as a falcon. According to Egyptian mythology, Horus was the child of Isis and Osiris, the fertility god who was killed by his brother Seth, the god of chaos (see "Isis *&* Osiris," p. 305). Ancient Egyptians believed that Horus avenged his father's death at Edfu by fighting and killing Seth. Many of the wall reliefs inside the temple deal with this cataclysmic battle, with Seth represented as a diminutive hippopotamus.

Immediately beyond the pylon is the immense, paved **peristyle court** surrounded by colonnades composed of columns with capitals sculpted with various forms. Also in the court, standing before the entrance to the first hypostyle hall, is a colossal black granite statue of Horus, portrayed as a falcon wearing the double crown of Egyptian kingship.

There are two **hypostyle halls,** each with 12 great columns supporting the roof, and beyond them an empty antechamber, off which is a doorway leading to a staircase. Long, straight, and narrow, this gives access to the roof with fine views over the town to the Nile and green fields beyond. It is usually necessary to pay one of the guardians some *baksheesh* (a tip) to get access.

Back downstairs, directly ahead from the antechamber, is the innermost core of the temple, the **sanctuary of Horus.** The shrine, carved from a single block of gray granite, stands 13 feet (4 m) high. As you face the sanctuary a doorway on the right leads out into a small unroofed court where a flight of steps leads up to what is known as the **New Year Chapel,** worth a look for the blue-colored image of the sky goddess Nut stretched across the ceiling.

To the other side of the temple, a flight of steps leads down to a small **Nilometer.**

Also, do not overlook the colonnaded **birth house,** across the forecourt from the temple's great pylon, which was a focus for an annual festival reenacting the divine birth of Horus and the reigning pharaoh. ■

Kom Ombo

Just 30 miles (48 km) north of Aswan, Kom Ombo occupies the Nile-side site of the ancient city of Pa-Sebek, the Domain of Sobek, a center for worship of the crocodile god of that name. All traces of the city are long gone—and the crocodiles that used to bask on nearby sandbanks have been hunted to extinction—but the remains of a fine waterfront temple are well worth a visit.

The best way to approach Kom Ombo is by river. If you are lucky enough to approach from the south by cruise ship, as your boat rounds the headland the ruins come spectacularly into view. Otherwise, reach the town by car, bus, or train from Aswan.

Like those at Esna and Edfu, the temple is postpharaonic, begun by Ptolemy VI (R. 180–145 B.C.) and completed during Roman times, probably replacing an earlier structure here. Unusually, it is dedicated to two gods, Sobek and Horus the Elder, the falcon-headed sky god. Symmetrical along its main axis, the temple has two of everything; each half is devoted to one god.

Cruise ships are the best way to get to Kom Ombo's ruins.

Kom Ombo After the High Dam

When it became clear that Nubia's Nile-side villages and towns would disappear beneath the waters of Lake Nasser following the construction of the High Dam in 1971, the Egyptian government launched a campaign to move thousands of Nubian families elsewhere. Most of the 50,000 Nubians displaced by the dam relocated to new villages in the area around Kom Ombo, now called New Nubia.

You approach from the side, via a small **Ptolemaic pylon** that formerly acted as a gate into the temple compound. This is at a right angle to what would have been the main pylon, now completely vanished, eroded by the river. Instead, the main remaining structure is, as at Esna, a **hypostyle hall** with eight great lotus-capital columns. It is fronted by a paved forecourt ringed with the stubs of columns bearing some well-preserved reliefs, complete with ancient coloring.

On exiting, look for the new **Crocodile Museum** out front, an installation displaying 40 mummified crocodiles, up to 16 feet long. Crocodiles, sacred to Sobek, may have been raised in the nearby deep well and a small pond. ∎

Temple of Kom Ombo

🅰 287 C4
✉ Corniche al-Nil
💲 $$

Nubian Culture

Nubian lands may have gone, drowned 200 feet (60 m) below the surface of Lake Nasser, but the culture of the Nubians remains very much alive and vibrant.

Nubians boast a rich musical culture; these women wearing embroidered gowns stage regular shows in Aswan as well as take part in wedding festivities.

When they were forced to abandon their villages in the 1960s and '70s, the Nubians re-created their traditional dwellings anew elsewhere. Made of mud-brick, their houses typically have domed or vaulted ceilings and are plastered or whitewashed. Each is decorated with claustrawork—moldings and tracery in mud. The distinctive decoration often includes ceramic plates set into the plaster of the external walls around the doorway. Such houses can be seen in the Nubian villages around Aswan and in Ballana near Kom Ombo. There is nothing else like them in Egypt.

Nubian Music

Just as unique is Nubian music, the fame of which has spread far beyond the Nile. Played on traditional instruments such as the *oud* (a pear-shaped guitar) and *douff* (a shallow drum), the music is characterized by a softly rolling, undulating rhythm, with a kind of swaying lilt. Melodies are simple and voices dry, twangy, and soulful. It's like an Egyptian form of the blues. One of the biggest names is Ali Hassan Kuban, a septuagenarian former tillerman from a small village near Aswan. He grew up playing at weddings and parties but is now a regular fixture on the international music scene. Almost as well-known was Hamza al-Din, a Nubian composer born in Wadi Halfa, the Sudanese town at the southernmost end of Lake Nasser. He was widely respected in the West for his compositions written for the oud. He died in 2006 in Oakland, California, where he'd been a long-time resident.

In Aswan, you can hear Nubian music as part of a floor show at a local restaurant or hotel, performed by troupes wearing gleaming white *galabiyyas* (gowns) and embroidered vests.

Wedding Traditions

It is also not uncommon to see a wedding in Aswan, particularly on a Thursday, which is the big wedding night throughout Egypt. Nubian wedding festivities last three days. On the first night, the bride and groom celebrate separately with their respective friends and families. On the second night, the bride takes her party to the groom's home and both

groups dance to traditional music until the small hours. Then the bride returns home and her hands and feet are painted in beautiful designs with henna. The groom's hands and feet also will be covered in henna, but without any design. On the third day, the groom and his party walk slowly to the bride's house in a singing and dancing procession.

INSIDER TIP:

At the handsome Nubian Museum in Aswan (see p. 296), take time to stroll through the gardens. Don't miss the stone ram's sarcophagus.

—ANN WILLIAMS
National Geographic magazine writer

Women visitors can have their hands "tattooed" with henna at some of the villages around Aswan—it looks great and provides an opportunity to spend time with Nubian women. Ask at the tourist office, which may be able to help. Expect to pay between $5 and $10 depending on the size of the design.

Women in front of the distinctively decorated wall of a Nubian mud-brick dwelling

Aswan

To most visitors Aswan is a one-night stopover en route to Abu Simbel. However, with a vibrant street market, a fascinating museum, idyllic midstream islands, and a couple of intriguing pharaonic sites in the vicinity, it is definitely worth a longer visit. If you can, take two or three days to enjoy what is one of the most peaceful and relaxing spots in Egypt.

Feluccas sail the Nile near Elephantine Island at Aswan, the sand hills of the Western Desert nearby.

Aswan

🗺 287 C4

Visitor information

✉ Railroad Station Sq.

☎ 097/231 2811

Historically, Aswan has always been Egypt's southern frontier town, the "gateway to Africa." It lies at the First Cataract, one of six sets of rapids in the Nile River (the other five are all in Sudan) between here and Khartoum that make the river impassable for boats. Hence waterborne traffic has always had to stop here, and the town has thrived over the centuries as a trading post. In ancient times the area was known as Swenet, but later the Copts called the place Souan, meaning "trade," from which the Arabic "Aswan" was derived.

Elephant caravans from the south once brought gold and perfumes; the skins of lions, leopards, and cheetahs; ostrich feathers and ivory tusks; and slaves, first for the pharaohs, then later for the harems of Islamic Cairo. Aswan was also an important military garrison, a base for expeditions into Nubia and Sudan. This garrison role continued right into the latter part of the 19th century, when the town was a marshaling point for Anglo-Egyptian forces sent down to Khartoum to quell the Mahdist Uprising (1881–1898) against the government.

About this time the town began to gain popularity among wealthy Europeans as a winter resort. The dry heat was deemed to be good for all kinds of ailments. Archaeologist Gaston Maspero (director of excavations in Egypt from 1899 to 1914) deplored the influx of foreigners, complaining that what once had been an unspoiled village was rapidly being turned into a copy of the French Riviera.

The main legacy of the early "excursionists" is the development of the Nile-side **Corniche,** created to provide moorings for the steamers. It is the most attractive waterfront boulevard in Egypt, looking over a beautiful stretch of the Nile, dotted with palm-crowded islands and with a backdrop of pure white sand hills rising from the water's edge on the far side.

One block inland from the Corniche is the *souq* (market), which, although no longer carrying the kind of unusual wares that once came in on the African caravans, is still a riot of bright colors and exotic fragrances. Things to look for include spices, patterned textiles, and local jewelry made in traditional Nubian designs.

At the southern end of the Corniche, at the point at which it curves sharply inland, are the **Ferial Gardens,** a peaceful little public park on a gentle rise of land. Beyond the gardens are the rather more private grounds of the **Old Cataract Hotel** *(Abtal al-Tahrir St., tel 097/231 6000; see p. 371),* another wonderful leftover from the early age of tourism. Opened in 1899, it is a great pink mansion of a place with Moorish interiors, vast high, wide corridors, and a magnificent of dining hall, which could double as a stage set for *The Thief of Baghdad.* Most splendid of all, though, is the setting, on a rocky outcrop high above the river. A big old wooden terrace makes the finest spot in Egypt to take an early-evening apéritif. The late French president François Mittérand was a frequent

INSIDER TIP:

Just north of the Old Cataract Hotel in Aswan is a shady public park, Ferial Gardens. You pay a small entrance fee, but the setting is great for relaxing and watching the river.

—CHIP ROSSETTI
National Geographic contributor

visitor, and other distinguished guests have included Winston Churchill, Jimmy Carter, Prince Charles and Princess Diana, and, perhaps most famously of all, Agatha Christie, who wrote part of *Death on the Nile* (1937) while staying here. The hotel appears prominently in both the book and the 1978 movie of the same

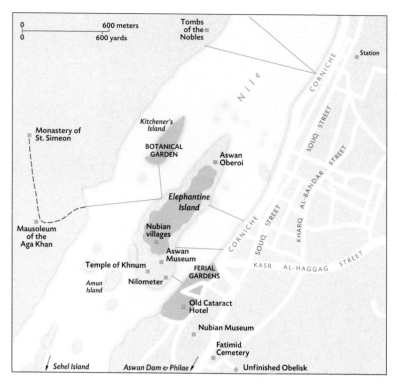

Nubian Museum

- 🅰 296
- ✉ Corniche al-Nil
- ☎ 097/231 3826
- 🕐 Open 9 a.m.–1 p.m. and 5 p.m.–9 p.m. (6 p.m.–10 p.m. in summer)
- 💲 $$

name, starring Peter Ustinov and Bette Davis. Unfortunately, in recent years the hotel has instituted a residents-only policy, and non-guests are allowed no farther than the main gate. It may, however, be possible to make a reservation for dinner (see p. 371).

South of the Center

Beyond the grounds of the Old Cataract Hotel stands a large, modern, light sandstone building, the **Nubian Museum,** opened in 1997. It represents a rather belated attempt to preserve and honor the culture of the region's indigenous people, a culture that was dealt a near fatal blow with the creation of the High Dam in

the 1960s (see p. 312–313). The lake that formed behind the dam completely submerged the Nubian heartland causing countless villages to be abandoned, forcing their inhabitants to migrate. The museum houses a collection of artifacts from the region, which are logically organized to tell the story of the development of this part of the Nile Valley, from prehistory through the pharaonic age, the coming of Christianity and Islam, right up to the building of the dam—although with no mention of the consequences. Exhibits are well displayed, and labeling is in several languages, English included. The large-scale models of Philae and of Abu Simbel are well worth seeing before a visit to those temples.

Most striking of all is a series of beautifully decorated facades, reconstructions of typical Nubian dwellings. In the museum's large, terraced garden there is a reconstructed Nubian house and a cave containing rock art rescued from areas now underwater.

High on top of the hill to the south of the museum is **Nubian House** (Nubian Museum Rd., tel 097/232 6226), a modest café with a terrace offering superb views over the Nile and First Cataract. It is a wonderful place for sunset drinks. To get there, turn left out of the museum and head straight on up the hill; it is a walk of about 20 minutes, or just a brief taxi ride. Ask the taxi driver to wait for you to avoid walking back along empty, unlit roads.

Below the museum is the vast **Fatimid Cemetery**, a burial ground with many small, domed mausoleums dating to the ninth century. Some of the tombs belong to local saints—these are usually strewn with flags and often visited by locals seeking blessings. Walk through the cemetery and out of a gate on the far side to reach what is known as the **Unfinished Obelisk.** One of Aswan's most curious sights, this is a huge obelisk perfectly shaped on three sides but still attached to the bedrock on the fourth. It was abandoned after a flaw was discovered in the stone. At nearly 140 feet (42 m) in length, had it been completed it would have been the largest, heaviest obelisk ever attempted. Archaeologists speculate that it was intended for Karnak (see pp. 242–249), a companion for the obelisk of Tuthmose III, which now stands on the Piazza San Giovanni in Rome. If you do not feel like walking (the quarry containing the obelisk is just over a mile/2 km from the center

EXPERIENCE: Make Your Own *Karkadeh*

At hotel breakfasts, you are likely to encounter the dark-red juice known as *karkadeh*. Made from dried hibiscus leaves, the cranberry-colored juice is a delicious morning drink, and it also is sometimes served hot as a tea. Because the plant is grown around Aswan, just about every spice store in the city has a crate of it out front. A bag of karkadeh leaves is a light souvenir to take with you, and it is very to easy to make the boiled drink once you're back home:

In a large saucepan, bring two quarts of water and two cups of loose hibiscus leaves to a boil. Simmer for 15 or 20 minutes, until the liquid is a rich red color.

Pour through a strainer to remove the leaves, and return the liquid to the pot. Over a low heat, add a cup of sugar (or less, if you prefer your karkadeh tarter). Stir until sugar is dissolved. To the resulting karkadeh—which will have the consistency of concentrated syrup—add water to dilute. Serve hot, or chilled over ice.

Karkadeh also makes a great drink mixer, particularly for a cocktail popular among expats in Egypt known as the Cairo Cosmopolitan: In a cocktail shaker, pour 1 oz. vodka, ½ oz. Triple Sec or Cointreau, the juice of half a lime, a splash of karkadeh, and ice. Shake, strain, and pour into a martini glass. Serve with a twist of lime.

Unfinished Obelisk

🔺 296

✉ Off Airport Rd.

💲 $$

of town), tours to Philae temple usually stop here on the way back. Alternatively, a taxi should cost no more than a couple of dollars.

The Nile & Its Islands

Shopping in the souq is fun, and the museum and obelisk are interesting, but the real attraction in Aswan is the river—broad and blue, and a conduit for cooling breezes that bring relief from the relentless heat. The best thing to do is get out on the water. One option is to rent a felucca, the traditional lateen-sailed boats that gracefully skim the Nile (see "Hire a Felucca in Aswan or Luxor," p. 301). Another alternative is to visit some of the many islands.

Preeminent among the local islands is **Elephantine Island,** so called for the giant gray granite boulders off its southern end, which resemble a herd of bathing elephants. A local ferry service shuttles across the Nile to it every 15 minutes or so between about 6 a.m. and 10 p.m., departing from the Corniche in front of Thomas Cook's office.

Long before the existence of Aswan, the pharaonic-era town of Swenet was on the southern end of the island, protected from attack by the turbulent waters of the First Cataract. It was known

INSIDER TIP:

The Aswan Moon, on a floating platform in the river (see p. 372), is one of the best places for atmosphere, good simple food, and sometimes live music.

—NEIL HEWISON

American University in Cairo Press

as the Gate of the South and was also the center of the cult of the ram-headed Khnum, creator of humankind. Partly excavated ruins cover this part of the island and include a late-dynasty temple devoted to Khnum, with the

Obelisks

Archaeologists believe that the obelisk originated as just an irregularly shaped, upright stone, which gradually developed into the familiar elongated, tapering, four-sided shaft with a point on top. Especially common during New Kingdom times, obelisks were often erected in pairs before temple entrances. They are always inscribed, and they generally commemorate victories, jubilees, or other notable events. Monolithic and regal, Egypt's obelisks have also always been regarded as something of collectors' items by powers abroad. The Assyrians removed two to Nineveh (in modern-day Iraq), the Romans carried off no less than three to Rome, and the Byzantines pilfered another to adorn the Hippodrome at Constantinople (now Istanbul).

The mighty industrial powers of the modern age also felt compelled to embellish their capitals with Egyptian megaliths. In the 19th century yet more obelisks were removed from Karnak in Luxor and Alexandria and then reerected in New York, London, and Paris.

This house is decorated in traditional Nubian style, more African than Middle Eastern.

remains of pillars painted by the Romans.

Overlooking the ruins is the modest **Aswan Museum,** which has lost its best artifacts to the Nubian Museum (see pp. 296–297). However, the museum building was formerly the residence of Sir William Willcocks, the English architect of the Aswan Dam (see p. 307), and it still has a fragrant flower-and-herb garden. From the museum a path goes southward to a sycamore tree, marking the location of an ancient **nilometer.** Steps incised in the rock lead down to a square chamber at water level. The walls are marked off in Arabic, Roman, and faint pharaonic numerals. You can also view the nilometer from the river, the only vantage point from which it is also possible to see inscriptions carved into the surrounding rock with cartouches bearing the names of Tuthmose III and Amenhotep III.

The central part of Elephantine Island is thick with palms, cut through by looping pathways. Among the groves are two **Nubian villages,** with houses painted in oranges, yellows, and blues, the tightly grouped buildings separated by narrow baked-earth alleys. The banks of the east side of the island make a fine place to sit with nothing but the river, a blue sky, and the palms of the next island as a view.

Elephantine Island's neighbor is **Kitchener's Island,** for Lord Horatio Kitchener (1850–1916), now chiefly remembered for Britain's famous "Your Country Needs You" World War I recruitment poster. He was given the island in the 1890s when, as consul general, he effectively ruled Egypt on behalf of the British. Although a military man, Kitchener also had a passion for horticulture, which he indulged here by turning the entire island into a botanical garden, importing

Aswan Museum & Nilometer

296

Elephantine Island

 $$

plants from other parts of Africa, from India, and from as far afield as Southeast Asia. With plenty of shade from the broad leaves overhead, it is a beautiful place to while away an afternoon. Get here by felucca from the Corniche or from the east side of Elephantine Island.

Also worth visiting is **Sehel Island,** a little less than 3 miles

Aswan is all about the river, and the best way to appreciate the place is to get on a boat.

(4 km) upriver from central Aswan. It is a beautiful run of about an hour in a felucca. The island has two summits, both of which provide superb views of the foaming waters around the First Cataract. There are pharaonic-era ruins and a picturesque Nubian village full of clamorous children eager to offer themselves as guides. All invitations should be firmly declined, as there is nothing to be guided around.

Across the River

Completely uninhabited, the West Bank of the Nile is pure desert. Fortunately, there are three unique attractions for those interested in crossing the river (take the local ferry from the Corniche opposite the railroad station.) Although it is not open to the public, the **Mausoleum of the Aga Khan**— the small, white, domed building high on the sandy slopes—is beautiful to photograph. The structure holds the body of Muhammad Shah Aga Khan III (1877–1957), the Pakistani-born 48th Imam, or spiritual leader, of the Ismaili sect of Islam. Once regarded as the richest man in the world and offered his weight in diamonds on his diamond jubilee in 1945, the Aga Khan liked to winter in Aswan. When he died, his wife, the Begum Aga Khan, a former French beauty queen, oversaw the construction of this fine monument in his honor, which in form is inspired by the Fatimid tombs in the cemetery over the river. Until her own death in July 2000, the Begum (or in her absence, the gardener) placed a red rose on his sarcophagus every day. She now lies entombed beside him.

About a mile into the desert from the ferry landing is the **Monastery of St. Simeon** (Deir Amba Samaan), founded in the seventh century, rebuilt in the tenth, and inexplicably abandoned some time in the 13th, never to be occupied again. Considering how long the monastery has lain abandoned, it remains in surprisingly good shape. Located at the head of a desert valley, it is an impressive sight, looking far more like a fortress in a movie set than a religious institution. Its outer walls are 30 feet (9 m) high in parts, with the lower courses composed of rock and the upper parts made of mud-brick. Inside are the remains of a church, with a painting of Christ in the domed apse, a central keep, a vaulted refectory, stables, and a rock chapel painted with saints. A fun way of getting to the monastery is to rent a camel from the pack down at the ferry landing. The round-trip including waiting time should cost about $10. Otherwise, it is a hard, extremely tiring trudge through soft sand.

The third of the interesting West Bank sights is the **Tombs of the Nobles,** a series of tombs in the high cliffs to the north of Kitchener's Island. These are the burial places of dignitaries of ancient Swenet. They date from the Old and Middle Kingdoms, with some much later Roman tombs lower down the cliff face. There's a ticket office at the site, and one ticket is good for all the tombs. The best preserved of them all is the **Tomb of Prince Sirenput II**

INSIDER TIP:

A quarry in Aswan contains an unfinished pink granite obelisk that the female pharaoh Hatshepsut may have commissioned. Find it near Mubarak Road.

—ANN WILLIAMS
National Geographic
magazine writer

(No. 31), dating from the 12th dynasty (1985–1795 B.C.), which contains six small Osiride statues of the tomb's occupant, as well as some fine wall paintings depicting Sirenput with his family. ∎

Monastery of St. Simeon

🅰 296

✉ West Bank

💲 $$

EXPERIENCE: Hire a Felucca in Aswan or Luxor

Felucca captains hustle for business along the Corniche in both Luxor and Aswan. Prices are almost wholly dependent on your bargaining skills, although the official government price for a boat capable of seating up to eight people is roughly $6 per hour. A three- or four-hour trip, for instance, to Sehel Island and back with an hour's wait by the captain included, costs about $18. By far the nicest time to be out on the water is at sunset. Pack a picnic and a few bottles of beer and feast while drifting, watching a blood red sun drop below the horizon.

Longer trips are also a popular option. Unlike the giant tourist cruises, feluccas are the much more authentic way to travel the Nile. Felucca trips usually begin in Aswan, heading north to Kom Ombo (overnight), Edfu (two nights), or Esna (three nights). When negotiating with a captain, make sure you spell out specifics: how far you're traveling, whether food is included in the price, and whether he himself will be piloting the boat. Bring plenty of bottled water, and bear in mind that feluccas usually don't have life jackets on board. A sail up the Nile by felucca has a timeless quality and is very relaxing. Other than the occasional cruise ship passing by, you won't see many reminders of the modern world around you!

Cruising the Nile

The Nile was ancient Egypt's highway. The pharaohs traversed their realm by river, it was the route for traders and invaders, and in death, the ancients even took boats to the underworld. Only over the last century, with the advent of first railroads, then air travel, has the river been surpassed as a mode of transport. And still, for anyone with time, a cruise on the Nile remains the best way to experience Egypt.

A boat on the Nile has long been the way to travel in Egypt, from pharaohs to traders and invaders to the Grand Tourists of the 19th century. Even though there are quicker ways to get from here to there, today's traveler should follow in their footsteps, embarking on a classic Nile journey.

Travelers have gazed out over the country from the deck of a boat since as far back as the fifth century B.C., when the Greek chronicler Herodotus took passage through Egypt. But it was a combination of Napoleon's expedition (1798–1801) and the firm, stabilizing rule of Muhammad Ali (R.1805–1847) that truly opened up the Nile to the curious traveler. At this time,

the Holy Land and Egypt came to supplant the Grand Tour of Europe as a part of any wealthy young gentleman's education. Each fall, when the temperatures cooled and the winds got up, intrepid tourists would arrive by ocean liner in Alexandria, from where they would travel down to Cairo, hire a dragoman (guide), select a suitable *dahabiyya* (large sailboat), scuttle it to get rid of the rats and vermin, gather provisions in the *souq*, retrieve the boat, and then set off. The pace was languid, taking anything from 6 to 12 weeks to cover the 530 miles (850 km) between Cairo and Aswan. Besides visiting the sights, these early tourists enjoyed such activities en route as picnicking in tombs and digging for antiquities.

From Sailboat to Steamboat

From the 1870s sailboats were replaced by steamers, all of which were owned by Thomas Cook, the Henry Ford of sight-seeing, who introduced the world to package tourism. Known as "excursionists," Cook's customers were looked down upon by more independent travelers, most notably by Mark Twain, writing in 1870 in his famous travel book *Innocents Abroad*: "In the morning the lost tribes of America came ashore and infested the hotels and took possession of all the donkeys . . . They went in picturesque procession; . . . tried to break a fragment off the upright [Cleopatra's] Needle." In another section of the book, Twain lambasted the

INSIDER TIP:

If you are thinking about a cruise up the Nile, consider traveling on one of the new *dahabiyya* boats. Built along traditional lines, they bring to mind Thomas Cook tours but with modern amenities.

—MARK LINZ
American University in Cairo Press

bumptious tourists by reporting that they "made noise for five hundred, collided with camels, dervishes, effendis, asses, beggars and everything else."

Since Cook made Nile cruising affordable, it has been the staple of any visit to Egypt. Unfortunately, the threat of terrorist attacks in Middle Egypt has meant that since the early 1990s cruise ships are no longer permitted to sail south of Cairo or much north of Luxor. These days, those wishing to journey by river have to be content with sailing between Luxor and Aswan, a voyage of three or four days, or a week including a return leg.

Nights are spent on the boat at dock, days are filled with excursions, typically including all the sights of Luxor, Esna, Edfu, and Kom Ombo, then Aswan. The temples of Philae and Abu Simbel are usually optional extras. Levels of luxury are as high as you are pre-pared to pay for. Top-of-the-line boats come with plush carpets, swimming pools, and icy air-conditioning.

The *Dahabiyya* Returns

Even better, recent times have seen the reintroduction of the *dahabiyya,* the masted sailboat once used by 19th-century Grand Tourists. These boats are new builds but they are fashioned along ancient lines, each with just a handful of luxury cabins and suites. Upper decks are equipped with cush-ioned divans and strung with hammocks (as the novelist William Golding, who voyaged down the Nile in the 1980s, wrote in his journal, "the rhythm of the Nile is the art of doing nothing"), and meals are taken alfresco—all the better to heighten the sense of time traveling that a slow glide along Egypt's great river evokes.

At the other end of the scale, there are plenty of boats on which conditions leave a lot to be desired. It is very much a case of get-ting what you pay for, so do your homework before settling on a vessel. The most reputable boats are managed by international hotel chains, for example Mövenpick or Sheraton. International travel agencies such as Aber-crombie and Kent (*www.abercrombiekent.com*), Bales Worldwide (*www.balesworldwide.com*), and, the people who started the whole busi-ness of tourists cruising the Nile, Thomas Cook (*www.thomascook.com*), also have their own boats with excellent reputations.

Philae

A temple complex on an island in the Nile devoted to the goddess Isis, Philae is arguably the most romantic of Egypt's monuments, harmonizing perfectly with its watery setting. Getting there is only possible by small motor launch, which is a wonderful experience in itself.

There is no setting to equal Philae, viewed here at night.

Philae

- 🅰 287 C4
- ✉ Aglika Island
- 💲 $$. Sound-and-light show $$$

"There are four great recollections of a traveler, which might tempt him to live forever: the sea view of Constantinople, the sight of the Coliseum by moonlight, the prospect from the summit of Vesuvius at dawn, and the first glimpse of Philae at sunset."

—DR. R. R. MADDEN, 1827

First, take a taxi to the boat landing at Shellal, just south of the old Aswan Dam (see p. 307), about 5 miles (8 km) south of Aswan town center. Then, after purchasing temple tickets, walk out to the jetty, off which is moored a flotilla of small boats with Nubian captains. These water taxis hover, waiting for a full complement of eight passengers before they cast off and ride low in the water, headed for Aglika Island and its splendid ruins.

But as recently as 30 years ago the launches would have been heading for Philae Island, which is where the temple complex was originally constructed back in the Ptolemaic era. After the building of the Aswan Dam at the end of the 19th century, the level of the Nile rose, completely submerging the temple for six months of the year. Visitors would row out to peer down through the translucent green waters to the courts and columns below. In the 1960s, when the new High Dam threatened to put the island underwater forever, the temples were dismantled and removed stone by stone and then reconstructed on the nearby higher terrain of Aglika Island, which was even landscaped to resemble the original Philae.

Philae rose to importance during the time of the Ptolemies

and was the main cult center of Isis (see below), drawing pilgrims from all over the Mediterranean basin. So popular was worship of Isis that the site survived well into the Christian era as one of the last outposts of the ancient religion. It was not officially closed until A.D. 550. Early Christians then transformed the main temple's hypostyle hall into a chapel and added churches to the island, but none of these have survived.

The motor launches dock at the ancient quay on Aglika Island. The first structure visitors pass, just off to the left, is a "kiosk," a small open temple, erected by Nectanebo I (R.380–362 B.C.). Although now little more than a paved area with a row of columns at the rear, it is the oldest monument on the island. Beyond is a large court enclosed by two long colonnades; that to the west has windows overlooking the river, while the one to the east is interrupted by a series of ruined structures. The most notable of these ruins is the Temple of

Arensnuphis, dedicated to a very obscure Nubian god.

At the head of the court is the first pylon of the **Temple of Isis,** the island's centerpiece. The pylon was raised by Ptolemy XII, the pharaoh responsible for the

INSIDER TIP:

Don't miss the Philae Sound & Light Show. The trip to the island by small boat at night is a spectacular way to approach the site.

—MARK LINZ
American University in Cairo Press

similarly grand gateway at Edfu (see pp. 289–290). It is decorated with scenes of the ruler dispatching enemies, which are also familiar from Edfu. On the walls of the passage leading between the two towers of the pylon are inscriptions left by Napoleon's troops. They commemorate a French victory

Isis & Osiris

Together Osiris and his consort/sister Isis ruled the country. However, the evil Seth, their brother, began to plot against them. He tricked Osiris into climbing into a chest, which he then sealed and flung into the Nile. The chest washed up on the shores of Lebanon (Byblos), where it was eventually found by Isis and returned to Egypt. Seth, however, intercepted the chest, hacked Osiris' body into 14 parts, and scattered them throughout the Nile Valley. Isis sought out each part and briefly revived Osiris to conceive a child, Horus, who used

the magic of his mother to defeat Seth and restore divine order.

As pharaohs identified themselves with Horus, Isis was their divine mother. She became identified as the goddess of women, sex, and purity, and Isis worship spread throughout the Roman empire, with cult temples as far afield as what is now Hungary. For the first two centuries of Christianity's history, she was its chief rival. Some scholars believe that the Virgin Mary cult was Christianity's attempt to win over the Isis worshipers.

over the Mamluks at the Battle of the Pyramids (see p. 38).

Beyond the pylon is a forecourt with elegantly carved columns; in fact, everything about this temple is extremely refined and delicate, making it a favorite with Egyptologists as well as casual visitors. Off to the left is what's known as the **birth house** (or *mammisi)*, which is where the pharaohs reinstated their legitimacy as mortal descendants of Horus by taking part in rituals celebrating the god's birth. At the bottom of the rear wall is a scene of Isis giving birth to Horus in the marshes, while on the left-hand wall she is shown suckling the infant. Unfortunately the goddess has suffered defacement at the hands of Christian iconoclasts.

Back in the forecourt, a second pylon gives access to the inner temple, where, beyond a small hy-postyle hall, a series of vestibules get lower and darker, culminating in the innermost holy sanctuary. Dimly lit by two apertures in the ceiling, the **sanctuary** contains a stone pedestal dedicated by Ptolemy III (*R*.246–221 B.C.) and his wife Berenice (portrayed in

INSIDER TIP:

Motor launches generally pass behind the island when leaving, so you can usually catch a great photo of the Kiosk of Trajan from the water as you go.

—CHIP ROSSETTI
National Geographic contributor

several beautiful mosaics at the Greco-Roman Museum in Alexandria; see pp. 176–177).

KEY TO SITE PLAN

Philae

1 Kiosk of Nectanebo1
2 Temple of Arensnuphis
3 Outer Temple Court
4 Gate of Ptolemy
5 First pylon
6 Birth house
7 Nilometer
8 Second pylon
9 Sanctuary
10 Gate of Hadrian
11 Temple of Harendotes
12 Temple of Hathor
13 Kiosk of Trajan
14 Gate of Diocletian
15 Roman Gate
16 Temple of Augustus

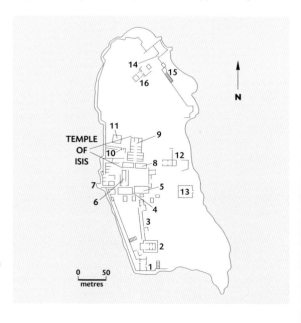

If the caretaker can be persuaded to open the gate, a staircase on the west side of the temple gives access to upper rooms decorated with reliefs dwelling on the resurrection of Osiris after his dismemberment by Seth (see "Isis & Osiris," p. 305). You can see Isis gathering up her brother's limbs. It is also possible to get up onto the roof.

Other Monuments

Beside the main Temple of Isis, east of the second pylon, is the small **Temple of Hathor.** It is in a fairly ruinous state, but you can still make out two Hathor-headed columns, distinguished by their flared wigs. It also possesses a particularly fine relief of musicians with the ugly dwarf-god Bes playing harp.

Just to the south is the most famous of Philae's monuments, the very distinctive **Kiosk of Trajan,** nicknamed the Pharaoh's Bedstead, for obvious reasons. Built under the Roman emperor of that name (ca A.D. 100), it served as a royal landing for the temple. The kiosk is a curious thing in that it combines a typically classical structure of columns and lintels with pharaonic trimmings, such as the floral column capitals. In its original form it would have had a wooden roof. Reliefs on the screen walls feature Emperor Trajan making offerings to Isis, Osiris, and Horus.

Philae, like all of Egypt's major monuments, hosts a bombastic **sound-and-light show,** but it is certainly the best of its kind. It consists of an hour-long tour through the floodlit ruins. The cost is $10, including the boat ride, but

The Kiosk of Trajan has come to symbolize Philae, but it is not part of the temple proper.

it is worth it for the magical ambience of being on the island after dark. There are three shows a night; performance times vary seasonally, so check the details with your hotel receptionist or at the Aswan tourist information office.

Aswan Dam

Just upriver from the First Cataract, the Aswan Dam was constructed by the British between 1898 and 1902. At the time it was the largest of its kind in the world. It released Egypt from being at the mercy of unpredictable fluctuations in the level of the Nile. It also opened up vast new areas to cultivation and provided the country with most of its hydroelectric power. Now surpassed both in function and as a tourist attraction by the High Dam (see pp. 308–309), it is still worth a brief visit for the views of the river below—access is by road atop the dam. ■

High Dam

Egypt has a long history of dam building. The earliest recorded dam is believed to have been on the Nile near Cairo, where a 49-foot-high (15 m) structure was built about 2900 B.C. to supply water to the capital at Memphis. A project to rival anything built by the pharaohs, the High Dam (Sadd al-Ali) contains almost 20 times the amount of building material used in the Great Pyramid.

Security is tight, as a dam burst would wash most of Egypt into the sea.

High Dam
A 287 C4

As early as the 1950s it was evident that the Aswan Dam (see p. 307) was not big enough to counter the annual flooding of the Nile. Nor could it any longer satisfy Egypt's needs for power. President Gamal Abdel Nasser had the answer: a bigger, more expensive dam. After the World Bank reneged on a promised loan under pressure from the United States, Nasser nationalized the Suez Canal to generate revenue for the project, precipitating the Suez Crisis during which France, the United Kingdom, and Israel invaded the canal zone (see p. 40). In the end, the Soviet Union offered funding and expertise. Work began on the High Dam in 1960 and was completed in 1971, outlasting Nasser by a year.

An Engineering Feat

The resulting structure is 12,562 feet (3,830 m) across the top, 3,214 feet (980 m) wide at its base, and 364 feet (111m) at its highest point. Over 35,000 people helped build it, and 451 of them died during the construction. It is by no means the largest dam in the world

(America's Hoover Dam is more than twice as high), but it is impressive nonetheless. The benefits of the dam also have been huge. Egypt's area of cultivable land has increased by more than 30 percent, while evaporation from Lake Nasser, the reservoir that backs up behind the dam, has brought rainfall to previously arid areas. The High Dam's hydroelectric station has doubled the country's power supply.

Since a dam burst would wash most of Egypt into the Mediterranean Sea, security is paramount. The surrounding hills bristle with antennas, radar, and missiles. Visitors are allowed, though, and a pavilion at the eastern end of the dam has models and photographs. At the western end a giant lotus-like tower stands as a monument to Soviet-Egyptian friendship.

Nearby Monuments

Visible from the dam, on the west side of Lake Nasser, is the **Temple of Kalabsha.** Like Philae, this temple was originally sited elsewhere (in this case, 30 miles to the south) but had to be moved to avoid being submerged by Lake Nasser. The German government financed the rescue project and was presented in return with the temple's gateway, which is now in the Berlin Museum. Kalabsha was built during the reign of the last of the Ptolemies and completed under the first Roman emperor of Egypt, Augustus, between 30 B.C. and 14 A.D. It was dedicated to the Nubian god Mandulis. Isis and Osiris were also worshiped here. An impressive stone causeway leads up from the lake to the entrance pylon, beyond which are a colonnaded court and hypostyle hall. Inscriptions on the walls show emperors and pharaohs worshiping with gods. Beyond the hall are three chambers, with stairs leading from one up to the roof. The view of Lake Nasser and the High Dam, across the hall and court, is fantastic.

Adjacent to the temple is the **Kiosk of Qertassi,** a smaller, less well-preserved version of Trajan's Kiosk at Philae. Also here is the **Temple of Bayt al-Wali,** carved from rock during the reign of Ramses II. On the walls of the forecourt are several reliefs detailing the pharaoh's victory over the

Temple of Kalabsha

🔼 287 C4
✉ Lake Nasser
$ $$

INSIDER TIP:

Even if you only know one or two words of Arabic, use all as well as you can. When you make your attempts, even stumbling, your Egyptian hosts will love you for it.

—NEIL HEWISON
American University in Cairo Press

Nubians (south wall) and his wars against the Libyans and Syrians (north wall). Like Kalabsha, both of the structures were removed here to escape being inundated.

The easiest way to visit the dam and temples is to hire a taxi in Aswan. A round-trip, 15 minutes each way, with an hour's wait by the driver, should cost about $8. ■

Lake Nasser

As the world's largest artificial body of water, Lake Nasser's dimensions are staggering. From the High Dam it stretches over 300 miles (480 km), down into Sudan, and in places spreads to over 22 miles (35 km) in width. It is also the most stunningly beautiful, unspoiled region of Egypt.

The massive expanse of Lake Nasser was created as a consequence of the construction of the High Dam.

Lake Nasser
287 C2

Sand-dune shores roll down to the water's edge. Elsewhere are jagged granite crags topped with white sand, looking for all the world like snowcapped alpine peaks. Skies are completely clear, cloudless, and the deepest of blues. At night, stars stretch from one horizon to the other, arrayed like a great open-air planetarium. The lack of human inhabitants has made the reedy lake shores a favorite with migrating birds, as well as with a variety of wildlife including gazelle, foxes,

and monitor lizards. The inlets of the lake are the habitat of the only surviving specimens of Nile crocodiles in Egypt, which in recent years have claimed the life of more than one local fisherman. At least 25 species of fish thrive in the lake, including the huge Nile perch (Lates niloticus). The current record is 510 pounds (232 kg). The area now draws visitors from Europe and America, purely on the strength of the **fishing.** It is possible to sign up for five-day fishing safaris (see p. 380–381), or just head out from Aswan for a day.

The only man-made structures anywhere on the lake are a series of ancient Egyptian temples, painstakingly moved out of the path of the rising waters in the 1960s (see pp. 312–313).

Almost the only drawback is how to visit, since the only possible way to explore Lake Nasser is by boat. Currently several outfits operate luxury cruises of three or four days' duration (see p. 349–350), sailing between the High Dam in the north and Abu Simbel in the south. They stop en route at all the various pharaonic sites.

Most northerly of these sites is **Wadi al-Sebua,** about 85 miles (140 km) south of the High Dam on the west bank of the lake. Built during the reign of Ramses II, its name means "valley of lions" and refers to the avenue of sphinxes that leads to the temple. Although the temple was only moved here from its original site in the 1960s, its inaccessibility meant that it was forgotten and allowed to fill with sand. When the first cruise ships started sailing Lake Nasser in the 1990s, though, it was re-excavated for visitors. Even so, fallen statues of kings still lie half buried in the sand, and the fact that there is nothing but desert around—no ticket office, no souvenir stalls, no guardian—allows visitors to imagine that they might be the first discoverers of the site.

Dedicated to the gods Amun-Re and Re-Horakhty, the temple is yet another work dating from the reign of the prolific Ramses II. A large statue of the great pharaoh stands to the left of the entrance, and ten more representations of him are attached to the columns around the first courtyard.

Less than a mile to the north are the remains of the **Temple of Dakka,** a Ptolemaic structure dating to the third century B.C., notable for its monumental pylon. Climb this pylon for amazing views over the surrounding landscape.

Oldest of all the Lake Nasser monuments is the **Temple of Amada,** about 30 miles (48 km) south of Wadi al-Sebua. This dates to the 18th dynasty, predating Ramses II by a couple of hundred years. Though it is small with a very simple plan, its wall paintings retain much of their original color.

The only monument to have remained on its original site is **Qasr Ibrim,** which once capped the top of a 235-foot (72 m) cliff. This has been transformed by the rising waters into a rocky island near the center of the lake. The Qasr, or fortress, is a pharaonic and Roman bastion, with a seventh-century sandstone cathedral. Ships generally moor alongside the island to allow passengers to peer over the remains, but because the site is the subject of intense archaeological work, it is off-limits to visitors. ∎

EXPERIENCE: Fish on Lake Nasser

It is ironic that some of the best fishing in the country bordered by the Red and the Mediterranean Seas is on the man-made lake south of the High Dam. Little visited by tourists, Lake Nasser is an excellent site for catching Nile perch, and it holds a thriving population of tilapia, tigerfish, and large catfish. Shore fishing and fly-fishing are best during the spring and early summer months, when Nile perch can be found in shallow water near the shores. From October to January, Nile perch can be found in deeper waters, rather than near the shore. (They are also bigger during those months.) Either way, fishing in such a serene environment will probably be one of your best angling experiences ever.

A British company, **The African Angler** *(tel 097/230 9748 or 097/233 0090, www. african-angler.co.uk)*, organizes fishing expeditions to Lake Nasser year-round, with prices depending on the number of days and anglers in each boat. They also do one-day fishing trips, picking you up from your hotel or cruise ship. Their excellent website has details on safari packages, logistics, and prices. Also based in Aswan is the environmentally responsible **Lake Nasser Adventure** *(tel 012/104 0266 or 012/104 0255, www.lakenasseradventure.com).*

Saving the Monuments

The Egyptian government's decision to build a new dam just upstream of Aswan in the 1950s threatened to submerge forever all the ancient sites and monuments along the Nubian stretch of the Nile. Drowning the past to save the future, they termed it. In the end, the monuments were saved by a UNESCO rescue effort that ranks as one of the greatest engineering feats of modern times.

Eventually the dam project got the go-ahead despite the risks. Archaeological missions from many countries, at the request of the Egyptian government, descended on Nubia. Teams of experts assisted the Egyptian authorities with planning, preservation, and excavation in the threatened area.

Moving the Temples

All portable artifacts were removed to museums. As the plan went forward, though some temples were surrendered and allowed to disappear beneath the rising waters of the newly formed Lake Nasser, more than a dozen temples were salvaged and moved to safety.

Ten of them, including the temples of Philae (see pp. 304–307), Kalabsha (see p. 304), and Abu Simbel (see pp. 314–318), were dismantled stone by stone and rebuilt as

INSIDER TIP:

Most of the temples are made from sandstone, the softest of all stone. Thus they are very sensitive to water, even in perspiration, so avoid touching them with your hands.

—TAYLOR KENNEDY
National Geographic photographer

close to the original sites as possible, but on higher ground. Several other smaller structures were donated to the countries that contributed to the rescue effort, including the Temple of Dendur, which now forms the centerpiece of the ancient Egypt collection at the Metropolitan Museum of Art in New York, and the Temple of Taffeh, housed at the Rijksmuseum van Oudheden in Leiden, The Netherlands.

The severed face of Ramses II, weighing 19 tons (17 tonnes), is carefully lifted at Abu Simbel before being transported to the new site.

Behind the Scenes at Abu Simbel

Beneath a man-made mountain, an immense concrete dome protects the great temple of Ramses II from the tons of rocks piled up in imitation of Abu Simbel's original setting. A concrete dome of this height and span (90 feet by 195 feet/59 m) had never previously been attempted at the time, and skeptics doubted that it could be built at all. But in the end, Swedish engineers produced a technical masterpiece that is almost the equal of the great pharaoh's achievement in building the temple.

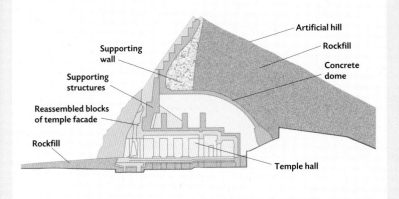

- Artificial hill
- Rockfill
- Concrete dome
- Supporting wall
- Supporting structures
- Reassembled blocks of temple facade
- Rockfill
- Temple hall

Sheltering Abu Simbel

Undoubtedly the most spectacular part of the whole ambitious project was the preservation of the temples at Abu Simbel. Hewn as they were out of a solid cliff face, there was no question of simply dismantling the temples and moving them to new sites where they would be reassembled. Instead various imaginative schemes were proposed. An Italian engineer submitted a plan to lift the temple the height of a 20-story building on hydraulic jacks. The British suggested enclosing the whole site in a vast clear dome under the water.

These ideas were explored, but proved prohibitively expensive, and in the end UNESCO accepted the plan of Swedish consulting engineers, which called for sawing up the temples and cutting them away from the mountain. In 1964 a cofferdam was built around the site to hold back the already encroaching water of the new lake, while engineers injected a strengthening synthetic resin into the brittle sandstone. The temples were then hand-sawn piece by precisely calculated piece.

At a cost of about 40 million dollars (a third of which was funded by the United States) the temples were cut up into more than 2,000 huge blocks, weighing around 22 tons (20 tonnes) each. They were moved, and then reconstructed like a giant jigsaw puzzle approximately 656 feet (200 m) inland of the water and 212 feet (65 m) higher than the original site. Two great concrete domes covered with rocks and sand were used to reconstruct the shape of the mountain out of which the temples had been cut. Great care was also taken to orient the temples in precisely the correct alignment to mimic their original position.

The project took just over four years. The temples of Abu Simbel were officially reopened in 1968, while the sacred site they had occupied for over 3,000 years disappeared beneath the waters of Lake Nasser.

Abu Simbel

Built by the mightiest of the pharaohs, Ramses II, with four massive colossi of himself adorning the facade, Abu Simbel is the most famous of the ancient Egyptian monuments after the Pyramids and the Sphinx. It marked the limit of Egypt's domain and was intended to convey the might of the pharaohs to any who approached from the south. More than 3,000 years later, its two temples have lost none of their power to inspire awe.

Abu Simbel at night. The enormous statues of Ramses II were carved from a sandstone cliff and still impress after 30 centuries.

Abu Simbel
 287 A1
 Lake Nasser
 Open 6 a.m.–
5 p.m.
$ $$$

Although it has the appearance of being a monument raised to the glory of is builder, Ramses II (1279–1213 B.C.), the larger of the two temples was dedicated to the gods Amun, Ptah, and Re-Harakhty. Carved from the mountainside on the West Bank of the Nile, it was begun in the pharaoh's fifth regnal year but was not completed until his 35th. With the passing of the great

age of the pharaohs, the upkeep of the temple was forgotten, and it gradually became almost completely buried in sand. It disappeared from history completely, mentioned by neither Greeks nor Romans, until its chance rediscovery by the Swiss explorer John Lewis Burkhardt in 1813. As he described the scene, "An entire head and part of the breast and arms of one of the statues emerge still above the surface. Of the adjacent statue, there is almost nothing to be seen, since its head has broken off and its body is covered in sand to above shoulder level. Of the two others, only their headdresses are visible. It is difficult to decide whether these statues are seated or standing."

With such a huge volume of sand piled up against the temple, initial efforts at clearance were limited to finding a doorway to gain entrance and see what treasures lay within. In 1817 the Italian adventurer in the employ of the British consul, Giovanni Belzoni (see p. 77), succeeded in digging his way inside. He was bitterly disappointed; aside from a few small statues, which he took away, the temple contained none of the hoped-for treasures. Belzoni and crew turned their backs on Abu Simbel and left for good. Over the next decades periodic attempts were made by various parties to clear more of the sand away, but always it blew back. It was not until as recently as 1909 that the temple was finally cleared for good.

Visiting the Temples

Abu Simbel is usually reached from Aswan. A road connects the two places, although most visitors make the trip here with EgyptAir, a brief 30-minute flight from Aswan. Flights are timed to allow visitors to spend a couple of hours at the temple before returning. Shuttle buses are

INSIDER TIP:

Egypt has huge and wonderful structures, but don't forget to take pictures of the small, of the details of hieroglyphs or of parts of statues.

—TAYLOR KENNEDY
National Geographic photographer

provided between the airport and the temples. An alternative option is to join a Lake Nasser cruise (see p. 310). These boats moor almost in the shadow of the Ramses colossi, giving passengers the chance to view

Ramses II: Archetype of Egypt's Power

Ramses II, "the Great," epitomized Egypt at the height of its power. Born about 1304 b.c., he was a king of imposing profile, with strong jaw and nose. Medical technology reveals that Ramses suffered from arthritis, dental abscesses, and poor circulation. He ruled for 66 years, living into his 90s. His architects chose a poor spot for his tomb, where the rock was soft. Wall collapses and floods have ruined the deep sepulchre and destroyed many of the superb wall paintings. Ramses did not lie in his tomb long. Necropolis priests snatched his mummy away in the face of looters. Eventually it came to rest in a deep rock cleft with other royal mummies. Ramses remained undisturbed until 1881, when tomb robbers discovered the hiding place. Fortunately recovered by archaeologists and stabilized by French conservators in 1976, Ramses now lies in the Cairo Museum.

them both by moonlight and by the first light of dawn.

At 69 feet (21 m) high, the four enthroned colossi are the largest surviving sculptures in Egypt. Their hands alone, resting on their knees, are longer than the average person is tall. They sit against a flattened area cut from the mountain to resemble the sloping walls of a temple's pylon. At the feet of the giant statues are bound captives—Africans and Asians—symbolic of the Egyptian kingdom's border foes. Either side of the kings' legs are smaller (though still much larger than life-size) statues of his mother, Tuya, his wife, Nefertari, and some of their children. Above the central entrance, between the heads of the colossi, is the figure of the falcon-headed sun god Re.

The interior of Ramses' temple is much less spectacular than its facade, however. Burrowed

The Temple of Ramses II at Abu Simbel

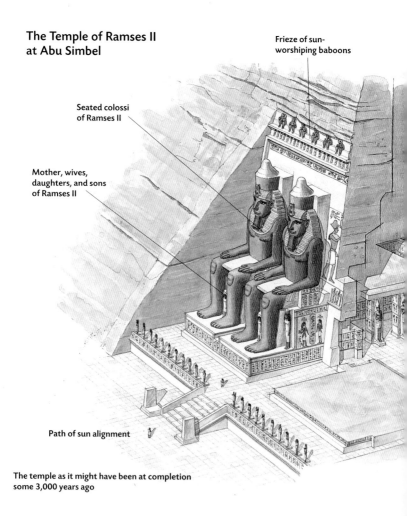

Frieze of sun-worshiping baboons

Seated colossi of Ramses II

Mother, wives, daughters, and sons of Ramses II

Path of sun alignment

The temple as it might have been at completion some 3,000 years ago

200 feet (60 m) into rock, the temple has the simplest of plans, with a large pillared hall leading to a small one, also with pillars, and a sanctuary at the rear. Nevertheless, the first pillared hall is still fairly imposing, with eight more statues of Ramses attached to columns supporting a ceiling decorated with Osiride vultures. Reliefs on the walls, some of which still have their original color, depict the pharaoh in battle.

The pharaoh, his chief wife, Nefertari, and gods decorate pillars in the small hall leading to the inner sanctuary.

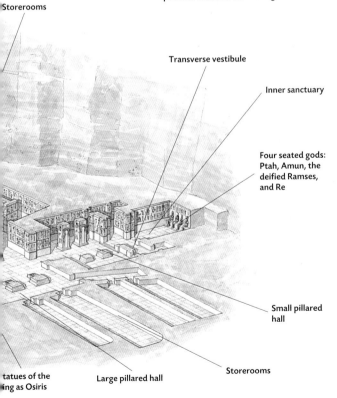

Storerooms

Transverse vestibule

Inner sanctuary

Four seated gods: Ptah, Amun, the deified Ramses, and Re

Small pillared hall

Storerooms

tatues of the ing as Osiris

Large pillared hall

Ankle-high to the pharaoh, children scramble over the colossi of Ramses II in front of his temple at Abu Simbel.

In the small pillared hall, Ramses and Nefertari are shown in front of the gods and their sacred barks. The innermost chamber is the Sacred Sanctuary, with four small statues of the gods Ptah, Amun-Re, the deified Ramses, and Re-Horakhty.

The temple is aligned in such a way that on February 22 and October 22 every year, the first rays of the rising sun penetrate the temple and illuminate the holy quartet—or at least three of them; Ptah, on the left, remains in shadow. Until the temples were moved up from the lake, this phenomenon happened one day

earlier. Some Egyptologists have speculated that these may be the anniversaries of Ramses' coronation and birth.

Temple of Hathor

To the north of Ramses' main temple is a far smaller second temple, built in honor of the pharaoh's beloved chief wife, Nefertari. It is dedicated to the goddess Hathor, the deity most closely associated with queenship in ancient Egypt. It, too, is fronted by a series of colossal figures. Standing about 32 feet (10 m) high, four of these statues are of Ramses and two of them are of his queen. Beside them are the more diminutive figures of the rest of the royal family.

Inside is a single hall with six pillars crowned with Hathor (cow-eared) capitals. The walls are adorned with scenes depicting Nefertari before Hathor and Mut. On the rear wall, the queen is shown as a cow with the king beneath her chin. What is striking is the importance granted to Nefertari, with the queen repeatedly shown on an equal footing with the king. As a pharaonic queen, she is unique in this respect.

A gray door in the mountainside to the right of the main temple offers quite a bizarre experience. Passing through and ascending a tubular steel staircase, you see the inside of the fake mountain, a vast domed space, filled on one side with cutstone blocks—the reverse of the monumental facade. The effect is a little like Dorothy pulling aside the curtain to reveal the puny reality of the Wizard of Oz. ■

Dichotomous marvels of an underwater world and a broad reach of desert canyons, either every bit as wondrous as Egypt's pharaonic heritage

Red Sea & Sinai

Introduction & Map   320–321

Monasteries of St. Anthony & St. Paul   322–323

Hurghada & South   324–327

Experience: Visit the Valley of the Camels   325

Feature: Reef Life   328–331

Experience: Help Protect Red Sea Wildlife   329

Northern Sinai   332–333

Southern Sinai   334–335

Experience: Take a Bedouin Ecotour
in the Sinai   335

Mount Sinai & St. Catherine's   336–339

Feature: The Bedouin   340–341

Sinai Coast   342–344

Hotels & Restaurants   372–375

A hawksbill turtle and scuba divers in the Red Sea

Red Sea & Sinai

In recent decades Egypt's tourism industry has been undergoing a dramatic shift. Where ancient history and the monuments of the pharaohs were once the big draw, an increasing number of visitors to the country now don't bother with the Pyramids of Giza or temples of Luxor. Instead, they are here for sun, white sands, and turquoise seas, all of which the Red Sea coast and the shores of Sinai have in abundance.

Remoteness from the life-sustaining Nile Valley has traditionally kept civilization away from Egypt's extreme eastern edges. Between the Nile and the Red Sea coastline, which extends for 775 miles (1,250 km) from the town of Suez to the Sudanese border, the Eastern Desert has proved a daunting barrier. The topography is one of lifeless rocky landscapes, with craggy mountains scored by parched wadis, the local term for dry riverbeds.

Sinai, the triangular peninsula bounded by the Gulf of Suez and the Suez Canal on the west, and the Gulf of Aqaba and Israel's Negev Desert on the east, is essentially a continuation of the desert. Until now the wild landscapes have been the domain of the Bedouin. During the early Christian era, hermits and ascetics valued the remote expanses a place in which they could seek religious enlightenment in solitude. The monasteries they founded still exist.

Sinai remains best known for its religious connections. The word itself probably derives from one of the Middle East's most ancient religious cults, that of the moon god Sin. But most people know the name from the Bible; Sinai is the "great and terrible wilderness" negotiated by Moses and his people in their epic 40-year journey from Egypt to the Promised Land. In the Book of Exodus, God first spoke to Moses in Sinai, from the burning bush, and Moses is believed to have received the tablets inscribed with the Ten Commandments on Mount Sinai.

Acting as both bridge and buffer between Egypt and the empires to the north in what we now call the Middle East, Sinai has historically served as a route for trade caravans and armies alike. Most recently that included the Israeli army, which captured the region during the Six-

> **NOT TO BE MISSED:**
>
> Diving around Giftun Island   **324**
>
> Wadi al-Gimaal nature preserve and Wadi Sekait's emerald mines   **325**
>
> The restored Ottoman fortress of Quseir   **327**
>
> Bird-watching at Zaranik Protectorate in northern Sinai   **333**
>
> The Thursday market at Al-Arish   **333**
>
> The ruins of Serabit al-Khadim   **335**
>
> A pre-dawn ascent of Mount Sinai to greet the sunrise   **336–337**
>
> St. Catherine's Monastery   **337–339**
>
> Diving in the Ras Muhammad national marine park   **343**

Day War of June 1967 and held it until 1982, when Sinai was returned to Egypt under the terms of the 1979 Camp David peace treaty.

Since then tourism has transformed this part of Egypt. Resorts in Sinai's Sharm al-Sheikh and Hurghada on the Red Sea have sprung up to offer warm recreation to northern Europeans escaping the cold. These resorts come complete with hotels, casinos, and golf courses, and a new set of commandments: from "Do not go topless on the beaches" to "Only drink bottled water."

Thankfully, the wilderness is far from tamed. Inland the desert remains virtually uninhabited, with bare mountains sheltering hidden oases. More dramatic still are the underwater landscapes of the Red Sea, where vast coral reefs provide some of the world's richest diving. ■

Mediterranean Sea

GAZA STRIP

Lake Bardawil

Rafah

200 kilometers

100 miles

Pelusium

6▷

Romani

Al-Arish

Qantara

ZARANIK PROTECTORATE

Cairo

Suez Canal

DELTA & SUEZ p. 159

ISRAEL

Bitter Lakes

S i n a i

Suez

Al-Shatt

Nakhl

Taba

JORDAN

Ain Sukhna

Gebel al-Tih

5▷

AROUND CAIRO p. 139

Zafarana

Gebel al-Igma

Monastery of St. Anthony

Serabit al-Khadim

Monastery of St. Catherine

Nuweiba

Gulf of Aqaba

Monastery of St. Paul

Al-Milga

2285m

SAUDI

2642m ▲ Mt. Sinai
(G. Musa)

Dahab

Ras Gharib

Mt. St. Catherine
(G. Katherina)

ST. CATHERINE PROTECTORATE

ARABIA

Wadi al-Tarfa

1762m
Gebel Gharib

Al-Tur

Gulf of Suez

*E a s t e r n
D e s e r t*

Gemsa

Ras Zeit

Strait of Gubal

Naama Bay
Sharm al-Sheikh

4▷

Mons Porphyritis

Al-Gouna

RAS MUHAMMAD NATIONAL PARK

MIDDLE EGYPT p. 209

Hurghada

Giftun Island

2187m
G. Shayib al-Banat

Mons Claudianus

Wadi Qena

Safaga

Red Sea Mountains

R E D

Qena

Bir Seiyala

Quseir

S E A

Luxor

1484m ▲
Gebel al-Sibai

Ras Abu Aweid

3▷

SOUTH OF LUXOR p.285

1160m ▲
Gebel Abu Diyab

Magal Umm Rus

Marsa Alam

1505m
Gebel Nugrus

Ras Samadai

*E a s t e r n
D e s e r t*

Wadi al-Kharit

1977m ▲
Gebel Hamata

Berenice

Ras Banas

Foul Bay

Cairo ⊛

Aswan

Bir Abu Hashim

1366m ▲
Gebel al-Faraid

Bir Shalatein

1165m ▲
Gebel Natitiai

Bir Abu Safa

Marsa Shaab

Ras Abu Dara

Wadi al-Allagi

Area of map detail

1▷

Halayeb

S U D A N

△
A

△
B

△
C

△
D

Monasteries of St. Anthony & St. Paul

Hidden in the barren hills of the Eastern Desert and dramatically set against backdrops of cliffs are what may be the world's two oldest monasteries. Black-robed monks welcome the few visitors who trouble to make it here to see the splendid ancient wall paintings and murals.

As there is no public transportation to the monasteries, they are best reached by taking an organized tour from either Cairo or Hurghada, both of which are slightly more than 200 miles (320 km) away. The national tour agency, Misr Travel

In spite of successive restorations, the Monastery of St. Anthony retains its original appearance.

(*Magawish Village, Hurghada, tel 065/344 2131*), organizes day trips from Hurghada that include visits to both monasteries.

St. Anthony Abbot (A.D. 251–356) is said to have become a hermit at the age of 18, traveling with a caravan into the Eastern Desert and settling in an isolated mountain cave, where he lived until the age of 105. Since he forbade his many followers from staying near the cave, they camped at the foot of the hill, creating a settlement that formed the basis of the **Monastery of St. Anthony** (Deir Anba Antonius), founded shortly after his death.

Entered through a double-arched gate between two towers topped by crosses, the monastery compound contains churches, housing quarters, and gardens. It has the pleasing appearance of a small, sandy-colored, walled village. Until quite recently it was largely empty, but since the current Coptic pope, Shenouda III, took office in 1971, all Egypt's monasteries have undergone a renaissance, attracting plenty of new, young would-be monks. From the four monks who maintained St. Anthony's in the early 1970s, numbers are now up to around 80. For the first time in more than a century, the monastery is actually expanding to accommodate the new interest from Coptic Christians in a life of spiritual contemplation.

The oldest structure is the **Church of St. Anthony,** built over the saint's tomb. It contains the largest array of Coptic wall paintings in Egypt, mostly dating from the 13th to 16th centuries, and all beautifully restored during the 1990s.

A path from the west side of the monastery winds steeply up to **St. Anthony's Cave.** The trip to the cave involves climbing some 1,158 wooden steps and the hike takes about an hour. Inside the cave is a small chapel with an altar,

INSIDER TIP:

There are rich archaeological remains (prehistoric to Roman) in the Eastern Desert, as well as interesting flora and fauna, but they can be difficult to access. Use Bedouin guides (ask staff at the big hotels).

—STEVE SIDEBOTHAM
National Geographic field researcher

but of more interest are the medieval graffiti on the walls. There is also a breathtaking view of the hills and valley below.

The **Monastery of St. Paul** (Deir Anba Bula) is smaller and even more remote than that of St. Anthony. It was built in and around the cave where Paul the Hermit lived for nearly 90 years

during the third and fourth centuries. Not to be confused with the Apostle Paul, this Paul was born into a wealthy Alexandrian family, but is said to have turned away from society at the age of 16, sickened by Roman inquisitions. Tradition has it that when Paul died, St. Anthony—past the age of 90—made the long trek through the mountains to bury him.

As the crow flies, the two caves and their monasteries are only about 22 miles (35 km) apart, but thanks to the cliffs and rocky hills between, they are around 50 miles (80 km) apart by road. It is possible to emulate St. Anthony's mission and walk between the two monasteries along a mountainous trail. It takes two full days, so camping gear is necessary. A map is available at St. Anthony's Monastery.

St. Paul's cave is contained within **St. Paul's Church,** which is strewn with a number of altars, candelabra, and icons. There is also a sarcophagus which, it is believed, contains the remains of the saint. Note the ostrich eggs, which the monks will tell you are kept as a symbol of Jesus Christ's resurrection. An alternative tale is that they were threaded onto the chains of the oil lamps hanging from the chapel ceilings to prevent rats from climbing down.

Also within the monastery, in the 17th-century **Church of St. Michael,** is an icon of the Virgin Mary claimed to have been painted from life by St. Luke in A.D. 40. Outside the monastery you can still see an ancient olive press, and the pulley that was used to hoist visitors and provisions over the wall in times of unrest. ∎

Monasteries of St. Anthony & St. Paul

🅰 321 B5

🕐 Closed Coptic Christmas (Jan. 6) & Lent

Hurghada & South

Hurghada (Al-Ghardaka in Arabic), 230 miles (370 km) southeast of Cairo on the Red Sea coast, is Egypt's pioneer tourist resort. From its humble beginnings as a small fishing village, the town has developed over the last 20 years into a thriving vacation destination filled with beachfront hotels, always full of guests drawn by the promise of year-round sunshine, crystal-clear waters, and good diving.

Two children make themselves secure on a camel in anticipation of a ride along a Hurghada beach.

Hurghada

🅐 321 B4

Visitor information

✉ Al-Korah Ave., after EgyptAir Office

☎ 065/344 4420 or 065/344 4421

🕐 Open 8 a.m.– 8 p.m.

Hurghada is a place wholly devoted to tourism. The beaches and sea provide the entertainment during the day, and by night the town lights up with streetside restaurants and bars, and gaudy souvenir shopping malls. Shorts, shades, and T-shirts are the accepted form of dress, and dance music sometimes drowns out the call to prayer. Burgers and pizza prevail over felafel and kabobs here, though dishes like borscht and *pelmeni* also appear on menus, catering to the huge flood of Russians who have taken to vacationing here since the collapse of the Soviet Union. There is probably more alcohol consumed in this one town than in the whole of the rest of the country combined. Most visitors fly in directly on charter deals, and their international hotel resorts—Hiltons, Marriotts, Sheratons—have a full range of amenities, plus their own strip of beach, so that guests need never wander beyond the grounds. The Egypt of ancient monuments doesn't exist here except as icons on T-shirts, and even Arab and Islamic cultures have only the most tenuous of footholds.

One thing that most guests like to do, however, is head out to sea. Nearly all the hotels offer snorkeling safaris out to the reefs that lie offshore. Many also visit **Giftun Island,** about a 40-minute boat ride from shore. This is a protected area, with a maximum of a hundred people allowed on the island each day. Several tourist camps provide dive centers, refreshment facilities, and rest rooms, but development has been kept to a minimum, and the island remains stunningly beautiful. Fish is usually provided for lunch as part of the package.

It is diving, however, that has really put Hurghada on the map. There are about ten coral islands within day-trip range, all harboring a fantastic array of marine life (see pp. 328–331), including sharks, manta rays, and giant moray eels, as well as myriad shoals of small, brightly colored fish. The numerous local dive centers offer first-timers' courses for novices and a wide array of one-day, overnight, and live-aboard options for the more experienced. Be wary when choosing a dive center, as some outfits are dangerously incompetent (see "Tips for Divers," p. 343). It is generally better to dive with centers attached to the larger hotels and vacation villages, which may be more expensive but keep better maintained equipment and employ professional instructors.

For the less adventurous, glass-bottom boats allow views of the coral marine life from the comfort of an air-conditioned cabin. Alternatively, the Sindbad Submarine dives to depths of below 66 feet (20 m) to drift among the fishes. It can be found moored offshore from the Sindbad Beach Resort. For a closer look at sea creatures if you don't want to dive, Hurghada is also home to the **Red Sea Aquarium**, with tanks containing a large number of species that are found swimming freely around the nearby reefs.

Red Sea Aquarium

- ✉ The Corniche, Al-Dahar
- ☎ 065/354 8557
- 🕐 Open 9 a.m.–10 p.m.
- 💲 $

EXPERIENCE: Visit the Valley of the Camels

One of the most overlooked spots in Egypt is in the deep south—the mountainous Eastern Desert. South of Marsa Alam lies the coastal opening to the Wadi al-Gimaal, an area rich in birdlife that extends 50 miles (80 km) inland. Driving along the coastal road, you will come across the stunning sight of camels wandering by the mangroves on the beach. The camels belong to local Ababda tribesmen, who brand them and let them graze freely, sometimes for months on end. The Eastern Desert is rocky rather than sandy and is filled with narrow valleys dotted with acacias and low grasses.

The entire region is also rich in minerals; like Mons Porphyrites and Mons Claudianus farther north, abandoned pharaonic and Roman mines can be found here, such as the emerald mining village of Wadi Sekait. The vein of emeralds (long since emptied out) sits atop a small hill the Romans called Mons Smaragdus—Mount Emerald—and you can easily climb to the top to look down the pit. Other Roman mining colonies nearby are littered with pottery fragments, and the stark, haunting landscape has a peaceful stillness to it.

Driving into the interior should not be done without guides, preferably organized by the outstanding **Red Sea Desert Adventures** *(tel 012/105 6593 or 012/399 3860, www.redseadesertadventures.com)*, based at the Shagra Village resort about 12 miles (20 km) north of Mersa Alam. This husband-and-wife team, Karen van Opstal, a Dutch geologist, and Thomas Krakhofer, have long experience in the Eastern Desert and they work with local Ababda guides to organize camel safaris, 4x4 day trips, and overnights. Half-day tours generally cost 45 euros, and full days are 90 euros, although longer expeditions are priced differently. When dining with the Ababda, be sure to try their *gabana* coffee, a variant of Arabic coffee made with fresh ginger, as well as their unique *gors* breads cooked in hot sand and ashes!

Some of Egypt's most attractive new hotels enjoy prime beachfront locations along the Red Sea coast.

Safaga
Ⓜ 321 C4

Quseir
Ⓜ 321 C3

Al-Gouna

An alternative to the unregulated development of Hurghada exists 12 miles (20 km) north at the resort center of Al-Gouna. Founded in the 1990s by one Egypt's biggest tycoons, it includes a number of international hotels, several clusters of villas, upscale shopping centers, and a brewery producing Sakkara beer and a winery producing Obelisk wine. This exclusive setup is a big hit with the jet set. Pick of the accommodations is the Sheraton Miramar (see pp. 372–373), which was built on nine islands connected by bridges and designed by Indianapolis-born architect Michael Graves. It is a pastel-colored, postmodern desert fantasy to turn the Disney Corporation—one of Graves's previous clients—green with envy.

South of Hurghada

Although south of Hurghada is off the tourist map of Egypt, that is all about to change, as much of the Red Sea coastline has already been sold to developers, modern-day alchemists aiming to transform white sands and turquoise seas into gold—or piles of the folding green stuff, at least.

The hottest spots: The hottest concepts in coastal development are tourist centers that incorporate not just hotels, restaurants, and entertainment facilities, but schools, hospitals, and housing for service workers and their families. Several are in advanced stages of completion along the coast between Hurghada and the port of **Safaga,** 32 miles (52 km) to the south. Of little interest to visitors, Safaga is a center for the export of phosphates from local mines, which comes to life once a year as a busy embarkation point for Muslims traveling to Mecca during the annual hajj (pilgrimage).

The mineral-rich Red Sea Mountains, which erupt south of Hurghada, were being quarried for their gold, copper, and other precious metals and stones as far back as pharaonic times. Though the area has no monuments to the ancient Egyptians, Roman-era quarries are at **Mons Claudianus,** 30 miles (48 km) inland of Safaga. Black-flecked granite was hacked out, transported to the Nile, and shipped to Rome, where it was used in the Pantheon and Trajan's Forum. For the prisoners sent to work here—and their guards—the experience was the ancient Near East equivalent of being banished to Siberia. You can still see the tiny cells that these unfortunates inhabited, plus an immense cracked pillar, left where it fell 2,000 years ago, a small temple, and partly formed columns and capitals. Some coastal hotels organize trips to the site and to **Mons Porphyritis,** north of Hurghada, where the Romans quarried porphyry, the precious white-and-purple crystalline stone often used for sarcophagi.

As developers have yet to travel south beyond Safaga, the scenery down here has a raw, untouched beauty. Few visitors appreciate it except for dedicated divers, and the best underwater landscapes are said to be toward the Sudanese border, where military permits are required to dive. A few companies take divers out; try Red Sea Diving Safaris *(tel 02/3337 9942, www .redsea-divingsafari.com)* or Wadi Gimal Divers *(tel 02/2417 0046).*

Quseir: The largest town of note is Quseir, 53 miles (85 km) south of Safaga. In pharaonic times, it was from here that boats sailed for the Land of Punt, as depicted in reliefs at the Temple of Hatshepsut (see pp. 268–270). Under the Romans, the Islamic leaders, and the Ottoman Turks, it remained a bustling port where Eastern spices were loaded onto caravans to continue west, and pilgrims rested en route to Mecca. Quseir ceded its status as a major port and shipbuilding center when the Suez Canal rendered it redundant. The town experienced a brief flourish of prosperity from phosphate processing early in the 20th century, but that has all but died out. Today, it has an end-of-the-world feel. Dominated by a 16th-century Ottoman fortress, the town center is sparse and low lying, with old coral-block buildings with wooden balconies lining the waterfront. A highlight is the waterfront Quseir Hotel (see p. 374), a former coffee merchant's house with *mashrabiyya* balconies. North of town, occupying the site of the old pharaonic-era harbor, is one of the most paradisical hotels in the country, the Mövenpick Resort Quseir (see p. 374). Designed to resemble a small stone village, it overlooks a sandy cove with gloriously clear waters, in which swim shoals of exotically patterned fish. ■

Bir Shalatein

If you've made it as far south as Marsa Alam, 160 miles (256 km) south of Hurghada, consider a day trip to Bir Shalatein—the farthest point south on Egypt's Red Sea coast to which foreigners are permitted. Bir Shalatein is a windswept market town, best known for its massive open-air camel market. The inhabitants of the region are the Bishari, nomadic herders whose lands extend into the Sudan, and who speak their own language, Beja. Most Egyptians don't consider them Egyptian at all. The coastal landscape is beautiful here, and there's something magical about being this far south: Bir Shalatein is as far as you can go and still be in Egypt.

Reef Life

The coral reefs of the Red Sea are Egypt's crowning natural glory—every bit as spectacular, in their own way, as pharaonic wonders like the Pyramids that usually head the itineraries of most visitors. No adjectives or glossy underwater photographs can adequately prepare you for that magical moment when you don a mask and poke your face into the warm waters of this seductive dreamscape.

Egypt has over 500 miles (800 km) of reef-lined Red Sea coastline, stretching from the border with Israel in the north down to the border with Sudan in the south.

A diver explores a coral-encrusted wreck, one of several sunken vessels resting on the bed of the Red Sea.

The Red Sea is essentially a water-flooded rip in the earth's crust, torn between the African and Asian landmasses. Along either side run chains of desert mountains. Narrow and constricted, the Red Sea is well over a mile (1.6 km) deep in places. Its reefs are mostly steep walls that plunge dizzyingly, rising at some spots to form offshore shoals and coral islands before plunging again. Because of the great depth, sediment never manages to drift upward, and as a result the waters are extremely clear. Between these subterranean cliffs and the shore are shallow fringe reefs, beginning where the water is no more than chest height on an average adult, and ideal for snorkeling.

Marine Life

Coral is what makes a reef. Thought for many centuries to be some form of flowering plant, it is in fact an animal. Corals are minute polyps, anemonelike creatures that have a calcareous or horny outer skeleton and feed off other small organisms that live in the sea. They group together in colonies and accumulate into beautiful formations of many shapes. When corals die, the next generation grows up on top of them. Over a long period of time, they build up into reefs. These coral reefs form a mini-ecosystem supporting more than a thousand species of marine life.

At its southern end, the Red Sea runs through narrow straits and shelves to a shallow sea, a geographical bottleneck that has effectively prevented much migration. As a result, the Red Sea is home to a huge number of endemic species (ones that are not found elsewhere). Many of the fish are brilliantly colored and swim in huge shoals that swathe the

EXPERIENCE: Help Protect Red Sea Wildlife

Since the 1980s, the annual number of visitors to the Red Sea has exploded, as the tourism industry has taken advantage of the assets of the Red Sea beaches: sun, white sands, azure waters, and stunning coral reefs. Such rapid expansion, coupled with hasty hotel construction, thoughtless tourists, and less-than-ideal local attitudes about waste disposal and recycling, has put enormous pressures on a fragile ecosystem, both underwater and on land.

Fortunately, there are ways for a visitor to help preserve this unique natural environment before it is too late. One way is simply to be more environmentally friendly in your behavior: When diving, for example, resist the temptation to touch the coral—they are remarkably fragile. And remember to stay on the marked roads when driving in the Sinai: The government has made off-road driving illegal in areas such as Ras Muhammad National Park in order to minimize damage to its environment. You can also ask at dive centers in Sharm and Dahab whether they sponsor "trash dives," days in which volunteer divers help to clear reefs of accumulated trash.

For an unforgettable experience you can feel good about, consider volunteering on a conservation project for Red Sea wildlife. Volunteering opportunities often are haphazard, so it's best to send out some queries and see what turns up. A good place to start, even before you arrive in Egypt, is the website for **HEPCA** (Hurghada Environmental Protection and Conservation Association; www.hepca.com). Started in 1992 by a consortium of local diving companies in an effort to protect the fragile coral reefs of the Red Sea from irresponsible diving, it oversees several conservation and public-awareness campaigns. Contact them directly about opportunities for volunteering.

Another good option is the **Red Sea Environmental Centre,** an Austrian marine conservation institute with field stations in Dahab and Quseir (www.redsea-ec. org). The center offers reef biology courses for both academics and laypeople, and will gladly accept volunteers interested in reef protection for the various conservation projects it organizes. Contact field station coordinator Christian Alter about volunteering (tel 010/784 7500).

---

reefs with blues, golds, and yellows, or glitter and shimmer like jewels against the background of ultramarine water. The blue-green parrotfish, numerous kinds of wrasses, beautiful yellow butterfly fish, and silvery damselfish graze the reef, gnawing away at the algae-clad surface. These are preyed on by predators such as groupers, scorpionfish, snappers, and morays. In turn, this group of fish form the menu for higher predators, including dolphins, barracuda, and sharks.

The most commonly encountered types of shark are white or black-tipped reef sharks. Hammerheads, tiger sharks, and the huge, plankton-eating whale sharks are generally found in deeper waters only. Turtles are common, especially the green turtle.

Such a high density of underwater life makes for a competitive environment. All species have necessarily evolved methods to prevent themselves ending up as dinner for some other, bigger fish. A large number carry some kind of spine or poisonous toxin to deter would-be predators. Few species are actually aggressive, but many can inflict painful, occasionally fatal injuries in self-defense. The stingray, for example, has sharp feather-shaped quills in its tail, which is whipped forward at any who get too close. The spiny lionfish, and the stonefish and scorpion fish, which are both well camouflaged to resemble seabed rocks, all have stout dorsal fins, which are erected when the fish is threatened and are strong and sharp enough to puncture skin. Even coral can be well armed. Fire coral can inflict irritating burns if it comes into contact with exposed flesh. The simple rule of thumb for divers and snorkelers is do not touch and you won't get hurt.

Exploring the Reef

Sinai and the Red Sea coast are perhaps second only to Australia's Great Barrier Reef when it comes to diving. If you want to learn to dive, plenty of courses are available along the coast, particularly in the tourist hubs such as Hurghada and Sharm al-Sheikh (see p. 380 for some recommendations). They vary greatly in professionalism and price, so shop around. Instructors should belong to an internationally recognized body, the largest of which is the Professional Association of Diving Instructors (PADI).

Most of Egypt's best diving is on the offshore reefs and islands: Some of the country's most famous diving sites include one known simply as **The Islands,** off the Sinai coast at Dahab; **Ras Muhammad,** just south of Sharm al-Sheikh; and, farther to the south off the mainland coast, **The Brothers, Daedelus Reef.** Serious divers will want to head down south of Quseir, where a series of dedicated dive camps are being established to take advantage of virgin reefs, until recently off-limits because of their proximity to the Sudanese border.

Dive resorts such as Kahramana around the small, dusty crossroads settlement of **Marsa Alam** give access to the **Abu Dabbab** reef, where a trail through a large underwater cavern leads to three huge coral towers rising up from the seabed.

If you don't dive, or don't want to, snorkeling can also reveal spectacular underwater sights. Most of the best displays of fish are in shallow water anyway, and if you simply paddle along the surface, face down, you'll be treated to vivid displays of tropical color and an eerie, dreamlike sensation of flying. You don't even have to get wet: Operators at resorts like Hurghada and Sharm al-Sheikh have glass-bottom boats, and even submarines, from which you can view the reef.

Humbug dascyllus

Yellowtail barracuda

male

female

Red Sea steephead parrotfish

Lionfish

Oceanic tip shark

Elkhorn

Red Sea coral-grouper

Fire coral

Giant moray

Common stonefish

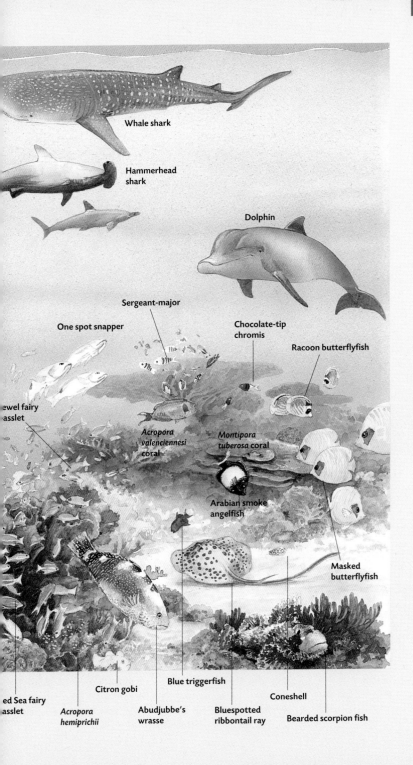

Whale shark

Hammerhead shark

Dolphin

Sergeant-major

One spot snapper

Chocolate-tip chromis

Racoon butterflyfish

Jewel fairy basslet

Acropora valenciennesi coral

Montipora tuberosa coral

Arabian smoke angelfish

Masked butterflyfish

Red Sea fairy basslet

Acropora hemiprichii

Citron gobi

Abudjubbe's wrasse

Blue triggerfish

Bluespotted ribbontail ray

Coneshell

Bearded scorpion fish

Northern Sinai

Sinai's northern and southern regions contrast greatly in character. Whereas the south is mountainous and fringed with beaches, the north is a great plateau that slopes downward toward the Mediterranean shore, where pale dunes rise from coastal salt marshes. There are few settlements, although Al-Arish is a popular resort with Egyptians and has ambitions to attract some of the foreign vacation trade.

Local Bedouin tribesmen limber up for camel races held regularly in northern Sinai.

About the only foreign traffic across northern Sinai is the nearly daily bus service running between Cairo and Tel Aviv, which crosses the border at the divided town of Rafah. The bus follows the ancient route for trade and invasions since pharaonic times. Buses to northern Sinai cross the Suez Canal over the Mubarak Peace Suspension Bridge at **Qantara,** sited midway between Port Said and Ismailia. The views from the bridge are impressive, and other than the passenger ferries at Port Said, this is about the only opportunity there is to get on the canal.

About 18 miles (30 km) east, just before the small settlement of Farma, is a signposted turnoff for **Pelusium.** The fortress town that guarded Egypt's eastern frontier for centuries has a colorful history. The Persian army of Cambyses is said to have captured the garrison here without a fight by driving cats (the sacred animal of the goddess Bastet; see p. 164) before them. Ptolemy XIII captured the Roman general Pompey here, then had him murdered, and presented the head to Julius Caesar (see p. 33).

Abandoned in the Islamic era, the town has weathered to nothing, unfortunately. Ongoing archaeological excavations have found little beyond a Roman amphitheater.

Continuing east, the coastal road passes ramshackle villages inhabited by Bedouin, their nomadic ways now abandoned. Much of the coast is dominated by the swampy lagoon of **Lake Bardawil,** separated from the Mediterranean by a limestone ridge. It acts as a huge fish farm; two gates close the lake off from the sea between April and October, when the fish breed. The rest of the year, it provides income for around 3,000 local fishermen.

Stretching from the eastern edge of the lake is the **Zaranik Protectorate,** an 85-square-mile (220 sq km) area of lagoons and

INSIDER TIP:

Don't be shy about approaching Bedouins in the Sinai. Respectfully put away your camera and acknowledge the elder man in the group. You may even be invited for a cup of tea under a tree!

—GAYLE YOUNG
National Geographic Television

marshes that provides a resting point for numerous species of migrating birds (see pp. 154–155) on their journey between Europe and Africa. Visiting is encouraged.

Al-Arish, about 22 miles (35 km) beyond Lake Bardawil, is

the peaceful, small-town capital of the North Sinai region. Its origins are as a Roman garrison town called Rhinocolorum (Noses Cut Off), after the fate of dissidents exiled there. However, its misfortune has been to lie in the path of every invading army, with the result that it has been razed and then rebuilt on countless occasions over the centuries. Most recently, the town was largely abandoned in 1967 when the Israelis captured Sinai, and only reinhabited after 1982.

The place comes to life every Thursday morning for the weekly market, as Bedouin from numerous tribes descend to buy and sell all manner of goods. Most interesting are the traditional Bedouin handicrafts: embroidered dresses, beadwork, rugs, silver, and jewelry—although much of the best work is transported directly to Cairo for sale.

The new **Al-Arish Museum** features exhibits on the many invading armies that have crossed Sinai (in both directions) over the millennia, as well as artifacts from modern excavations. The museum also offers displays of colorful Bedouin handicrafts, including clothing, jewelry, and pottery. There is also a garden with an outdoor theater, a cinema, and a library.

The other main attraction is the beach, which is lined with endless groves of bowed palms. Although the water is significantly cooler than that of the Red Sea and there are no reefs to afford good snorkeling, Al-Arish has the advantage of being undeveloped and quiet. However, because Al-Arish is not used to foreigners, women should not wear bikinis. Local women swim clothed. ∎

Zaranik Protectorate
🗺 321 B6

Visitor information
✉ Just off main highway
🕐 Open sunrise to sunset

Al-Arish
🗺 321 B6

Visitor information
☎ 068/336 3743
🕐 Closed after 2 p.m. & Fri.

Al-Arish Museum
✉ East side of Al-Arsih
☎ 068/332 9344
🕐 Open 9 a.m.– 4 p.m. (until 5 p.m. in summer)
💲 $$

Southern Sinai

Southern Sinai is a great, jagged, rust-colored expanse of mountains, with drifting sands carpeting its valleys and plains. Almost completely uninhabited and bisected by a single surfaced road, this region is difficult to explore but extremely rewarding.

An adventure tour group steps out of their 4WD vehicles to admire the starkly beautiful Sinai desertscape.

St. Catherine Protectorate

🅼 321 B4/B5/ C4/C5

Sinai's booming tourist industry is based on its beaches and reefs (see pp. 328–331), but a trip into the interior can be every bit as spectacular and memorable. Many of the larger resort hotels organize inland safaris, ranging from half-day excursions by jeep to week-long treks on camels.

An alternative is to go trekking on foot. This is certainly the most rewarding way to experience the terrain. The base for a number of good hikes is the village of **St. Catherine,** near the monastery (see p. 337–339) of the same name. The village lies right at the heart of the mountainous region of the peninsula, but is readily accessible by bus. It is also

at the center of the **St. Catherine Protectorate,** a 1,680-square-mile (4,350 sq km) mountain park created by prime ministerial decree in 1996. The park contains a unique high-altitude desert ecosystem, as well as stunning scenery and a number of historical sites. The protectorate has set up three half-day walking trails, which start and finish in the village. Each has its own trail guide describing the flora and fauna. The trail up to **Wadi Arbaeen** takes in the Rock of Moses, with 12 fissures said to have gushed water when struck by the prophet, and passes the house of a Bedouin named Ramadan. Some years ago Ramadan rescued four hyrax, an indigenous but very elusive rabbitlike creature that is actually a distant relative of the elephant. He now has a colony of some 40 of these animals. Trail booklets, available from the visitor center at the monastery, can direct you to Ramadan.

Ambitious treks requiring the services of Bedouin guides and camels can be organized at the village of **Al-Milga,** near St. Catherine, through Sheikh Musa, a local tribal leader *(ask at the monastery visitor center)*. One worthwhile excursion that can be arranged through the sheikh is to **Blue Valley,** a round-trip of about 8 miles (13 km). It owes its name to Belgian "landscape artist" Jean Verame, who in 1980–1981 painted all the large rocks in the valley a deep blue to symbolize peace. It makes a very surreal sight.

Roughly 40 miles (64 km) west of St. Catherine is **Wadi Feiran,** a twisting, high-walled valley full of palms. The Cairo–St. Catherine bus passes through without stopping, but if you have your own transportation you can explore the area. This was the earliest Christian stronghold in Sinai, and a convent is set high up (no visitors).

Continuing west toward the coast, motorists can detour north to the remains of a pharaonic temple at **Serabit al-Khadim.** It dates to the 12th dynasty and is dedicated to the goddess Hathor. Next to it is a New Kingdom shrine to Sopdu, god of the Eastern Desert. Throughout the temple's many courts, inscriptions list the temple's benefactors, who included Hatshepsut and Tuthmose III. The temple also marks the site of ancient mines. Despite its remote location, turquoise was mined here as far back as the Old Kingdom. In the mines, archaeologists found crude carvings of a fish, an ox-head, and a square. These signs are quite different from Egyptian hieroglyphics. The Semitic people who carved them were perhaps writing in the earliest known phonetic alphabet— one where each character represents a sound, not an object.

In nearby **Wadi Mukattab** (Valley of Inscriptions), there are more rock inscriptions and stelae, some dating to the 3rd dynasty. These provide further evidence of the turquoise mining that was carried out here. ∎

EXPERIENCE: Take a Bedouin Ecotour in the Sinai

In addition to the walking trails around St. Catherine's, there is a growing interest in ecotourism in the Sinai, and in developing a travel economy that works hand in hand with local Bedouin, who have often been excluded from tourism developments in the region. Taking a tour of the Sinai interior under the guidance of local Bedouin—by camel safari, by 4x4, or on foot—is a great way to encounter this peninsula and come to know the traditional way of life of its inhabitants. However, bear in mind Sinai's climate when planning your trip: Trekking in the interior is impossible in the winter because of snow, and Sinai's extreme heat during the summer makes it quite unpleasant.

The St. Catherine Protectorate now has several Bedouin-run ecolodges and safari companies, such as the **El Milga Guesthouse,** run by a member of the local Gabaliya Bedouin tribe named Sheikh Mousa (tel 010/641 3575 or 010/688 0820 or 069/347 0457, www.sheikmousa.com). Sheik Mousa organizes extended hiking and camel tours around St. Catherine's. A local Bedouin guide is required, and Sheik Mousa will handle the necessary paperwork (such as registering trekkers with local authorities). Guides cost about 50LE per day, as do camels. El Milga is the closest village to the Monastery, about 2 miles (3 km) away.

If you are in Dahab, contact **Centre for Sinai,** a non-governmental organization that works to preserve Sinai's Bedouin heritage and which organizes multiday tours into the Sinai interior in conjunction with Bedouin guides (tel 069/364 0702 or 010/666 0835, www.cen tre4sinai.com.eg). They also run clean-ups to clear once pristine areas of trash left by other tour groups.

Mount Sinai & St. Catherine's

Mount Sinai is revered by Jews, Christians, and Muslims alike as the place where Moses received the Ten Commandments. And, according to belief, it was in the valley below that God spoke to him from a burning bush. The area was designated a UNESCO World Heritage site in 2002.

Tourists and pilgrims witness dawn from atop Mount Sinai.

Mount Sinai (in Arabic, Gebel Musa, the Mountain of Moses) is identified with the biblical Mount Horeb, where Moses spent 40 days and received the tablets bearing God's commandments. Some archaeologists and historians dispute this claim and place Mount Horeb variously in Jordan and Saudi Arabia; that doesn't deter the hordes of pilgrims. Visitors here are not just the religious; watching the spectacular sunrise views from the top of Mount Sinai after visiting the monastery is de rigueur for almost all travelers. Consequently the predawn hours on the mountain can be a distinctly unsacred mix of tour groups tripping over sleeping backpackers and church groups singing rival hymns.

There are two ways up the 7,500-foot (2,285 m) mountain. For the fit, there are the 3,750 **Steps of Repentance,** supposedly hewn by a penitent monk; this is the most direct route. There are several votive sites en route, including the **Gate of Confession,** where a monk once heard pilgrims' confessions. More meandering but slightly easier on the leg muscles is the **camel path,** which begins behind the monastery (see "Tips for Climbing Mount Sinai," p. 337). On average, depending on your fitness, it takes about two to three hours to climb to the summit. Bedouin with camels place themselves strategically along the route to offer their services to anyone with faltering legs.

The camel path joins up with the last 750 Steps of Repentance at **Elijah's Basin.** This mountainside hollow is dominated by a 500-year-old cypress tree marking the spot where the Bible recounts that God spoke to Elijah as he hid from Jezebel. If you spend the night, you are asked to sleep here. There are self-composting toilets and stands selling tea and snacks. Even in summer it gets cold and windy in the early hours of morning, so warm clothes and a sleeping bag are a must. There is no space to pitch a tent. From here it is a short climb to the summit to watch the sunrise.

On the summit itself is the Greek Orthodox **Chapel of the Holy Trinity,** built in 1934 on the ruins of a fourth-century church. It contains beautiful paintings and ornaments, and a small mosque. However, these were so desecrated by tourists in the 1980s that the chapel is usually kept locked. The summit also offers a breathtaking panorama of southern Sinai, right across to the Gulf of Aqaba.

Monastery of St. Catherine

Nestled in the shadow of the sacred mountain is the Monastery of St. Catherine (Deir Sant Katreen), where communities of monks have lived almost uninterruptedly since its founding in the sixth century A.D. Before the monastery, there was a chapel on this site, established in the fourth century by the Empress Helena at the place where tradition says that Moses saw the burning bush. This soon became a place of pilgrimage, and in the sixth century a fortified monastery was added by the Emperor Justinian to protect the monks and pilgrims from raiders. It was not until much later that the establishment was dedicated to St. Catherine. She was an early Christian saint who was martyred in Alexandria in the fourth century. After being tortured on a spiked wheel (hence the catherine wheel firework), she was beheaded. According to legend her body was carried away by angels, to be found, uncorrupted, six centuries later by monks on Mount St. Catherine (Gebel Katarina), a neighbor of Mount

Sinai and at 8,665 feet (2,642 m) the highest mountain in Egypt.

Once entailing a difficult and dangerous journey for would-be visitors, the monastery is now connected by a good road to the Red Sea resorts. Many people visit on a half-day trip arranged by their hotel and, as a consequence, the small village of St. Catherine near the monastery is often choked with tour buses and people, especially in the mornings. You can avoid the crowds by making your way to St. Catherine's by regular public transportation and finding accommodations in the village.

Visitors enter the monastery through a postern in the imposing curtain wall, which in places is nearly 9 feet (3 m) thick. Because of the monastery's working nature, most of it is off-limits to the public.

Monastery of St. Catherine

🅰 321 B5/C5

✉ St. Catherine, South Sinai

☎ 069/470 341 or 069/470 343

🕐 Closed after noon & Fri. and Sun.

💲 Donation

www.sinai monastery.com

Tips for Climbing Mount Sinai

If you don't want to walk up the camel path, hire a camel from a Bedouin at the base of Mount Sinai. If you plan to ascend in the middle of the night, arrange to hire a camel earlier in the evening (rather than seeking one at 2 a.m.). Some of the tea stands just below the summit offer semi-sheltered rooms where you can drink your tea and stay warm before making the final ascent. If you have good knees, take the Steps of Repentance down the mountain, for a great view of the monastery from above.

NOTE:
Monastery of
St. Catherine
Remember that St. Catherine's is still a functioning monastery, not a museum piece. It is home to about 20 monks. They are Greek Orthodox and not Coptic, and most are from the monasteries of Mount Athos in Greece.

The only building open is the **Basilica of the Transfiguration** (or the Church of St. Catherine), added by Justinian in the sixth century. Though much of this is roped off, it is worth visiting for the splendid display of priceless icons in the antechamber—a small sample of about 2,000 icons held by the monastery, including some of the oldest in existence, dating to the fifth century. St. Catherine's library also has the most important collection of religious manuscripts after

the Vatican. The monks' reluctance to allow access to these valuable documents is understandable. In the 19th century a German scholar borrowed one of their rarest, the fourth-century *Codex Sinaiticus,* and never returned it: The British Library now holds two-thirds of the folios and the University of Leipzig the remainder. However, scholars will soon be able to access parts of the monastery's collection online, as the monks are adding manuscripts to St. Catherine's website.

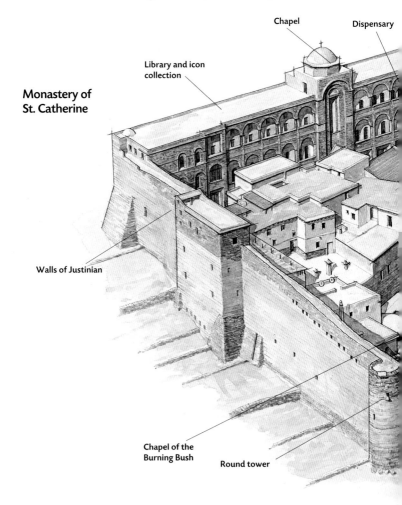

Monastery of
St. Catherine

Chapel

Dispensary

Library and icon
collection

Walls of Justinian

Chapel of the
Burning Bush

Round tower

Behind the basilica, the **Well of Moses** marks the place where the patriarch is believed to have met his future wife, Zipporah. Close by is a large bush protected by a wooden lattice; this is a transplant of what was claimed to be the original burning bush. Uniquely for a Christian monastery, St. Catherine's contains a **mosque** within its walls, opposite the entrance to the basilica. The mosque was built for a Bedouin who worked for the monks. It has probably also helped avoid attacks by Muslims over the centuries.

Outside the high walls are the monastery gardens, with an orchard of olive and apricot trees shading a cemetery, from which the monks' bones are periodically exhumed and transferred to the nearby **Charnel House.** This rather macabre display of skulls and assorted bones is usually open to visitors. The robed skeleton is Stephanos, a sixth-century guardian of the Mount Sinai path. ■

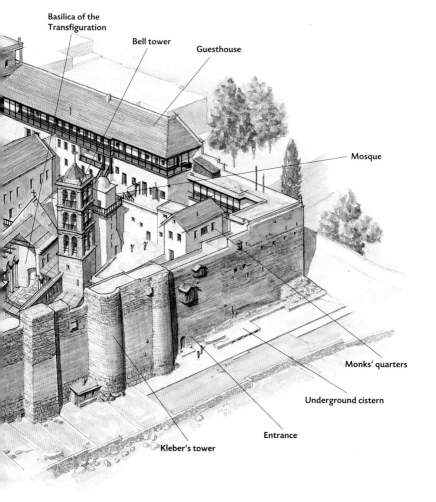

Basilica of the
Transfiguration

Bell tower

Guesthouse

Mosque

Monks' quarters

Underground cistern

Entrance

Kleber's tower

The Bedouin

Although increasingly they are a settled people and have largely traded their camels for pickup trucks, the original inhabitants of Sinai, the Bedouin, still maintain many of their nomadic traditions.

Bedouin men in typical attire of white head scarves gather for a feast.

Most of the 14 Bedouin tribes on the peninsula claim ancestry from the horsemen of Arabia (now Saudi Arabia) and refer to themselves as Arabs rather than Egyptians. One significant exception is the Jabaliya, who are said to be descended from 200 soldiers brought from Romania in the sixth century to defend the monks of St. Catherine's Monastery.

Traditionally, Bedouin lifestyle has involved a constant search for pasture for their livestock, then moving on as an area of vegetation was exhausted, to return the next year. Herding was supplemented by a little cultivation, fishing, and some trading. Each tribe roamed its own territory and had exclusive use of particular oases. At every new grazing spot, the tribe pitched its black, goat-hair tents, known as *bayt shaar*, or hair houses.

With no permanent settlements, strong emphasis was—and still is—placed on family and tribal structures. A nomadic existence also meant owning no more than a person was able to carry. Wealth was accrued in terms of goats or camels, or in the weight of a wife's jewelry. For this reason, the jewelry is large and chunky, valued by mass rather than workmanship.

Equally distinctive is Bedouin clothing. Girls under the age of 12 wear bright peacock dresses, but beginning at puberty they must cover up in black cloaks. The colorful stitched embroidery on these robes and their hoods also has a meaning; Red means the wearer is married, blue means she is not. Some tribal women still sport distinctive leather face masks, hung with coins, and have their faces tattooed and eyes ringed with kohl like raccoons. Even the most urbanized of men still prefer the practical flowing white robes to trousers and shirts.

Though Muslim, the Bedouin also have their own superstitions and practices and their own common law (*urf*), according to which they administer their own justice. Since the 1960s, there have been continued attempts to change all this and bring the Bedouin under central government. Schools, clinics, and housing settlements have been provided. Although this outside interference has been resisted, and some tribes do still roam the desert with their flocks, particularly in northern Sinai, most have now forsaken their nomadic ways. Stone houses with tin roofs and TV antennae have replaced the tents. Beginning in the 1980s, tourism has also had a profound effect. Exposure to massive numbers of not just Westerners, but also urban Egyptians, has, unsurprisingly, led to many Bedouin giving up age-old means of earning income for jobs in construction, taxi driving, or the service industries. Resort towns such as Dahab are full of "Bedouin" hotels and restaurants.

Fortunately, many Bedouin have been able to parlay their traditional skills—finding water,

INSIDER TIP:

Wind, Sand, and Stars (www.windsandstars.co.uk), a British company, can immerse you in Bedouin culture with an unforgettable desert trek.

—PAM GROUT
National Geographic author

navigating by the stars, tracking, and exercising an extensive knowledge of Sinai's plant and animal life—into a living as tourist guides. A number are also employed as rangers looking after the St. Catherine Protectorate. Future development in Sinai, it is to be hoped, can continue using the former nomads' unique abilities.

Women prepare to weave the highly distinctive cloth of the Sinai Bedouin.

Sinai Coast

The southeast coast of Sinai, from the border with Israel at Taba down to Ras Muhammad at the tip of the peninsula, features some of the world's most incredible underwater scenery. It is a scuba-diving and snorkeling paradise that has spawned an increasing number of specially built small resorts, all whitewashed and pristine because the builders have only just moved out.

Once the domain only of Bedouin, coastal Sinai is fast developing into a beach tourism hot spot.

Thirty years ago nothing was here. The most venerable resort, **Sharm al-Sheikh,** is little more than 20 years old. Neighboring **Naama Bay** is half that age. The two occupy bays either side of a rocky headland. Both are Las Vegas-style strips, a single highway lined with hotels and shopping centers. On one side is the sea, on the other the jagged, purplish mountains, and, beyond those, the desert. A palm-fringed boardwalk skirts the beach, lined with cafés and bars. Sunshine is guaranteed, although given that summer temperatures frequently top 105°F (40°C), peak seasons are fall, winter, and early spring, before the heat builds.

Most visitors are young Europeans (predominantly French, German, and Italian), here for the diving and snorkeling. Despite the growing number of visitors, the offshore reefs remain teeming with fish. Every hotel has its own boats, dive centers, and instructors, and there are many independent outfits. You don't have to be an expert to dive: You can be taught on the spot. Popular local dive spots include the stunning **Near** and **Middle Gardens,** and the even more incredible Far Garden, all reached by boat.

Serious divers sign up for a day trip to **Ras Muhammad,** Egypt's first national marine park, which lies 18 miles (30 km) southwest of Sharm al-Sheikh at the very southernmost point of Sinai. It is a protected area of 320 square miles (829 sq km) of land and sea, including Tiran Island, of which only a small part is accessible to visitors. All of the thousand-plus species of marine life found in the Red Sea are represented here, including sharks, barracuda, and giant rays, making a trip here an experience not to be missed. Both snorkeling and diving are possible, but the number of boats allowed each day is limited, so make reservations in advance with one of the dive operators in Sharm al-Sheikh or Naama Bay (see p. 380).

Back in Sharm, other activities include sailing lessons, windsurfing, parasailing, and glass-bottom-boat trips. Most hotels also offer a wide variety of excursions into the Sinai interior to places such as the Monastery of St. Catherine (see pp. 337–339) and Mount Sinai (see pp. 336–337), and farther afield to Wadi Feiran and Serabit al-Khadim (see p. 335).

Vacationers who have jetted directly into Sharm even head off on day trips to Cairo for a quick peek at the Pyramids, involving a grueling 14 hours' travel time there and back. Evenings are more than adequately filled dining at any of a plethora of open-air restaurants, which take valiant stabs at cuisines from Japanese to Mexican. After

INSIDER TIP:

Wear a T-shirt when snorkeling. It's easy to forget the time, and this will help protect you from sunburn.

—NEIL HEWISON
American University in Cairo Press

dessert there are numerous discos, bars, and clubs to sample.

Sharm al-Sheikh and Naama Bay are the most complete of Sinai's resorts, but plenty more are coming. About 50 miles (80 km) to the north, **Dahab** has long been a

Sharm al-Sheikh
🗺 321 C4

NOTE: There are no visitor centers in Sinai. Hotel receptionists will be able to offer advice and assistance in planning and booking trips.

Tips for Divers

Most resorts have their own diving centers, which tend to be the most reliable, but you can choose from plenty of dive clubs and operators in Dahab, Sharm, and Hurghada, some better than others. Safety—not cost—should be the primary concern. Before signing on with a dive center, make sure its equipment is in good condition. Diving suits left out in the sun, for example, can crack. Poorly maintained scuba equipment can also be dangerous, and occasionally, fatal.

If you are a first-time diver, there are plenty of places in the Red Sea and Sinai where you can train for your PADI (Professional Association of Diving Instruction) certificate. Check that the instructor has a card proving that he is qualified to teach diving, and make sure he speaks your language; miscommunication can have dire consequences. Divers who haven't dived for three months should do a refresher dive, although operators will often require this in any case.

A stretch of unspoiled Sinai coastline at Sharm al-Sheikh

shaft that has been known to claim several lives in a year.

Farther north along the coast is **Nuweiba,** which is several small settlements strung together with a backdrop of beautiful mountain scenery. It started life during the Israeli occupation as a farming cooperative *(moshav)* and has since become a full-fledged small town with a commercial center, Nuweiba City. It has also spawned a neighboring Bedouin village, Tarabeen, and a port area to the south, from where there are twice-daily sailings to Aqaba in Jordan.

Less polished than Naama Bay and Sharm al-Sheikh, Nuweiba caters more to moderately affluent Egyptians, partly because the diving is not as good here as it is to the south. However, Nuweiba is the best base for excursions into the interior, including the Blue Valley, St. Catherine's Monastery, and Wadi Mukattab (see p. 335).

Sinai's newest resort lies about 15 miles farther up the coast: **Taba Heights**, a chic gathering of newly built luxury hotels, a casino, shops, restaurants, dive centers, and an 18-hole golf course. From the greens it is possible to look out over the Red Sea to the coastlines of Saudi Arabia, Jordan, and Israel. It is also possible to take an excursion to Pharaoh's Island, a small offshore outcrop of rock, crowned by a much restored Crusader fortress that later fell to Salah ad-Din (Saladin).

The northernmost Sinai resort, **Taba,** is on the border with Israel—the Israeli resort of Eilat is just a few miles past the checkpoints. Taba offers a pleasant strip of beach, a five-star hotel, and a bus station. ■

favorite with budget travelers and backpackers, who pay just a few dollars a night for a bamboo hut on the beach. The place exists in a late-1960s time warp: Most visitors are content to sprawl on cushions beneath the palms, dozing, reading, and letter-writing to a sound track of Jimi Hendrix, Bob Marley, and Pink Floyd, occasionally raising themselves for a bite at one of the many small beachfront cafés.

Yet there is also a modern resort area here, known as Dahab City, with tranquil beachside hotels and chic restaurants, and not a hint of a hippie influence. Dahab also has the requisite fine diving, with the most famous—and most dangerous—of sites being the Blue Hole, a 215-foot-deep (66 m)

Travelwise

Travelwise Information   346–388

Planning your Trip   346–347

How to Get to Egypt   347–348

Getting Around   348–350

Practical Advice   350–353

Emergencies   353

Further Reading   354–355

Movies   355

Hotels & Restaurants   356–375

Shopping in Egypt   376–378

Activities & Entertainment in Egypt   379–383

Language Guide   384

Menu Reader   385

Glossary   386

Who's Who   387

Cairo Metro Map   388

Spices piled in the shape of
pyramids on a stall in Luxor

TRAVELWISE

PLANNING YOUR TRIP
When to Go
Climate

Egypt is good for vacations year-round. However, summer temperatures can be extreme, especially in the south of the country, where the majority of the pharaonic sites are concentrated. If at all possible, avoid June, July, and August, when daytime temperatures in this area can regularly top 100°F (38°C). If you do visit at this time, be prepared for early rising, as dawn is the best time for exploring the sites.

Luxor and Aswan make for ideal winter destinations, as even in January skies are clear and temperatures are balmy. Unfortunately, the north of the country does experience the cold; winter days in Cairo can be overcast and evenings chilly, while it rains frequently in Alexandria. The best times to visit the country as a whole are spring and fall, which manage to avoid both clouds in the north and extreme heat in the south.

Ramadan

Try not to visit during the holy month of Ramadan, in which all observant Muslims fast during daylight hours. Many restaurants and cafés are closed, stores and offices keep erratic hours, and all schedules are disrupted.

The exact dates of Ramadan change every year as Islam follows a lunar calendar, but in 2010 it begins on August 11.

Calendar of Events

See also National and Religious Holidays (on p. 352). For more information about these events, consult the Egyptian Tourist Authority (see p. 353; www.touregypt.com).

January
Cairo Book Fair
A two-week festival of literary culture with displays by local and foreign publishers held at the Cairo Exhibition Grounds.

Wust al-Balad Art Festival
A two-week-long program of exhibitions, theater, poetry, and music at galleries, cafés, and other venues in downtown Cairo.

February
International Fishing Tournament
Held at Hurghada on the Red Sea and attended by anglers from all over the world.

Ascension of Ramses II
On February 22 each year the sun penetrates into the inner sanctuary of the temple at Abu Simbel, illuminating the statues of the gods within.

May
South Sinai Camel Festival
Thrilling Bedouin camel races in Sharm al-Sheikh.

July
International Festival of Oriental Dance
Belly dancing festival throughout Cairo in which famous Egyptian practitioners give showcase performances and lessons to international attendees.

August
Tourism and Shopping Festival
Countrywide promotion of Egyptian products, with participating stores offering discounted prices.

September
Experimental Theater Festival
Ten days of international fringe theater performed at a variety of venues throughout Cairo.

October
Alexandrias of the World Festival
Four-day celebration attended by delegations from all the cities named Alexandria (there are over 40 in the world).

Pharaohs' Rally
An 11-day, 2,900-mile (4,700 km) motor vehicle race through the desert, beginning and ending at the Pyramids and attracting competitors from all over the world.

Birth of Ramses II
On October 22 the sun's rays penetrate the temple at Abu Simbel.

Commemoration of the Battle of Al Alamein
Services are conducted at this pivotal World War II battle site attended by former combatants of Allied and Axis countries.

November
Arabic Music Festival
A ten-day festival of traditional Arabic music held at venues throughout Cairo.

December
Cairo International Film Festival
A 14-day festival with screenings of recent films from all over the world, plus celebrity guests.

What to Take

Pack clothing that covers your legs and—especially if you are female—as much skin as possible. Not only will this help protect against sunburn, but it will also provide an appropriate degree of modesty in an Islamic country whose citizens cover up and appreciate their visitors doing the same.

Of course, if you are hitting the beaches of Sinai or the Red Sea coast, then pack a bikini or swimming shorts. Women need head scarves inside mosques, and it is wise to get into the habit of carrying one at all times.

Leave the portable drugstore at home—pharmacies are easy to find in Egypt and are very well stocked. Most pharmacists speak English and are competent to make basic diagnoses. Stomach ailments are the biggest concern, so you might want to bring along a suitable drug for immediate use. Consult your doctor before leaving home.

Other handy items include a small flashlight for poorly lit tombs and museums, earplugs for noisy hotels, an alarm clock (wake-up calls rarely happen), and perhaps a notebook to write down addresses—locals love keepsake photographs.

Travel Insurance

Always take out adequate insurance when you travel, especially for medical needs. Costs for emergency surgery or medical repatriation home can be exorbitant. Make sure that the policy covers all the activities that you are likely to undertake, for example diving.

Entry Formalities

Visas

You need a valid passport and a visa obtainable in advance from an Egyptian embassy or consulate in your country. Apply at least one month in advance.

Alternatively, you can acquire a visa on the spot on arrival at Cairo or Luxor airport for $15. The visa is good for a stay of up to three months.

Customs

Travelers over the age of 18 may bring one liter of alcohol, one liter of perfume, 200 cigarettes, and 25 cigars into the country.

Travelers may be asked to declare video cameras, music players and laptop computers if customs officials require it, and all of these items may be subject to an import tax. Alternatively, the items may be written into the traveler's passport to ensure that they leave the country again and are not sold in Egypt.

Currency Restrictions

There are no restrictions on the import of foreign currencies; you are supposed to declare all you have when you enter, but in practice this is never required.

Drugs & Narcotics

Medicines you bring to Egypt for personal use should be clearly labeled, preferably in their original packaging or prescription bottle. Obtain a statement from your doctor if you are importing a large number of pharmaceuticals, or if they are of a restricted type.

Embassies

For details and information on visas, customs controls, and restrictions, contact the relevant Egyptian embassy or consulate.

United States
3521 International Court NW
Washington D.C. 20008
Tel 202/895-5400
Fax 202/244-4319
Consulates in Chicago, Houston, New York, and San Francisco

Canada
454 Laurier Ave., East
Ottawa, Ontario, K1N 6R3
Tel 613/234-4931
Fax 613/234-4398
Also in Montreal

United Kingdom
2 Lowndes St.
London SW1
Tel 020/7235 9777

Australia
1 Darwin Ave., Yarralumla
Canberra, ACT 2600
Tel 02/6273 4437
Fax 02/6273 4279
Consulates in Melbourne and Sydney

HOW TO GET TO EGYPT

Choosing a Ticket

Egypt is a relatively cheap destination, and you can also save money by shopping around for the airline ticket, going out of season, and planning ahead. At the minimum you should investigate the savings available through advance purchase ticketing, such as Apex. Some of the major airlines flying to Egypt are:

EgyptAir
United States
19 W. 44th St.
New York, NY 10036
Tel 212/315-0900
Fax 212/315-0967
www.egyptair.com

Canada
151 Bloor St.
Toronto, Ontario M5S 1S4
Tel 613/960-3203
Fax 613/960-1436

United Kingdom
63 Conduit St.
London W1S 2GD
Tel 020/7734 2864
Fax 020/7287 1728

British Airways
United States
Tel 800/247-9297
United Kingdom
Tel 0870/850 9850
www.britishairways.com

Delta Airlines
United States and Canada
Tel 800/221-1212
www.delta.com

United Airlines
United States
Tel 800/538-2929
www.united.com

Package Tours

It can be invaluable to have a local agent while traveling in Egypt. Confirming flights, negotiating for better hotel rooms, arranging for drivers and guides, and securing hard-to-get tickets all waste untold hours that could be more usefully spent seeing the sights. There are two main ways of achieving this. The first is to fly independently and then spend your time with a tour company. Among the best companies are:

Abercrombie & Kent
U.S.: 1520 Kensington Rd.,
Suite 212
Oak Brook, IL 60523-2141
Tel 800/554-7016
Fax 630/954-3324
www.abercrombiekent.com
Cairo: Tel 02/2393 6255

American Express
www.americanexpress.com
Cairo: 15 Qasr al-Nil
Tel 02/574 3656

Misr Travel
U.S.: 1270 Avenue of the
Americas, Suite 604
New York, NY 10020
Tel 212/332-2600 or
800/223-4978

Fax 212/332-2609
www.misrtravel.org
Cairo: 1 Talaat Harb St.
Tel 02/2393 0010
e-mail: csheraton@misrtravel.net

National Geographic Expeditions
P.O. Box 65265
Washington, D.C., 20035-5265
Tel 888/966-8687
www.nationalgeographic.com

Thomas Cook
U.K.: 30 St. James's St.
London SW1A1HB
Tel 0845/308 9570
www.thomascook.com
Cairo: 17 Mahmoud Bassiouni,
Downtown
Tel 02/2574 3955

Expect to pay between $200 and $300 per person per day, all inclusive, for a customized itinerary.

The second way to save planning time is to buy a vacation package that includes flights, hotels, and sight-seeing from one of the many companies that advertise their packages in travel magazines.

Arriving by Air

Most visitors arrive in Cairo, though international flights also arrive at Alexandria, Luxor, Hurghada, and Sharm al-Sheikh airports. Cairo International Airport is located 15 miles (25 km) northeast of the city center. Most hotels arrange pick-ups for guests. For detailed information, see www.cairo-airport.com.

Although a regular bus service to central Cairo exists, it departs from the domestic terminal some distance away. There is no effective link between the international and domestic terminals.

If you need to make your own way to the city center, the best option is a taxi. Official "limousines" make the trip for $15. The journey can take anything between 30 minutes and an hour, depending on the traffic.

Note: There is a departure tax, but this is usually prepaid as part of your air ticket. For more details, see www.cairo-airport.com.

GETTING AROUND
By Air

The national carrier EgyptAir, along with its subsidiary Air Sinai, has a comprehensive network of domestic services linking the major cities and tourist areas. At present Alexandria, Asyut, Aswan, Abu Simbel, Al-Arish, Hurghada, Kharga Oasis, St. Catherine's, and Sharm al-Sheikh all have domestic airports. Marsa Alam on the Red Sea and Taba in Sinai both have international airports, currently served only by European charter flights.

Round-trip ticket prices are roughly double the one-way fare, and there are no special deals or passes. In Cairo, all domestic flights depart from terminal one. If possible, arrange with your tour company for pick-ups and drop-offs, as public transportation to and from regional airports is often nonexistent. Confirm each flight locally, as overbooking is common.

Signs at airports are poor and often wrong, so don't rely on them. To be safe, when a flight boards, show your boarding pass to the gate attendant, who will either nod yes or turn you away.

EgyptAir has offices at:
Cairo: Nile Hilton Hotel,
tel 02/2579 3049
Alexandria: 19 Midan Zaghloul,
tel 03/482 5938
Luxor: Winter Palace Arcade,
tel 095/338 0580
Aswan: Corniche, tel 097/231 5000

Sharm al-Sheikh: Al Hadaba, near the old market, tel 069/366 5061
For EgyptAir overseas offices see p. 347.

By Train
Egypt's rail network is, to all practical effect, limited to a single extended line shadowing the Nile from Alexandria on the northern coast all the way down to Aswan in the south.

Services between Cairo and Alexandria are excellent. There are three types of train: *turbini, fransawi,* and local. The first two are express services, and there are several of each every day, while the local makes numerous stops at small Delta towns. The faster services make just one or two stops, completing the journey in around two and a half hours. Passenger coaches are air-conditioned and seating is comfortable.

Beware when traveling to Alexandria because there are two stations; the first is Sidi Gaber, in the eastern suburbs of the city, and then the train continues on to terminate at Cairo Station (Mahattat Masr), in the center of town.

Heading south from Cairo, three tourist trains depart daily for Luxor (a ten-hour journey) and Aswan (13 to 16 hours depending on the service), the best of which is the luxurious Wagon Lits sleeper ($80 for a single, including dinner and breakfast). One-way fares on the other two less comfortable trains (one a morning departure, the other overnight, but with no sleeping berths) are $16 to Luxor and $19.50 to Aswan.

Tickets for all three services must be bought at least two or three days in advance. In the case of the Wagon Lits, reservations are made at a ticket office to your left as you enter Cairo's main train station. Seats for the other two services are bought from the ticket office beside platform 11.

Cairo's metro (subway) system is a good way to get around the city (see map on p. 388). It is efficient and clean, though often crowded. Unfortunately for visitors, the metro has been designed with the commuter in mind and the lines primarily service the suburbs, stopping at few places of interest (although there are convenient stations for Coptic Cairo, the Opera House, and Ramses train station). A third line, currently under construction, will be of greater value to the visitor because it will connect downtown with Islamic Cairo and Zamalek. Stations are easily identified by signs with a big red M in a blue star.

Tickets are bought down in the underground concourses and cost 1LE (17 cents) for a ride of up to nine stops. Signing is in Arabic and English and the system is extremely easy to use. The service starts at about 5 a.m. and closes around 11:30 p.m. The first carriage is reserved for women only. Women who want to ride in this carriage should make sure they're standing at the right place on the platform, as the trains don't stop for long.

By Bus
When it comes to getting around, if you aren't flying, then the way to go is trains for any travel north–south, but buses when it comes to going east and west. So from Cairo, if you want to head out to the Western Desert and its oases, or over to the Red Sea coast and Sinai, the best means of transportation is the bus.

The country is covered by several companies, each of which has its own territory. In Cairo they all operate out of one giant bus station, called Turgoman Garage, which is in the district of Bulaq, north of downtown between the city center and the Nile. To call it a bus station is a bit of an exaggeration because it's nothing more than a huge parking lot with a few wooden cabins where tickets are sold. It is an exceptionally confusing place, and it is essential to be accompanied by a guide, or have your hotel or a tour company purchase tickets for you ahead of time, particularly for popular destinations like Sinai and the Red Sea coast. Most of the buses are modern and air-conditioned, and departures to most destinations are frequent. Some buses may be old, with worn seat cushions, however, and depending on the driver's tastes, you may be listening to a tape of Umm Kolthum, a Koranic reciter, or an Arabic comedy album for much of your trip.

Nile Cruises
Visiting Egypt without cruising the Nile is like going to Las Vegas and not gambling. The traditional cruise has always been from Cairo down to Luxor (see pp. 302–303), but since the early 1990s fears for tourists' safety have meant that boats are no longer allowed to sail through Middle Egypt. Instead, cruisers sail for three or four nights between Luxor and Aswan, typically stopping off at Esna, Edfu, and Kom Ombo en route.

Every big hotel company or tour operator has a boat on the Nile. In particular, Abercrombie & Kent's 40-passenger *Sun Boat III* and 84-passenger *Sun Boat IV* are notably luxurious and serve excellent food.

Lake Nasser Cruises
Even better than taking a Nile cruise is sailing the length of Lake Nasser from the High Dam at Aswan down to the magnificent temple of Abu Simbel.

Five boats currently sail the lake and two of them stand out far above the rest. The M.S. *Eugénie* and M.S. *Qasr Ibrim* are supremely luxurious, designed to look like late 19th-century floating palaces. Both have pools, Jacuzzis, and fantastic French cuisine. Their passengers are pampered with such treats as cocktails served in the desert and their own private sound-and-light performance in front of the temples at Abu Simbel. These boats are run by Belle Epoque Tours of Cairo (tel 02/2516 9653 or 02/2516 9654 or 02/2516 9656, fax 02/2516 9646, www.kasribrim.com.eg).

By Car

There are very few places in Egypt where you would want to rent a car and drive yourself. Traffic in and around Cairo and Alexandria is nightmarish. Local drivers' observance of traffic rules is negligible, and almost every vehicle carries the bumps and dents to prove it.

Driving in the south of the country is less harrowing, but the continued threat of terrorism means that private cars must travel in police-escorted convoys that travel at set times. Therefore, opportunities for sight-seeing are limited, as the traditional freedoms of having your own transportation are severely curtailed.

Perhaps the only parts of the country in which driving is an attractive option are Sinai and the Red Sea coast. Many of the major hotels in resorts such as Hurghada, Sharm al-Sheikh, and Naama Bay have international car rental desks.

Rental rates are not particularly cheap, typically $50 to $60 a day, depending on the model. If you think you may want to rent a car, remember to take your driver's license with you.

PRACTICAL ADVICE
Business Hours

Banks, government offices, and most businesses are open Sunday through Thursday from 8:30 a.m.

to 2 p.m. They close on public and religious holidays. It is usually possible to find a hotel bank that is open 24 hours.

Stores normally do not open until at least 10 a.m. but often remain open until 10 p.m. or later, especially during summer. Many close on Friday, the Islamic holy day, or at the very least for Friday prayers, which occupy an hour around noon.

Many stores and private businesses also close on Saturdays, including consulates and foreign embassies. Christian businesses close on Sunday.

Communications
Mail

Stamps may be purchased at post offices and hotel bookstalls. Postcards and letters up to half an ounce (15g) cost the equivalent of 25 cents to most countries and take around a week to ten days to reach the United States, and four or five days to reach Europe. Sending mail from the mailboxes at major hotels instead of from those on the street helps ensure quicker service.

If possible, avoid sending packages home. These can only be mailed from a city's central post office (which in Cairo is close to Ramses train station) and it involves a long, tortuous process of paperwork and customs inspection. When you are buying in the bazaar, some shopkeepers will offer to handle mailing as part of the deal.

General Delivery

Larger post offices have a free general delivery (poste restante) service. The letter needs to have the recipient's name and be addressed "Poste Restante, Central Post Office" and the name of the town. Take proof of identity, preferably a passport, when collecting mail. American

Express has a client mail service at its main offices.

Telephones

Probably the best thing that can be said about Egypt's telephone system is that it is improving. The easiest way of making a call is to use the card phones that are found on most street corners. There are two kinds of card phones, of which the distinctive yellow-and-green booths of Menatel are by far the most common.

Phone cards are sold at shops and kiosks flagged with a little sticker in the window, and come in units of 10, 20, and 30 Egyptian pounds. Rates for calling Europe and the U.S. via Menatel are 5.6 Egyptian pounds (roughly $1) for the first minute and then 4.5 Egyptian pounds for each additional minute. Calls made from your hotel carry a heavy surcharge.

The international dialing code for Egypt is 20. To call from Egypt to the U.S. or Canada, the code is 00 1. To call from Egypt to the U.K., the code is 00 44.

Fax

Fax machines are available at main post offices and at most three- to five-star hotels. From a telephone office, a one-page fax to the U.S. or U.K. costs about $3.50. Hotel rates are a lot more.

E-mail & Online Services

Cairo, Alexandria, Aswan, Dahab, Hurghada, Sharm al-Sheikh, and Luxor all offer privately owned Internet cafés. These allow you to get online and send e-mail at a quarter-hour, half-hour, or hourly rate (typically one hour costs the equivalent of $3). Connections can be infuriatingly slow, a result of too much demand on insufficient international bandwidth.

If you are traveling with a laptop and want to connect to the Internet, you may have problems because of the variety of phone sockets in use in Egypt. In older hotels, phone cables are usually wired right into the wall.

Electricity

Egyptian electrical appliances have plugs with two round pins. Electrical voltage is 220 volts AC, 50 Hz. American and British appliances will need adaptors.

Conversions

Egypt uses the metric system. Useful conversions are:

1 mile = 1.6 kilometers (km)
1 kilometer = 0.62 mile
1 quart = 0.95 liter
1 liter = 1.06 quart
1 U.S. gallon = 3.79 liters
1 pound = 0.37 kilograms (kg)
1 kilo = 2.2 pounds
1 ounce = 28 grams (g)
1 foot = 0.3 meter (m)
1 meter = 39.37 inches

Etiquette

Though Egypt is an Islamic country, few special rules apply to the visitor. The main concern is to be sure that you dress modestly. For women this means avoiding shorts and sleeveless tops and wearing pants or skirts that come below the knee. In more conservative areas, such as Islamic Cairo, and when visiting mosques or churches, shoulders and sometimes heads must be covered. Women might want to carry scarves with them.

Because Western women are perceived to be more lax in their modesty, they are frequently hit on by Egyptian men. It is usually harmless, but can nevertheless be annoying. It is also generally easy to shrug off: Avoid eye contact;

do not beam wide smiles; do not respond to invitations, come-ons, or obnoxious comments.

One advantage for women travelers is that they often have their own lines, at train station ticket offices, for example, and these are always much shorter than the corresponding men's lines. Not that Egyptians are very good at standing in line anyway—it does not pay to be too polite or you will never get to the front.

In central Cairo and Luxor, in particular, beware of touts who will stop you on the street to ask where you are from. Invariably, stopping to chat with one of these friendly fellows ends up leading to a time-consuming visit to a perfume or papyrus shop.

Beware also of shopowners who tell you that the museum or temple to which you are obviously heading is closed, and why not spend time and have tea at my shop instead? Of course, the museum or temple is not closed, but you would be amazed how many people fall for this ploy. Not all Egyptians are looking to part visitors from their cash, but a healthy dose of skepticism is useful.

Liquor Laws

Few Egyptians consume alcohol because the Koran warns against substances that cloud the mind. At the same time, they generally are tolerant of others who wish to do so, particularly foreign visitors who drink.

Locally produced beer and wine and imported hard liquor are readily available in hotel bars and in many restaurants, especially those in more touristed areas. The farther you get from the big cities and resorts, however, the harder it is to find alcohol. Until recently alcohol could not be found at Siwa Oasis at all. Discretion should still be shown anywhere in Egypt, and

alcohol should never be consumed on the streets.

Media

Newspapers

The English-language daily (no Sunday edition, though) *Egyptian Gazette* is available throughout the country, as is the *Al-Ahram Weekly;* they are both government-owned newspapers. *The Daily News Egypt,* is a better read; it is sold both inside the *International Herald Tribune* and separately. *Egypt Today,* a monthly glossy magazine, is worth picking up for its what's-on listings. The same publishers also put out useful pocket-size quarterlies: *Alex Today, Red Sea Today,* and *Sinai Today.*

TV Channels

Cairo-based Nile TV broadcasts news and current affairs exclusively in English and French from early each morning until past midnight. In addition, most hotels offer satellite TV with CNN, BBC World, and MTV at the very least.

Radio

FM95 broadcasts news in English on 557 kHz at 7:30 a.m. and 2:30 and 8 p.m. daily. BBC and Voice of America (VOA) broadcasts can be picked up on medium wave at various times of the morning and evening. The BBC can be heard on both 639 kHz and 1320 kHz, and VOA on 1290 kHz.

Money

The country's unit of currency is the Egyptian pound (LE), which is divided into 100 piastres (pt). Bills come in denominations of 25 pt, 50 pt, and 1, 5, 10, 20, 50, 100, and 200 pounds. Different colors and sizes make them easy to identify. There are also coins of 5, 10, 25 and 50 pt and 1 LE, although the smaller ones have little value and are rarely encountered by most visitors. Egypt is a cash economy, so carry lots of small-denomination notes (50 pt and LE1) for taxis and tipping.

Major international credit cards are widely accepted in most hotels, restaurants, and tourist establishments. ATMs are common in all larger centers and tourist resorts, and allow cash withdrawals on American Express, Visa, and MasterCard. Other than in remote regions such as the Western Desert, it is becoming increasingly easy to travel in Egypt on just plastic.

National & Religious Holidays

National Holidays
January 1 (New Year's Day)
April 25 (Sinai Liberation Day)
May 1 (May Day)
July 23 (Revolution Day)
October 6 (National Day)

Religious Holidays
Egypt's major holidays are all religious holidays. Because the Islamic calendar is 11 days shorter than the Gregorian (Western) calendar, its holidays fall 11 days earlier each year. Dates of Islamic holidays are also approximate because they depend on the sighting of the moon. The following are public holidays in Egypt:

Eid al-Adha, the Great Feast (November 27–29 in 2009 and November 16 in 2010)
Moulid an-Nabi, Prophet's Birthday (February 26 in 2010)
Ramadan (August 11 to September 9 in 2010)
Eid al-Fitr, the Small Feast (September 9 in 2010)

Photography & Video
Although quality film and processing are available throughout Egypt, some stores do not always take good care of their stock. Film is often stored in direct sunlight and high temperatures, which adversely affects the quality, so be careful where you buy your film.

When you're shooting, be aware that the intense glare from the sun and its reflection on the water may bleach your photographs or digital images of color. To minimize this problem, make use of the best times to shoot—the early morning and late afternoon.

Note that most ancient sites in Egypt charge an additional camera fee of two to three dollars. If you do not wish to pay to take photos, you may be forced to surrender your camera at the ticket office during your visit. For video cameras the fee rises up to $20 to $30 per site, so think twice about taking the camera with you to these places.

In this guide, information about these fees where applicable is given in the sidebar for each site.

Be cautious when pointing your camera at anything other than tourist sights. It is forbidden to photograph airports, bridges, railroad stations, and anything related to the military, as well as many other seemingly innocuous public structures, including factories. Anybody who does so risks having their film or their digital memory card confiscated.

Egyptians are also sensitive about visitors recording images of what may be perceived as backward aspects of the country, such as donkey carts or dilapidated buildings. Always ask before photographing people, especially women.

Rest Rooms
Toilets in most hotels and restaurants are the Western sit-down variety and are generally clean and well maintained, but public rest rooms elsewhere can be fairly awful.

Some toilets are of the squat kind and are very uncomfortable if you have never used this kind of facility before. Only in better hotels will toilet paper be provided; most toilets simply come equipped with a water squirter for washing yourself when you are finished. For this reason, it is a good idea to carry packets of disposable tissues with you (these are available cheaply all over Egypt).

Time Differences
Egyptian time is seven hours ahead of Eastern Standard Time, and two hours ahead of British Summer Time.

Tipping
For most services, *baksheesh*, (tipping) is expected. Ten percent is customary in restaurants. Tip LE1 to LE2 for small services, such as a porter carrying your bags or when a guard shows you something off the beaten track at an ancient monument. However, do not be intimidated into tipping when you do not believe that it is warranted.

Tourist Offices
The Egyptian Tourist Authority runs tourist offices in most countries. Ones in major English-speaking nations follow:

United States
630 5th Ave., Suite 1706
New York, NY 10111
Tel 212/332-2570
Fax 212/956-6439
Also in Los Angeles & Chicago.

Canada
1253 McGill College Ave.
Suite 250,
Montreal, Quebec H3B 2Y5
Tel 514/851-4606
Fax 514/861-8071

United Kingdom
Egyptian House,
170 Piccadilly
3rd Floor West,
London W1V 9DD
Tel 020/7493 5283
Fax 020/7408 0295

Australia
1 Darwin Ave., Yarralumla
Canberra, ACT 2600
Tel 02/6273 4260
Fax 02/6273 4629

Internet Information
The Egyptian Ministry of Tourism
has a good website with travel
information and reservation
advice at: www.touregypt.com

Travelers with Disabilities

Although some of the larger
hotels are wheelchair accessible,
generally speaking Egypt is a
difficult place for anyone with a
mobility problem. Sidewalks are
high with a plethora of steps,
and many of them are badly
maintained. Ramps are few,
public facilities don't necessarily have elevators, and gaining
entrance to many of the ancient
sites is all but impossible owing
to their narrow entrances and
steep stairs.

Public transportation is also
basically inaccessible. Anybody
with mobility problems wishing
to visit Egypt should make special
arrangements with their tour
operator.

EMERGENCIES
Emergency Telephone Numbers

For the **tourist police** call 126.
For an **ambulance** call 123.
For the **fire service** call 125.

Embassies & Consulates

Most countries have an embassy
in Cairo, and several (including

the United States and United
Kingdom) also maintain a consulate in Alexandria.

United States
5 Latin America St.
Garden City, Cairo
Tel 02/2797 3300
Fax 02/2797 3200

Canada
26 Kamel El Shenawy St.
Garden City, Cairo
Tel 02/2797 8700
Fax 02/2797 8860

United Kingdom
7 Ahmed Ragheb St.
Garden City, Cairo
Tel 02/2791 6000
Fax 02/2791 6133

Australia
World Trade Centre,
11th floor
1191 Corniche al-Nil, Cairo
Tel 02/2575 0444
Fax 02/2578 1638

Health

Medical care in Egypt is not
very good. If you become ill,
the best advice is to fly home.
If you are in immediate need of
medical attention, your embassy
will have a list of recommended
doctors.

Inoculations

No inoculations are essential for
travel to Egypt. It is sensible to
be vaccinated against tetanus
and hepatitis (A and B), but that
is true whether you are traveling
or not.

Egypt is not in a malarial zone,
but there is a risk of malaria in the
Fayoum area from June through
October. If you intend to travel to
this region, you should consider
taking antimalarials. Other insect-
borne diseases, such as dengue
fever, typhus, filariasis, and West

Nile fever, do occur along the Nile
but the risk to travelers is minimal.
It is wise, however, to take steps
to avoid insect bites by using an
effective repellent.

If you require a particular
medication, take an adequate
supply, as it may not be available
locally. For peace of mind, take
part of the packaging showing
the generic name rather than the
brand, which will make getting
replacements easier.

Food & Water

Doctors recommend sticking
to mineral water only. There
are several good local brands
widely available such as Baraka
or Siwa. Avoid unpeeled fruit
and vegetables, unless cooked.
Avoid salads in restaurants where
it is impossible to tell how clean
the ingredients are.

Sunburn & Heat Sickness

Do not underestimate the power
of the Egyptian sun. Try to stay
out of the sun between 11 a.m.
and 3 p.m. At the very least,
always wear properly applied,
high SPF sunscreen and a broad-
brimmed hat. Keep your neck
and arms well covered, and protect your eyes with good-quality
sunglasses.

Drink plenty of fluids to
prevent dehydration. Long,
continuous periods of exposure to
high temperatures and insufficient
fluids can leave you vulnerable to
heatstroke, a serious, occasionally
fatal, condition.

Lost Property

To report a crime or loss of
belongings, report to the tourist
police rather than the local
police. Tourist police generally
speak English. Even so, filling out
the necessary forms is a long and
tedious process and can take up
half a day.

FURTHER READING

There is a vast and growing array of publications on all aspects of Egypt and Egyptology. Many of these titles are available in book-shops in Egypt, often at prices cheaper than those you will find at home.

Fiction & Literature

Al-Aswany, Alaa
The Yacoubian Building (2004)
A runaway bestseller in Arabic, now in English, tells the story of modern Egypt through the varied lives of the inhabitants of one Cairo building.

Cavafy, Constantine
Collected Poems (1935)
The Alexandrian Greek poet who inspired Lawrence Durrell.

Christie, Agatha
Death on the Nile (1937)
Detective Hercule Poirot inves-tigates the murder of an heiress onboard a Nile steamer. Christie herself cruised the Nile.

Durrell, Lawrence
Alexandria Quartet (1960)
Made up of *Justine, Balthazar, Mountolive,* and *Clea,* these four novels tell the tale of cosmopoli-tan life in 1930s Alexandria.

El Sadaawi, Nawal
Woman at Point Zero (1979)
Novella about an abused young woman who was forced into prostitution, set in prison as she is awaiting execution after murdering her pimp.

Gedge, Pauline
Lords of the Two Lands (2001)
This ancient Egyptian trilogy brings to life the little docu-mented 17th dynasty and the struggle of the prince Kamose to expel the foreign Hyskos rulers from Egypt.

George, Margaret
The Memoirs of Cleopatra (1997)
A novelization of the life of Egypt's legendary queen, with impressive attention to detail, presents her as a mother and a diplomat, rather than the schem-ing seductress she's so often taken to have been.

Jacq, Christian
Ramses Quintet (1999)
A five-volume populist work by a French Egyptologist that put ancient Egypt's greatest pharaoh at the top of the best-seller lists. Also the author of the *Magnificent Queen of Freedom Trilogy.*

Mahfouz, Naguib
Cairo Trilogy
The judges who awarded Mahfouz the Nobel Prize for Literature considered *Between the Palaces, Sugar Street,* and *Palace of Desire,* the novels that make up the trilogy, to be the laureate's finest work.

Smith, Wilbur
Egyptian Series
This series of books written with mass appeal is historical fiction set in ancient Egypt.

Ondaatje, Michael
The English Patient (1992)
An award-winning story of love and destiny in World War II, set in Italy and Egypt. The central character, Laszlo Almasy, was based on a real desert explorer.

Soueif, Ahdaf
The Map of Love (2000)
Soueif is an Egyptian, raised in Cairo but educated in English and now very much part of the London literary scene. This massive family saga was short-listed for Britain's prestigious Booker Prize.

Nonfiction

Aciman, André
Out of Egypt (1996)
A memoir of eccentric family life in prerevolutionary cosmopolitan Alexandria by an occasional con-tributor to *The New Yorker.*

Atiya, Nayra
Khul-Khaal (1984)
Five women from vastly different backgrounds tell their life stories. Published by the American Uni-versity in Cairo (AUC) Press and widely available in Egypt.

Empereur, Jean-Yves *Alexandria Rediscovered* (1998)
Beautifully illustrated exploration of Alexandria's history through its archaeological remains, written by the leader of one of the two teams currently diving the harbor.

Foreman, Laura
Cleopatra's Palace (1999)
A profusely illustrated history of the queen and how her legend has grown over the years, brought up to date with the story of the ongoing dives in Alexan-dria on what is thought may be the ancient royal palace.

Ghosh, Amitav
In an Antique Land (1994)
Account of time spent by the author in a small Delta farming village. Affectionate, sympathetic, and extremely illuminating about the life of the Egyptian peasant.

Hawass, Zahi
Mountains of the Pharaohs (2006)
An engaging narrative account of the 4th dynasty pharaohs that built the Giza and Dahshur pyramids, by Egypt's head archaeologist.

Lehner, Mark
The Complete Pyramids (1997)
Everything you ever wanted to know about pyramids, not

just those at Giza but the other 80-plus scattered throughout Egypt, written by one of the world's foremost pyramid experts.

Quirke, Stephen, and Jeffrey Spencer (editors)
The British Museum Book of Ancient Egypt (2007)
The authoritative who's who and what's what of ancient Egypt in encyclopedic form.

Reeves, Nicholas
Ancient Egypt: The Great Discoveries (2000)
Fascinating chronological account of all the major landmarks in the science of Egyptology, from the deciphering of the Rosetta Stone right up to date with robots crawling into the pyramids.

Rodenbeck, Max
Cairo: The City Victorious (1998)
Entertaining and highly anecdotal meander through 5,000 years of the city's history, but especially informative on the Cairo of today.

Sattin, Anthony
The Pharaoh's Shadow (2000)
Travel literature with a twist as Sattin searches for "survivals" of pharaonic traditions in modern Egypt.

Steegmuller, Francis (editor)
Flaubert in Egypt (1996)
Extracts from diaries French novelist Gustave Flaubert kept when he visited the country for a few months in 1849. Bathhouses and bordellos are preferred over ancient monuments.

Tiradritti, Francesco and DeLuca, Araido
Egyptian Treasures From the Egyptian Museum in Cairo (1999)
Hefty and expensive, but the hundreds of magnificent full-color photographs make this just about the most sumptuous book

on the artifacts of ancient Egypt. The pictures are backed up by informative essays.

Twain, Mark
The Innocents Abroad (1869)
Twain liked Egypt about the same as he liked most places (very little) and turns his cantankerous wit on Alexandria, the Pyramids, and the Sphinx, all of which are found lacking.

Vivian, Cassandra
The Western Desert of Egypt: An Explorer's Handbook (2008)
Third edition of the definitive trekker's guide to the starkly beautiful desert.

MOVIES

For such a cinematic country with spectacular monuments, exotic bazaars, and striking desert scenery, Egypt is rather poorly served on the big screen. The major reason for this is punitive taxes, put in place in the early 1980s, which have kept foreign filmmakers away ever since.

Cairo Road (1950)
Anti-drug-smuggling escapade, with Eric Portman and Laurence Harvey, actually shot in Cairo and Port Said.

Cleopatra (1963)
A four-hour marathon of a film, remembered more for the on-set affair between stars Richard Burton and Elizabeth Taylor.

Death on the Nile (1978)
Nostalgic period re-creation with Peter Ustinov as Poirot and a cast that includes Bette Davis, Mia Farrow, and David Niven, all filmed against fantastic Nile scenery.

The English Patient (1996)
Winner of seven Oscars, particularly notable for some sensuous

desert photography. Alas, the desert was in Tunisia, and Venice stood in for Cairo.

Lawrence of Arabia (1962)
David Lean's epic biopic of T. E. Lawrence takes place mainly in the deserts of Jordan, but includes episodes crossing Sinai and at military headquarters in Cairo (actually shot in Seville).

The Mummy (1932)
The first and best of the mummies, with Boris Karloff in the title role. Some scenes were shot in Cairo's Egyptian Museum.

The Mummy (1959)
Produced by Britain's Hammer Studios, this time with Christopher Lee taking the title role, lumbering around London.

The Mummy (1999) and *The Mummy Returns* (2001)
Comic Saturday matinee-style takes on ancient horror. The Tunisian desert stands in for Egypt, while Cairo is a mix of studio work and clever montage.

The Prince of Egypt (1998)
Animated version of the story of Moses and the Jews' escape from Egypt.

The Spy Who Loved Me (1977)
Bond goes to Egypt. Roger Moore dispenses with the bad guys at the Pyramids, in Islamic Cairo, and at Karnak, all of which look ravishing.

The Yacoubian Building (2006)
An award-winning film based on the bestselling novel, reputedly the biggest-budget Egyptian film ever made.

Hotels & Restaurants

Egypt offers visitors a broad range of accommodations; construction in the tourism industry is booming and the number of beds is rising rapidly. There is less of a choice when it comes to restaurants. Cairo, Aswan, Luxor, and the established coastal resorts of Hurghada and Sharm al-Sheikh all have a wide choice of hotels from luxury to modest, but it is only in the capital that visitors find anything like an equivalent range of dining options. Elsewhere—in Middle Egypt and the Western Desert, for example—accommodation and dining standards are generally lower.

ACCOMMODATIONS

Hotels

Rooms in international luxury chain hotels may usually be reserved through the hotels' international network, or over the Internet. Reservations at more modest establishments can sometimes be made via the Internet or by e-mail. Try the Egyptian Ministry of Tourism website (see p. 353) for links to useful sites. It is always advisable to make advance reservations, although often far better deals can be arranged once you are in Egypt—perhaps through a local agent—if you are flexible and prepared to shop around.

The big international five-star chains are well represented in Egypt; most have several hotels dotted throughout the country. The Sheraton, Marriott, Hilton, and InterContinental hotels in Egypt have facilities every bit as good as you'll find in any other country in the world. All have air-conditioning, banks, shops, swimming pools, and a full complement of bars and restaurants. Some have fitness centers; others golf courses or diving schools; one even has butlers who wait on guests in its most exclusive rooms. Unfortunately, service is the one area that disappoints. Do not rely on that early-morning alarm call from reception, and always double-check all arrangements.

In smaller hotels, service can often be better because of the personal factor. At the same time, facilities are wildly variable. While most mid-range options will have air-conditioning and a restaurant, and perhaps a pool, expect little more. Hot water is not always a given, or might only be available at certain times of the day. It is wise to check before accepting a room.

One of the greatest pleasures of a stay in Egypt can be the historic hotels. Mass tourism came early to Egypt, and as a result the country has some splendid, near-palatial accommodations, built when travel still involved steamer trunks and servants and drinks on the veran-dah. Alexandria's Cecil (see p. 364), Cairo's Mena House (see p. 358), Luxor's Winter Palace (see p. 368) and Aswan's Old Cataract (see p. 371) are places that, even if you are not staying there, are worth a visit as sights in themselves.

Hotel Rates

The range of prices given for hotels is based on the standard full price for a double room. During the off season, which in central and southern Egypt covers the summer months, many hotels are prepared to offer guests special rates. It is always worth asking if any such arrangements are available.

Note that quoted prices are usually exclusive of a series of taxes and service charges that can add a further 19 to 23 percent to the final bill.

Hostels

Egypt has 15 hostels recognized by Hosteling International (HI). These are located in Cairo, Alexandria, al-Fayoum, Aswan, Asyut, Hurghada, Ismailia, Luxor, Marsa Matruh, Port Said, and Sharm al-Sheikh. Standards are not very good, but prices are as little as $1 to $5 per night. In a few there are rooms for couples or families, but on the whole the sexes are segregated. Reservations are not usually needed. For fur-ther details contact the Egyptian Youth Hostels Association (tel 02/2796 1448, fax 02/2795 0329).

Camping

Officially, camping is allowed at only a very few places in Egypt, such as the desert oases and Ras Muhammad National Park in Sinai. Facilities tend to be very rudimentary. There is a YMCA campsite in Luxor (tel 095/372 425). There is no Egyptian camping organization.

RESTAURANTS

Only Cairo has anything that could be described as a wide variety of eating places. There it is possible to eat at vegetarian cafés, pizza parlors, Western-style fast-food joints, and ethnic restaurants from a bewilderingly large and varied number of countries. Alexandria is notable for the excellence of its seafood. Outside these main cities, you may find yourself becoming overly reliant on the cafés, bistros, brasseries, and restaurants in your hotel. Reservations at restaurants are rarely necessary, and outside of Cairo they are almost unheard of.

Traditional Egyptian restaurants are fairly rare because, on the whole, Egyptians are not frequent restaurant goers. Instead, what you do find are a great many street food stalls selling *fuul* and *falafel* (called *taamiyya* in Cairo), the two Egyptian staples, which are eaten for breakfast, lunch, and dinner. You will also see eateries where the windows are filled with great vats of rice, lentils, and macaroni; these three constituents are ladled into a bowl and topped with fried onions and hot tomato sauce to make a dish called *kushari*. It's excellent for a quick fill-up.

On the occasions when Egyptians sit down to dine, it tends to be a very social affair. They begin with many small dishes, known as *meze*, which may include *taamiyya*, eggplant (*bedingan*), stuffed vine leaves, *hummus*, green salads, and plenty of bread. After that may come soup or a slightly more filling dish such as bread stuffed with ground beef. Only when this has been consumed is the main course served, typically roast chicken or grilled meats, usually served with both potatoes and rice.

In order to digest all that, there follows a lengthy period after a meal during which coffee, and maybe sticky, syrupy pastries and fruit, are taken. Some of the company may even smoke a water pipe. The whole procedure can take most of an evening, and as evening meals are eaten late, it's not unusual for Egyptians to still be at the table at midnight. Most local restaurants do not close until the early hours of the morning, and there are some in Cairo that stay open until dawn. Egypt is not a place for the overly health conscious or for those keeping a watch on their figures.

Alcohol

Many tourist-oriented restaurants and hotel bars serve alcohol (see section on Liquor laws on p. 351), but some smaller restaurants listed here may not.

CREDIT CARDS & ORGANIZATION

Large hotels and most tourist oriented restaurants accept the major credit cards. Abbreviations used are AE (American Express), DC (Diners Club), MC (Mastercard), V (Visa).

In the following section, hotels are listed under each location by price, then in alphabetical order, followed by restaurants, also by price and alphabetical order.

■ CAIRO

HOTELS

🏨 FOUR SEASONS HOTEL CAIRO AT NILE PLAZA
$$$$$
1089 CORNICHE AL-NIL
GARDEN CITY
TEL 02/2791 7000
FAX 02/2791 6900
www.fourseasons.com/
caironp
In the embassy-laden enclave of Garden City, this most recent luxury hotel shares the elegance of its sister in Giza, but with stunning Nile views on the Corniche. Directly opposite is the dock with felucas for hire to sail the river.
🛈 365 🛏 🕃 🛋 🍹
🕾 All major cards

🏨 CAIRO MARRIOTT HOTEL & OMAR KHAYYAM CASINO
$$$$
16 SARAY AL-GEZIRA
ZAMALEK
TEL 02/2728 3000
FAX 02/2728 3001
www.marriott.com/caieg
The Egyptian ruler Khedive Ismail built this palace on an island in the Nile to house

France's Empress Eugénie and her suite when she was guest of honor at the grand opening of the Suez Canal in 1869. The palace (furnished with antiques) and 6 acres of gardens form the core of the hotel, while two modern towers contain the bedrooms, which have all up-to-date facilities. Most have views of the Nile. The garden is a wonderful place to eat lunch even if you aren't a guest at the hotel.
🛈 1,124 🛏 🕃 🛋 🍹 🕾 All major cards

🏨 CAIRO SHERATON
$$$$
AL-GALAA SQ.
DOKKI
TEL 02/3336 9800
FAX 02/3336 4601
www.starwoodhotels.com/
sheraton
This sizable 1970s hotel lies on the river, so most rooms have excellent views. Unfortunately it is on the wrong side of the river—the West Bank—which means you have to take taxis everywhere because it's just a bit too far to walk.
🛈 605 🛏 🕃 🛋
🕾 All major cards

🏨 CONRAD CAIRO
$$$$
1191 CORNICHE AL-NIL
BULAQ
TEL 02/2580 8000
FAX 02/2580 8080
www.conradhotels.com
This is one of Cairo's newer luxury hotels, with a Nile-side location (all rooms overlook the river) just north of the city center—too far to walk to most of the sights but only a couple of minutes in a taxi. The elegant rooms and suites have many amenities. Next door is the Arkadia Mall, the largest in central Cairo with more than 500 stores.
🛈 617 🛏 🛋 🕾 All major cards

🕃 Nonsmoking 🕃 Air-conditioning 🕿 Indoor Pool 🛋 Outdoor Pool 🍹 Health Club 🕾 Credit Cards

FOUR SEASONS HOTEL CAIRO AT THE FIRST RESIDENCE

$$$$

35 GIZA ST.

GIZA

TEL 02/3573 1212

FAX 02/3568 1616

www.fourseasons.com/cairofr

One of Cairo's most luxurious hotels is part of the exclusive First Residence complex, the most expensive real estate in the city, with shops, luxury apartments, and a casino. Though the levels of service here are unmatched, the location in Giza is not particularly convenient for the major sights except the Pyramids and the Sphinx.

🛈 271 ⊟ 🅢 🖼 🔻 🕸 All major cards

GRAND HYATT CAIRO

$$$$

CORNICHE AL-NIL

MANIAL

TEL 02/236 51 234

FAX 02/236 21927

www.cairo.grand.hyatt.com

By virtue of the hotel's location on the northern tip of the island of Roda, all rooms have great Nile views. There are all the usual facilities and several restaurants, cafés, bars, and a cinema in the attached shopping complex.

🛈 1,100 ⊟ 🅢 🖼 🕸 All major cards

HILTON CAIRO WORLD TRADE CENTER RESIDENCE

$$$$

1191 CORNICHE AL-NIL

BULAQ

TEL 02/2580 2000

FAX 02/2579 0577

www1.hilton.com

Part of the World Trade Center complex—a cluster of office buildings on the Corniche north of downtown—this top hotel has a pool (heated in winter) and en suite kitchens.

🛈 104 ⊟ 🅢 🖼 🕸 All major cards

SOMETHING SPECIAL

MENA HOUSE OBEROI

A former royal hunting lodge belonging to Khedive Ismail (R. 1863–1879), turned into a hotel in the late 19th century, the Mena House boasts wonderful views courtesy of its location beside the Pyramids; you can float in the garden pool while gazing up at one of the Seven Wonders of the World. The interior is an opulent Orientalist fantasy, enjoyed by a list of past guests that has included Charlie Chaplin, Cecil B. DeMille, British Prime Minister Winston Churchill and U.S. President Franklin Roosevelt, who met here to finalize plans for the Allied invasion of Europe that would end World War II. If possible, avoid rooms in the modern garden annex, which are quite characterless. Restaurants include The Moghul Room and Khan al-Khalili. The hotel has its own golf course.

$$$$

PYRAMIDS RD.

GIZA

TEL 02/3377 3222

FAX 02/3376 7777

www.oberoihotels.com

🛈 523 ⊟ 🅢 🖼 🕸 All major cards

MÖVENPICK RESORT CAIRO-PYRAMIDS

$$$$

CAIRO-ALEXANDRIA DESERT HWY.

GIZA

TEL 02/3377 2555

FAX 02/3377 5006

www.moevenpick-pyramids.com

If you want to get away from the noise and pollution of the city, this pleasant, modern, low-rise hotel out by the Pyramids

is a good bet. The Mövenpick makes a convenient base for trips to sights in the environs of Cairo such as Saqqara, Memphis, Abu Sir, and Dahshur.

🛈 240 ⊟ 🅢 🖼 🕸 All major cards

RAMSES HILTON

$$$$

1115 CORNICHE AL-NIL

DOWNTOWN

TEL 02/2577 7444

FAX 02/2575 2942

www1.hilton.com

A towering Nile-side hotel, the Ramses Hilton is behind the Egyptian Museum. It has good facilities (including six restaurants), and the views are terrific—there's a rooftop cocktail bar. But the tangle of four-lane highways surrounding the hotel is discouragingly ugly and makes getting anywhere on foot potentially lethal.

🛈 859 ⊟ 🅢 🖼 🕸 All major cards

🏨 Hotel   🍴 Restaurant   🛈 No. of Guest Rooms   🛏 No. of Seats   🅟 Parking   🕒 Closed   ⊟ Elevator

SEMIRAMIS INTER-CONTINENTAL

$$$$

CORNICHE AL-NIL

DOWNTOWN

TEL 02/2795 7171

FAX 02/2796 3020

www.intercontinental.com

One of Cairo's most attractive modern hotels, the Semiramis has a bright, airy foyer and elegant, generously sized rooms, most with good river views. The hotel has an excellent Nile-side location, just a few minutes' walk from the Egyptian Museum.

730 🔲 🔄 🏊 All major cards

BARON

$$$

8 MAAHAD AL-SAHARA

HELIOPOLIS

TEL 02/2291 5757

FAX 02/2291 7077

www.baronhotelsegypt.com

Located just off Airport Road in the northern suburb of Heliopolis, this modest three-star overlooks the bizarre Hindu architecture of the Baron's Palace (Baron Empain was the founder of the new town of Heliopolis in 1903). The hotel is convenient for the airport or business in the north of the city.

126 🔲 🔄 AE, DC, V

GOLDEN TULIP HOTEL FLAMENCO

$$$

2 GEZIRA AL-WUSTA

ZAMALEK

TEL 02/2735 0815

FAX 02/2735 0819

www.flamencohotels.com

This modest but comfortable neighborhood hotel is situated among the busy backstreets on the west side of Zamalek. The river-facing rooms look down on a sweep of houseboats moored along the Nile.

157 🔲 🔄 All major cards

HOTEL LONGCHAMPS

$$$

21 ISMAIL MUHAMMAD ST.

ZAMALEK

TEL 02/2735 2311

FAX 02/2735 9644

www.hotellongchamps.com

A friendly hotel (located in the same building as the Horus House below), the Long-champs has a pleasant terrace bar overlooking Zamalek. All of the rooms have air-conditioning and king-size beds, and there Is Internet access.

22 🔲 🔄 MC, V

NOVOTEL CAIRO AIRPORT

$$$

CAIRO AIRPORT

TEL 02/2291 8520

FAX 02/2291 4794

www.novotel.com

The airport hotel is the most convenient place to stay for anyone who is on a short stayover in Cairo or taking an early morning flight. For other visitors to Cairo, however, it is a long way away from the city center and sights.

207 🔲 🔄 🏊 All major cards

COSMOPOLITAN

$$

1 IBN TAALAB ST.

DOWNTOWN

TEL 02/3392 3845

FAX 02/3393 3531

A grand 1910 art nouveau building in the heart of downtown Cairo, the Cosmo-politan has been renovated and updated. However, the remodeling project did not extend to all the rooms, some of which are still very basic, so it is worth asking to view a few before making a choice.

84 🔲 🔄 All major cards

GARDEN CITY HOUSE

$$

23 KAMAL AD-DIN SALAH

DOWNTOWN

TEL 02/ 2794 8400

FAX 02/2794 4126

www.gardencityhouse.com

This budget hotel with plenty of character is located just north of Tahrir Square and behind the Semiramis InterContinental. Though the place has seen better days, the friendly service compensates for its faded glory. Visiting academics and archaeologists affiliated with the nearby American University often stay here.

38 🔲 🔄 None

HORUS HOUSE

$$

21 ISMAIL MUHAMMAD ST.

ZAMALEK

TEL 02/2735 3634

FAX 02/2735 3182

www.horushousehotel.4t.com

The Horus House is a small, friendly family hotel on the 4th floor of an apartment block in the backstreets of the leafy island neighborhood of Zamalek. It may be some way from the sights, but the area is full of small boutiques, cafés, bars, and some of the city's better restaurants.

35 🔲 🔄 AE, MC, V

HOTEL HUSSEIN

$$

AL-HUSSEIN SQ.

ISLAMIC CAIRO

TEL 02/2591 8089

This is one of only two hotels in the historic area of Islamic Cairo. The interior is a little institutional, but it has plenty of atmosphere as the rooms overlook bustling Al-Hussein Square and the Khan al-Khalili bazaar, but noise levels are high as a result.

56 🔲 🔄 None

🚭 Nonsmoking 🔄 Air-conditioning 🏊 Indoor Pool 🏊 Outdoor Pool 🏋 Health Club 🔳 Credit Cards

WINDSOR
$$

19 ALFY BEY ST.
TEL 02/2591 5810
FAX 02/2592 1621
www.windsorcairo.com
A British officers' club in the early part of the 20th century, the Windsor retains a distinctly colonial air. This is particularly so in the reception area with its creaky old wooden elevator, and the splendid "barrel bar," one of the finest places in Cairo for a post-sight-seeing drink. Old-fashioned rooms are characterful but occasionally verging on shabby, so look at a few before choosing.

🛈 55 🛗 🄲 🄰 All major cards

PENSION ROMA
$

169 MUHAMMAD FARID ST.
DOWNTOWN
TEL 02/2391 1088
FAX 02/2579 6243
This immaculately run establishment is by far the best of Cairo's budget options. The Roma occupies the uppermost floors of an old apartment building in mid-downtown. Its rooms are high ceilinged with wooden floors and fans, and there is a lovely breakfast area. As the Roma is always busy, advance reservations are essential.

🛈 32 🛗 🄰 None

RESTAURANTS

THE GRILL
$$$$

SEMIRAMIS INTERCONTINENTAL HOTEL
DOWNTOWN
TEL 02/2795 7171
Cairo's best restaurant for carnivores, within the Semiramis InterContinental Hotel (see p. 359), also earns top billing for service and has marvelous panoramic views of the river. As if all that wasn't enough, it also has one of the best wine lists in the country.

🕐 Open 7 p.m.–11:30 p.m.
🄲 🄰 All major cards

JUSTINE
$$$$

FOUR CORNERS COMPLEX
4 HASSAN SABRY ST.
ZAMALEK
TEL 02/2735 1647
A candidate for the title of the best French restaurant in Egypt, Justine is a long-established favorite with Cairo's diplomatic community. Reservations are advisable.

🕐 Open 12:30 p.m.–3 p.m. & 7:30 p.m.–11 p.m 🄲
🄰 All major cards

THE REVOLVING RESTAURANT
$$$$

GRAND HYATT CAIRO
RODA
TEL 02/2365 1234
Located on the 41st floor of the Hyatt (see p. 358), this French-menu luxury eatery claims to be the highest restaurant in the Middle East. The views over Cairo and the Nile are stellar.

🕐 Open 7 p.m.–1 a.m. 🄲
🄰 All major cards

VILLA D'ESTE
$$$$

CONRAD CAIRO
1191 CORNICHE AL-NIL
BULAQ
TEL 02/2580 8000
This supremely elegant and highly recommended Italian restaurant sits on the first floor of the Nile-side Conrad International Hotel (see p. 357). The restaurant operates an admirable policy of no mobile phones—a rarity and a blessing in Cairo.

🕐 Open 7 p.m.–midnight
🄲 🄰 All major cards

PRICES

HOTELS
An indication of the cost of double room in the high season is given by **$** signs.

$$$$$	Over $200
$$$$	$120–$200
$$$	$60–$120
$$	$30–$60
$	Under $30

RESTAURANTS
An indication of the cost of three-course meal without drinks is given by $ signs.

$$$$	Over $35
$$$	$20–$35
$$	$10–$20
$	Under $10

SOMETHING SPECIAL

ABU AL-SID

One of Cairo's most sumptuous restaurants, Abu al-Sid is decked out in stage-set Orientalia: padded cushions, brass lamps, and spangly bric-a-brac. Lucky diners get to sit cross-legged at low slung *tabliya*. The food here is traditional Egyptian. Choose from the likes of *sharkassiyya* (chicken breast with walnut sauce), *sayadiyya* (fish with tomatoes, onions, and red rice), or *molokhiyya*, the summer soup made of the eponymous leaves, served with rabbit. It's all exceptional. Reservations are necessary.
$$$

57 26TH OF JULY ST.
ZAMALEK
TEL 02/2735 9640
🍴 🕐 Open 11 a.m.–2 a.m. 🄲
🄰 All major cards

🏨 Hotel 🍴 Restaurant 🛈 No. of Guest Rooms 🍴 No. of Seats 🅿 Parking 🕐 Closed 🛗 Elevator

ARABESQUE

$$$

6 QASR AL-NIL ST.

DOWNTOWN

TEL 02/2574 7898

Entered through a small art gallery, Arabesque exudes intimacy and exclusivity, and is favored by Egyptian movie stars. The menu mixes accomplished Continental cuisine with local specialties, such as kabobs and pigeon.

🕐 Open 12 p.m.–4 p.m. & 7:30 p.m.–midnight 🅰

🅰 AE, MC, V

LA BODEGA

$$$

157 26TH OF JULY ST.

ZAMALEK

TEL 02/735 6761

La Bodega is an elegant and unusual combination of a restaurant, bar, and cocktail lounge with fabulous decor. The menu ranges wide and includes Middle Eastern and international dishes. The selection of liquor here is possibly the best in town, and the lounge even has its own cigar humidor.

🕐 Open noon–1 a.m. 🅰

🅰 All major cards

CITADEL VIEW

$$$

SALAH SALEM ST.

AL-AZHAR PARK

TEL 02/510 9150

Arguably one of the most beautiful restaurants in Cairo, especially the terrace on a balmy evening. The food is Lebanese and Egyptian and extremely well prepared.

🕐 Open 11 p.m.–midnight 🅰

🅰 All major cards

KHAN AL-KHALILI RESTAURANT/NAGUIB MAHFOUZ COFFEE SHOP

$$$–$

5 SIQQAT AL-BADESTAN

KHAN AL-KHALILI

TEL 02/2590 3788

This restaurant/coffee shop complex buried deep in Khan al-Khalili is operated by the Oberoi hotel group. Named for Egypt's Nobel Prize-winning author, the coffee shop offers good sandwiches and snacks (and has the only decent toilets in the area). The attached restaurant has attractive Oriental decor and a menu of Eastern and international dishes.

🕐 Open 10 a.m.–2 a.m. 🅰

🅰 All major cards

MAZMAZA

$$$

LE PACHA 1901 BOAT SARAY

AL-GEZIRA ST.

ZAMALEK

TEL 02/2735 6730

Mamaza is one of four excellent restaurants on board a restored turn-of-the-20th-century paddleboat moored just north of the 6th October Bridge. The specialty here is *meze*, small dishes of Egyptian, Lebanese, and Turkish origin. Ideal for sharing.

🕐 Open 7 p.m.–2 a.m.

🅰 All major cards

THE MOGHUL ROOM

$$$

MENA HOUSE OBEROI

PYRAMIDS RD.

GIZA

TEL 02/3377 3222 EXT. 6840

Some of the best Indian cuisine in the entire Middle East is served here in a sumptuously decorated dining room. French and Italian wines are available, too. Also in the same hotel is the Khan al-Khalili (see below), serving Egyptian cuisine in a dining room with views of the Pyramids.

🕐 Open 12:30 p.m.–3 p.m. & 7:30 p.m.–12:30 a.m. 🅰

🅰 All major cards

LA PIAZZA

$$$

FOUR CORNERS COMPLEX

4 HASSAN SABRY ST.

ZAMALEK

TEL 02/2736 2961

This airy, conservatory-like Italian restaurant overlooking the Gezira Club serves good soups, salads, and pastas. It is particularly popular for lunch.

🕐 Open 12:30 p.m.–12:30 a.m.

🅰 🅰 All major cards

ANDREA

$$

59-60 MARYOUTIA CANAL

GIZA

TEL 02/3383 1133

If you fancy eating out in the vicinity of the Pyramids, try this extremely popular garden restaurant. It specializes in grilled chicken and quail, served with a selection of meze, and accompanied by hot, flat disks of bread that are baked in clay ovens on the premises.

🕐 Open noon–12:30 a.m.

🅰 None

L'AUBERGINE

$$

5 SAYYED AL-BAKRY ST.

ZAMALEK

TEL 02/2738 0080

L'Aubergine is a backstreet bar/restaurant popular with the local young fashionable set and with expatriates. Unusually for Cairo, the menu recognizes the existence of vegetarians. It changes regularly but is generally an eclectic mix of Lebanese and other international cuisines.

🕐 Open noon–2 a.m. 🅰

🅰 AE, DC, V

CAFÉ RICHE

$$

17 TALAAT HARB ST.

DOWNTOWN

TEL 02/2392 9793

A survivor of prerevolution

days but extensively renovated in the 1990s, the Café Riche serve s traditional Egyptian fare in a room hung with portraits of Egypt's revered cultural pantheon. It's open for breakfast as well. In the evenings, it's still favored as an intellectuals' drinking den and salon.

🕒 Open 8 a.m.–midnight 📋
💳 AE, MC, V

🍴 CHANTILLY
$$
11 BAGHDAD ST.
HELIOPOLIS
TEL 02/2290 7303
This reliable Swiss Air–owned restaurant has a bakery attached and a pleasant garden out back.

🕒 Open 7 a.m.–midnight 📋
💳 All major cards

🍴 CRAZY FISH
$$
22 MARYOUTIA CANAL
GIZA
TEL 02/3388 6288
Located opposite the Siag Pyramids Hotel, near the Pyramids, this place specializes in seafood, but with meat on the menu in the form of kofta, kabobs, and chicken. It's a big favorite with tour groups.

🕒 Open 9 a.m.–1 a.m.
📋 💳 AE, MC, V

🍴 SAMAKMAK
$$
24 AHMED ORABI
MOHANDISEEN
TEL 02/3302 7308
This excellent fish restaurant is hidden away among the residential blocks in western Cairo. Appetizers include fried calamari and jumbo shrimp, then you choose your own fish from the catch of the day displayed on ice. The house lime juice is refreshing, and beer is available; there are even water pipes for an after-dinner smoke.

🕒 Open 10 a.m.–4 a.m. 📋
💳 All major cards

🍴 ABU TAREK
$
40 CHAMPOLLION ST.
DOWNTOWN
This is arguably Cairo's finest *kushari* restaurant—it sells nothing else (see pp. 357 and p. 385). Take a table and order a bowl; ask for *kebir* (big), *meta-wasit* (medium), or *sughayyar* (small). Dessert is excellent cold rice pudding (*roz bileban*).

🕒 Open 24 hours 📋
💳 None

🍴 ALFY BEY
$
3 ALFY BEY ST.
DOWNTOWN
TEL 02/2577 4999
The Alfy Bey is a simple, old-fashioned restaurant, little changed since it opened in the 1930s. It specializes in basic Egyptian fare, particularly grilled meats. Choose from *kofta* (spicy ground meat grilled on a skewer), kebab, lamb chops, and grilled pigeons stuffed with crushed wheat.

🕒 Open 1 p.m.–1:30 a.m.
💳 None

🍴 EGYPTIAN PANCAKE HOUSE
$
AL-HUSSEIN SQ.
The Egyptian take on the pancake is called a *fiteer*, and it's made of layers of flaky pastry. Watching the cook prepare one, as he whirls the dough around his head and pounds it, is quite an experience. You can have a savory *fiteer*, served with cheese, egg, tomato, olives, or ground beef in any combination, or the sweet version, dusted with powdered sugar and coconut.

🕒 Open 24 hours 💳 None

PRICES

HOTELS
An indication of the cost of double room in the high season is given by $ signs.

$$$$$	Over $200
$$$$	$120–$200
$$$	$60–$120
$$	$30–$60
$	Under $30

RESTAURANTS
An indication of the cost of three-course meal without drinks is given by $ signs.

$$$$	Over $35
$$$	$20–$35
$$	$10–$20
$	Under $10

SOMETHING SPECIAL

🍴 FELFELA
Its inexpensive local cooking has made Felfela a long-time favorite with tourists and Egyptians alike. Try the *fuul* (mashed beans), served up with garlic, oil, egg, and tomato, or *fuul hosnia*, made with cream and eggs and then baked in the oven. Order plenty of meze—like *baba ghanoug* (mashed eggplant), *hummus* (chickpea paste), *tahina* (sesame seed paste), and *felafel*, all of which are eaten with bread. Grilled meats offered here include pigeon. The decor is fun (tree trunk tables, aquariums, caged birds), and there is a lively atmosphere. Beer is served.

$
15 HODA SHAARAWI ST.
DOWNTOWN
ALSO 27 CAIRO-
ALEXANDRIA HWY.
GIZA

🏨 Hotel 🍴 Restaurant 🛏 No. of Guest Rooms 🪑 No. of Seats 🅿 Parking 🕒 Closed 🛗 Elevator

TEL 02/2392 2833
🕐 Open 8 a.m.–midnight 🄴
🅒 None

🍴 MAISON THOMAS
$
157 26TH OF JULY ST.
ZAMALEK
TEL 02/2735 7057
You get decent pizzas and generously filled baguettes, as well as breakfasts here, in the closest approximation you'll find in Egypt of a Continental-style delicatessen.
🕐 Open 24 hours 🅒 None

■ AROUND CAIRO

🏨 SAQQARA COUNTRY CLUB
$$
SAQQARA RD.
BADRASHEIN
TEL 02/3381 1282
FAX 02/3381 0571
This small, comfortable hotel is set amid palm gardens in the Egyptian countryside. It has a lovely lagoon-style pool. The location is convenient for traveling to see the sights at Saqqara, Memphis, and Abu Sir, but you will need to arrange your own transportation to get around.
🄸 20 🄴 ⛱ 🅒 All major cards

🏨 ZAD AL-MOSAFER
$$
TUNIS, LAKE QARUN
FAYOUM
TEL 084/682 0180
A new rustic ecolodge in Fayoum's expatriate artists' colony by the lake. The restaurant serves excellent fresh-caught fish.
🄸 13 🅒 None

■ THE DELTA & SUEZ

ISMAILIA

🏨 MERCURE FORSAN ISLAND
$$$
GEZIRAT AL-FORSAN
TEL 064/391 6316
FAX 064/391 8043
www.accorhotels.com
Large and modern in a green setting on the shores of Lake Timsah, this hotel has its own beach and fine views across the water.
🄸 138 🄴 ⛱ 🅒 AE, MC, V

🍴 GEORGE'S
$$
11 THAWRA ST.
TEL 064/391 8327
Opened in 1950 and scarcely changed since then, George's is an atmospheric little fish restaurant and bar on Ismailia's main street.
🕐 Open noon–11 p.m.
🅒 AE, MC, V

PORT SAID

🏨 HELNAN PORT SAID
$$$$
ATEF AL SADAT ST.
CORNICHE
TEL 066/332 0890
FAX 066/332 3762
www.helnan.com
This large, but somewhat aging, hotel is situated on the beach a few minutes' walk north of the town center, overlooking the point at which the canal joins the Mediterranean. There are several restaurants and a nightclub, as well as many other amenities.
🄸 202 🄴 ⛱ 🅒 AE, MC, V

🏨 SONESTA PORT SAID
$$$$
SULTAN HUSSEIN ST.
TEL 066/332 5511

FAX 066/332 4825
www.sonesta.com
Most of the rooms overlook the canal in this fairly modest, business-oriented hotel on one of Port Said's main streets.
🄸 110 🄴 ⛱ 🅒 All major cards

🏨 HOTEL DE LA POSTE
$
42 GOMHURIYYA ST.
TEL/FAX 066/322 4048
The fading old Greek-run establishment in the center of town is a little creaky around the edges, but it's well maintained and has been recently renovated.
🄸 44 🄴 🅒 None

🍴 AL-BORG
$$
CORNICHE
Some Egyptians will tell you this very modest beachfront restaurant serves the best and freshest fish and seafood in the country. The specialty is a wonderful seafood soup.
🕐 Open noon–midnight
🅒 None

🍴 NORAS FLOATING RESTAURANT
$$
PALESTINE ST.
TEL 066/332 6804
About the only way to sail the Suez Canal is to sign up for a 75-minute tour on the Noras. Sailings are for lunch and dinner, and the menu invariably features seafood.
⛱ 3 p.m. & 8:30 p.m.
🅒 None

■ ALEXANDRIA

HOTELS

🏨 AL SALAMLEK PALACE HOTEL
$$$$$

🄴 Nonsmoking 🄴 Air-conditioning 🅐 Indoor Pool ⛱ Outdoor Pool 🄷 Health Club 🅒 Credit Cards

MONTAZAH PALACE GARDENS
TEL 03/547 7999
FAX 02/547 3585
EMAIL: SALAMLEK@SANGIO-VANNI.COM

The Egyptian president's summer palace is next door to this former royal hunting lodge set in beautiful gardens with fine views over the sea. The rooms are opulently furnished, and there is a casino as well as two fine restaurants on site. Also, the beach is nearby.

[i] 20 🚇 📶 🅰️ DC, MC, V

SOMETHING SPECIAL

🏨 **CECIL HOTEL**

The famous Cecil Hotel was built in 1929 in an elegant Moorish style overlooking Alexandria's Eastern Harbor. It featured in Lawrence Durrell's *Alexandria Quartet* as a haunt of the enigmatic Justine. It also was used by the British Secret Service as its headquarters during World War II. The signatures of Noel Coward and Somerset Maugham are among those in the guest book. Now managed by the Sofitel chain, the hotel retains plenty of period charm—notably the grand wrought-iron and wood central elevator—combined with modern five-star facilities. The rooftop Chinese restaurant is very good, and the Monty Bar is a nice spot to have drinks.

$$$$
SAAD ZAGHLOUL SQ.
TEL 03/487 7173
FAX 03/485 5655
www.sofitel.com

[i] 83 rooms 🚇 📶 🅰️ All major cards

🏨 **HELNAN PALESTINE**
$$$$
MONTAZAH PALACE GARDENS
TEL 03/547 4033
FAX 02/547 3378
www.helnan.com

The uncompromising architecture of this modern hotel on the otherwise sublime Montazah Palace grounds blights the view for everyone else but offers superb Mediterranean vistas to its guests.

[i] 222 🚇 📶 🅰️ 🍷 🅰️ All major cards

🏨 **RENAISSANCE ALEXANDRIA**
$$$$
544 AL-GEISH AVE.
SIDI BISHR
TEL 03/549 0935
FAX 03/549 7690
www.marriott.com

Most rooms have a sea view in this modestly sized, modern, comfortable hotel situated in the eastern suburbs not far from the Royal Jewelry and Mahmoud Said Museums.

[i] 171 🚇 📶 🅰️ 🅰️ All major cards

🏨 **SHERATON MONTAZAH**
$$$$
CORNICHE
MONTAZAH
TEL 03/548 0550
FAX 02/540 1331
www.starwoodhotels.com

The Sheraton is located in the far eastern suburb of Montazah. Rooms overlook the palace grounds and the sea, as does the Caesar Bar. There's a restaurant and disco.

[i] 296 🚇 📶 🅰️
🅰️ All major cards

🏨 **METROPOLE**
$$$
52 SAAD ZAGHLOUL SQ.
TEL 03/484 0920
FAX 02/486 2040

This is a fine period hotel (built in 1902), recently renovated and very comfortable. The Metropole has a good, central location and most rooms have a sea view. Beneath the hotel is the famous Trianon café,

a fine place for breakfast with outdoor seating.

[i] 66 🚇 📶 🅰️ All major cards

🏨 **CRILLON HOTEL**
$$
5 ADIB ISHAQ ST.
TEL 03/480 0330

The best of Alexandria's budget lodgings is a modest pension occupying several floors of a downtown apartment block. Some of the rooms have French windows opening onto great harbor views, but others are significantly less attractive. Have a look before you accept a room.

[i] 36 🚇 🅰️ None

🏨 **HOTEL UNION**
$$
164 26TH OF JULY ST.
TEL 03/480 7350
FAX 03/480 7350

A good budget option on the Corniche overlooking the harbor. Some rooms have sea

---

🏨 Hotel   🍴 Restaurant   [i] No. of Guest Rooms   🛏️ No. of Seats   🅿️ Parking   🕐 Closed   🚇 Elevator views, some have bathrooms, some have both. Ask to view a few before choosing.

🛈 37 ⮟ 🚭 None

RESTAURANTS

🍴 CHINA HOUSE
$$$

CECIL HOTEL
SAAD ZAGHLOUL SQ.
TEL 03/487 7173

The rooftop restaurant of the city's venerable downtown hotel does very passable Cantonese-style cuisine. The harbor views are magnificent, but avoid on windy nights.

🕐 Open 11 a.m.–11:30 p.m.
🚭 All major cards

SOMETHING SPECIAL

🍴 QADOURA

When in Alexandria, the thing to do is to eat seafood at a streetside restaurant. Of the many places where you can do this, Qadoura is one of the best. It is on a backstreet out toward the Fortress of Qaitbey, one block from the sea. The tram rumbles by the outdoor tables.

As is standard, there is no menu. Instead you pick your fish from the ice-packed selection (which may include sea bass, red and grey mullet, bluefish, sole, squid, and shrimp), and tell the waiter how you want it cooked: baked or grilled. A selection of *meze* comes with all orders, and there is beer and wine. Take a seat after the sun goes down and make a night of it.

$$$

33 BAIRAM AL-TONSI ST.
ANFUSHI
TEL 03/480 0405

🕐 Open 24 hours 🚭 V

🍴 SAMAKMAK
$$$

42 QASR RAS AL-TIN ST.

ANFUSHI
TEL 03/480 9523

The name is a play on the Arabic word for fish, *samak*. It's a toss-up whether this or the Qadoura is the better seafood restaurant. However, Samakmak is certainly the better known of the two, courtesy of the owner, a famous former belly dancer.

🕐 Open 10 a.m.–2 a.m. 🚭
🚭 MC, V

🍴 SANTA LUCIA
$$$

40 SAFIYYA ZAGHLOUL ST.
TEL 03/486 4240

Service is black tie at Alexandria's most exclusive restaurant. Even though not quite as glamorous as it once was, the Santa Lucia serves a Mediterranean menu that is still good, and the food is certainly a cut above average.

🕐 Open noon–4 p.m. & 7 p.m.–2 a.m. 🚭 🚭 AE, MC, V

🍴 BA'ASH
$$

SAFER PASHA ST.
ANFUSHI
TEL 03/480 2815

Safer Pasha is the most wonderful of streets, lined with fish and meat restaurants, all producing great clouds of aromatic smoke from their busy open-air grills. Most places are open around-the-clock and the best time to visit is late. Of the restaurants here **Ba'ash** does great pigeon, while **Abu Ashraf** (tel 03/481 6597) at No. 28 is recommended for fish, and **Muhammad Hosni** at No. 48 for grilled meats.

🕐 24 hours 🚭 🚭 V (at Abu Ashraf only)

🍴 ELITE
$$

43 SAFIYYA ZAGHLOUL ST.
TEL 03/486 3592

The Elite used to be a favorite

of intellectuals and artists when Alexandria still had an intellectual and artistic scene to speak of before the revolution of 1952. Still run by the redoubtable Madam Christina, it maintains a raffish air and is the only place in Alexandria where you can drink beer and watch the street through large picture windows. The food, though not fine cuisine, is satisfying.

🕐 Open 11 a.m.–midnight 🚭
🚭 None

🍴 MALEK AL-SAMAAN
$$

ATTAREEN ST.
ATTAREEN

If you don't read Arabic, look for the street sign showing a tiny bird. The bird is a quail, which is all that is served at this rough, awning-covered, open-air courtyard restaurant, one of Egypt's most unusual dining venues.

🕐 Open 8 p.m.–late 🚭 None

🍴 L'OSABUCCO
$$

14 HORREYA AVE.
TEL 03/487 2506

Run by the same people as Cairo's L'Aubergine (see p. 361), this is a recently opened chic bar-restaurant on two floors, with drinking downstairs and candlelit dining upstairs. The menu changes frequently and is inventive and wide ranging, from salmon felafel to Cajun chicken.

🕐 Open noon–midnight 🚭
🚭 AE, DC, V

🍴 ATHINEOS
$

21 MIDAN SAAD ZAGHLOUL
TEL 03/486 0421

An Alexandria institution, this old-fashioned Greek eatery is both a pastry café and a restaurant. As you sip your coffee, you might think you're

---

🚭 Nonsmoking 🚭 Air-conditioning 🏊 Indoor Pool 🏊 Outdoor Pool 🏋 Health Club 🚭 Credit Cards

back in the 1930s.
🕐 Open noon–midnight
🚫 None

🍴 CAP D'OR
$
4 ADIB ST.
OFF SAAD ZAGHLOUL ST.
TEL 03/486 5177
Primarily a bar—and an
excellent one at that—the
Cap d'Or also serves first-rate
seafood snacks such as prawns
and calamari.
🕐 Open noon–2 a.m. 🚫 None

🍴 HASSAN BLEIK
$
18 SAAD ZAGHLOUL ST.
The tiny, venerable Lebanese
restaurant is through the back
of a pastry shop. It may look
a little basic, but the food is
beautifully prepared. While
here, it's worth visiting the
wonderful Sofianopoulo
Coffee Store next door.
🕐 Open noon–6 p.m.
🚫 None

🍴 MUHAMMAD AHMED
$
17 SHAKOUR PASHA ST.
DOWNTOWN
TEL 03/487 3576
Alexandrians rate this as the
city's best restaurant for *fuul*
and *felafel*. It also offers a range
of omelettes and fried cheese,
plus all the usual salad and
dip accompaniments. You can
eat in or take out. Find this
place one street west of main
Safiyya Zaghloul Street, just
north of Saad Zaghloul.
🚫 None

■ WESTERN DESERT

BAHARIYYA OASIS

🏨 INTERNATIONAL
HOT SPRINGS HOTEL
$$$

BAWITI
TEL 02/3847 2322
Located about 3 miles (5 km)
outside the oasis on the road
to Cairo, this is a three-star spa
built around a sulfur spring,
supposed to have therapeutic
qualities. There are also a gym,
a sauna, and a restaurant.
ℹ️ 27 🚫 None

🏨 AL-BESHMO LODGE
$$
BAWITI
TEL/FAX 02/3847 3500
Basic huts are arranged around
a courtyard beside a palm
grove watered by Al-Beshmu
spring. Some of the huts have
air-conditioning and private
bathrooms, and the rest are
equipped with fans and share
spotlessly kept facilities.
ℹ️ 25 🔲 🚫 None

DAKHLA OASIS

🏨 MEBAREZ HOTEL
$$
MUT
TEL/FAX 092/782 1524
This modern concrete hotel
on the edge of Mut is reason-
able value for money. Some of
the rooms are on the shabby
side, but they are air-condi-
tioned and have their own
fairly clean bathrooms.
ℹ️ 29 🔲 🚫 None

🍴 MUT INN
$$$
MUT
TEL 092/792 7982
FAX 092/792 7983
www.solymaregypt.com/mutte
This small complex consisting
of a salmon pink central villa,
six chalets, and three canvas
tents sits beside a hot spring
a couple of miles outside Mut,
the main center of the oasis. It
is under the same management
as the Pioneers Hotel in Kharga.
ℹ️ 11 🚫 None

🍴 AHMED HAMDY
$
MUT
TEL 092/782 0767
Look for this very basic, tiny
open-air restaurant on the
main road through the oasis,
near the Mebarez Hotel.
There is no menu; instead
there are just two dishes of
the day served, with salad and
beer, but the food is always
fresh and wholesome.
🕐 Open noon–late 🚫 None

FARAFRA OASIS

🏨 AL-BADAWIYA
SAFARI & HOTEL
$$–$$$
TEL 092/751 0060
www.badawiya.com
This tastefully designed
mud-brick hotel is owned
by Bedouin brothers (who also
own a hotel in Dakhla) and
managed by a Swiss woman.
There are various styles of

rooms from shared dormitories to suites with their own living rooms, and the whole package is excellent value. The brothers who own the hotel also organize jeep, camel, and walking safaris into the White Desert. Both the hotel and the safaris are very popular, so it is essential to reserve rooms well in advance.

ℹ 32 �šNone

KHARGA OASIS

🏨 PIONEERS
$$$
GAMAL ABDEL NASSER ST.
TEL 092/792 7982
FAX 092/792 7983
www.solymaregypt.com/ pioneer
The only luxury accommodations in all the oases except for the Adrere Amellal in Siwa, the Pioneers is a postmodernist, pink-painted, low-rise hotel. Attractive terraces overlook a central pool area and there are a bar, café, and restaurant. Desert safaris can be arranged.

ℹ 102 🚽 ⚑ � None

🏨 KHARGA OASIS HOTEL
$$
KHARGA OASIS
TEL 092/792 1500
FAX 092/792 1611
This modernist high-rise hotel has a pleasant palm-filled garden and terrace. The rooms are comfortable; most have balconies overlooking the garden and are equipped with air-conditioning and private bathrooms.

ℹ 30 🚽 ⚑ � None

MARSA MATRUH

🏨 BEAU SITE
$$$$
CORNICHE
TEL 046/493 2066
FAX 046/493 3319
www.beausitehotel.com
Among the many bland

concrete blocks that deface this quiet Mediterranean town, the Beau Site stands out as somewhat individual. Run by the same family since the 1950s, it has a pleasingly personal quality, comfortable rooms, and its own private beach. The restaurant is also very good.

ℹ 170 🚽 ⚑ ⚑ ⚠ AE, MC, V

SIWA OASIS

SOMETHING SPECIAL

🏨 ADRERE AMELLAL
Twelve miles (19 km) outside the center of Siwa, this is possibly the most unique and enchanting accommodations in all Egypt. Lying in the lee of a chalky mountain beside a lake on the edge of the desert, it's a remote ecolodge built in a traditional Siwan mud-brick and palm-beam fashion. It resembles a small village. Promoting a real back-to-nature ethic, the lodge has no electricity or phone lines; at night the place is lit by candles and flaming torches. A Roman spring in a nearby palm grove serves as a swimming pool. The price includes all meals (gourmet-standard organic food), drinks, and excursions to visit hot springs in the desert.
$$$$$
SIDI JAFAR
TEL 02/2736 7879
FAX 02/2735 5489
www.adrereamellal.net

ℹ 32 ⚑ ⚠ AE, V

🏨 SHALI LODGE
$$$
SIWA TOWN
TEL 046/460 1299
FAX 046/460 1799
In this intimate mud-brick hotel, set in a palm garden just off the main square in central Siwa, the rooms are arranged around a central pool.

ℹ 7 🚽 ⚑ ⚠ None

🏨 SIWA SAFARI PARADISE
$$$–$
TEL 046/460 1590
FAX 046/460 1592
www.siwaparadise.com
This is a three-star complex in a palm garden setting close by the Temple of Amun. It has a variety of accommodation choices: You can enjoy the luxury of a bungalow with air-conditioning, TV, and fridge; pay less for a bungalow without air-conditioning; or go native in a reed hut.

ℹ 54 🚽 Some rooms ⚠ AE, V

🏨 AROUS AL-WAHA HOTEL
$$
SIWA TOWN
TEL 046/460 2100
Despite its utilitarian concrete appearance, this is a comfortable place to stay in the center of Siwa. Rooms with private bathrooms are well maintained and have constant hot water; and, although there's no air-conditioning, the rooms do have fans.

ℹ 20 ⚠ None

▪ MIDDLE EGYPT

ASYUT

🏨 ASSIUTEL HOTEL
$$
AL-THAWRA ST.
TEL 088/231 2121
FAX 088/231 2122
The hotel is of middling quality but it's as good as it gets for Asyut. However, it has an excellent riverside position and lovely views from the rooms.

ℹ 28 🚽 Some rooms ⚠ None

MINYA

🏨 MERCURE NEFERTITI & ATON

$$$

CORNICHE AL-NIL

TEL 086/233 1515

FAX 086/232 6467

The only real contender in town is this four-star hotel with Nile-side location just north of the center. It has a full range of facilities including gym, swimming pool, tennis courts, bar, and restaurants.

ⓘ 96 🅢 🕭 🕭 AE, MC, V

SOHAG

🏨 **MERIT AMOUN HOTEL**

$$

EAST BANK

TEL 093/460 1985

FAX 093/460 3222

The Merit Amoun is a large three-star hotel, which has the advantage of possessing a restaurant (finding somewhere decent to eat can be a problem in Middle Egypt). Also consider the nearby **Cazalovy Hotel,** which is of similar quality to the Merit Amoun but around half the price.

ⓘ 28 🅢 Some rooms🕭 None

◾ LUXOR

HOTELS

SOMETHING SPECIAL

🏨 **AL-MOUDIRA**

This is an extraordinary boutique hotel out in a desert setting on the West Bank, which was built using traditional mud-brick styles but in a grand manner that recalls Italianate villas. Rooms are arranged off a series of courtyards and each has a trompe d'oeil theme. Other beautiful touches include the use of salvaged architectural pieces, such as old doors and wrought-iron balconies. By far Luxor's most magical accommodations.

$$$$$

DABAIYYA

WEST BANK

TEL 012/325 1307

www.moudira.com

ⓘ 54 🅢 🕭 All major cards

🏨 **MARITIM JOLIE VILLE LUXOR HOTEL & RESORT**

$$$$$

KINGS ISLAND

TEL 095/227 4855

FAX 095/ 227 4936

www.jolieville-hotels.com

Occupying its own island in the Nile, 2.5 miles (4 km) south of town, this is Luxor's top hotel in terms of setting, service, and facilities. Accommodations are bungalows set on a lush banana plantation; the well-equipped rooms each have their own terrace. There are several good restaurants on-site, including the Nileside Sherezade Terrace (see p. 370), and two tennis courts. Feluccas (traditional Nile sailing boats) are available for the use of guests; there is even a little zoo and playground.

ⓘ 326; 21 bungalows 🅢 🕭 🕭 All major cards

SOMETHING SPECIAL

🏨 **WINTER PALACE HOTEL**

This grand old hotel was built to accommodate the aristocracy of Europe who were flocking to discover ancient Egypt at the turn of the last century. More recently, the hotel has been tastefully refurbished by the Sofitel chain and now has all modern facilities. Half of the rooms overlook the Nile, while the rest overlook a splendid garden. There is also a considerably less charming new annex, the New Winter Palace.

$$$$$–$$$$

CORNICHE AL-NIL

TEL 095/238 0425

FAX 095/237 4087

www.sofitel.com

ⓘ 356 🅢 🕭 All major cards

🏨 **HILTON LUXOR RESORT & SPA**

$$$$

KARNAK ST.

TEL 095/237 4933

FAX 095/237 6571

www.hilton.com

Located 2.5 miles (4 km) north of town, the Hilton is convenient for the great temple complex of Karnak, but little else of interest is within walking distance. However, there are shuttle services to the town center, and the hotel has recently added luxury spa facilities.

ⓘ 261 🅢 🕭 🕭 All major cards

🏨 **HOTEL MERCURE CORALIA**

$$$$

CORNICHE AL-NIL

TEL 095/237 4944

FAX 095/237 4912

www.mercure.com

This attractive, mid-rise hotel

---

has a superb location on the Nile-front Corniche, midway between Luxor Temple and Luxor Museum. Rooms at the front have a glorious view of the West Bank across the river.

🛈 314 ❄ 🏊 🗗 All major cards

SHERATON LUXOR
$$$$
KHALID IBN AL-WALID ST.
TEL 095/237 4544
FAX 095/237 4941
www.sheraton.com
The location 2 miles (3 km) south of town, necessitating lots of taxi rides, is a drawback of this hotel. However, the Sheraton has a pleasant garden setting beside the Nile and good facilities, and it offers daily yacht excursions to the temple at Dendara.

🛈 290 ❄ 🏊 🗗 All major cards

SONESTA ST. GEORGE
$$$$
KHALID IBN AL-WALID ST.
TEL 095/238 2575
FAX 095/238 2571
www.sonesta.com/luxor
This stylish hotel is only a few years old. It has the disadvantage of being some distance south of the town center but is redeemed by its beautiful Nile-side setting. The St. George is known for its excellent Japanese restaurant, which is open to guests and nonguests alike.

🛈 224 ❄ 🏊 🗗 All major cards

PYRAMISA ISIS HOTEL
$$$
KHALID IBN AL-WALID ST.
TEL 095/237 0100
FAX 095/237 2923
www.pyramisaegypt.com
Overlooking the Nile cruise ships docked below, this luxury complex stands in

beautiful gardens beside the Nile. It's about a mile (1.5 km) south of the center, but it has its own excellent Chinese and Italian restaurants, plus a couple of pools (and a heliport on the roof).

🛈 480 ❄ 🏊 🗗 MC, V

EMILIO
$$
YOUSEF HASSAN ST.
TEL 095/237 3570
FAX 095/237 0000
This mid-range hotel in the center of town is convenient for Luxor Temple and the West Bank ferry. All of the rooms have private bathrooms and air-conditioning, and there's a pleasant rooftop terrace for relaxing.

🛈 101 ❄ 🏊 🗗 AE, MC, V

GADDIS HOTEL
$$
KHALID IBN AL-WALID ST.
TEL 095/238 2838
FAX 095/238 2837
A mile (1.5 km) south of the center of town, the Gaddis offers good value with clean and stylish rooms. There are a smallish pool, three restaurants, and a bar.

🛈 55 ❄ Some rooms 🏊 🗗 MC, V

HOTEL EL-GEZIRA
$$
BAYARAT AL-GEZIRA
WEST BANK
TEL/FAX 095/231 0034
www.el-gezira.com
Just up from the West Bank ferry landing is this modest, modern hotel, with rooms overlooking the river. Some rooms have air-conditioning, others just fans. Private bathrooms. Excellent Egyptian food is served in a rooftop restaurant.

🛈 11 ❄ Some rooms 🗗 None

NUR AL-GURNA
$$
BAYARAT
WEST BANK
TEL 095/231 1430
A recent addition to the West Bank, this small hotel is built around a mud-brick courtyard hidden in a palm grove across from the West Bank ticket office. Rooms are decorated with local crafts and fabrics.

🛈 9 🗗 None

PHARAOH'S HOTEL
$$
BAYARAT
WEST BANK
TEL/FAX 095/231 0702
Pharaoh's is the most upscale of the West Bank hotels, located between the West Bank ticket office and the temple of Medinat Habu. Rooms have air-conditioning or a fan, some have private bathrooms, and some have views of the temple. There is a nice beer garden.

🛈 29 ❄ Some rooms 🗗 None

AMUN AL-GEZIRA
$
BAYARAT AL-GEZIRA
WEST BANK
TEL 095/231 0912
FAX 095/231 1205
This modest family-run establishment is in a back alley of a West Bank village just uphill from the ferry landing. The rooms have fans and bathrooms and are kept immaculately clean. There's a lovely roof terrace and small garden. You'll have to compete for rooms with archaeologists who favor the place.

🛈 12 🗗 None

RESTAURANTS

🍽 MIYAKO
$$$

SONESTA ST. GEORGE HOTEL
KHALED IBN AL-WALID ST.
TEL 095/238 2575
This attractive Japanese restaurant is centered on a teppanyaki grill at which up to ten people can sit and watch the chef at work. The decor is stylish, and if the food wouldn't quite pass muster in Tokyo, it makes a welcome change in Egypt.
🕐 Open 7 p.m.–11 p.m. 🔌
🚫 All major cards

🍴 **SHEREZADE TERRACE**
$$$
MARITIM JOLIE VILLE LUXOR
HOTEL & RESORT
KINGS ISLAND
TEL 095/237 4855
Nonguests are invited to take the hotel shuttle launch and head to Kings Island for lunch or dinner at the Sherezade. All are served on a beautiful terrace overlooking the Nile. It is by far the most pleasurable eating out experience to be found in Luxor.
🚫 All major cards

🍴 **JAMBOREE RESTAURANT**
$$
SHARIA AL-MONTAZA
TEL 095/235 5827
This friendly restaurant, run by a British couple, offers a mixed menu of Egyptian grills, tagens, and European fare. It's popular with tourists, and the small downstairs area fills up quickly. The shady upstairs terrace is perfect for a cold beer and relaxing lunch after a morning of sight-seeing.
🚫 None

🍴 **LA MAMA**
$$
SHERATON LUXOR
KHALID IBN AL-WALID ST.
TEL 095/237 4544
Pastas, pizzas, and other assorted Italian dishes are served in the hotel garden

beside a pool with ducks and pelicans.
🕐 Open noon–11 p.m.
🚫 AE, MC, V

🍴 **TUTANKHAMUN RESTAURANT**
$$
BAYARAT AL-GEZIRA
WEST BANK
TEL 095/231 0118
Just up from the local ferry landing, this open-air Nile-side restaurant is run by Aam Mahmoud, a former cook at one of the French archaeological missions. There's no menu, just a couple of dishes of the day, often tagens (stews cooked in a clay pot), plus salads and sides.
🚫 None

🍴 **KING'S HEAD PUB**
$
KHALID IBN AL-WALID ST.
TEL 095/237 1249
The King's Head is an English-style pub, but the king in question is Akhenaten, wearing a Tudor hat. The food ranges from dishes of French fries to a Sunday lunch special of roast beef and Yorkshire pudding. The authentic pub atmosphere extends to traditional games such as darts and billiards.
🕐 Open noon–midnight 🔌
🚫 None

🍴 **RESTAURANT MUHAMMAD**
$
NEXT TO THE PHARAOH'S HOTEL
BAYARAT
WEST BANK
TEL 095/231 1014
You are basically a guest at Muhammad Abdel Lahi's mud-brick house, where he cooks up good, basic Egyptian food, including chicken, kebab, duck, and molokhiyya, the glutinous green-leaf soup that is very much an acquired taste.
🕐 Open noon–10 p.m.
🚫 None

PRICES

HOTELS
An indication of the cost of double room in the high season is given by $ signs.

$$$$$	Over $200
$$$$	$120–$200
$$$	$60–$120
$$	$30–$60
$	Under $30

RESTAURANTS
An indication of the cost of three-course meal without drinks is given by $ signs.

$$$$	Over $35
$$$	$20–$35
$$	$10–$20
$	Under $10

◼ SOUTH OF LUXOR

ABU SIMBEL

🏨 **SETI FIRST ABU SIMBEL**
$$$$
TEL 02/2736 9820
A pricier but more elegant alternative to the state-owned Nefertari Hotel, the Seti First is beautifully sited atop a promontory with Nubian-style architecture and magnificent views of the lake.
ℹ️ 138 🔌 🏊 🚫 All major cards

🏨 **NEFERTARI HOTEL**
$$$
TEL/FAX 097/240 0508
Of only two accommodation options at Abu Simbel, this is less expensive—and closer to the temples. It has the advantage of a garden with a tree-shaded pool.
ℹ️ 120 🔌 🏊 🚫 AE, MC, V

ASWAN

🏨 MÖVENPICK RESORT ASWAN
$$$$$
ELEPHANTINE ISLAND
TEL 097/230 3455
FAX 097/230 3485
www.moevenpick-hotels.com
Though the Mövenpick's ugly tower dominates the Aswan skyline, if you stay here you will enjoy the full complement of five-star facilities in the setting of a luscious Nile island. There's an excellent riverside pool, too.
🛈 244 🆂 🌊 🆂 All major cards

SOMETHING SPECIAL

🏨 OLD CATARACT
Arguably Egypt's most romantic hotel, the Old Cataract is an opulent Moorish mansion set amid beautiful gardens on a rocky bluff above the Nile. It's a period piece belonging to the days when Aswan was a winter resort for the rich and titled of Europe. Agatha Christie wrote part of *Death on the Nile* here. The hotel is currently being refurbished and is expected to reopen in May 2010. Most of the large rooms have balconies with fantastic views of the river. The dining room is of palatial proportions with great horseshoe arches supporting the ceiling. Best of all is the terrace, perfect for drinks while watching the sun sink below the desert hills on the far bank.
$$$$$–$$$$
ABTAL AL-TAHRIR ST.
TEL 097/231 6000
FAX 097/231 6011
www.sofitel.com
🛈 131 🆂 🌊
🆂 All major cards

🏨 AMOUN ISLAND HOTEL
$$$$

AMOUN ISLAND
TEL 097/231 3800
FAX 097/231 7190
This small, island hotel run by Club Med is centered on a former royal hunting lodge. Rooms are modest but all have river views, and the garden setting is stunning. Small motorboats shuttle guests across the river from shore to shore.
🛈 50 🆂 🌊 🆂 MC, V

🏨 NEW CATARACT
$$$$
ABTAL AL-TAHRIR ST.
TEL 097/231 6000
FAX 097/231 6011
www.sofitel.com
It may be an unattractive, modern high-rise, but guests at the New Cataract get to share the garden, splendid swimming pool, and, above all, the view with those staying at its illustrious neighbor, the Old Cataract (but note that the Old Cataract building is undergoing renovation until about May 2010). The New Cataract also has two restaurants and a bar.
🛈 144 🆂 🌊 🆂 All major cards

🏨 BASMA
$$$
ABTAL AL-TAHRIR ST.
TEL 097/231 0901
FAX 097/231 0907
www.basmahotel.com
The Basma is a somewhat impersonal hotel south of town, beside the Nubian Museum. However, the rooms are comfortable with good views, the staff is friendly, and the rates are highly competitive. On-site restaurant and bar.
🛈 200 🆂 🌊 🆂 AE, MC, V

🏨 CLEOPATRA HOTEL
$$$
SOUQ ST.
TEL 097/231 4003
FAX 097/231 4002
The rooms are clean and comfortable (although occasionally gloomy, so look at a few before choosing) and have air-conditioning and private bathrooms. There's also a rooftop pool. The hotel is located close to the railroad station in the market area.
🛈 109 🆂 🌊 🆂 AE, MC, V

🏨 HAPPI HOTEL
$$
ABTAL AL-TAHRIR ST.
TEL 097/231 4115
FAX 097/230 7572
One block back from the Corniche, the Happi is right in the center of town amid the busy market streets. Rooms have private bathrooms and air-conditioning, and guests have use of the rooftop pool at the nearby Cleopatra Hotel for a discounted fee.
🛈 64 🆂 🆂 None

🏨 HOTEL KEYLANY
$$–$
SOUQ ST.
TEL/FAX 097/231 7332
This is an excellent budget option. It is located in the thick of the market and has a variety of rooms ranging from dormitories to new doubles with private bath. There's a small pool on the roof. Internet access is also available to guests.
🛈 28 🆂 Some rooms 🌊 🆂 None

🏨 RAMSES HOTEL
$$
ABTAL AL-TAHRIR ST.
TEL 097/230 4000
FAX 097/231 5701
This is a good value. The rooms are old, and a little shabby in some cases, but they are air-conditioned and

---

🆂 Nonsmoking 🆂 Air-conditioning 🌊 Indoor Pool 🌊 Outdoor Pool 🆂 Health Club 🆂 Credit Cards

come with private bathrooms, fridge, and Nile views.
 112 None

🍴 1902 RESTAURANT
$$$
OLD CATARACT HOTEL
ABTAL AL-TAHRIR ST.
TEL 097/231 6000
In a stunning dining room, under a huge domed ceiling, eat a four-course fixed-price menu with French-inspired dishes. The restaurant is sometimes closed to nonresidents, when the hotel is full. Like the rest of the hotel, the 1902 is slated to fully reopen in May 2010.
Open 7 p.m.–midnight
All major cards

🍴 ILE AMOUN
$$
AMOUN ISLAND
TEL 097/231 3800
Nonresidents are welcome to dine at the Amoun Island Hotel restaurant, which offers an excellent dinner buffet of meat and fish dishes, plus plenty of *meze* and salads. Free boats to the island run from in front of the EgyptAir office on the Corniche.
Open 7 p.m.–late
All major cards

🍴 NUBIAN RESTAURANT
$$
ESSA ISLAND
SOUTH OF ELEPHANTINE
This is a complete Nubian experience. You eat a three-course meal—including meat stews cooked in clay dishes—to the accompaniment of music and dance performed by a Nubian troupe. Free boats shuttle to the island from the Al-Dokka landing stage on the Corniche opposite the telecom building.
Open 7 p.m.–midnight
None

🍴 AL-MASRI
$
AL-MATAR ST.
TEL 097/230 2576
On a side street off the souq, this place serves kebabs and *kofta* only. The meat is excellent and comes with bread, salad, and *tahina*. Very popular with local families, the restaurant is clean, with attractive Arabesque tiled walls.
Open noon–midnight
None

🍴 ASWAN MOON
$
CORNICHE AL-NIL
TEL 097/231 6108
The Aswan Moon is the best of a string of floating restaurants. The food here is basic (soup, kebabs, chicken, some vegetarian dishes) but good, and the service is friendly. It's also a popular beer-drinking haunt for local *felucca* captains.
Open 8 a.m.–midnight
None

■ RED SEA & SINAI

DAHAB

🏨 HILTON RESORT
$$$$
DAHAB BAY
TEL 069/364 0310
FAX 069/364 0424
www.hilton.com
Far less developed than nearby Sharm al-Sheikh and Naama Bay, Dahab makes for a quieter getaway, and this is the newest and best of the big hotels there. Most rooms are whitewashed and domed and arranged around a central artificial lagoon. There's a fine strip of beach, and water sports and diving facilities are good.
163 All major cards

🏨 NESIMA HOTEL & DIVING CENTER
$$$
MASHRABA
TEL 069/364 0320
FAX 069/364 0321
www.nesima-resort.com
Accommodations are simple but comfortable domed rooms, some with air-conditioning. The Nesima has a great pool with a juice bar overlooking the beach. The hotel's diving center has an excellent reputation; as a consequence, the hotel is often quite packed with dive groups.
51 MC, V

EL GOUNA

🏨 SHERATON MIRAMAR
$$$$$
AL-GOUNA RESORT
TEL 065/354 5606
FAX 065/354 5608
www.sheraton.com

Designed by internationally renowned architect Michael Graves, this is one of Egypt's most outstanding modern hotels. A pastel-painted postmodern creation, it looks stunning in its seaside desert setting. Service is exceptional, and in addition to rooms and suites there are 25 "palace" rooms served by butlers.
🛈 338 🆂 ✈ 🅂 All major card

🏨 DAWAR AL-UMDA
$$$$
KAFR AL-GOUNA
TEL 065/354 5060
FAX 065/354 5061
Part of the exclusive Al-Gouna resort, this is a modestly scaled boutique hotel designed along traditional lines with domes and vaults and adobe walls. Guests have full use of the resort's facilities, including swimming pools, water sports, and a golf course.
🛈 64 🆂 ✈ 🅂 All major cards

HURGHADA

🏨 HURGHADA INTERCONTINENTAL
$$$$$
NEW HURGHADA
TEL 065/346 5100
FAX 065/346 5101
www.ichotelsgroup.com
Hurghada's most splendid resort complex has rooms overlooking a garden with several pools. It has a fine private beach, a good dive center, water sports, and numerous bars and restaurants.
🛈 244 ✈ 🅂 🅂 All major cards

🏨 JASMINE VILLAGE HOTEL
$$$
NEW HURGHADA
TEL 065/346 0460
FAX 065/344 6441
www.jasminevillage.com

At the southernmost end of Hurghada's sprawling hotel strip, Jasmine is a family resort of bungalow-style accommodations. It has a reputable dive center with its own boats, good water sports facilities, and a small zoo and playground for children.
🛈 460 🆂 ✈ 🅂 All major cards

🏨 TRITON EMPIRE HOTEL
$$
MUSTASHFA ST.
AL-DAHAR
TEL 065/354 9200
FAX 065/354 9212
www.threecorners.com
Despite being an unattractive concrete building, the Triton Empire nevertheless has an excellent location among the bars and restaurants on the busiest street in central Hurghada (Al-Dahar). Guests have access to a private beach a few minutes' walk away. It has several on-site restaurants and bars, including one by the pool..
🛈 366 🆂 ✈ 🅂 All major cards

🍴 BIER KELLER
$$
IBEROTEL ARABELLA
SIGALA
TEL 065/354 5086
More a bar than a restaurant, the Bier Keller has a fixed-price menu special every evening. This takes the form of Germanic-type fare such as veal escalope, braised beef, or cabbage roll filled with ground meat. It's raucous and fun.
🕘 Open noon–midnight 🆂
🅂 All major cards

🍴 FELFELA
$$
SHERATON ST.
SIGALA
TEL 065/344 2410
OR 065/344 2411
This branch of the ever

popular Egyptian-cuisine Cairo restaurant (see p. 363) overlooks the Red Sea.
🕘 Open 8 a.m.–midnight
🅂 None

🍴 PORTOFINO
$$
GENERAL HOSPITAL ST.
AL-DAHAR
TEL 065/354 6250
Right on Hurghada's main street, this is an extremely good Italian and seafood restaurant offering interesting specialties such as fish baked in rock salt.
🕘 Open 12.30 p.m.–12.30 a.m. daily 🆂 🅂 AE, MC, V

🍴 YOUNG KANG
$$
5 EL SHEIKH SEBAK ST.
AL-DAHAR
TEL 065/354 6623
For a change of pace, try this popular and good-value Chinese-Korean restaurant, located near the Tourist Bazaar in Al-Dahar.
🕘 Open 12 p.m.–11 p.m. 🆂
🅂 None

NUWEIBA

SOMETHING SPECIAL

🏨 BASATA
Basata means "simplicity," and that's the ethic behind Egypt's oldest eco-resort, founded in the 1980s by engineer and owner Sherif Ghamrwy. Some 16 bamboo and mud-brick huts stand on a beautiful, secluded beach 15 miles (24 km) north of Nuweiba. At the resort's heart is a central communal hut with kitchens and lounge area. Guests cook their own food from provisions supplied by Sherif (log what you use and pay later) or eat whatever the designated cook prepares. No alcohol, TV, loud music, or scuba diving are allowed to disturb the

New Age atmosphere.
$
RAS AL-BURQA
TEL 069/350 0480
FAX 069/350 0481
www.basata.com
ⓘ 16 ♿ AE, MC, V

QUSEIR

SOMETHING SPECIAL

🏨 **MÖVENPICK RESORT QUSEIR**

The Quseir Mövenpick is a
beautiful, environmentally
friendly, resort complex 3 miles
(5 km) north of the town
center, set around an aquama-
rine bay. The majority of the
accommodations are pretty
stone bungalows. There's a
gorgeous terraced pool area,
from where you can look
down into the crystal-clear sea-
water and watch large, colorful
fish dart around. There are lots
of activities for children, too.
$$$$
SIRENA BEACH
AL-QADIM BAY
TEL 065/333 2100
FAX 065/333 2128
www.moevenpick.com
ⓘ 175 🅿 🛗
♿ All major cards

🏨 **QUSEIR HOTEL &
RESTAURANT**
$$
138 PORT SAID ST.
TEL/FAX 065/333 2301
Here you can stay in an attrac-
tively restored Ottoman house
on the waterfront with creaky
wooden stairs and clean-lined
rooms with decor of exposed
stone and blonde pine. Some
rooms have air-conditioning,
others have fans only. Bath-
rooms are shared. The ground
floor restaurant specializes in
seafood.
ⓘ 6 🅿 ♿ All major cards

SHARM AL-SHEIKH

🏨 **RITZ CARLTON RESORT**
🍴 **$$$$**
RAS UMM SID
TEL 069/366 1919
FAX 069/366 1920
www.ritzcarlton.com
This clifftop hotel boasts
sumptuous rooms overlook-
ing the sea or mountains (the
latter are slightly cheaper).
There are also a garden
with pools, waterfalls, and
fountains; a private beach
with its own stretch of reef;
and a golf course. La Luna
restaurant (see p. 375) is one
of Egypt's finest. ⓘ 307 🅿
🛗 ♿ All major cards

🏨 **SOFITEL CORALIA
SHARM AL-SHEIKH**
$$$$
NAAMA BAY
TEL 069/360 0083
FAX 069/360 0085
www.sofitel.com
One of the best hotels in
southern Sinai, the Sofitel
Coralia is located at the
northern edge of the resort
cluster, with stunning views
across the bay from its
Moorish-styled rooms.
The hotel has three pools
and a very good array of
bars and restaurants.
ⓘ 302 🅿 🛗
♿ All major cards

🏨 **SANAFIR**
$$$
NAAMA BAY
TEL 069/360 0197
FAX 069/360 0196
At the heart of Naama Bay,
surrounded by shops, cafés,
and bars, and just a stone's
throw from the beach, the
Sanafir is one of the resort's
older hotels. However, it is
well maintained, and, with
several popular nightspots, is a
favorite with a younger crowd.
ⓘ 74 🅿 🛗 ♿ All major cards

PRICES

HOTELS
An indication of the cost
of double room in the high
season is given by **$** signs.

$$$$$	Over $200
$$$$	$120–$200
$$$	$60–$120
$$	$30–$60
$	Under $30

RESTAURANTS
An indication of the cost of
three-course meal without
drinks is given by $ signs.

$$$$	Over $35
$$$	$20–$35
$$	$10–$20
$	Under $10

🏨 **AMAR SINAI**
$$
RAS UMM SID
TEL 069/366 2222
FAX 069/366 2233
Up on the rocky headland
that divides Sharm al-Sheikh
Bay and Naama Bay, Amar has
been designed by its owner to
look like an Egyptian village.
The facilities are good for a
budget hotel, with a pool,
Jacuzzi, and Oriental café.
Some of the rooms have
excellent views.
ⓘ 91 🅿 🛗
♿ All major cards

🏨 **PIGEON HOUSE**
$$–$
NAAMA BAY
TEL 069/360 0996
FAX 069/360 0995
Inexpensive places to stay are
scarce in Sharm al-Sheikh and
Naama Bay. This is about the
best offer. Room types range
from basic huts with fans and

shared facilities to superior rooms with air-conditioning and private bathrooms. There's a small beach-type bar/café—which is nice, but the sea is a good 15-minute walk away.

🛏 68 ❄ Some rooms
🚫 None

🍴 LA LUNA
$$$$
RITZ CARLTON RESORT
RAS UMM SID
TEL 069/366 1919
Reputedly one of the best restaurants in the whole of Egypt, La Luna is supervised by Italian chef Marco Aveta, who gets some of his ingredients flown in from his home country. He serves a mouth-watering mix of pastas, steaks, and seafood.

🕐 Open for dinner only ❄
🃏 All major cards

🍴 BUA KHAO
$$$
SHARM HOTEL
NAAMA BAY
TEL 069/360 1391
This is the Sinai branch of an award-winning Cairo restaurant specializing in Thai food, here with a seafood slant. Pleasant decor and friendly service complement authentically spiced dishes.

🕐 Open noon–midnight ❄
🃏 All major cards

🍴 AL-FANAR
$$
RAS UMM SID
TEL 069/366 2218
Members of the local diving community favor Al-Fanar for its out-of-the-way but on-the-beach location. The restaurant itself is decorated in attractive, Bedouin tent style, but with sunken alcoves offering privacy. The food is, unsurprisingly, mostly choices from the sea, and thoroughly excellent—try the baked snap-

per, washed down with chilled Stella beer.

🕐 Open 10.30 a.m.– midnight
🃏 MC, V

🍴 DANANEER
$$
SHAMANDOURA
SHOPPING CENTER
NAAMA BAY
TEL 069/360 0321
You'll find this popular place above the Benetton store. It's simple but appealing, with an inviting *mashrabiyya*-style (carved wood window) decor. The menu is a nice mix of seafood and traditional Egyptian fare.

🕐 Open noon–midnight
🃏 All major cards

🍴 SAFSAFA
$$
OLD SHARM MALL
TEL 069/366 0474
One of the oldest restaurants in town, the Safsafa is badly located way inland from the sea and is very small (only eight tables). Despite these disadvantages, it's worth seeking out to indulge in some of the freshest and best seafood in town at great prices.

🚫 None

🍴 SINAI STAR
$
DOWNTOWN MARINA
This is an unpretentious restaurant run by a local Bedouin sheikh. There are no menus but the likes of shrimp, calamari, red snapper, and lobster, either baked, steamed or fried, are typically available. All entrees come with bowls of nutty-tasting brown rice and crisp salad. Simple but excellent food.

🕐 Open noon–midnight
🚫 None

SINAI INTERIOR

🏨 ST. CATHERINE'S TOURIST VILLAGE
$$$$–$$$
ST. CATHERINE'S VILLAGE
TEL 069/347 0333
FAX 069/347 0325
The resort consists of stone bungalows on a rocky hillside about a mile (1.5 km) from St. Catherine's Monastery. All of the rooms are air-conditioned, but not all have their own bathroom.

🛏 118 ❄ 🏊 🃏 AE, V

🏨 AUBERGE ST. CATHERINE
$$$
ST. CATHERINE'S MONASTERY
TEL 069/347 0353
FAX 069/347 0543
This basic hostel is actually part of the monastery complex and was originally intended to provide lodgings for pilgrims. It now offers 150 beds in single, double, and triple rooms on a dinner-bed-and-breakfast basis.

🛏 52 🃏 V

SOMA BAY

🏨 SHERATON SOMA BAY RESORT
$$$$
TEL 065/354 5845
FAX 065/354 5885
www.sheraton.com
Located 32 miles (52 km) south of Hurghada, Soma Bay is a new resort complex dominated by this enormous hotel, built to resemble an ancient Egyptian temple. The Sheraton has every imaginable amenity, including an 18-hole golf course.

🛏 310 ❄ 🏊
🃏 All major cards

🚭 Nonsmoking ❄ Air-conditioning 🏊 Indoor Pool 🏊 Outdoor Pool 🏋 Health Club 🃏 Credit Cards

Shopping in Egypt

The best shopping in Egypt is at the bazaar, or *souq*. These places overflow with gold and silver jewelry, hieroglyphic paintings, cotton goods, alabaster figurines, copper- and brassware, musical instruments, and wooden boxes inlaid with mother-of-pearl.

Biggest and most famous of the souqs is Cairo's Khan al-Khalili, a 500-year-old maze of commerce at the heart of the old Islamic city, but there are also good examples in Alexandria, Aswan, and Port Said. All are interesting to visit even if you don't intend to buy.

When shopping in the souq, remember that the starting price is generally high, and bargaining is expected (except at fixed-price artisans' boutiques). Take your time and enjoy the sport, always remaining cordial. If you can't get a price that you think is fair, just walk away.

Tip: An Arabic phrase to remember is *la shukran* (no, thank you), effective at turning away that street peddler intent on selling you just one more set of postcards.

Antiques & Antiquities

In Egypt an antique is defined as an object up to a hundred years old. Antiquities are those over a hundred years old; they cannot be taken out of the country except with a license from the Department of Antiquities.

Do not be fooled into buying "antiquities." To begin with, most antiquities offered to visitors are anything but old. For example, black "basalt" figurines for sale outside many tombs at Luxor are actually painted plaster and will disintegrate if dropped. "Ancient" scarabs are often newly carved from old bone.

Shopping for antiques is more worthwhile. Hoda Shaarawi Street in downtown Cairo and the side streets of Zamalek both have a number of antiques emporiums that are fun to browse. In Alexandria, the Attarine district is a warren of narrow alleyways all lined with

cave-like establishments piled high with furniture and fittings, paintings, and historical bric-a-brac, much of it sold to the dealers by wealthy foreign families fleeing the country in the wake of the 1952 revolution.

Art Galleries

Several of Cairo's commercial galleries sell works by local painters, photographers, and sculptors. Prices are often very affordable.

Ebdaa Art Gallery
17 Aswan Sq., Mohandiseen
Tel 02/3345 2263

Mashrabia Gallery
8 Champollion St.,
off Tahrir Sq., Cairo
Tel 02/2578 4494

Townhouse Gallery
Hussein Pasha St., off Mahmoud Bassiouni St., Downtown Cairo
Tel 02/2576 8086

Books

You can find excellent pictorial books of the sights of Egypt and a first-class range of more scholarly works on all things Egyptian from pharaohs to mosques. The American University in Cairo (AUC) Press has a prodigious output of quality titles sold throughout the country, as well as in its bookstores in Cairo. The AUC Press is also the English-language publisher of the works of Naguib Mahfouz (see p. 53).

Most five-star hotels have a small bookshop (where you can also usually get a selection of international newspapers that are just a couple of days old), but other good places to include:

Aboudi
Tourist Bazaar,
Corniche al-Nil, Luxor
Tel 095/237 3390

AUC Press Downtown Bookstore
AUC Downtown Campus,
Tahrir Sq., Cairo
Tel 02/2797 5929

Diwan Bookstore
159 26th July St.
Zamalek, Cairo
Tel 02/736 2598
American-style bookstore

Ezbekiyya Book Market
Ezbekiyya Gardens, Midan Ataba,
Downtown Cairo
Antiquarian to modern stock,
much in English.

Gaddis
Corniche al-Nil, next to Winter Palace Hotel, Luxor
Tel 095/237 2142

Lehnert & Landrock
44 Sherif St., Downtown Cairo
Tel 02/2393 5324
Upstairs are prints of early 20th-century photos of Egypt.

L'Orientaliste
15 Kasr al-Nil St., Downtown Cairo
Tel 02/2575 3418
Antiquarian bookshop specializing in Egypt and the Middle East. Also carries prints, maps, and old photos.

Carpets & Rugs

Unlike Morocco and Turkey, Egypt is not a big producer of carpets. What you do find here are brown-and-beige striped, hardwearing Bedouin camel-hair rugs, sold in the narrow covered alleys that run south of the Al-Ghouri Mosque across from Khan al-Khalili in Islamic Cairo, and in some of the handicraft shops below. Perhaps more distinctive are the carpets from the school of Wissa Wassef, an art and teaching center on the road to Saqqara. Carpets, rugs, and wall hangings produced here depict rural and folkloric scenes in beiges, browns, and greens.

Wissa Wassef Art Centre
Next to the Motel Salma, Saqqara Rd., Harraniyya, 2.5 miles (4 km) south of Al-Ahram Street, Cairo
Tel 02/3381 5746

Clothes

Cotton is Egypt's biggest cash crop (much of it exported), so it is possible to find bargains on quality products, including shirts, blouses, and pants. Look in particular for branches of **On Safari,** found in the malls and some hotel shopping complexes. For quality linens, **Galerie Hathout** in downtown Cairo proudly sells Egyptian goods only, and has beautifully embroidered sheet sets (with a made-in-Egypt tag, of course), tablecloths and matching napkins, down to simple kitchen towels.

Down in Middle Egypt, across the Nile from the town of Sohag, the village of **Akhmim** is the center of an ancient weaving tradition. Legend has it that pharaohs were buried in shrouds of Akhmim silk. The cloth comes in deep, rich colors, with elaborate floral and paisley-style patterns. You can find it at the **Akhmim Gallery** in the arcade of the Old Winter Palace in Luxor.

For something even more exotic, try the sequined bras, beaded hip bands, veils, and filmy skirts that make up a belly dancer's outfit. Several specialist emporiums are devoted to dressing dancers. Most famous is the studio of Amira al-Kattan, who makes costumes to order, but there are also a couple of

suppliers in Cairo's Khan al-Khalili at the northernmost end of Muski Street. To complete the outfit, pick up a pair of *sagat*, or finger cymbals.

Cairo
Amira al-Kattan
27 Basra St., Mohandiseen, Cairo
Tel 02/3349 0322

Galerie Hathout
Mustafa Kamel Sq.
Downtown Cairo

On Safari
10 Lotfalla St., Zamalek, Cairo
Tel 02/2735 1909

Handicrafts

Khan al-Khalili and the souqs are good for souvenirs, but for better quality crafts try specialist shops.

Cairo
Al-Ain Gallery
73 Hussein St., Doqqi
Tel 3349 3940
A favorite for intricate metalwork lamps by designer Randa Fahmy, jewelry by Azza Fahmy, clothing and furnishings, fabrics from Akhmim, and rugs from Sinai.

Al-Khatoun
Sheikh Muhammad Abdu St.
Islamic Cairo
Tel 02/2514 7164
In a restored Ottoman house behind Al-Azhar Mosque, Al-Khatoun sells wrought-iron furniture made in a village just outside Cairo, soft wall hangings, glassware, and local leather goods.

Egypt Crafts Center
27 Yehia Ibrahim St.
Zamalek, Cairo
Tel 02/2736 5123
Here you can buy Bedouin rugs and embroidery from Sinai and the northern Western Desert, handmade paper from Muqattam, and Upper Egyptian shawls.

Nagada
8 Dar al-Shifa, Garden City, Cairo
Tel 02/2792 3249
A favorite of Cairo's expatriate community, Nagada is a treasure trove of gorgeous handwoven textiles from Upper Egypt, jewelry, pottery, and other craftwork.

Khan Misr Touloun
17 Ahmed Ibn Tulun St.
Islamic Cairo
Tel 02/2365 2227
Near the Mosque of Ibn Tulun, this French-owned gallery sells handicrafts from the villages and oases, including wooden chests, dishes, blown glass, clay figurines, scarves, and woven clothing.

Nomad
14 Saraya al-Gezira St.
Zamalek, Cairo
Tel 02/2736 1917
Nomad specializes in jewelry and traditional Bedouin craft and costumes. It is on the first floor of an apartment tower overlooking the Nile.

Luxor
Egypt Crafts Center
Manshiyya St., Luxor town
This craft center offers products made by village women all over Egypt, who share in the profits.

Sinai
Aladin
Camel Hotel, Naama Bay
Tel 069/360 0700 ext. 355
This shop located in the hotel specializes in Bedouin textiles and lovely Egyptian glass.

Bedouin House
St. Catherine's Village, Sinai
Tel 069/345 0155
Owned and run by Bedouin women, this handicraft shop sells embroidery, bead jewelry, and small stone carvings.

Jewelry

Egypt's gold and silver shops are concentrated in the center of Khan al-Khalili. Jewelry is sold by weight, with a little extra added for workmanship. The day's gold prices are listed in the *Egyptian Gazette.* The most popular souvenirs are gold or silver cartouches with your name engraved in hieroglyphs—most shops in Khan al-Khalili can arrange it for you.

For something far more original, artist Azza Fahmy produces individual pieces of jewelry inspired by facets of Egyptian history and culture. Her work is sold at the Al-Ain Gallery in Cairo (see Handicrafts, above) and at First Residence Mall (tel 02/3573 7687). For chunky Bedouin jewelry, visit Nomad (see Handicrafts, above) or visit the Thursday market at Al-Arish in Northern Sinai (see p. 333).

Malls

In bigger cities like Cairo and Alexandria, malls are becoming popular places to shop. Although they contain little of interest for the visitor, they can be good places to pick up cheap cotton clothing. Malls' air-conditioning offers respite from the heat, and they have food courts and cinemas.

Talk of the town is the **First Residence Mall** in the Cairo suburb of Giza, which is part of one of the most expensive bits of real estate in the country, the First Residence Towers. Shop here for Gucci and Louis Vuitton. Farther afield in Nasr City is the upscale **Citystars Mall,** popular with wealthy Egyptians and filled with international brand clothing stores and restaurants. The **Ramses Hilton Mall,** beside the Ramses Hilton hotel in the city center, is more family oriented, with lots of cheap clothing and shoes.

Citystars Mall
Off Tariq al-Nasr, Nasr City Cairo

First Residence Mall
Giza St., Giza, Cairo

Ramses Hilton Mall
Abdel Moniem Riad Sq., Cairo

Papyrus

Banana-leaf papyrus (see Antiques & Antiquities, p. 376) can be bought everywhere in Egypt, typically painted in sweatshops with crude copies of pharaonic wall paintings. For this kind of quality, pay no more than 50 cents a sheet. For real papyrus, painted with some artistry, visit any of the galleries in the upscale hotels.

For a wider choice, and to learn something about the process of making papyrus and its historical use, visit one of Dr. Ragab's papyrus institutes, which are actually sales centers but with an educational spin—staff takes the trouble to explain what it is that you're buying. A good alternative in Cairo is **Said Delta Papyrus Centre** in Islamic Cairo on Al-Muizz li-Din Allah Street, north of Bab Zuweyla. It's on the third floor above a shoe shop; look for a yellow sign at first floor level.

Dr. Ragab's Papyrus Institute
Nile Corniche, Doqqi, Western Cairo
Tel 02/3571 8675

Perfume

Egypt is a big producer of many of the essences that make up French perfume, and places like Cairo's Khan al-Khalili offer a chance to pick up the scents at source. Pure essences cost anywhere from $3 to $10 per ounce. Beware though of cheaper substances, which are diluted with alcohol or oil. The essences are often sold in small decorated glass vials, which in themselves make a very attractive gift.

Souvenirs

Pharaonic knickknacks of all sorts fill Egypt's souqs: Tutankhamun on a T-shirt, Nefertiti lampshades, pyramid paperweights, Abu Simbel painted on ashtrays. Some items are more worthwhile than others; there are attractive castings of artifacts from the Egyptian Museum, cute little scarabs, and interesting jewelry inspired by ancient Egypt. All of this can be found in Cairo's Khan al-Khalili souq in the old Islamic quarter.

The Khan is also a good source of more inventive mementos of Egypt. It's the place to find marquetry backgammon boards for game enthusiasts. Cooks and kitchen genies might appreciate a copper or brass coffeepot and set of cups from the **Coppersmith's Market.** Many visitors choose to lug home *sheeshas,* the cumbersome water pipes (buy from Khan al-Khalili, around the Bayn al-Qasreen area), but remember you'll also need a plentiful supply of tobacco and the little pottery tobacco holders.

Children back home may appreciate a Monopoly board game (in Arabic, of course) or a hieroglyph stamp set, available from the many toy stores that line Muski, the market street running between Khan al-Khalili and downtown Cairo.

Spices

Khan al-Khalili in Cairo and the souqs in Luxor and Aswan are the places for spices. They come in every conceivable color, and the smell around the stalls is fantastic. Generally they are fresher and better quality than packaged spices you'll find in the West, and considerably cheaper. Look for black pepper (*filfil*), cumin (*kamoon*), saffron (*zaafaran*), and a purplish dried leaf, which is hibiscus; boiled up, strained, and sugared, this makes *karkadeh,* a sweet crimson drink (see p. 297).

Activities & Entertainment

From diving and sailing to fishing and golf, from hot air ballooning and bird-watching to desert four-wheel-drive safaris and walking treks, Egypt offers a broad range of activities. In the realm of entertainment, visitors outside Cairo almost exclusively rely on their hotels for evening distractions. In Cairo, however, you'll discover a wealth of fare, from movies to music and bars. The magazine *Egypt Today* has listings of events in and out of the capital.

ACTIVITIES

Traditionally, activities in Egypt have focused solely on the sea, in the form of diving and water sports. In recent years, however, tour operators, in conjunction with the Egyptian authorities, have been looking to diversify and to broaden the country's appeal. Desert safaris are one exciting recent development, with several agencies and individuals now making accessible dramatic sandy landscapes previously little seen by visitors.

More unexpected is the rise of golf. This is, after all, a blisteringly hot country with a shortage of fresh water and cultivatable land. Despite these factors, the Egyptian Ministry of Tourism is determinedly grooming the country as a golf holiday destination, with the creation of several courses in recent years and more on the drawing board.

Ballooning

In Luxor several companies now offer early morning balloon flights over the West Bank monuments. The package, which includes a champagne breakfast, costs about $250 per person. Reservations can be made through reception at all the larger hotels, or directly (see p. 268).

Balloons Over Egypt
Tel 095/237 0638

Hod Hod
Tel 095/227 1116 or 012/585 7028

Magic Horizons
Tel 012/226 1697 or 010/568 8439
www.magic-horizon.com

Birding

Egypt's strategic location at the crossroads of three continents and abundance of ecosystems provide an ideal environment for migrating birds. Birds, ranging from herons to passerines, which breed in Europe and winter in sub-Saharan Africa, migrate through Egypt via the Nile River Valley, the Gulf of Suez, and the Red Sea during the fall and spring months to water at oases, restore their fat deposits, and rest before continuing their journey. It is possible to view these birds on your own (see "Go Bird-watching," p. 155), but for longer, guided tours of various areas and ecosystems try the following list of providers.

Egyptian Birding Tours for Independent Travelers
Tel 02/2360 8160
E-mail baha@internetegypt.com
Mindy Baha el Din, in conjunction with Thomas Cook, has been the leading expert on birds and bird tourism in Egypt for the last ten years. Tours are designed for independent travelers or small groups.

Travel Egypt
4015 Nine McFarland Dr.
Alpharetta, GA
Tel 877-778-3497
www.travelegypt.com/egyptbirdingtour.htm
Operating weekly November through March, Travel Egypt presents a 2-week, fully escorted trip through Cairo, Fayoum, Luxor, Aswan, and the Sinai. Pairs bird-watching with visits to top Egyptian destinations

Wings: Birding Tours Worldwide
1643 N. Alvernon, Ste. 109
Tucson AZ
Tel/888-293-6443
www.wingsbirds.com/tours
Offering one two-week, escorted tour in the spring, Wings, partnered with their British counterpart Sunbird, provides a tour through Cairo, Suez Delta, Sinai, Luxor, and Aswan. Highlights are stops at prime bird-watching areas and ecosystems and important archaeological sites. The tour starts in London and prices include travel to and from London and Egypt.

Desert Safaris

Egypt's stunning desert scenery remains one of the country's greatest little seen treasures. Few visitors get to experience the magnificent sandscapes because of the difficulty of getting to these remote areas. However, a growing number of local tour operators are now offering trips into Sinai and the far more impressive Western Desert. Though some of these are simply half-day expeditions into the desert from popular resorts, others are true safaris of three or four days, undertaken in 4WD vehicles, with tents for accommodations (see p. 205 for more suggestions).

In Sinai, local Bedouin lead treks into the interior from resorts such as Naama Bay, Dahab, and Nuweiba. Trips usually last half a day and can be arranged at short notice by your hotel. Similarly, there are some wonderful treks with Bedouin guides to be done from St. Catherine's village (see p. 335). Possibly the best of the Sinai operators is Abanoub Travel, based in Nuweiba. The company runs tours that cost about $35 per person per day, including food. Camel treks are about $10 more.

Abanoub Travel
Tel 069/352 0201
Fax 069/352 0206
To see the most spectacular desert scenery, it is necessary to head into the Western Desert, to the oases. Many hotels in Siwa, Farafra, and Dakhla organize one-day and overnight expeditions, such as those offered by the Al-Badawiya Hotel (see p. 366) in Farafra; the Bedouin brothers who own the hotel arrange highly recommended treks throughout the Western Desert and other areas of Egypt. They also run a sister property in Dakhla that offers desert treks (see p. 205).

Amr Shannon
Tel 02/2518 6894
Based in Cairo, Amr Shannon is an artist who has been leading small groups into the deserts for more than 30 years. You will need to provide your own camping equipment and 4WD, but Shannon and his wife can help with renting what you will need for the trip. He leads groups of up to a dozen people at a flat rate of $300 per person per day. Shannon's trips are made several times a year and must be booked well in advance.

Egypt Off-Road
Tel 012/174 5462
www.egyptoffroad.com
This company, run by expatriate

Peter Gaballa, also has long experience organizing deep desert expeditions into the Great Sand Sea and to the Gilf al-Kabir.

Diving
Egypt's Red Sea is a diver's paradise of beautiful clear waters filled with teeming marine life. It attracts thousands of visitors each year. Diving is concentrated around the southern tip of the Sinai Peninsula, centered on the resorts of Dahab, Naama Bay, and Sharm al-Sheikh, and especially around the fabulous Ras Moham-med National Park. The other big dive center is the Red Sea coast resort of Hurghada. Serious divers head farther south to a few scat-tered dive centers along the barely developed stretch of coast down toward Marsa Alam, where the best reefs are found around the proliferation of offshore islands.

A vast number of dive clubs cater to visitors wanting to explore underwater worlds. Almost every large hotel in Sinai and on the Red Sea coast has its own dive center. These places offer introductory dives for first-timers, accredited courses for those who want to get into the sport, as well as more ambitious expeditions for the experienced diver. Some clubs also organize dive safaris to remote sites ranging from one night to two weeks. All equipment is provided. Most clubs are well-equipped and staffed by professionals, but not all, so take care when choosing whom to dive with. Prices vary, but not greatly. Don't choose a dive center purely on the grounds of cost. Most visitors organize diving trips once they arrive in Egypt, but if you wish to make some inquiries in advance, following are a few recommended outfits.

Also, there is a lengthy index of dive centers on the website www.red-sea.com.

African Divers
Sharm al-Sheikh/Naama Bay
Tel/fax 069/366 4884

Aquanaut Blue Heaven
Hurghada
Tel 065/344 0892
www.aquanaut.net

Camel Dive Club & Hotel
Sharm al-Sheikh/Naama Bay
Tel 069/360 0700
www.cameldive.com

Divers International
Dahab, Hurghada, & Sharm al-Sheikh/Naama Bay
Tel 069/360 0865
www.diversintl.com

Oonas Dive Club
Sharm al-Sheikh/Naama Bay
Tel 069/360 0581
www.oonasdiveclub.com

Red Sea Diving College
Sharm al-Sheikh/Naama Bay
Tel 069/360 0145
www.redseacollege.com

Red Sea Diving Safari
Southern Red Sea coast
Tel 02/3337 9942
www.redsea-divingsafari.com

Fishing
The prize place for fishing in Egypt is Lake Nasser. The silt-rich depths of this artificially created lake are home to fish of massive proportions, particularly the Nile perch.

Because the lake is difficult to get to, and the area around it is completely uninhabited, specialist help is required to mount a fishing expedition. There are two compa-nies that offer either boat trips or overland safaris:

The African Angler
Tel 097/230 9748 or
097/233 0900
www.african-angler.co.uk

Lake Nasser Adventure
Tel 012/104 0266 or
012/104 0255

For more details on these two
companies, see p. 311.

Golf

The British introduced golf to
Egypt back in the 19th century.
After the 1952 revolution, when
the British were sent packing,
there was no one left to play.
However, in the last decade
there has been a renewed interest in the sport among Egypt's
nouveau riche. New suburban
desert housing developments
on the fringes of Cairo are being
built with attached courses, and
there are no fewer than three
"golf villages" along the Desert
Highway that connects Cairo and
Alexandria.

Al-Gouna Golf Course
Al Gouna Resort, Red Sea coast
Tel 065/354 9702
www.elgouna.com

Dreamland Golf Resort
6th of October City,
Cairo–Alexandria Desert Hwy.
Tel 02/3855 3164
www.dreamlandgolf.com

Jolie Ville Golf Resort
Sharm al-Sheikh
Tel 069/360 3200
www.jolieville-hotels.com/
golf_welcome.php

Luxor Royal Valley Golf Club
Tel 095/238 0522

Mirage City Golf Club
Cairo–Alexandria Desert Hwy.
Tel 02/3412 5041/43
http://golf.jwmarriottcairo.
com/golf

Pyramids Golf & Country Club
Cairo–Alexandria Desert Hwy.
Tel 02/3335 3688

Sailing

A highlight of a trip to Egypt is
drifting on the Nile in a *felucca,*
the small, lateen-sailed boats
that have been in use here since
ancient times. They're frequently
portrayed in tomb paintings.
Boats and their captains are
found for rent by the hour all
along the Nile, from Corniche-
side landings in central Cairo
right down to Aswan.

Although taking to the Nile
at sunset is a wonderful end to a
day's sight-seeing in the capital,
the best place to enjoy the languid
pleasures of sailing is in Aswan,
where the riverside scenery is at
its most stunning, and you can
employ the boat for an afternoon
or evening of island-hopping.
Prices should be negotiated for
the boat per hour; for an idea of
the going rates, check with the
local tourist office.

The more adventurous might
consider a trip of two or three
days on a felucca, sailing from
Aswan downriver to Edfu. Days
are spent visiting sights en route
(including Kom Ombo), often with
a stop-off for tea at your captain's
village somewhere along the way.
Food is bought in the market
before departure and prepared by
the captain. Nights are spent on
the boat or camping on an island.
Though it's a very basic existence
with no facilities or comforts, it
makes for a memorable experience. Arriving at Edfu, you can
catch a bus back to Aswan or
onward to Luxor.

Feluccas carry a minimum of
six passengers and a maximum of
eight, and the cost per person is
about $20 to Edfu from Aswan,
although this is negotiable. There
is also a small fee for police reg-
istration, and you must buy your
own food. Finding
a good captain is essential; it is
wise to consult with the local
tourist office.

Hermes Travel
Tel 02/3303 5105
Fax 02/3345 4711
Hermes Travel operates a 50-foot
(15 m) yacht on Lake Nasser, with
five double cabins. In addition
to sailing to all the temples on
the lake (see p. 311) on request,
it can also be captained to the
Eastern Desert protectorate of
Wadi al-Alagi to link up with
4WDs that can take guests across
the desert to the usually off-
limits Red Sea port of Berenice.
Prices are in the range of $50 per
person per day.

ENTERTAINMENT

Outside of Cairo, visitors will
find themselves relying mostly
on hotels for their evening
entertainments, especially in
Luxor and Aswan. Most of the
larger hotels put on nightly floor
shows of folkloric dancing or
belly dancing, or there's always
the bar, and sometimes a disco.
Cairo, on the other hand, has a
vibrant cultural scene with plenty
of films, music performances,
nightclubs, and bars. For information on what's going on, seek
out the glossy monthly magazine
Egypt Today, on sale at most hotel
bookstores, which has extensive
coverage of events throughout
the country.

Bars, Cafés, & Clubs

The majority of Egyptians are
Muslims and do not ever drink
alcohol. So while alcohol is available, it is generally restricted to
places frequented by tourists,
such as hotel bars and cafés and
upscale restaurants.

Cairo
After Eight 6 Qasr al-Nil,
Downtown, tel 02/2574 0855.
This popular spot fills up quickly
nightly for live music.

Bullseye 32 Geddah St., Mohandiseen, tel 02/3761 6888. This is an English pub where you can play darts, as the name hints.

Cairo Jazz Club 197 26th of July St., Mohandiseen, tel 02/3345 9939. Jazz and blues are played here nightly.

Absolute Casino al Shagara, Maspero, Corniche al-Nil, tel 02/2579 6511. Crowded on weekends with pumping club music; a quiet place to chill on weeknights.

Deals Sayed al-Bakry St., Zamalek, tel 02/2736 0502. For a quieter night out, try this neighborhood bar.

Harry's Bar Marriott Hotel, Saray al-Gezira, Zamalek, tel 02/2735 8888. You can let your hair down at this popular pub with karaoke and DJs.

Purple Imperial Boat, opposite Marriott Hotel, Zamalek, tel 02/2736 5796. Upscale dance club on a boat, featuring house and retro grooves, with the occasional live band.

Le Tabasco 8 Amman Sq., Mohandiseen, tel 02/3336 5583. For more sedate revelers, this is a fashionable bar/restaurant.

Alexandria
Cap d'Or 4 Adib St., off Salah Salem St., Downtown, tel 03/487 5177. Bar with seafood snacks.

Monty's Bar second floor, Cecil Hotel, Saad Zaghloul Sq., tel 03/480 7224. This classy hotel bar is named for the British general (Montgomery).

Spitfire Bar 7 Bursa al-Qadima St., off Saad Zaghloul St., Downtown, tel 03/480 6503. Seafarers' bar.

Luxor
King Dude Gaddis Hotel, Khalid ibn al-Walid St., tel 095/238 2838. There are regular karaoke nights in the bar.

King's Head Pub Khaled ibn al-Walid St., tel 095/237 1249. An English-style pub with meals, darts, and billiards.

Mars Bar Venus Hotel, Youssef Hassan St., tel 095/238 2625. Draft beer, satellite TV, a pool table, and Western music are all to be found here.

Pub 2000 Khalid ibn al-Walid St. This English-style pub pulls in the visitors with its popular happy hour.

Aswan
Aswan Moon Corniche al-Nil, tel 097/231 6108. This restaurant by day becomes boozier as the night wears on.

Isis Hotel Corniche, tel 097/231 5200. There's a disco here nightly.

Royal Restaurant, Pub, & Coffeeshop Corniche al-Nil. Beers, snacks, Internet, and satellite TV.

Red Sea & Sinai
Bus Stop Bar & Disco Sanafir Hotel, Naama Bay, Sinai, tel 069/360 0197. It's the liveliest place in town.

Café Bedouin Sharm Panorama, Naama Bay, Sinai. No alcohol but romantic and quirky late-night venue for tea and a waterpipe

Hard Rock Café Naama Bay, Sinai, tel 069/360 2665. Rock memorabilia and burgers

Papa's Bar New Marina, Sigala, Hurghada, tel 010/512 9051. Recently moved to the New Marina, this Sigala standby is popular with expats and divers.

Peanuts Bar Market Place Complex, near Three Corners Hotel, Ad-Dahar, Hurghada. Loud and beery, the bar is open 24 hours.

Pirates Bar Hilton Fayruz, Naama Bay, tel 069/360 0136. This terrace bar with mini-lights is a big hit with divers.

Belly Dancing
The best dancers perform at the nightclubs attached to Cairo's five-star hotels. Venues such as the Haroun el-Rashid Club (Semiramis InterContinental Hotel, Garden City, Cairo, tel 02/2795 7171) and La Belle Epoque (Grand Hyatt Cairo, Roda, Cairo, tel 02/2365 1234) attract the biggest names, including Dina, Lucy, and the irrepressible Fifi Abdou. But a night in the presence of the ladies does not come cheap. A seat for such a show costs about $50 a head, with buffet included. At these belly dancing performances, the main act generally doesn't appear until at least 2 a.m., and the band doesn't call it a night until the sun is creeping up over the Nile. Far less accomplished dancers can be seen at most hotels and tourist restaurants throughout the country, for considerably less cash.

Casinos
Most of Egypt's international five-star hotels have casinos. These are open to non-Egyptians only, which means that you will have to show your passport to gain admission to the casino. All games are conducted in U.S. dollars or other major foreign currencies, with a minimum stake of a dollar. Smart casual attire is required.

For Children

Egypt is a very child-friendly place, and the locals really warm to youngsters. Keeping them entertained while you're here, though, is another story. In Cairo, kids will enjoy the Pharaonic Village (see p. 127). A trip to Cairo Zoo (see pp. 126–127) is less inspiring, although unlike Western zoos, visitors can feed the animals and that can be fun. Donkeys and camels can be ridden at the Pyramids.

Folkloric Dance

Folkloric dance often forms part of dinner entertainment at hotels and tourist restaurants, especially in Upper Egypt.

In Luxor the most elaborate folkloric dancing shows are put on at the "Fellah's Tent" in the Maritim Jolie Ville (King's Island, tel 095/227 4855, fax 095/227 4936, adm. $45) and every Saturday evening at the Sheraton for the "Nubian Night" (Khalid ibn al-Walid St., tel 095/237 4544, adm. $35). The performances at these two places include belly dancing and "stick dancing," performed by men in a highly stylized pantomime of combat involving clashing staves. The price of admission includes a buffet meal; drinks are extra. Stick dancing is also on the agenda at Aswan's Nubian Restaurant (Essa Island; see p. 372), where there is no admission or cover charge.

There are also a few cultural venues with regular performances, including the municipality-run Palace of Culture (17 Corniche al-Nil, tel 097/231 3390) in Aswan, and the Sayyid Darwish Concert Hall (Gamal ad-Din al-Afghani St., off Al-Ahram St., Giza, Cairo, tel 02/560 2473) in Cairo. See also the Sufi Whirling Dervish performances that are described on page 101.

Music

Egypt's premier music venue for classical Western and classical Arabic music is the Cairo Opera House (Tahrir St., Gezira, Cairo, tel 02/2739 8144) on the island of Gezira. Its main hall hosts regular performances from a variety of visiting international and local artists. On such occasions a jacket and tie are compulsory for men. The small hall has nightly recitals by ensembles, quartets, and soloists, and it is also used by the Cairo Symphony Orchestra, which gives concerts there every Saturday from September to mid-June.

In Islamic Cairo, music evenings, and sometimes theater performances, are occasionally held at the House of Zeinab Khatoun (Mohamed Abdu St., Islamic Cairo, tel 02/2510 4174) and the Al-Ghouri Complex (Al-Azhar St., Islamic Cairo, tel 02/2510 0823, see p. 91), especially during Ramadan, when there are nightly shows.

In Alexandria, the Sayyid Darwish Theater (22 Horeyya St., Alexandria, tel 03/486 5602) hosts occasional classical Western and classical Arabic concerts, often organized by the French, Italian, or German consulates.

In Aswan, the Palace of Culture (see Folkloric Dance) sometimes hosts performances of Nubian and other local musicians.

Sound-and-Light Shows

Many major sights in Egypt present an evening son et lumière, or sound-and-light show, in which the monuments are illuminated by floodlight while a recorded voice narrates history and legends. It is often worth attending for the chance to see these places by moonlight. Sound-and-light shows take place at the Pyramids, the Temple of Karnak in Luxor, Philae at Aswan, and Abu Simbel.

Timetables of performances are displayed at the sights, or visit www.sound-light.egypt.com.

Sport

Soccer is the national sport, and nothing else comes close in inspiring passions. On big match days, streets empty as fans crowd into coffeehouses to watch the action. The two top clubs both hail from Cairo (Ahly and Zamalek), and meetings of these teams are the high points of the sporting calendar. Major games are played at Cairo Stadium in the northeast of the city, but because of high demand, tickets can be hard to get. Still, it's fun to join the crowd watching at the coffeehouse.

Squash also has a sizable following and is the sport of choice of the Egyptian president, Hosni Mubarak. The annual Al-Ahram International Squash Tournament draws competitors from all over the world to the glass-enclosed courts set up beside the Pyramids. The Pyramids also feature as the start and finishing point in the annual Pharaoh's Rally. Held every October, this is a desert race for souped-up 4WDs and trail bikes.

Language Guide

The official language in Egypt is Arabic, but English is taught in schools and most people speak a little, especially in Cairo and in the areas with many tourists. However, any attempts on your part to speak even a few words in Arabic will be met with an enthusiastic response. The following list gives a phonetic transliteration from the Arabic script. Words or letters in parentheses indicate the different form that is required when a woman is speaking or being addressed.

Greetings & Common Words

yes *aywa, naam*
no *la*
please *min fadlak (fadlik)*
thank you *shukran*
you're welcome *afwan*
hello *salaam aleikum*
    response *aleikum al-salaam*
goodbye *maa al-salaama*
good morning *sabaah al-kheir*
    response *sabaah al-nur*
how are you? *izzayak (izzayik)*
fine *kwayyis(a) al-hamdulillah*
God willing *inshallah*
no problem/don't worry
    maalesh
tomorrow *bukra*
tomorrow morning *bukra sobh*
after tomorrow *bada bukra*
today *innaharda*
sorry *ana aasif (asfa)*

do you speak English?
    bititkallim(i) Ingleezi?
I don't understand *Ana mish faahem (fahma)*
I don't know Arabic *Ana mish aarif (arfa) arabi*
go away *imshee*
leave me alone *bass kifaaya*
don't/enough *balesh*
slowly/bit by bit *shwaya shwaya*

Emergency

help! *al-haooni!*
thief! *haraami!*
police *bulees*
hospital *mustashfa*

where is the toilet?
    feyn el-twalet?
I'm sick *ana ayyaan(a)*
we need a doctor
    ayzeen duktor

Shopping

shop *dukkan*
market/bazaar *souk*
I would like *ana aiyz(a)*
I'm just looking *ana batfarrag bass*
how much? *bikam?*
may I? *mumkin?*
that's too much *da ketir awi*
change *fakka*
do you have change? *maak fakka?*
no change *maafish fakka*

good *kwayyis*
bad *mish kwayyis*
big *kebir*
small *sughayyar*
hot *sukn*
cold *baarid*
many *kitiir*
few *olayyel*
up *foq*
down *taht*
more *kamaan*
enough *kefaya*

Getting Around

street *sharia*
square *midan*
stop here *hina kwayyis*
straight *ala tuul*
left *shimel*
right *yemeen*
next to *gamb*
behind *wara*
ticket *tazkara*
wait *istanna*
where is the...? *fein el...?*
how many kilometers to...?
    kaam kilu illa...?
airport *mataar*
boat *markeb*
bridge *kubri*
bus station *mahattat al-autobees*
car *sayara*

church *kineesa*
embassy *sifaara*
hotel *fonduk*
hospital *mustashfa*
museum *mathaf*
post office *busta*
railroad station *mahatta*

Numbers

0 *sifr*
1 *wahid*
2 *itneyn*
3 *telaata*
4 *arbaah*
5 *khamsa*
6 *sittah*
7 *sabbaah*
8 *tamanya*
9 *tisah*
10 *ashara*
11 *hidaashar*
12 *itnaashar*
13 *telataashar*
14 *arbaatashar*
15 *khamastaashar*
16 *sittaashar*
17 *sabbahtaashar*
18 *tamantaashar*
19 *tisahtaashar*
20 *ashreen*
21 *wahid waashreen*
22 *itneyn waashreen*
30 *telaateen*
40 *arbaheen*
50 *khamseen*
100 *mia*
200 *mitayn*
1,000 *alf*

Eating Out

what's that? *eh da (di)?*
bill *al-hisab*
the bill please *al-hisab lau samaht*
breakfast *iftar*
dinner *asha*

Menu Reader

baba ghanoug purée of eggplant, grilled and mashed, seasoned with tahina, olive oil, and garlic

felafel (taamiyya in Cairo) mashed broad beans and spices balled up and deep fried

fisiikh salty dried fish

fuul beans mashed into a thick, lumpy paste, usually ladled into a piece of pita-type bread as a sandwich

gibna cheese
   gibna beyda soft, white, like feta
   gibna ruumi hard, yellow, and sharp

hummus paste of ground chick-peas mixed with olive oil

kebda liver, often chickens' liver (kebda firekh), usually sautéed with lemon or garlic

kellawi kidneys

kubeba minced lamb, burgul wheat, and pine seeds shaped into a patty and deep-fried

kushari rice, macaroni, black lentils, fried onions, and tomato sauce

labneh cheesy, yogurt paste that is often heavily flavored with garlic or mint

mahshi stuffed vegetable leaves, typically filled with ground meat, a spicy mix of rice, chopped tomatoes, onion, and spices

shwarma strips of lamb or chicken sliced from a spit, sizzled on a hot plate with chopped tomatoes and garnish, and then stuffed in a pocket of pita-type bread

tahina sesame seed paste

zeitoun olives

Main Courses

bamya tomatoey stew of okra, sometimes with lamb

fatteh boiled lamb or chicken served over bread and rice in a garlicky, vinegary sauce

firakh chicken, usually spit roasted

kebab skewered, flame-grilled chunks of meat, usually lamb

kofta ground meat peppered with spices, shaped into small sausages, skewered and grilled

hamam pigeon, usually served stuffed with rice and spices

loubiah French beans cooked in a tomato sauce as a stew with other vegetables and lamb

molokhiyya gluey soup made from the molokhiyya leaf, often served with rabbit

samak fish

shish tawouk flame-grilled kebab of marinated, spiced chicken, onions, peppers, and tomato

tagen oven-baked dish containing vegetables and/or meat

Fish & Seafood

barbuuni red mullet

buuri grey mullet

gambari shrimp

istakooza lobster

kaborya crabs

kalamari/subeit squid

muusa sole

salamuun salmon

tuuna tuna

Sweets & Desserts

atayif filled sweet crêpe, deep-fried and dipped in syrup

basboosa a semolina cake drenched in sugar syrup, often flavored with coconut or orange-blossom syrup

konafa vermicelli pastry on a soft cheese or cream base

muhalabiyya milk cream thickened by corn flour or ground rice, often flavored with rose water and served with chopped almonds or coconut sprinkled on

umm Ali Egyptian version of bread pudding: layers of pastry, with nuts and raisins, soaked in cream and milk, and baked in the oven

Fruit

ananas pineapple

balah date

batikh watermelon

bortuaan orange

fraula strawberry

gooz al-hind coconut

guafa guava

khookh peach

kummitra pear

limoon lemon

manga mango

mishmish apricot

mooz banana

rumaan pomegranate

tufaah apple

tiin fig

Drinks

ahwa coffee
   ahwa saada with no sugar
   ahwa mazbuut with medium sugar
   ahwa ziyaada very sweet

shai tea
   shai lipton teabag tea

mayya water

aseer juice

nibiit wine

biira beer

sahlab milky drink thickened with the powdered bulb of a type of orchid, and flavored with chopped nuts and cinnamon

karkadeh made from boiled hibiscus leaves, served hot or cold

yansoon hot drink made from aniseed

Breakfast

aish bread in general

aish baladi whole wheat bread, comes in big round disks

aish shammi white flour bread, like pita

beid egg

ishta cream

laban milk

zabaadi yogurt

zibda butter

Glossary

abu father of

ain well, spring

Aten sun disk, worshiped by Akhenaten

bab gate or door

baksheesh tip

baladi adjective meaning "country" or "local"

bawab porter or doorman, common at Egyptian apartments

bayt house

bir spring, well

birket lake

bismillah in the name of God

Books of the Dead ancient theological compositions and the subject of most colorful paintings and reliefs on tomb walls

burg tower

calèche horse-drawn carriage

caliph Islamic ruler

canopic jars pottery jars holding embalmed internal organs and viscera of a mummified body

caravanserai merchants' inn

cartouche oblong figure enclosing the hieroglyphs of royal or divine names

corniche seafront or riverfront promenade

deir monastery

eid feast

emir Islamic ruler

false door fake, seemingly half-open *ka* door in a tomb wall which enabled the pharaoh's spirit, or life force, to come and go at will

fatwa a religious ruling

fellaheen rural workers who make up the majority of Egypt's population

felucca sailing boat

galabiyya full-length robe worn by both men and women

gebel mountain

gezira island

haj pilgrimage to Mecca

hamman bathhouse

hantour horse-drawn carriage

haramlik women's quarters

hieroglyphs ancient Egyptian form of writing, which used pictures and symbols to represent objects, words or sounds

hypostyle hall hall in which the roof is supported by columns

imam prayer leader in a mosque

iwan vaulted hall, opening into a central court, in the madrassa of a mosque

ka spirit, or "double," of a living person

khan another name for a caravanserai

khanqah Sufi monastery

khedive Egyptian viceroy under Ottoman suzerainty (1867–1914)

kom heap of rubble over an ancient settlement

Koran Muslim holy book

kuttab Koranic school

madrassa school where Islamic law is taught

mammisi ancient Egyptian symbolic birth house

mashrabiyya ornate carved wooden panel or screen, typical of Islamic architecture

Masr Egypt (also means Cairo)

mastaba Arabic word for "bench"; a mud-brick structure above tombs from which the pyramids were developed

mihrab niche in the wall of a mosque that indicates the direction of Mecca

minbar pulpit in a mosque

moulid festival celebrating the birthday of a local saint or holy person

muezzin mosque official who calls the faithful to prayer five times a day from the minaret

papyrus paper-like material made from the papyrus reed's pith

pasha Ottoman title bestowed on politicians and men of rank

pharaoh ancient Egyptian ruler; strictly speaking the term only came into use in the New

Kingdom, the rulers before that being kings

pylon monumental gateway at the entrance to a temple

pyramid texts paintings and reliefs on the walls of a pyramid's rooms and burial chamber

qasr palace

Ramadan holy month during which Muslims fast from sunrise to sunset

sabil public drinking fountain

Saidi a native of Upper Egypt

sarcophagus large stone coffin that typically encases smaller wooden coffins

scarab dung beetle regarded as sacred in ancient Egypt; represented on amulets or in hieroglyphs as a symbol of the sun-god Re

serdab chamber containing a life-size, painted statue of the dead pharaoh, provided so that the deceased's ka could communicate with the outside world

sharia street, literally "way."

sharm bay

solar bark wooden boat placed in or around the pharaoh's tomb; the symbolic vessel of transport for his journey into the eternal afterlife

stela (pl: stelae) stone slab decorated with inscriptions or figures

Sufi follower of an Islamic mystical order that emphasizes dancing, chanting, and trances in order to attain unity with God

sultan secular title meaning ruler or king

tell mound of earth covering an ancient site

umm mother of

Upper Egypt general term for the country south of Cairo

wadi dry riverbed

wikala synonym for caravanserai

Who's Who

For more pharaohs see "Timeline of the Pharaohs," pp. 52–53.

Akhenaten (R.1352–1336 B.C.)
Formerly Amenhotep IV, the
pharaoh who ushered in a revolutionary period in ancient Egyptian
history when he replaced worship
of the traditional pantheon of
gods with the cult of the sun
disk Aten.

**Al-Ghouri, Sultan Qansuh (died
1516)** Penultimate Mamluk
sultan, killed in battle with the
Ottoman Turks; left behind a fine
architectural legacy.

Amenhotep III (R.1390–1382 B.C.)
The Sun King whose 38-year
reign represented the zenith
of ancient Egypt's power and
prestige.

Belzoni, Giovanni (1778–1823)
Italian strongman turned ancient
Egyptian treasure hunter who
supplied the British Museum with
key pieces for its ancient Egypt
collection.

Carnarvon, Lord (1866–1923)
British Egyptologist who was
the patron and associate of
archaeologist Howard Carter
in the discovery of the tomb of
Tutankhamun (1922).

Carter, Howard (1873–1939)
British archaeologist who made
one of the richest and most celebrated contributions to Egyptology: the discovery of the largely
intact tomb of Tutankhamun.

**Champollion, Jean-François
(1790–1832)** French linguist who
cracked the code of hieroglyphics
when he deciphered the Rosetta
Stone.

Cleopatra (69–30 B.C.)
To be precise, Cleopatra VII,
queen of Egypt and last of the
Ptolemaic line. Defeated by the

Romans, who then absorbed
Egypt into their empire.

Eugénie, Empress (1826–1920)
Wife of Napoleon III and empress
of France (1853–1870) who
was guest of honor at the grand
celebrations for the inauguration
of the Suez Canal.

Farouk (1920–1965)
Playboy king of Egypt, reigning
from 1936 to 1952, when his
administration was brought to an
end by a republican coup.

Ismail Pasha (1830–1895)
Descendant of Muhammad Ali
who ruled Egypt from 1863
to 1879 and presided over the
building of modern Cairo and the
grand celebrations for the inauguration of the Suez Canal.

Lesseps, Ferdinand de (1805–1894)
French diplomat famous
for building the Suez Canal
(1859–1869).

Mahfouz, Naguib (1911–2006)
Egyptian novelist who was
awarded the Nobel Prize for
Literature in 1988.

Mariette, Auguste (1821–1881)
First serving head of the Egyptian
Antiquities Service and founder
of Cairo's Egyptian Museum.

**Mubarak, Muhammad Hosni (born
1928)** Current president of the
Arab Republic of Egypt.

Muhammad Ali (1769–1849)
Albanian mercenary who seized
power in 1805 in the wake of
Napoleon's failed Egyptian expedition, establishing a dynasty that
would rule until toppled by the
1952 republican coup.

Napoleon Bonaparte (1769–1821)
French general who led an army

of soldiers, scientists, and artists
to Egypt (1798–1801). In military
terms the expedition was a failure, but it launched the fledgling
science of Egyptology.

Nasser, Gamal Abdel (1918–1970)
Charismatic army officer who
was one of the ringleaders of
the 1952 coup, prime minister
(1954–56) and then president
(1956–1970) of Egypt.

Nefertari (ca1300–1250 B.C.)
Principal wife of Ramses II, often
depicted at his side.

Nefertiti (ca 1380-1340 B.C.)
Prinicpal wife of Akhenaten.

Ramses II (R.1279–1213 B.C.)
Mightiest of the New Kingdom
pharaohs and a supreme egotist
responsible for some of ancient
Egypt's grandest monuments.

Sadat, Anwar (1918–1981) Succeeded Nasser as Egyptian president and signed the Camp David
peace deal with Israel. Assassinated by Islamic extremists.

Said Pasha (1822–1863) Descendant of Muhammad Ali who
ruled Egypt from 1854 to 1863
and gave the go-ahead for the
construction of the Suez Canal.

Tuthmose III (R.1479–1425 B.C.)
The "Napoleon of Ancient Egypt"
who led numerous successful
military campaigns into Palestine
and Syria.

Umm Kolthum (1904–1975)
The voice of 20th-century Egypt
and the Arab world's most popular singer. Known reverentially as
Al-Sitt, or The Lady.

Cairo Metro Map

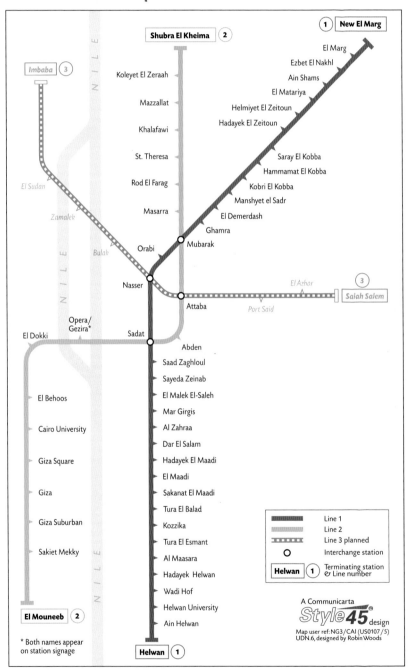

* Both names appear on station signage

INDEX

Bold page numbers indicate illustrations.
CAPS indicates thematic categories.

A

Abdeen Palace, Cairo 79–80
Abdel Rassoul family 265
Abdou, Fifi **59**
Aboudi's Bookshop, Luxor Town 230
Abu al-Abbas al-Mursi Mosque, Alexandria 192
Abu al-Haggag Mosque, Luxor Town 234–35, **237**
Abu Mena 197
Abu Qir 192
Abu Simbel 314–18
 hotels 370–71
 Ramses II colossi **318**
 relocation 313, **313**
 temple 314–18, **316–17**
 Temple of Hathor **314**, 318
Abu Sir (south of Giza) **142**, 142–43
Abu Sir (Western Desert) 196–97
Abydos **222**, 222–23
Activities 379–81
Aga Khan II, Muhammad Shah 300
Aghurmi, Western Desert 200
Agricultural Museum, Cairo 137
Agriculture 22, 24, **25**
Ahmed Shawqi Museum, Cairo 137
Air travel 347–48
Akhenaten (Amenhotep IV) 30–31, 214–17, 241, 387
Akhenaten Museum, Minya 212
Akhmim 221, 377
Al-Abd bakery, Cairo 84
Al-Alamein, Western Desert 197
Al-Aqmar Mosque, Cairo 96, 98
Al-Arish 333
Al-Azhar Mosque, Cairo 91–92, **92, 94–95**
Al-Azhar Park, Cairo 111, **111**
Al-Bagawat, Kharga Oasis **208**, **208**
Al-Din, Hamza 293
Al-Ghouri, Sultan Qansuh 37
Al-Ghouriyya, Cairo 101
Al-Gouna 327
 hotels 373
Al-Hakim Mosque, Cairo 93–95, **102**
Al-Kharga, Kharga Oasis 208
Al-Milga 334
Al-Muayyad Mosque, Cairo 102
Al-Muizz li-Din Allah Street, Cairo 95–96, 98
Al-Muzawaka tombs, Dakhla Oasis 207
Al-Nasir Muhammad Mosque, Cairo 108–9
Al-Qahira *see* Cairo
Al-Qasr, Dakhla Oasis 207
Al-Qusiya 220
Al-Rifai Mosque, Cairo 107
Alcohol 351, 356
Alexander the Great 33, 177, 200–201
Alexandria **11**, 173–92
 Abu Qir 192
 Alexander the Great's tomb 177
 Alexandria National Museum 187, **187**

An-Nabi Daniel Street 186, 189
Anfushi 192
archaeology **178**, 178–79
Attarine Street 186
bars, cafés, and clubs 381
Bibliotheca Alexandrina 188, **188**
bookstalls 189
Catacombs of Kom al-Shuqafa **180**, 180–81
Cecil Hotel 184, **184**, 364
Cinema Metro 186
Constantine Cavafy Museum 186
diving 179
Durrell's House 192, **192**
Eastern Harbor **178**, 178–79
fish market **173**
Fortress of Qaitbey **182**, 182–83
Great Synagogue 185
Greco-Roman Museum 176–77
history 33–34
hotels and restaurants 363–66
introduction 174–75
Kom al-Dikka **176**, 177
Mahmoud Said Museum 190
maps 174–75, 185
Marine Aquarium 183
Marine Life Museum 183
Montazah Palace 191, **191**
Mosque of Abu al-Abbas al-Mursi 192
Mosque of an-Nabi Daniel 186
movie theaters 186
music 383
Mustafa Kamel Necropolis 192
necropolises 192
Pharos Lighthouse 176–77, 183
Pompey's Pillar 181
Ramla Square 184
Roman Theater 186
Royal Jewelry Museum 189
Serapeum 181
Shatby Necropolis 192
shopping 376
Tahrir Square 186
transportation 190, 349
walk 184–86
Alexandria National Museum, Alexandria 187, **187**
Amarna **214**, 214–17, **217**
Amenhotep II 280–81
Amenhotep III **250**, 387
Amenhotep IV *see* Akhenaten (Amenhotep IV)
American University in Cairo 79, 103
Amir Cinema, Alexandria 186
Amr ibn al-As Mosque, Cairo 117
An-Nabi Daniel Mosque, Alexandria 186
An-Nabi Daniel Street, Alexandria 186, 189
Anfushi, Alexandria 192
Anfushi Necropolis, Alexandria 192
Antiques and antiquities
 fakes 231
 looting 77
 shopping 376
 smuggling 231

Antony, Mark 34
AQUARIUMS
 Alexandria 183
 Hurghada 325
Arab identity 21
Arabic language
 alphabet **103**
 glossary 386
 lessons 103
 menu reader 385
 useful phrases 16, 384
Archaeological Museum, Al-Kharga 208
Archaeology, volunteering on a dig 44
Architecture
 contemporary 60–61
 Delta style 167
 Mamluk 37, 98–101
 Nubian 292, **299**
ART GALLERIES AND MUSEUMS *see* MUSEUMS AND GALLERIES
Arts 54–61
 architecture 60–61
 art 60
 belly dancing 58, 59, **59**, 377, 382
 film 57–58
 Islamic 61, 104–5
 literature 54, 56
 music 56–57
 shopping 376
Aswan 294–301
 Aswan Museum 298–99
 bars, cafés, and clubs 382
 Corniche 295
 Elephantine Island 298–99
 Fatimid Cemetery 297
 felucca boats 301
 Ferial Gardens 295
 hotels and restaurants 371–72
 Kitchener's Island 299–300
 Mausoleum of the Aga Khan 300
 Monastery of St. Simeon 300–301
 Nile River and islands 298–300, **300**
 nilometer 299
 Nubian House 297
 Nubian Museum 296–97
 Nubian villages 299, **299**
 Old Cataract Hotel **294**, 295–96, 371
 Sehel Island 300
 souq 295
 Tombs of the Nobles 301
 train service 349
 Unfinished Obelisk 297
Aswan Dam 307
 see also High Dam
Aswan Museum, Aswan 298–99
Aswany, Alaa Al 61
Asyut 218, 220, **220**
 hotels 367
ATMs 351
Attarine Street, Alexandria 186
Auberge du Lac, Fayoum Oasis 152
Automobiles 140, 350
Avenue of Sphinxes, Luxor Town 231, **233**, 234

B

Bab al-Futuh, Cairo 93
Bab al-Nasr, Cairo 93
Bab Zuwayla, Cairo 102
Badr's Museum, Farafra Oasis 206
Bahariyya Oasis, Western Desert **202**, 202–3
  hotels 366
Balat, Dakhla Oasis 207
Ballooning **23**, 268, **269**, 379
Banana Island, Luxor 233
Banking hours 350
Bardawil, Lake 333
Bargaining 87, 89–90
Baron's Palace, Heliopolis 136
Bars, cafés, and clubs 381–82
Bashandi, Dakhla Oasis 207
Basilica of the Transfiguration,
  Monastery of St. Catherine 338
Bawiti, Western Desert 202–3
Bayn al-Qasreen, Cairo 98–101
Bayt al-Suhaymi, Cairo 96, **99**
Bedouin **332**, 335, **340**, 340–41, **341**, 379–80
Begum Aga Khan 300
Belly dancing 58, 59, **59**, 377, 382
Belzoni, Giovanni 77, 315, 387
Ben Ezra Synagogue, Cairo 117
Beni Hasan 212–13
Bent Pyramid, Dahshur 151, **151**
Bible **35**
Bibliotheca Alexandrina, Alexandria 188, **188**
BICYCLE TRIPS
  West Bank **252**, 252–53
Bir al-Ghaba, Western Desert 203
Bir Shalatein 327
Bir Sitta, Western Desert 206
Birding 379
BIRD-WATCHING 152, 154–55, 156
Birqash Camel Market 157
Bishari people 327
Blue Valley 334–35
BOAT TRIPS
  felucca boat to Banana Island,
    Luxor 233
  felucca boats **285**
  felucca boats from Aswan 301, 381
  felucca boats from Luxor 301
  felucca boats in Cairo 81
  ferry to Qanater 158
  glass-bottom boats 325
  Lake Nasser cruises 349
  Nile River cruises **302**, 302–3, 349
  sailing 381
  Sindbad Submarine 325
Books
  recommended reading 354–55
  shopping 85, 189, 376
Bourse, Cairo 83
Breasted, James H. 216
Brooke Animal Hospitals 231
Bubastis 164
Burkhardt, John Lewis 314–15
Burnt Monastery, near Asyut 220
Bus travel 349
Business hours 350

C

Caesar, Julius 33–34
Caesarion 34
  statue **279**

Café Riche, Cairo 82
Cairo 65–138
  Abdeen Palace 79–80
  Agricultural Museum 137
  Ahmed Shawqi Museum 137
  Al-Abd bakery 84
  Al-Aqmar Mosque 96, 98
  Al-Azhar Mosque 91–92, **92, 94–95**
  Al-Azhar Park 111, **111**
  Al-Ghouriyya 101
  Al-Muayyad Mosque 102
  Al-Muizz Ii-Din Allah Street 95–96, 98
  Al-Nasir Muhammad Mosque 108–9
  Al-Rifai Mosque 107
  American University in Cairo 79
  Amr ibn al-As Mosque 117
  Bab al-Futuh 93
  Bab al-Nasr 93
  Bab Zuwayla 102
  bars, cafés, and clubs 381
  Bayn al-Qasreen 98–101
  Bayt al-Suhaymi 96, **99**
  belly dancing 382
  Ben Ezra Synagogue 117
  bookstores 85
  Bourse 83
  bus service 349
  Café Riche 82
  Cairo Marriott Hotel and Omar
    Khayyam Casino 122, **124**, 357
  Cairo Opera House 121, 383
  Cairo Tower 121
  Cairo University **125**, 126
  Cairo Zoo 126–27
  central Cairo **78**, 78–81, **80**
  Child Museum 137
  Church of St. George 114
  Church of St. Sergius 116–17
  Church of the Virgin Mary **114**, 115–16
  Citadel **108**, 108–10
  City of the Dead 110
  Clot Bey Street 85
  coffeehouses 97, **97**
  Coptic Cairo **114**, 114–17, **116**
  Coptic Museum 115
  Cosmopolitan Hotel 83, 359
  daily life 16–17
  downtown **82**, 82–85
  Dr. Ragab's Papyrus Institute 137
  Egyptian Museum **68–76**
  Egyptian National Railways
    Museum 85
  entertainment district 84
  Entomological Society Museum 137–38
  felucca boats 81
  First Residence 127
  Fish Garden 124
  Fishawy's Café 90
  Gayer-Anderson Museum 113
  Gezira **120**, 120–21
  Gezira Art Center 123
  Gezira Club 121, 155
  Groppi 82–83, **84**
  Heliopolis 136, **136**
  history 35–38
  hotels 357–60

Hunting Museum 80
Ibn Tulun Mosque **112**, 112–13
introduction 66–67
Islamic Cairo **86–102**
Jewish community 84, 117
Khan al-Khalili **86**, 87–91, **90**
language schools 103
Madrassa and Mausoleum of al-
  Nasir Muhammad 99
Madrassa and Mausoleum of
  Sultan Qalawun **100**, 99–100
Madrassa of Sultan Barquq 99
Maison Thomas 124
Manyal Palace **80**, 80–81
maps 66–67, 83, 89, 109, 115, 123, 388
metro 79, 349, 388
Mokhtar Museum 120
Monasterli Palace 119
Mosque of Al-Hakim 93–95, **102**
Muhammad Ali Mosque 108
Muhammad Mahmoud Khalil
  Museum 125–26
Museum of Islamic Art **104**, 104–5
music 383
National Military Museum 110
National Museum of Egyptian
  Modern Art 121
National Postal Museum 138
Nile Hilton 79
Nilometer **118**, 118–19
Nomad Gallery 123
northern walls 92–96, 98
October War Museum 138, **138**
Opera Square 84–85
oud lessons 98
Pharaonic Village **126**, 127
Police Museum 109
pyramids **128–35**
Qasr al-Nil Bridge 120
Ramses Square 85
restaurants 360–63
riverboat 117
Sednaoui department store 85
Shaar Hashamaim Synagogue 84
Shepheard's (hotel) 81
shopping 376–78
southern city gate 100–2
Street of the Tentmakers 102
Suleyman Pasha Mosque 110
Sultan Hassan Mosque **106**, 106–7
Taha Hussein Museum 138
Tahrir Square 78–79
taxis 96
train service 81, 349
as travel base 8
Trieste Insurance Building 84
Umm Kolthum Museum 119
walks 82–85, 122–24
western Cairo **125**, 125–27, **126**
Wikala of al-Ghouri 91
Zamalek **122**, 122–24, **124**
Cairo environs 139–58
  Abu Sir **142**, 142–43
  Birqash Camel Market 157
  Dahshur 151, **151**
  Dreamland City 158
  Fayoum Oasis **152**, 152–53
  Golf City 158

hotels 363
introduction 140–41
map 141
Memphis 150, **150**
Qanater 158, **158**
Saqqara 139, **144,** 144–47, **146**
Wadi al-Rayyan 156, **156**
Cairo Marriott Hotel and Omar
Khayyam Casino, Cairo 122, **124,** 357
Cairo Opera House complex, Cairo
121, 383
Cairo Tower, Cairo 121
Cairo University, Cairo **125,** 126
Cairo Zoo, Cairo 126–27
Camels
markets 157, 288
riding tips 147
safaris 205, 335
Valley of the Camels 325
Cameras 10, 352
Camping 356
Car rental 140, 350
Carioca, Tahiyya 59
Carnarvon, Lord 276–77, 387
Carpets and rugs **90,** 376–77
Carter, Howard 253, 273, 276–77, 387
Cartouches 50–51, **51**
Casinos 382–83
Catacombs of Kom al-Shuqafa,
Alexandria **180,** 180–81
Cecil Hotel, Alexandria 184, **184,** 364
Chahine, Yousef 58
Champollion, Jean-François 167,
262, 387
Chapel of the Holy Trinity, Mount
Sinai 337
Charnel House 339
Child Museum, Cairo 137
Children
activities for **126,** 127, 137, 383
Christianity
Coptic 21, 34, **35, 159,** 162–63
Gnosticism 225
history 34
Holy Family sites 218–19
Christie, Agatha 295
CHURCHES
Basilica of the Transfiguration,
Monastery of St. Catherine 338
Chapel of the Holy Trinity, Mount
Sinai 337
Church of St. Anthony 323
Church of St. George, Cairo 114
Church of St. Michael 323
Church of St. Sergius, Cairo
116–17
Church of the Virgin Mary, Cairo
114, 115–16
clothing suggestions 351
St. Paul's Church 323
Cinema 57–58, 84, 186, 355
Cinema Metro, Alexandria 186
Citadel, Cairo **108,** 108–10
City of the Dead, Cairo 110
Cleopatra VII **32,** 33–34, 178–79, 387
Cleopatra's Bath, Western Desert 201
Cleopatra's Needles 185
Climate 346
Clot Bey Street, Cairo 85
Clothes
for church visits 351

for mosque visits 87, 93, 351
packing suggestions 346–47
shopping 377
Clubs 381–82
Coffeehouses 64, 97, **97,** 105
Colossi of Memnon, West Bank **250,**
251, 252, 254
Communications 350
Constantine Cavafy Museum,
Alexandria 186
Consulates 353
Conversion table 351
Coptic Cairo 114–17, **116,** 218, 219
Amr ibn al-As Mosque 117
Ben Ezra Synagogue 117
Church of St. George 114
Church of St. Sergius 116–17
Church of the Virgin Mary **114,**
115–16
Coptic Museum 115
map 115
Coptic Christianity 21, 34, **35, 159,**
162–63
Coptic Museum, Cairo 115
Corals and coral reefs **326,** 328–31,
328–31
Corniche, Aswan 295
Cosmopolitan Hotel, Cairo 83, 359
Credit cards 351, 357
Crocodile Museum, Kom Ombo 291
CRUISES *see* BOAT TRIPS
Crystal Mountain, Western
Desert 204
Currency 10, 347, 351
Customs regulations 347
Cycling tour, West Bank **252,** 252–53

D
Dahab 343–44
hotels 372–73
Dahabiyya (sailboats) 303
Dahshur 151, **151**
Dakhla Oasis, Western Desert 207,
207
hotels and restaurants 366
Dance
belly dancing 58, 59, **59,** 377, 382
folkloric dancing 383
Deir al-Bahri *see* Hatshepsut, Temple
of, West Bank
Deir al-Haggar, Dakhla Oasis 207
Deir al-Kashef, Kharga Oasis 208
Deir al-Medina, West Bank 256–59,
257
tomb paintings **45, 155**
Deir al-Suriani 163
Deir Anba Bishoi 162–63
Deities 44–46, 305
Delta 159–72
Bubastis 164
fishing industry **166**
geography 22
hotels and restaurants 363
introduction 160–61
map 160–61
Port Said **170,** 170–71
rice farm **25**
Rosetta 166–67
sailing trips 381
Tanis 165, **165**
Wadi Natrun **162,** 162–63

Dendara **224,** 224–26
Desert safaris 205, **205,** 335, 379–80
Disabilities, travelers with 353
DIVING AND SNORKELING 380
Alexandria 179
Hurghada 325
Red Sea **328,** 330
Sinai Coast 342–43
south of Safaga 327
tips 343
Djoser, King 145–46
Donkeys **193**
Dr. Ragab's Papyrus Institute,
Cairo 137
Dreamland City 158
Dress code
for church visits 351
for mosque visits 87, 93, 351
packing suggestions 346–47
Driving 140, 350
Durrell, Lawrence 175, 184, 186
home, Alexandria 192, **192**

E
E-mail 350
Eastern Desert 24–25, 325
Eaton, William 197
Edfu **289,** 289–90
Egyptian Museum, Cairo 68–76, 77
artifacts **43, 52, 68, 73, 74, 76**
Central Court 71, **71**
exterior **70**
floor plan 70
mummies 74–75, **239**
Tutankhamun Galleries 75–76
Egyptian National Railways Museum,
Cairo 85
Egyptians 21
Egyptology 278–79
Eid al-Kebir 20
Electricity 350
Elephantine Island 298–99
Embassies 347, 353
Emergencies 353, 384
Empain, Edouard 136
Empereur, Jean Yves 179
Entertainment 379, 381–83
Entomological Society Museum,
Cairo 137–38
Esna 288
Etiquette
clothing suggestions 87, 93, 351
photography 10, 352
Eugénie, Empress (France) 387
EXPERIENCES
Alexandria bookstalls 189
Arabic language lessons 103
Bedouin ecotour in the Sinai 335
belly dancing lessons 58
bird-watching 155
City of the Dead 110
coffee 105
desert safari 205, **205**
diving in Alexandria's harbor 179
fishing on Lake Nasser 311
foods to try 62
Holy Family tours 219
horseback riding in Giza 129
hot-air balloons over Luxor 268
karkadeh (juice) 297
monastery lodgings 163

moulids (street fairs) 164
oud lessons 98
pottery-makers in the Fayoum 153
protecting Red Sea wildlife 327
sailing to Banana Island,
    Luxor 233
sand baths in Siwa 199
see the landscape by boat 24
soccer 137
spirituality tours 132
volunteering on an archaeologi-
    cal dig 44
Wadi al-Gimaal (Valley of the
    Camels) 325
weddings 121

F
Family life 19
Farafra Oasis, Western Desert 206,
    206
    hotels 366–67
Farma (Pelusium) 218, 219, 332–33
Farouk, King 189, 387
Fathy, Hassan 60–61
Fatimid art 105
Fatimid Cemetery, Aswan 297
Fatnas Spring, Western Desert 201
Fax machines 350
Fayoum Oasis **152,** 152–53, 213
Fayoum Portraits 153
Feluccas see BOAT TRIPS
Ferial Gardens, Aswan 295
FESTIVALS AND HOLIDAYS
    Abu al-Haggag 235
    calendar of events 346
    Feast of Shenouda 221
    Feast of the Virgin 220
    national 352
    Opet Festival 236
    Ramadan 20, 346
    religious 20, 352
Fez (hat) 102
First Residence, Cairo 127
Fish Garden, Cairo 124
Fishawy's Café, Cairo 90
Fishing **166,** 310, 311, 380–81
Folkloric dance 383
Food and drink
    alcohol 351
    coffee 105
    cultural influences **63**
    drinks 64
    fruit 127
    karkadeh (juice) 297
    local favorites 62
    overview 62–64
    safety 353
    spices 378
    sweets 64
    useful phrases 384, 385
    see also Restaurants
Fortress of Qaitbey, Alexandria **182,**
    182–83
Fruit 127

G
GARDENS
    Fish Garden, Cairo 124
    Kitchener's Island, Aswan 299–300
    Montazah Palace Gardens,
        Alexandria 191

Gayer-Anderson Museum, Cairo 113
Gebel al-Mawta, Western Desert 201
Gebel Zeit 155
Geography 22–25
Gezira, Cairo **120,** 120–21
Gezira Art Center, Cairo 123
Gezira Club, Cairo 121, 155
Giftun Island 324
Giza
    Great Pyramid of Khufu **2–3,** 128,
        130–34
    horseback riding 129
    Pyramid of Khafre **2–3,** 133
    Pyramid of Menkaura 133–34
    pyramids **2–3, 128**
    site plan 135
    Sphinx **134,** 134–35
    visiting the pyramids 128–34
Gnosticism 225
Goddio, Franck 178
Gods and goddesses 44–46, 305
Golding, William 303
Golf City 158
Golf courses 158, 380
Grand Egyptian Museum, Giza 77
Gratuities 259, 352
Great Pyramid of Khufu **2–3,** 128,
    130–34
Great Sand Sea, Western Desert 201
Great Synagogue, Alexandria 185
Greco-Roman Museum, Alexandria
    176–77
Groppi, Cairo 82–83, **84**
Gurna, West Bank 264–65, **265**
    bike tour 252–53
    wall art **60,** 264, **264**
Gurnawis **209,** 264, **264**

H
Haggling 87, 89–90
Handicrafts 377
Hart, George 240–41
Hatshepsut, Temple of, West Bank
    260, 268–70, **269**
Hawass, Zahi 179, **278,** 279
Health 260, 347, 353
Heliopolis, Cairo 136, **136**
Henna tattoos 293
Hermopolis 216
Herodotus 26
Hieroglyphics **50,** 50–51, 167
High Dam 291, **308,** 308–9, **312,**
    312–13, **313**
History 26–41
    Alexandria and the Ptolemies
        33–34
    Arab Republic of Egypt 40–41
    Cairo (Al-Qahira) 35–38
    Muhammad Ali 38–39
    Napoleon 38
    pharaonic culture 42–53
    pyramid builders 26–29
    Suez Canal 39–40
    Thebes and Karnak 29–33
    who's who 387
HOLIDAYS
    see FESTIVALS AND HOLIDAYS
Holy Family 218–19, 220
Horemheb **48–49,** 281–82
Horseback riding 129
Horus (deity) **155**

Hostels 356
Hot-air balloons **23,** 268, **269,** 379
Hot springs 203, 206
Hotels 356–75
    accommodations 356
    Alexandria 363–64
    Aswan **294,** 295–96
    Cairo 357–60
    Cairo environs 363
    Delta and Suez Canal 363
    Luxor 368–70
    Middle Egypt 367–68
    monastery stays 163
    rates 356
    Red Sea and Sinai 372–75
    South of Luxor 370–72
    Western Desert 366–67
Howard Carter's House, West Bank
    253
Hulsman, Cornelis 219
Hunting Museum, Cairo 80
Hurghada **324,** 324–25
    hotels and restaurants 373
Hussein, Taha 138

I
Ibn Tulun Mosque, Cairo **112,** 112–13
Idfu *see* Edfu
Imhotep (high priest and architect) 145
Imhotep Museum, Saqqara 147
Information, tourist 352
Inoculations 353
Insurance, travel 347
Internet 350, 352
Isis (deity) 305
Islam 19–20, **20–21,** 34–35
Islamic Cairo 86–102, **88**
    Al-Aqmar Mosque 96, 98
    Al-Azhar Mosque 91–92, **92,**
        94–95
    Al-Ghouriyya 101
    Al-Muayyad Mosque 102
    Al-Muizz li-Din Allah Street
        95–96, 98
    Bab al-Futuh 93
    Bab al-Nasr 93
    Bab Zuwayla 102
    Bayn al-Qasreen 98–101
    Bayt al-Suhaymi 96, **99**
    Fishawy's Café 90
    introduction 86–87
    Khan al-Khalili **86,** 87–91, **90**
    Madrassa and Mausoleum of al-
        Nasir Muhammad 99
    Madrassa and Mausoleum of
        Sultan Qalawun **100,** 99–100
    Madrassa of Sultan Barquq 99
    map 89
    Mosque of Al-Hakim 93–95, **102**
    northern walls 92–96, 98
    oud lessons 98
    planning your visit 87
    southern city gate 100–2
    Street of the Tentmakers 102
    Wikala of al-Ghouri 91
Ismail Pasha 39, 82, 387
Ismailia 172, **172**
    hotels and restaurants 363
Ismailia Museum, Ismailia 172
Isna *see* Esna
Itineraries 8–11

J
Jed-Khenso-Iufankh, King 203
Jewelry 378

K
Karanis, Fayoum Oasis 152–53
Karkadeh (juice) 297
Karnak, Luxor 232, 242–49
    Cachette Court 248–49
    Festival Temple of Tuthmose
       III 248
    Great Hypostyle Hall **27, 242,** 246
    history 29–33
    introduction 242–43
    Obelisks of Hatshepsut 247
    Precinct of Amun **242,** 243,
       245–48
    Precincts of Mut and Montu
       248–49
    Ramses II colossus **247**
    Sacred Bark Shrine 247
    Sacred Lake 248, **248**
    site plan **244–45**
    sound-and-light show 246
    Temple of Ptah 249
    visiting tips 243
Khaemwaset 259
Khan al-Khalili, Cairo **86,** 87–91,
  90, 376
Kharga Oasis, Western Desert 208
    hotels 367
Khufu (Cheops) **149**
Kiosk of Qertassi 309
Kiosk of Trajan, Philae 307, **307**
Kitchener, Lord Horatio 299
Kitchener's Island, Aswan 299–300
Kolthum, Umm **56,** 56–57, 119, 387
Kom al-Dikka **176,** 177
Kom Ombo 291, **291**
Kom Oshim 152–53
Kuban, Ali Hassan 293
KV 5 (tomb), Valley of the Kings
  277, 279

L
Language *see* Arabic language
Lesseps, Ferdinand des 168–69, 387
  house 172, **172**
Libraries
    Bibliotheca Alexandrina 188, **188**
Liquor laws 351
Literature 54, 56, 354–55
Lost property 353
Luxor 227–84
    antiquities 231
    bars, cafés, and clubs 382
    boat trips 233, 301
    cycling trips 252–53
    folkloric dance 383
    food and drink **4, 345,** 382
    history of Thebes 29–33
    hot-air balloons 268, **269,** 379
    hotels and restaurants 368–70
    introduction 228–29
    Karnak **242–49**
    Luxor Town **230–37, 240,**
      240–41
    maps 228–29, 232, 253
    shopping **345,** 377
    train service 349

Valley of the Kings **271–73, 276,**
  276–77, **281–83**
    West Bank **250–63, 266–69**
Luxor Museum, Luxor Town 231, **240,**
  240–41
Luxor Temple, Luxor Town 230,
  233–37, **235**
    Bark Shrine 237
    central sanctuary 237
    grand processional colonnade
      236
    Great Court of Ramses II 234
    hypostyle hall 236
    Opet Festival 236
    site plan 234
    Sun Court of Amenhotep III 236
Luxor Town **230–37, 240,** 240–41
    Aboudi's Bookshop 230
    Avenue of Sphinxes 231, **233,** 234
    festivals 235, 236
    Karnak 232
    Luxor Museum 231, **240,** 240–41
    Luxor Temple 230, 233–37, **235**
    Luxor Wena Hotel 231
    map 232
    Mosque of Abu al-Haggag
      234–35, **237**
    Mummification Museum 231, 239
    Winter Palace Hotel 230, **230,** 368
Luxor Wena Hotel, Luxor Town 231

M
Maadi 218
Madrassa and Mausoleum of al-Nasir
  Muhammad, Cairo 99
Madrassa and Mausoleum of Sultan
  Qalawun, Cairo **100,** 99–100
Madrassa of Sultan Barquq, Cairo 99
Mahfouz, Naguib 54, 56, 90, 387
Mahmoud Said Museum,
  Alexandria 190
Mail service 350
Maison Thomas, Cairo 124
Malaria 353
Malls, shopping 378
Mamluks 35–37, 98–101
MANSIONS AND PALACES
    Abdeen Palace, Cairo 79–80
    Baron's Palace, Heliopolis 136
    Bayt al-Suhaymi, Cairo 96, **99**
    Manyal Palace, Cairo **80,** 80–81
    Montazah Palace and Gardens,
      Alexandria 191, **191**
    Ramadan House, Rosetta 167
    Uruba Palace, Heliopolis 136
Manyal Palace, Cairo **80,** 80–81
Maps
    Alexandria 174–75, 185
    Cairo 66–67, 83, 89, 109, 115,
      123, 388
    Cairo environs 141
    Luxor 228–29, 232, 253
    Luxor Town 232
    Middle Egypt 211
    Nile Delta 160–61
    Port Said 171
    Red Sea and Sinai 321
    South of Luxor 287, 296
    Suez Canal 160–61, 171
    West Bank, Luxor 253
    Western Desert 195

Mariette, Auguste 77, 144, 147, 387
Marsa Matruh 198, **198**
    hotels 367
Mashrabiyya windows **99,** 104–5
Maspero, Gaston 295
Mastaba of Ti, Saqqara 147
Matariyya 218
Mausoleum of the Aga Khan, Aswan
  300
Medicine and health 260, 347, 353
Medinat Habu, West Bank **254,**
  254–56
Mediterranean Coast **196,** 196–97
Memphis 28–29, 150, **150**
Menes 28
Menkaura **52**
Merenptah 282–83
Metaphysical tourism 132
Metro, Cairo 79
    map 388
Middle Egypt 209–26
    Abydos **222,** 222–23
    Amarna **214,** 214–17, **217**
    Asyut 220, **220**
    Dendara **224,** 224–26
    hotels 367–68
    introduction 210–11
    map 211
    Minya **212,** 212–13
    police escorts 213
    Sohag 221, **221**
Middle Kingdom 29–30
Military Museum, Port Said 170
Minya **212,** 212–13
    hotels 367–68
Mit Rahina 150
Mokhtar Museum, Cairo 120
MONASTERIES 162–63
    Burnt Monastery, near Asyut 220
    Monastery of the Syrians 163
    Monastery of the Virgin, near
      Asyut 220
    overnight stays 163
    Red Monastery, near Sohag 221
    St. Anthony **322,** 322–23
    St. Bishoi 162–63
    St. Catherine 337–39, **338–39**
    St. Paul 322, 323
    St. Simeon, Aswan 300–301
    White Monastery, near Sohag
      218, 221, **221**
Monasterli Palace, Cairo 119
Money
    ATMs 351
    banking hours 350
    credit cards 351, 357
    currency 10, 347, 351
Mons Claudianus 326
Mons Porphyritis 327
Montazah Palace and Gardens,
  Alexandria 191, **191**
Montet, Pierre 278–79
Montgomery, Bernard 197, 198
MOSQUES
    Abu al-Abbas al-Mursi Mosque,
      Alexandria 192
    Abu al-Haggag Mosque, Luxor
      Town 234–35, **237**
    Al-Aqmar Mosque, Cairo 96, 98
    Al-Azhar Mosque, Cairo 91–92,
      92, 94–95

Al-Hakim Mosque, Cairo 93–95, **102**
Al-Muayyad Mosque, Cairo 102
Al-Nasir Muhammad Mosque, Cairo 108–9
Al-Rifai Mosque, Cairo 107
Amr ibn al-As Mosque, Cairo 117
An-Nabi Daniel Mosque, Alexandria 186
clothing suggestions 87, 93, 351
decorative arts 61
etiquette 87, 93
Ibn Tulun Mosque, Cairo **112,** 112–13
Monastery of St. Catherine 339
Muhammad Ali Mosque, Cairo 108
Suleyman Pasha Mosque, Cairo 110
Sultan Hassan Mosque, Cairo **106,** 106–7
Mostorod 218
Moulids (street fairs) 164
Mount Sinai **336,** 336–37
Movies 57–58, 84, 186, 355
Mubarak, Hosni 41, 387
Muhammad Ali 38–39
Muhammad Ali Mosque, Cairo 108
Muhammad Ali Tewfik, Prince 80
Muhammad Mahmoud Khalil Museum, Cairo 125–26
Mummies
  animals 74, 146–147, 164, 203, 239
  children **238**
  in the Egyptian Museum, Cairo 74–75, **239**
  mummification 238–39
  Valley of the Golden Mummies, Western Desert 203
Mummification Museum, Luxor Town 231, 239
Museum of Islamic Art, Cairo **104,** 104–5

MUSEUMS AND GALLERIES
  Agricultural Museum, Cairo 137
  Ahmed Shawqi Museum, Cairo 137
  Akhenaten Museum, Minya 212
  Al-Arish Museum, al-Arish 333
  Alexandria National Museum, Alexandria 187, **187**
  Archaeological Museum, Al-Kharga 208
  Aswan Museum, Aswan 298–99
  Badr's Museum, Farafra Oasis 206
  Child Museum, Cairo 137
  Constantine Cavafy Museum, Alexandria 186
  Coptic Museum, Cairo 115
  Crocodile Museum 291
  Dr. Ragab's Papyrus Institute, Cairo 137
  Egyptian Museum, Cairo **68–76**
  Egyptian National Railways Museum, Cairo 85
  Entomological Society Museum, Cairo 137–38
  Gayer-Anderson Museum, Cairo 113

Gezira Art Center, Cairo 123
Grand Egyptian Museum, Giza 77
Greco-Roman Museum, Alexandria 176–77
Hunting Museum, Cairo 80
Imhotep Museum, Saqqara 147
Ismailia Museum, Ismailia 172
Luxor Museum, Luxor Town 231, **240,** 240–41
Mahmoud Said Museum, Alexandria 190
Marine Life Museum, Alexandria 183
Military Museum, Port Said 170
Mokhtar Museum, Cairo 120
Muhammad Mahmoud Khalil Museum, Cairo 125–26
Mummification Museum, Luxor Town 231, 239
Museum of Islamic Art, Cairo **104,** 104–5
National Military Museum, Cairo 110
National Museum of Egyptian Modern Art, Cairo 121
National Postal Museum, Cairo 138
Nomad Gallery, Cairo 123
Nubian Museum, Aswan 296–97
October War Museum, Cairo 138, **138**
Police Museum, Cairo 109
Port Said National Museum, Port Said 170
Rosetta Museum, Rosetta 167
Royal Jewelry Museum, Alexandria 189
Siwan House Museum, Siwa 200
Taha Hussein Museum, Cairo 138
Umm Kolthum Museum, Cairo 119
Music and musicians
  Nubian culture 292–93
  oud lessons 98
  shopping 57
  traditional **55**
  Umm Kolthum **56,** 56–57, 387
  venues 383
Muslims 19–21, **20–21,** 34–35
Mustafa Kamel Necropolis 192
Mut, Dakhla Oasis 207

N
Naama Bay 342–43
Nag Hammadi 225
Napoleon Bonaparte **36–37,** 38, 77, **77,** 387
Narmer, King 26, 28
Nasser, Gamal Abdel 40–41, **41,** 387
Nasser, Lake **310,** 310–11
  cruises 349
  fishing 310, 311, 380–81
National Military Museum, Cairo 110
National Museum of Egyptian Modern Art, Cairo 121
National Postal Museum, Cairo 138
Necropolis of al-Bagawat, Kharga Oasis 208, **208**
Necropolises, Alexandria 192
Nefertari, Queen **227,** 387
  tomb **258,** 260–62, **261**

Nefertiti, Queen 387
New Gurna, West Bank 252, 265
New Kingdom 30–33
Newspapers 351
Nightlife 381–82
Nile Delta *see* Delta
Nile Hilton, Cairo 79
Nile River
  in ancient Egypt 34
  Aswan area islands 298–300, **300**
  Aswan boat trips 301, 381
  Cairo boat trips 81, 117, 158
  cruises **302,** 302–3, 349
  flooding 118–19
  geography 22
  Luxor boat trips 233, 301
  women washing clothes **210**
NILOMETERS
  Aswan 299
  Cairo **118,** 118–19
  Edfu 290
Nomad Gallery, Cairo 123
North Pyramid, Dahshur 151
Nubian culture 291, **292,** 292–93, **293**
Nubian Dynasty 249
Nubian House, Aswan 297
Nubian Museum, Aswan 296–97
Nubian villages, Aswan 299, **299**
Nuweiba 344
  hotels 373–74
Nyuserra 143

O
OBELISKS 298
  Cleopatra's Needles 185
  Obelisks of Hatshepsut 247
  Unfinished Obelisk, Aswan 297
Octavian, Emperor 34
October War Museum, Cairo 138, **138**
Old Cataract Hotel, Aswan **294,** 295–96, 371
Old Gurna, West Bank *see* Gurna, West Bank
Old Kingdom 29
Online services 350
Opera Square, Cairo 84–85
Opet Festival 236
Osiris (deity) 305
Oud (musical instrument) 98
"Ozymandias" (Shelley) 256

P
Package tours 348
Packing tips 346–47
PALACES *see* MANSIONS AND PALACES
Papyrus 69, 378
Passports and visas 347
Pelusium 218, 219, 332–33
Perfume 378
Pharaonic culture 42–53
  hieroglyphs and cartouches 50–51
  overview 26, 28–29
  religion 42–49
  temples 46–50
  timeline 52–53
  tomb art 49–50
Pharaonic Village, Cairo **126,** 127
Pharmacies 347

Pharos Lighthouse, Alexandria 176–77, 183
Philae **304,** 304–7, **307**
 Kiosk of Trajan 307, **307**
 site plan 306
 sound-and-light show 307
 Temple of Hathor 306–7
 Temple of Isis 305–6
Photography 10, 352
Place of the Dead, Minya 212, **212**
Police escorts 213
Police Museum, Cairo 109
Pompey's Pillar, Alexandria 181
Port Said **170,** 170–71
 hotels and restaurants 363
 map 171
Port Said National Museum, Port Said 170
Post offices 350
Pottery 153
Ptolemaic dynasty 33–34
Ptolemaic temple, Deir al-Medina 258–59
Ptolemy XIII 33–34
Public transportation *see* Transportation
PYRAMIDS
 Abu Sir **142,** 142–43
 Bent Pyramid, Dahshur 151, **151**
 builders 148–49
 cut-away view **130–31**
 Dahshur 151, **151**
 excavations **148**
 Fayoum Oasis 153
 Giza **2–3, 128–35**
 Great Pyramid of Khufu **2–3,** 128, **130–34**
 history 29
 inner passage **133**
 introduction 128
 mysteries 134
 Pyramid of Khafre **2–3,** 133
 Pyramid of Meidum, Fayoum Oasis 153
 Pyramid of Menkaura 133–34
 Pyramid of Neferirkare 143
 Pyramid of Nyuserra 143
 Saqqara 144–46
 Step Pyramid, Saqqara **144,** 145, **146**
 visiting 128–34

Q
Qaitbey Fortress, Alexandria **182,** 182–83
Qanater 158, **158**
Qaran, Lake 152, **152**
Qasr al-Dush, Kharga Oasis 208
Qasr al-Ghueita, Kharga Oasis 208
Qasr al-Nil Bridge, Cairo 120
Qasr al-Zayyan, Kharga Oasis 208
Qasr Ibrim 311
Qasr Qarun, Fayoum Oasis 152
Quseir 327
 hotels 374

R
Radio 351
Rail travel 81, 348–49
Ramadan 20, 346

Ramadan House, Rosetta 167
Ramesseum, West Bank 252, 262–63, **263**
 site plan 262
Ramses II 31–32, 315, 387
 Ramesseum, West Bank **262,** 262–63, **263**
 statues 85, 150, **150, 165,** 234, **235, 312, 318**
Ramses III 283
Ramses IV 283–84
Ramses VI **276,** 284
Ramses IX 284
Ramses Square, Cairo 85
Ramses Station, Cairo 81
Ras Muhammad 343
Reading, recommended 354–55
Red Monastery, near Sohag 221
Red Sea and Sinai 319–44
 bars, cafés, and clubs 382
 Bir Shalatein 327
 diving 380
 hotels and restaurants 372–75
 Hurghada **324,** 324–25
 introduction 320
 map 321
 Monasteries of St. Anthony and St. Paul **322,** 322–23
 Monastery of St. Catherine 337–39, **338–39**
 Mount Sinai 336–37
 northern Sinai **332,** 332–33
 reef life **319, 328,** 328–31, **328–31**
 Sinai Coast **342,** 342–44
 south of Hurghada 326–27
 southern Sinai **334,** 334–35
Red Sea Aquarium, Hurghada 325
Religions
 Coptic Christianity 21, 34, **35, 159,** 162–63
 holidays 20, 352
 Islam 19–20, **20–21,** 34–35
 overview 19–21
 pharaonic 42, 44–46
 Sufism 101
 see also Churches; Mosques; Synagogues
Rest rooms 352
Restaurants 356–75
 alcohol 356
 Alexandria 365–66
 Cairo 360–63
 Delta and Suez Canal 363
 introduction 356–57
 Luxor 370
 menu reader 385
 Red Sea and Sinai 372–75
 seafood 186
 South of Luxor 370–72
 useful phrases 384
 Western Desert 366–67
 see also Food and drink
Roda (island) 118
Roman Theater, Alexandria 186
Rommel, Erwin 197, 198
Rosetta 166–67
Rosetta Museum, Rosetta 167
Rosetta Stone 167
Royal Jewelry Museum, Alexandria 189

S
Sadat, Anwar 41, 387
Safaga 326
Safaris, desert 205, **205,** 335, 379–80
Safety
 food and water 353
 police escorts 213
 for women travelers 11, 351
Sahure, King 142
Said, Mahmoud 190
Said Pasha 77, 387
Sa'idis 241
Sailing 381
St. Anthony (church) 323
St. Anthony's Cave 323
St. Catherine 334
 hotels 375
St. Catherine Protectorate 334, 335
St. George, Cairo 114
St. Michael (church) 323
St. Paul's Church 323
St. Sergius, Cairo 116–17
Saint-Saëns, Camille 80
Sakha 218
Sand baths 199
Sand dunes 201
Saqqara **139,** 144–47
 archaeology 279
 Imhotep Museum 147
 Mastaba of Ti 147
 Philosophers' Circle 147
 Pyramid of Teti 146
 Pyramid of Unas 146
 Serapeum 146–47
 site plan 145
 Step Pyramid **144,** 145–46, **146**
 Tomb of Ankh-ma-Hor 146
 Tomb of Mereruka 146
 tomb paintings 146
Scarabs **8**
SCUBA DIVING *see* DIVING AND SNORKELING
Sednaoui department store, Cairo 85
Sehel Island, Aswan 300
Selket **43**
Serabit al-Khadim 335
Serapeum, Alexandria 181
Serapeum, Saqqara 146–47
Seti I
 temple 270
 tomb 274–75, **274–75, 281,** 282
Sèves, Joseph 38
Sexual harassment 11
Shaar Hashamaim Synagogue, Cairo 84
Shali (ruins), Siwa Oasis 199–200
Shamma, Naseer 98
Sharif, Omar 58
Sharm al-Sheikh 342–43, **344**
 hotels and restaurants 374–75
Shatby Necropolis 192
Shawqi, Ahmed 137
Sheeshas (water-pipes) 124
Shelley, Percy Bysshe 256, 262
Shepherd's (hotel), Cairo 81
Shopping 376–78
 antiques and antiquities 376
 art 376
 books 85, 189, 376
 carpets **90,** 376–77
 clothing 377
 haggling 87, 89–90

handicrafts 377
jewelry 378
Khan al-Khalili, Cairo **86,** 87–91, **90,** 376
malls 378
markets and bazaars 124
music 57
papyrus 69, 378
perfume 378
souvenirs 378
spices 378
store hours 350
Street of the Tentmakers, Cairo 102
textiles 221
useful phrases 384
what to buy 91
Sinai Peninsula
Bedouin 335, **340,** 340–41, **341**
desert safaris 379–80
ecotours 335
geography 25
introduction 320
map 321
Monastery of St. Catherine 337–39, **338–39**
Mount Sinai **336,** 336–37
Northern Sinai **332,** 332–33
shopping 377
Sinai Coast **342,** 342–44
Southern Sinai **334,** 334–35
Siwa, Western Desert 199–201, **200**
crafts **199,** 201
hotels 367
sand baths 199
Siwa House Museum, Siwa 200
Smoking 124
Sneferu, Pharaoh 151
Snorkeling 330
Soccer 137, 383
Sohag 221, **221**
hotels 368
SOUND-AND-LIGHT SHOWS 383
Karnak 246
Philae 307
Souq, Aswan 295
South of Hurghada 326–27
South of Luxor 285–318
Abu Simbel **314,** 314–18, **316–17, 318**
Aswan **294,** 294–301, **299, 300**
Edfu **289,** 289–90
Esna 288
High Dam 291, **308,** 308–9
hotels and restaurants 370–72
introduction 286
Kom Ombo 291, **291**
Lake Nasser **310,** 310–11
maps 287, 296
Philae **304,** 304–7, **307**
Souvenirs 378
Speos Artemidos (temple) 213
Sphinx **134,** 134–35
Spices 378
Spirituality 132
Spoonbills **154**
Sports 137, 383
Squash (sport) 383
Stamps, postage 350
Step Pyramid, Saqqara **144,** 145, **146**
Storytelling 54

Street of the Tentmakers, Cairo 102
Suez Canal 160–61, 168–72, 308
construction **169**
hotels and restaurants 363
introduction 160–61
Ismailia 172, **172**
maps 160–61, 171
nationalization 40
opening celebration **168,** 169
Port Said **170,** 170–71
Suez Canal House, Port Said **170,** 171
Suez Crisis 40, 308
Sufism 101
Suleyman Pasha Mosque, Cairo 110
Sultan Hassan Mosque, Cairo **106,** 106–7
Sun safety 353
SYNAGOGUES
Ben Ezra Synagogue, Cairo 117
Great Synagogue, Alexandria 185
Shaar Hashamaim Synagogue, Cairo 84

T
Taba 344
Taba Heights 344
Taha Hussein Museum, Cairo 138
Tahrir Square, Alexandria 186
Tahrir Square, Cairo 78–79
Tanis 76, 165, **165**
Tanta 164
Tarboosh (hat) 101
Taxis 96, 348
Telephones 350
Television 351
Tell al-Amarna *see* Amarna
TEMPLES
Abu Simbel **314,** 314–18, **316–17, 318**
Abydos **222,** 222–23
in ancient Egypt 46–50
architecture **46–47**
Dakhla Oasis 207
Deir al-Medina 258–59
Dendara **224,** 224–26, **226**
Edfu **289,** 289–90
Esna 288
Fayoum Oasis 152
Karnak 242–49
Kharga Oasis 208
Kom Ombo 291
Lake Nasser 309, 311
Luxor 265, 268–70, **269,** 270
Medinat Habu 254–56
Minya 213
Philae 305–7
Serabit al-Khadim 335
Siwa Oasis 200, 201
Theban Hills 23
Thebes *see* Luxor
THEME PARKS
Dreamland City 158
Pharaonic Village, Cairo **126,** 127
Theophilus 218, 219
Thoth (deity) 216
Time differences 352
Tipping 259, 352
Toilets 352
TOMB ART 49–50, 274–75
Al-Qusiya 220

Amarna 215–16
Beni Hasan 212–13
Deir al-Medina **45, 155,** 257–58
Gebel al-Mawta 201
Hermopolis 217
Saqqara 146
Tombs of the Nobles **266,** 266–68
Valley of the Kings **48–49, 274–75, 276,** 280–84, **281**
Valley of the Queens **258,** 259–61, **261**
TOMBS
Abu Sir (south of Giza) **142,** 142–43
Al-Muzawaka, Dakhla Oasis 207
Al-Qusiya 220
Amarna 215–16
Anfushi Necropolis, Alexandria 192
Aswan 257–58, 301
Bahariyya Oasis **202,** 202–3
Beni Hasan 212–13
Bubastis 164
Catacombs of Kom al-Shuqafa, Alexandria **180,** 180–81
Deir al-Medina **45, 155,** 257–58
discoveries 277
funerary offerings **48–49,** 49, 75, 239, 272
Gebel al-Mawta 201
Hermopolis 216
Mausoleum of the Aga Khan, Aswan 300
Minya 212, **212**
Mustafa Kamel Necropolis 192
Necropolis of al-Bagawat, Kharga Oasis 208, **208**
Necropolises, Alexandria 192
Saqqara 146
Shatby Necropolis 192
Tanis 165
tomb building 274–75
Tomb of Ankh-ma-Hor 146
Tomb of Inherkhau **155,** 257
Tomb of Jed-Khenso-Iufankh 203
Tomb of Mereruka 146
Tomb of Peshedu 258
Tomb of Sennedjem **45,** 257–58
Tomb of Sirenput II 301
tomb of workers 257–58
Tombs of the Nobles **266,** 266–68, 301
Valley of the Golden Mummies 203
Valley of the Kings **48–49,** 271–84
Valley of the Queens **258,** 259–62, **261**
Tourist offices 352
Tozzi, Anna 110
Trains 348–49
Transportation
air travel 347–48
Alexandria tram system 190
buses 349
Cairo metro 79, 388
driving 140, 350
trains 348–49
useful phrases 384

Travel insurance 347
Trianon, Alexandria 184–85
Trieste Insurance Building, Cairo 84
Tuna al-Gebel 216–17
Tutankhamun
  artifacts **8, 30–31, 43, 68,** 69, 75–76, **76**
  history 31
  tomb 273, **273,** 276–77, 280
Tuthmose I 30
Tuthmose III 280, 387
Tuthmose IV 281
Twain, Mark 64, 303

U

Umm Kolthum **56,** 56–57, 387
Umm Kolthum Museum, Cairo 119
Underwater archaeology **178,** 178–79
Unfinished Obelisk, Aswan 297
Upper Egyptians **13**
Uruba Palace, Heliopolis 136

V

Valley of the Camels 325
Valley of the Golden Mummies, Western Desert 203
Valley of the Kings **271,** 271–84, **283, 284**
  site plan 272
  tickets 272–73
  tomb art **48–49**
  Tomb KV 5 277, 279
  Tomb of Amenhotep II 280–81
  Tomb of Horemheb 281–82
  Tomb of Merenptah 282–83
  Tomb of Ramses III 283
  Tomb of Ramses IV 283–84
  Tomb of Ramses VI **276,** 284
  Tomb of Ramses IX 284
  Tomb of Seti I 274–75, **274–75, 281,** 282
  Tomb of Tutankhamun 273, **273,** 276–77, 280
  Tomb of Tuthmose III 280
  Tomb of Tuthmose IV 281
Valley of the Queens 259–62
  Tomb of Amunherkhepshep 259–260
  Tomb of Khaemwaset 259
  Tomb of Nefertari **258,** 260–62, **261**
  Tomb of Titi 260
Videotaping 10, 352
Visas and passports 347
Volunteer opportunities 44

W

Wadi al-Gimaal 325
Wadi al-Rayyan 156, **156**
Wadi al-Sebua 310–11
Wadi Arbaeen 334
Wadi Feiran 335
Wadi Hennes, Western Desert 204
Wadi Mukattab 335
Wadi Natrun **162,** 162–63
WALKS
  Alexandria 184–86
  Cairo 82–85, 122–24

Water-pipes *see Sheeshas* (water-pipes)
Weather 9
Weaving 221
Weddings 121, 293
Weeks, Kent 277, 279
West Bank, Luxor 250–63, 266–70
  Colossi of Memnon **250,** 251, 252, 254
  cycling tour **252,** 252–53
  Deir al-Medina 256–59, **257**
  Gurna 252–53
  hot-air balloons 268, **269,** 379
  Howard Carter's House 253
  introduction 250–51
  map 253
  Medinat Habu **254,** 254–56
  New Gurna 252
  Old Gurna 252
  Ramesseum 252, 262–63, **263**
  Temple of Hatshepsut 268–70, **269**
  Temple of Seti I 270
  ticket information 251
  Tombs of the Nobles **266,** 266–68
  Valley of the Kings **271,** 271–84, **283, 284**
  Valley of the Queens **258,** 259–62, **261**
Western Desert 193–208
  Abu Mena (site) 197
  Abu Sir 196–97
  Aghurmi 200
  Al-Alamein 197
  Bahariyya Oasis **202,** 202–3
  Bawiti 202–3
  Bir al-Ghaba 203
  Bir Sitta 206
  Cleopatra's Bath 201
  Crystal Mountain 204
  Dakhla Oasis 207, **207**
  donkey **193**
  Farafra Oasis 206, **206**
  Fatnas Spring 201
  Gebel al-Mawta 201
  geography 24
  Great Sand Sea 201
  hotels and restaurants 366–67
  introduction 194
  Kharga Oasis 208
  map 195
  Marsa Matruh 198, **198**
  Mediterranean Coast **196,** 196–97
  Necropolis of al-Bagawat **208**
  safaris 205, **205,** 379–80
  Siwa Oasis **199,** 199–201, **200**
  Temple of Amun 201
  Temple of the Oracle 200
  Valley of the Golden Mummies 203
  Wadi Hennes 204
  White Desert 204, **204, 205**
Whirling Dervishes 101
White Desert, Western Desert 204, **204, 205**
White Monastery, near Sohag **218,** 221, **221**
Wikala of al-Ghouri, Cairo 91
WILDLIFE-VIEWING
  Wadi al-Rayyan 156

Winter Palace Hotel, Luxor Town 230, **230,** 368
Women, Egyptian 19, **99,** 104–5
Women travelers 11, 351
Workers' Village, Deir al-Medina 256–57

Y

Yousef, Hany Halim 110

Z

Zaghloul, Saad 184
Zamalek, Cairo **122,** 122–24, **124**
  map 123
Zaranik Protectorate 333
Zawiyyet al-Mayyiteen 212, **212**
ZOOS
  Cairo Zoo 126–27

ILLUSTRATIONS CREDITS

National Geographic
TRAVELER
Egypt

Published by the National Geographic Society
John M. Fahey, Jr., *President
and Chief Executive Officer*
Gilbert M. Grosvenor, *Chairman of the Board*
Tim T. Kelly, *President, Global Media Group*
John Q. Griffin, *Executive Vice President;
President, Publishing*
Nina D. Hoffman, *Executive Vice President;
President, Book Publishing Group*

Prepared by the Book Division
Barbara Brownell Grogan, *Vice President and Editor in Chief*
Barbara A. Noe, *Senior Editor*
Marianne R. Koszorus, *Director of Design*
Carl Mehler, *Director of Maps*
R. Gary Colbert, *Production Director*
Jennifer A. Thornton, *Managing Editor*
Meredith C. Wilcox, *Administrative Director, Illustrations*
Cinda Rose, *Series Art Director*

Staff for 2009 Edition:
Brooke C. Stoddard, *Project Editor*
Kay Kabor Hankins, *Art Director*
Jennifer Frink, *Designer*
Paula Kelly, *Text Editor*
Michael McNey, Nicholas P. Rosenbach, and Mapping
Specialists, *Map Production*
Al Morrow, *Design Assistant*
Richard Wain, *Production Project Manager*
Rob Waymouth, *Illustrations Specialist*
Connie Binder, *Indexer*
Bridget A. English, Susan Hannan, Maura Walsh,
Contributors

Manufacturing and Quality Management
Christopher A. Liedel, *Chief Financial Officer*
Phillip L. Schlosser, *Vice President*
Chris Brown, *Technical Director*
Nicole Elliott, *Manager*
Rachel Faulise, *Manager*

First edition: Edited and designed by AA Publishing
(a trading name of Automobile Association Developments Limited, whose registered office is Norfolk House,
Priestley Road, Basingstoke, Hampshire, England RG24
9NY. Registered number: 1878835).

Area map illustrations drawn by Chris Orr Associates,
Southampton, England.
Cutaway illustrations drawn by Maltings Partnership,
Derby, England.

The National Geographic Society is one of the
world's largest nonprofit scientific and educational
organizations. Founded in 1888 to "increase and
diffuse geographic knowledge," the Society works
to inspire people to care about the planet. It
reaches more than 325 million people worldwide
each month through its official journal, *National
Geographic*, and other magazines; National
Geographic Channel; television documentaries;
music; radio; films; books; DVDs; maps; exhibitions;
school publishing programs; interactive media;
and merchandise. National Geographic has funded
more than 9,000 scientific research, conservation
and exploration projects and supports an education
program combating geographic illiteracy. For more
information, visit nationalgeographic.com.

For more information, please call 1-800-NGS LINE
(647-5463) or write to the following address:

National Geographic Society
1145 17th Street N.W.
Washington, D.C. 20036-4688 U.S.A.

Visit us online at www.nationalgeographic.com

For information about special discounts for bulk
purchases, please contact National Geographic
Books Special Sales: ngspecsales@ngs.org

For rights or permissions inquiries, please contact
National Geographic Books Subsidiary Rights:
ngbookrights@ngs.org

National Geographic Traveler: Egypt (Third Edition)
ISBN: 978-1-4262-0521-7

Printed in China

The information in this book has been carefully
checked and to the best of our knowledge is accurate.
However, details are subject to change, and the
National Geographic Society cannot be responsible for
such changes, or for errors or omissions. Assessments
of sites, hotels, and restaurants are based on the
author's subjective opinions, which do not necessarily
reflect the publisher's opinion.

10/TS/2

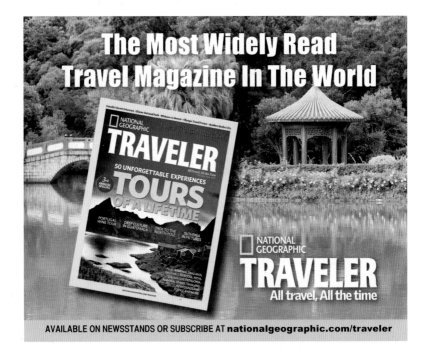